TEXT EDITION

ADVANCES IN
MEDICAL SOCIAL SCIENCE

Advances in Medical Social Science

A series edited by Julio L. Ruffini,
Medical Anthropology Program, University of California,
San Francisco, USA

Volume 1 1983

Additional volumes in preparation

ISSN: 0275–5742
The publisher will accept continuation orders which may be cancelled at any time and which provide for automatic billing and shipping of each title in the series upon publication. Please write for details.

---

† Deceased.

ADVANCES IN MEDICAL SOCIAL SCIENCE

Edited by

JULIO L. RUFFINI

Medical Anthropology Program,
University of California, San Francisco

Volume 1 1983

GORDON AND BREACH SCIENCE PUBLISHERS
New York London Paris Montreux Tokyo

Copyright © 1983 by Gordon and Breach, Science Publishers, Inc.

Gordon and Breach, Science Publishers, Inc.
One Park Avenue
New York, NY 10016

Gordon and Breach Science Publishers Ltd.
42 William IV Street
London WC2N 4DE

Gordon & Breach
58, rue Lhomond
75005 Paris

Gordon and Breach Science Publishers SA
Case Postale 161
CH-1820 Montreux 2

Gordon and Breach, Science Publishers, Inc.
48-2 Minamidama
Oami Shirasato-machi
Sambu-gun
Chiba-ken
Japan 299-32

Contents

Acknowledgements

I WOULD like to express my sincere thanks to the many people who have given me valuable help during the several years of work that have preceded publication of this first volume in the series *Advances in Medical Social Science*. The distinguished members of my editorial advisory board have proven invaluable in providing the series with multidisciplinary and international perspectives and visibility. Many of them have been particularly active in providing me with assistance and useful advice concerning topics and potential authors. In this regard, the death of Manfred Pflanz is a significant loss, as he was especially helpful, and I feel a personal loss in his passing.

In addition to the Editorial Advisory Board members, Frederick Dunn and Arthur Kleinman were most helpful in the initial stages of developing the series. I am grateful to the publishers, in fact, for enthusiastically supporting this effort in interdisciplinary collaboration. I also wish to express my grateful thanks to the authors for their contributions which, in my opinion, represent provocative ideas, and, for the most part, truly significant achievements.

*　　*　　*

The editor and publisher also wish to thank the copyright holders for permission to print excerpts from the following material already published.

*　　*　　*

Culliton, B.J. 1976. Kennedy hearings: year-long probe of biomedical research begins, *Science* **193**: 32–35. Copyright © 1976 by the American Association for the Advancement of Science.

Foster, George M., 1953. Relationships between Spanish and Spanish-American folk medicine, *Journal of American Folklore* **66**: 201–217. Washington D.C.: American Folklore Society Inc.

Young, Allan, 1976. Some implications of medical beliefs and practices for social anthropology, *American Anthropologist* **78**: 5–24. Washington D.C.: American Anthropological Association.

Young, James E., 1978. Illness categories and action in a Tarascan town, *American Ethnologist* **5**: 81–97. Washington D.C.: American Anthropological Association.

Janzen, John M., 1978. *The Quest for Therapy in Lower Zaire*, Berkeley: University of California Press. © 1978 by The Regents of the University of California, reprinted by permission of University of California Press.

Koss, Joan D., 1977. Social progress, healing, and self-defeat among Puerto Rican spiritualists, *American Ethnologist* **4**: 453–469. Washington D.C.: American Anthropological Association.

Garrison, Vivian, 1977. Doctor, espiritista, or psychiatrist?: health-seeking behavior in a Puerto Rican neighbourhood of New York City, *Medical Anthropology* **1**: 2, Part 3, 65–191. Redgrave Publishing Company, P.O. Box 67, South Salem, New York 10590.

Mensforth, Robert P. *et al.*, 1978. The role of constitutional factors, diet and infectious disease in the etiology of porotic hyperostosis and periostal reactions in prehistoric infants and children, *Medical Anthropology* **2**: Part 2, 1–59, Redgrave Publishing Company, P.O. Box 67, South Salem, New York 10590.

Black, Francis L., 1975. Infectious diseases in primitive societies, *Science* **187**: 515–518. Copyright © 1975 by the American Association for the Advancement of Science.

Young, T. Kue, 1979. Changing patterns of health and sickness among the Cree-Ojibwa of North-western Ontario, *Medical Anthropology* **3**: 191–223. Redgrave Publishing Company, P.O. Box 67, South Salem, New York 10590.

Messing, Simon D., 1975. Health care, ethnic outcasting, and the problem of overcoming the syndrome of encapsulation in a peasant society, *Human Organization* **34**: 395–397. University of West Virginia: American Anthropological Association.

Marwick, Max (ed.), 1970. *Witchcraft and Sorcery: Selected Readings*, pp. 54–70. Harmondsworth, Middlesex: Penguin Books. Copyright © Max Marwick, 1970, 1982. Introduction and notes copyright © Max

Marwick, 1970, 1982. Reprinted by permission of Penguin Books Ltd.

Selby, Henry A., 1974. *Zapotec Deviance: The Convergence of Folk and Modern Sociology*, Austin, Texas: University of Texas Press.

Hay, Thomas H., 1971. The windigo psychosis: psychodynamic, cultural, and social factors in aberrant behavior, *American Anthropologist* **73**: 1–19. Washington D.C.: American Anthropological Association.

Culture, Disease and Healing: Studies in Medical Anthropology by David Landy. Copyright © 1977 by David Landy.

Foulkes, Edward F., 1972. *The Arctic Hysterias of the North Alaskan Eskimos*, Anthropological Studies No. 10. Washington D.C.: American Anthropological Association.

Foster, George M., 1976. Disease etiologies in non-western medical systems, *American Anthropologist* **78**: 773–6. Washington D.C.: American Anthropological Association.

Weaver, Thomas, 1970. Use of hypothetical situations in a study of Spanish American illness referral systems, *Human Organization* **29**: 140–154. University of Pittsburgh Press.

Williamson, William, 1966. Life or death – whose decision?, *Journal of the American Medical Association* **197**: 793–795. Copyright 1966, American Medical Association.

Hamburg, David, 1978. *Disease Prevention: The Challenge of the Future*. The Sixth Annual Matthew B. Rosenhaus Lecture. Washington D.C.: American Public Health Association.

Eberstadt, Nick, 1981. The health crisis in the USSR, *The New York Review of Books* **XXVIII**: 26–33, 19 February. Reprinted with permission from The New York Review of Books. Copyright © 1981 by Nyrev Inc.

Introduction to the Series

SINCE I became coeditor of the *Medical Anthropology Newsletter* in 1975 I have felt the need for closer relations and exchange between the various social science disciplines specializing in health. Many of my colleagues, of course, share this view and there are few who would actively oppose it. Yet it is easier to express pious hopes in this regard than to make significant achievements. The forces working against integration are strong. With the mushrooming of research and the increase in scholars, it is much easier to specialize narrowly within one subdiscipline than to attempt to master a number. If any trend is discernible, it is toward greater fragmentation.

Nevertheless, my goal continues to be an increased communication between health social scientists and a greater awareness among them of activities and achievements in related disciplines. The ultimate goal, I think, would be an integrated theory and grand unifying theoretical scheme or major methodological breakthroughs. A worthwhile interim goal, much more modest to be sure, is the juxtaposition, in a convenient format, of the most recent advances in the various areas of study.

Thus, this series of annual volumes seeks to present the latest developments in social science research in health and illness. The first volume is devoted to a summary of the state of the art at the disciplinary level – anthropology, geography, psychology, sociology, economics, and politics. One paper is devoted to the social (or behavioral) sciences as a whole.

This volume does not itself present a unified synthetic model of the field, but it does, I think, represent a significant description of the issues and achievements of the various disciplines and offers the reader an excellent opportunity to become familiar with the contributions social science has made to our understanding of health and illness.

Future volumes will report on advances in specialized areas of research at the subdisciplinary and cross-disciplinary levels of investigation. At the time of writing this the papers for the second volume have been received. Together with those of the first volume, they represent thoughtful analyses of major problem areas, written by scholars who have made significant contributions to their particular areas and who have impressive knowledge of developments in their areas of expertise. It is my firm hope that these and future volumes will provide a valuable resource for scholars, students, health care providers, and interested lay persons concerned with increasing their knowledge of the social, cultural, psychological, and geographical factors which affect, and in turn are affected by, the central human concerns of health and illness. I seek and welcome the cooperation of my colleagues in this endeavor.

Julio L. Ruffini

Preface

WHEN I solicited the manuscripts for the introductory volume to the series, I gave the authors some fairly general guidelines, intending that the articles, singly and as a whole, would provide a comprehensive view of the state of the art of the social sciences of health and illness. I wished to provide a coherent and unifying framework so there would be consistency and continuity, which many collections of articles lack.

At the same time, I was aware that each discipline *is* different – in scope, development, traditions of data gathering and analysis, and style. Furthermore, I had, with the help of my Editorial Advisory Board, sought out highly respected or representative and knowledgeable leaders in each discipline to contribute the articles. I felt that such people should be given considerable freedom to develop their papers in ways they considered meaningful.

There was, in most cases, considerable dialogue between the authors and myself, and while I may have wished, in several cases, for greater comprehensiveness, or a bit more emphasis on this or that approach, I feel that the results offered here are, for the most part, a genuine reflection of the goals I had set myself at the outset of this project.

While several papers explicitly or implicitly limit themselves to particular topics or approaches, others make truly heroic efforts to be comprehensive and, in my estimation, succeed admirably. Adler and Stone, and Armstrong, for example, succeed in providing non-specialists with the feeling that they are obtaining a sound, thorough overview of their fields, respectively health psychology and medical geography. Hughes and Kennedy contribute an excellent review of the social or behavioral sciences approach to health as a whole.

Most remarkable, from my personal perspective as an anthropologist, is the contribution of David Landy, which I consider to be a true masterpiece. Medical anthropology is a broad, varied, and large field, and while Landy states that he focused primarily on the areas which he knows best, I was (and continue to be) awed by the very impressive mastery of such a vast and complex body of literature and concepts.

Bloom and Zambrana provide an excellent overview of several important topics in the sociology of medicine; Krause offers a fine example of the state of the fascinating field of the politics of health; McCready gives the reader an introduction to the generally badly neglected (by most medical social scientists) discipline of health economics; and, finally, Reiser offers a brief but tantalizing glimpse of the value of the historical approach to our understanding of health and illness.

I am grateful to these authors for contributing to this introductory effort. I think they have succeeded beyond reasonable expectations in laying the groundwork for the future volumes which will hopefully build upon, complement, refine, and, ultimately, integrate, these excellent initial efforts.

Julio L. Ruffini

About the Contributors

About the Editor

JULIO L. RUFFINI received his Ph.D. in anthropology from the University of California, Berkely, in 1974. His early fieldwork took place in Sardinia and among San Francisco Bay Area Samoans, whose health care behavior was his focus of study. More recently, his research has been among the elderly in San Francisco.

Dr. Ruffini has been at the University of California, San Francisco, since 1974, where he is affiliated with the Medical Anthropology Program and the School of Nursing. He was coeditor of the *Medical Anthropology Newsletter*, the official organ of the Society for Medical Anthropology, and an ex-officio member of the Society's Executive Committee, from 1975 to 1981, and was coeditor of *Teaching Medical Anthropology: Model Courses for Graduate and Undergraduate Instruction.*

About the Authors

NANCY ADLER is Associate Professor of Psychology in the Department of Psychiatry at the University of California, San Francisco. In addition to teaching in the Health Psychology Program, she is an associate of the Adolescent Health Program, an interdisciplinary training program in the Department of Pediatrics.

R. WARWICK ARMSTRONG is Professor of Public Health and of Geography at the University of Hawaii at Manoa, Honolulu. He holds a joint appointment in the School of Public Health in health services administration and planning and in the Department of Geography in medical geography.

SAMUEL W. BLOOM is Professor of Sociology and Community Medicine at Mount Sinai School of Medicine of the City University of New York (CUNY), where he is Director of the Division of Behavioral Sciences in the Department of Community Medicine. He holds a joint appointment at the Graduate Center of CUNY in the Ph.D. Program in Sociology as Professor and Director of the training program in medical sociology. He is currently a member of the Behavioral Sciences Test Committee of the National Board of Medical Examiners.

CHARLES CAMPBELL HUGHES is Professor of Behavioral Sciences and Director of Graduate Studies, Department of Family and Community Medicine, and Professor of Anthropology in the Department of Anthropology, University of Utah.

DONALD ALEXANDER KENNEDY has taught at Tufts Medical School, at the Harvard School of Public Health in health services administration, and Pennsylvania State University College of Medicine in the field of behavioral sciences and family medicine. Since 1977, he has served as Professor of Behavioral Science and Assistant Dean for Behavioral Sciences at the College of Human Medicine, University of Wyoming.

ELLIOTT A. KRAUSE is Professor of Sociology at Northeastern University. He is the author of *The Sociology of Occupations, Power and Illness: The Political Sociology of Health and Medical Care,* and *Division of Labor: A Political Perspective.*

DAVID LANDY is Professor of Anthropology at the University of Massachusetts, Boston, and was formerly Chair of the Department. He was formerly Professor and Chair of the Department of Anthropology, University of Pittsburgh and Professor of Anthropology in the Graduate School of Public Health at Pittsburgh. He has been on the Executive Boards of the American Society for Ethnohistory and the Society for Medical Anthropology, was Associate Editor of *Ethnology,* and a member of the Editorial Advisory Council of *Behavioral Science.*

DOUGLAS McCREADY has served as an Assistant and Associate Professor at Wilfrid Laurier University in Waterloo, Ontario, since 1969, where he has been active in the formation and as a charter member of the Waterloo Region District Health Council.

STANLEY JOEL REISER is currently Associate Professor of Medical History, and Co-Director of the Kennedy Interfaculty Program in Medical Ethics at Harvard Medical School. He is coeditor of the anthology *Ethics in Medicine: Historical Perspectives and Contemporary Concerns* and author of *Medicine and the Reign of Technology*.

GEORGE STONE is currently Professor of Psychology at the Langley Porter Institute and Director of the Graduate Academic Program at the University of California, San Francisco. Through his leadership, the program in health psychology was initiated at the university, and a recent book by Stone, Cohen, Adler and associates was the first comprehensive review of the field. In 1980 he was appointed editor of a new journal, *Health Psychology*.

RUTH E. ZAMBRANA is currently the Dean of the Graduate School of Psychology at Wright Institute, Los Angeles. She is an Assistant Professor of Sociology at the Mount Sinai School of Medicine, Division of Behavioral Science, New York.

1 Psychology and the Health System

Nancy Adler and George Stone

HEALTH PSYCHOLOGY is a relatively new field. Even as recently as five years ago, a chapter reviewing the state of the field would have been relatively easy to write and would have been extremely brief. Since that time there has been an exponential growth in the number of psychologists engaged in health-related research, and in the number of books, journals and articles addressing themselves to issues of health psychology. This chapter will give a brief overview and history of the field, summarize the major areas of research, and consider the relationship of health psychology to other disciplines investigating psycho-social aspects of health and illness.

Although the field of health psychology is new, many of the topics with which it concerns itself have long histories, having been first addressed by physicians or by persons in other disciplines of the behavioral and social sciences. Many topics that health psychologists take up have sociological and anthropological aspects as well, and because of the earlier emergence of medical sociology and medical anthropology as identified specialties in their respective disciplines (Adler and Stone 1979), these aspects have often been considered before psychologists have come on the scene. It is our view that the sharing of topics among disciplines is not only proper, but useful. Without unduly stressing differences among the disciplines, it does appear appropriate to recognize the different perspectives and emphases that each brings to its analyses.

While most of the writings we cite in this chapter are by psychologists, a good many are not. It is not feasible, nor probably desirable, to distinguish the disciplinary origin of the data that we cite. In a few places we do point to areas that have been worked almost entirely by members of other disciplines, and we then defer to their reviews rather than incorporating them into ours. But for the most part we have considered the data to be common domain, and our interpretation of them to be psychological.

History of Health Psychology

It is difficult to pinpoint the moment when an area becomes recognized as a coherent field or discipline. One way to demarcate the emergence of a field is through formal organizations or institutions. Using this guideline, health psychology became a field in 1978 with the establishment of a Division of Health Psychology within the American Psychological Association. By the end of the first year, this Division already had over 700 members, and by 1980 had almost 1500 members.

While an organized field of health psychology is new, awareness of psychological factors in health and illness is not. As far back as 5000 B.C. early writings reveal a concept of mind and body attuned to one another (Matarazzo 1980). Views of illness dating to 500 B.C. include a concept of the whole body, including ideas of will, faith, and behavioral effects on disease (Stone 1979a).

More recent history shows psychologists engaged in the health field soon after the turn of the century. In 1911 a symposium on psychology and medical education was sponsored by the American Psychological Association. Since that time, psychologists have been involved in the education of health professionals, conducted psychological research in the health system, and been engaged in clinical practice in health settings. The vast majority of psychologists who have worked in the health system work in departments of psychiatry where they have been concerned with issues of mental health and not with other aspects of health care (Nathan et al. 1979; Schofield 1969). However, there has been a move in recent years to examine the relationship of physical and mental health and to provide coordinated services. Several studies have demonstrated the effectiveness of psychotherapy in reducing utilization of other health services (Follette and Cummings 1967; Goldberg et al. 1970). In addition, clinical psychologists have become more involved in providing services such as biofeedback, relaxation training, and behavior modification to patients with specific disorders as well as to individuals seeking preventive care (Gambrill 1977; LeBow 1975; Schwartz 1979). A number of psychologists are working with patients or with individuals at risk of developing diseases related to lifestyle to help them deal more effectively with stress and to modify potentially self-destructive habits. In terms of areas of medical practice, psychologists have shown particular impact in the areas of family practice and pediatrics; in fact, a special field of pediatric psychology has emerged in recent years (Drotar 1977; Routh 1977).

Psychologists have been involved in other aspects of the health system, but in a more limited degree. The major focus of psychology is the individual and it is not surprising that the field of health psychology has been relatively less involved in research on system-level questions. Given the joint function of the profession as practitioners within the system and as researchers on it, the involvement of psychologists in activities such as health planning has been addressed more to planning for the delivery of psychological services than for the psychological aspects of planning for health services (see, for example, Dorken and Associates 1976). However, the two are related as evidenced by growing emphasis on integrated mental and physical health services and by research demonstrating the impact of provision of mental health services on utilization of physical health services (Follette and Cummings 1967; Cummings and Follette 1976). In addition, psychologists are starting to address psychological issues in the planning, delivery, and evaluation of health services.

Much of the research and application by psychologists in the health system has been in the area of program evaluation. Contributions of methods and approaches from psychological research have been made to this multidisciplinary field. Psychologists have addressed questions regarding methods of evaluating health programs, and assessing outcomes in health care, the roles of the evaluator in the system, ways of feeding back the results into the system and making it useful, and setting up information systems so that organizations can conduct ongoing evaluation (see Attkisson, Hargreaves, Horowitz, and Sorensen 1978; Sechrest and Cohen 1979).

Psychologists have also been involved in research on need assessment which is central to health planning. While many planning decisions are made on the basis of planners' beliefs about needed services, greater emphasis is being given to empirical methods of obtaining accurate representation and granting an effective voice to consumer wants and needs (Adler and Milstein 1979). Gaining an accurate assessment of individual needs is basically a psychological question and the measurement of need and preference involves complex psychological processes (Parker and Srinivasan 1976). Researchers as well as planners have noted biases inherent in such traditional methods for measuring consumer preference as the use of key informants, telephone interviews, mail questionnaires, and cross-sectional field interviews (e.g. Delbecq 1976; Kahn 1969; Schwartz 1973; Warheit 1976). Alternatives to these approaches have been developed by psychologists or by others with working knowledge of psychological theory and research. For examples, social indicators have been developed to provide a detached overview with a nonreactive measure of a community's needs (Bloom 1976). Another method is the "nominal group approach" developed by Delbecq (1976). This approach draws on knowledge concerning group dynamics to develop procedures for getting groups of individuals to indicate consumer preference in a specific area. Finally, psychological researchers have proposed that, given the problems inherent in any one approach to measurement, a broader approach be used. Nguyen, Attkisson, and Bottino (1976) have proposed a process of convergent analysis which involves an integration of information from a number of viewpoints and value perspectives, based on a variety of assessment procedures, and which is gathered collectively over time.

In addition to work done by psychologists in health settings, health providers' need to know about psychological dimensions of health and illness has resulted in greater involvement of psychologists in medical training. Following the initial symposium on psychology and medical education, periodic reviews of the involvement of psychologists in medical school teaching have been conducted (Bott 1928; Dennis 1950; Franz 1913; Glover 1934; Lubin et al. 1978; Matarazzo 1955; Matarazzo and Daniel 1957; Webster 1971). From the early reviews through the 1950's there appears to have been slow but increasing growth in the number of hours in medical school curricula devoted to psychiatry and behavioral science. However, the direct involvement of psychologists in such teaching was not shown and seems not to have been substantial. In the latter half of the 1950's the involvement of psychologists in medical student teaching and the actual number of psychologists in medical schools expanded. Nathan et al. (1979) documented this increase. In 1955 there were only 346 psychologists working in medical schools. This rose to 993 in 1964; 1,300 in 1967–1969; and to 2,336 in 1976. At the same time, psychologists expanded the scope of their activities. They can now also be found on the faculties of schools of dentistry (Kleinknecht et al. 1976) and pharmacy (Blaug et al. 1975).

In the past few years, research in health psychology has increased at an even greater rate than has either the number or involvement of psychologists in medical school faculties. Research is being done not only by psychologists who are on the faculties of schools of medicine, nursing, and dentistry, but also by those in academic departments of psychology who are interested in problems of health and illness or who are interested in using health settings to test theoretical predictions.

As recently as the mid-1970's surveys showed a rather limited research literature in health psychology. The American Psychological Association Task Force on Health Research (1976) conducted a computer search of the *Psychological Abstracts* covering the years 1966–1973. They found 3,500 abstracts in this period which related to psychological aspects of physical illness, physical disability and health. However, of these articles, only 350 fit the criteria that they be direct reports of research and not deal primarily with mental health issues. Approximately two-thirds of the 350 articles concerned psychobiological aspects of health. The remaining third were almost equally divided into articles dealing with health care delivery and those investigating health-related attitudes. There is no similar survey of such publications in the late 1970's, but we are sure that any such survey would reveal a dramatic increase in the number of publications. In addition to an increasing number of health-related articles appearing in the usual psychology journals, there have been special issues on health psychology in journals such as *Journal of Social Issues* and *National Forum*. New journals addressing aspects of health psychology, such as *Health Psychology* and the *Journal of Behavioral Medicine*, have recently been established or proposed. A number of books on psychological aspects of health (e.g., Cullen *et al.* 1976; Garfield 1979; Insel and Moos 1974; McNamara 1979; Moos 1977) have been released and there is at least one new book on Health Psychology as a field (Stone *et al.* 1979).

Given the amount of activity in "Health Psychology" it may be useful to consider definitions of the field before turning to a consideration of the research itself.

Definitions of health psychology

In a kind of excess fostered by their long infatuation with logical positivism and operationalism, psychologists have sometimes defined significant terms with empirical recursiveness, though they may claim to do so with tongue in cheek: for example, "educational psychology is what educational psychologists do" or, even "intelligence is what intelligence tests measure." In a field so new to self-awareness as health psychology, it would be especially inappropriate to set boundaries by this device. The first semi-official definition was that proposed by Joseph Matarazzo, first president of the Division of Health Psychology, in the inaugural issue of its newsletter, *The Health Psychologist*: "Health Psychology is the aggregate of the specific educational, scientific and professional contributions of the discipline of psychology to the maintenance of health, the prevention of illness and dysfunction, and the rehabilitation of those already disabled" (Matarazzo 1979).

Matarazzo appropriately indicated the preliminary nature of his definition, saying that it would require augmentation and refinement. Interpreted narrowly, Matarazzo's definition might appear to focus almost exclusively on the activities of the person whose health is at issue and those of providers of health services. We believe that this definition does not necessarily limit health psychology to applications in the health *care* system (Stone 1979a). Rather, it can encompass the entire health system, including the whole complex of logistic support for the health care system, and the individuals and the political and corporate entities who engage in or support research into health problems, design new tools for use by providers, and participate in the recruitment and education of new workers in the health care system. The health system also includes environmental hazards to health – toxins, pollutants, natural phenomena such as storms, avalanches, and cliffs, and man-made hazards such as vehicles and rupturable dams.

The concept of health *care* is extended beyond meaningful bounds if we incorporate within it hurricane watches, the engineering design of earthen dams, and the politics of food production and distribution, and yet these are clearly aspects of the total geobehavioral system that affects our health. Are there any aspects of our world that do not have potentially significant implications for our health? And if there are not, are we then able to conclude that health psychology is all of psychology?

The bounds that we propose for defining the term "health psychology" are between those that focus only on the health care system and those suggested in the preceding paragraph. We consider the total health process to begin with the individual's potential and actual interactions with health hazards, and to extend through the identification, treatment, and rehabilitation of problems that arise from encounters with these hazards. Thus, the health system is made up of those aspects of the total environment that bear principally on the regulation of the hazards and the support of efforts to ameliorate health problems. Health psychology is that branch of psychology that deals with attempts to reduce or regulate health hazards, whether by individual or social action, with the psychologically mediated impact of these hazards on individuals, and with attempts to minimize the impact of such hazards upon persons who fall victim to them.

Health psychology exists in relation to one of the great human values: health. Other psychologies exist (or are potential) in relation to other values such as materialism, aesthetic and religious expression, and the acquisition of fundamental knowledge. While there are many interactions among these spheres of value, there are reasons to keep them distinct. It is part of the task of health psychology to discover generic properties of the health system that set it apart in a meaningful way from other systems such as the aesthetic or the religious system. Are there special attributes of planning for health activities that require a specialized knowledge of the health system such that a person experienced only in planning for religious activities, for example, would be at a disadvantage? While one task facing health psychologists is to differentiate this field from others, another task is to apply what is known about human behavior from these other fields of psychology to problems of health and health care.

Present day psychology is divided into many groupings on the basis of methods used (experimental, psychometric, survey, clinical), the kinds of organisms studied (comparative [animal], child, adolescent, geriatric), the locus of the problems studied (industrial, school, military), the conceptual level addressed (physiological, cognitive, personality, social), and the theoretical predilections of the psychologists (experimental analysis of behavior, psychoanalytic, field theoretic). Some of the older subdivisions, reflected in named fields of specialization, appear to lie wholly within the logical domain of health psychology (rehabilitation psychology, pediatric psychology – perhaps clinical psychology). Others offer concepts and methods that are essential to the pursuit of health psychology, but are equally significant for other psychologies. Still others have intersections with health psychology, as in the health aspects of military, industrial, or school psychology.

How can these various subdivisions be related to the new field of health psychology? To answer this question, we make an analogy to the first computer program written with the capability to solve a great variety of problems, "The General Problem Solver" (Newell *et al.* 1960). This program was designed in two major segments. One, the "problem solving core," was composed of the procedures for handling any problem in terms of abstract symbols and processes. The other contained the specific propositions, interrelationships and constraints of a particular "task environment". Psychology is a discipline that provides methods, concepts and theories for understanding the experience and the behavior of individuals in any situation. Health psychology is what results when the specifics of health problems and health system settings are superimposed as the task environment.

This chapter will identify major areas of research within the domain of health psychology. Research on psychobiological and mental health aspects of health and illness is excluded, however, since a review of these large areas is beyond the scope of a single chapter.

Even with this exclusion the field is already far too large to review exhaustively within the scope of a chapter, or even an oversize book. Many sections are highly schematized, with very few references to individual work, while others give more detail, which we hope can give a richer sense of the field. A number of major topics appear only in the form of a sentence or two indicating that work on the topic does exist. Even the most thoroughly documented topics are not covered exhaustively, although they will provide a good entry to the literature. The research to be reviewed will be divided into three major categories: studies of psychological factors in the etiology of health problems, studies of responses to disease or the threat of disease, and studies of psychosocial issues of health care delivery.

Psychological Factors in the Etiology of Health Problems

Most of the research in health psychology has focused on psychological dimensions of health and the development and course of illness. Researchers have investigated the extent to which psychological factors and associated behaviors contribute to development of illness or disease in general (or, conversely, contribute to the establishment and maintenance of health) and to the development of specific diseases. In addition, psychological dimensions of responses to the threat or occurrence of illness have been examined.

Life style or behavioral issues that contribute to diseases in general

A major category of etiological factors leading to illness has to do with behaviors of individuals with respect to the hazards and risks of the environment. These may range all the way from the precautionary measures taken (or not taken) in response to storm warnings to behaviors in relation to food or stressful circumstances.

From the viewpoint of a cognitive psychologist, it is important to consider these behaviors in light of the degree to which the risk factors are known to the individual engaging in the behavior. Eating patterns that lead to excessive body weight, according to our current understanding of the health implications of such weight, may have identical health consequences in a traditional culture, where such patterns are the norm, and in our culture, where they are seen as "self-destructive." The psychological aspects of these two situations are, however, quite different. In the first case, we would design interventions to make the risks known, in the second case, we would have to deal with "irrational" behavior.

The recommendation of health promoting behaviors dates back as far as Hippocrates (Ackerknecht 1968). During most times, it has been recognized that people do not always do what is, by whatever sources of evidence are currently in vogue, demonstrably good for them. Despite this, most attempts at health education have been limited to the presentation of information and recommendations.

With the advent in the twentieth century of a functional psychology concerned with the adaptiveness of behavior and then of a professional psychology committed to changing it, the issues of self-destructive behaviors such as over-eating, alcoholism, smoking and other substance abuse engaged the attention of psychologists from varying theoretical backgrounds. Now, with the emergence of health psychology as a self-conscious field of specialization, it is beginning to be realized that these patterns of behavior represent phenomena whose thorough understanding can bring a resolution to many of the theoretical controversies that have troubled the field of psychology for the past 75 years. To what extent can humans be regarded as rational organisms that self-consciously proceed to maximize expected attainment of value? To what extent are they driven by urges from the unconscious that may even impel them toward their own destruction? To what degree are they machines driven by the exigencies of reinforcing mechanisms? Is it possible, by becoming aware of the conditioning processes explicitly, to gain some measure of freedom from them or control over them? The apparently non-adaptive, often intractable behaviors that we call "self-destructive" offer a wealth of opportunities for the study of these and many related questions.

In this section, we review briefly the history and present status of psychological investigations of the problems of excesses of eating, smoking, drinking and drug use, and the deficiencies of exercise and nutritional concerns that are generally recognized to be harmful to our health. We then attempt to integrate the generalizations from these several areas with those from the scanty research literature on the seeking and avoiding of risks in general.

The history of psychological approaches to each of the areas mentioned here is essentially the history of efforts to change behavior. Most recent overviews of the problems of self-destructive behaviors (Brownell and Stunkard 1978; Henderson *et al.* 1979; Pomerleau 1979) are also presented in the context of appraising the possibility for and the success of attempts at intervention. They tend to focus almost entirely on methods derived either from the behavioral theories of Skinner (1953), or the social learning theories of Bandura (1969), and others. Tracing these efforts further back in time eventually involves us in the task of distinguishing the non-psychological practice of techniques now believed to be justified by psychological theory from those that have been explicitly derived from such theories. It is only the latter, of course, that can be claimed as a part of health psychology.

Obesity Standards regarding body weight vary among cultures and over time. In western society there are clearly both social and physical costs to be borne by those whose weights are more than 20 percent above the established norms for their age and sex (Brownell and Stunkard 1978; Millman 1980). Efforts to disentangle the contribution of constitutional, environmental, cultural and personality factors in the etiology of obesity have not yet led to a consensual view (Garrow 1975). Current treatments of obesity range from those emphasizing education in nutrition and messages about the dangerous consequences of obesity (Becker *et al.* 1977b) to surgical removal of portions of the gastrointestinal tract to reduce the area of absorptive tissues (Knecht 1978). While conceding that nutritional information is essential if appropriate eating behavior is to be learned, and acknowledging the psychological impact of the weight loss that follows ileostomy (Schiebel and Castelnuovo-Tedesco 1977), health psychologists have focused mainly on studies that make use of psychological interventions. Henderson *et al.* (1979) identified three principal psychological approaches to the problem: 1) The rational model views the person as a decision-maker who weighs the consequences of various forms of behavior (not always with full awareness) and selects that which will best achieve personal goals. Interventions may involve confronting the client with discrepancies between asserted intentions and behavior (Rokeach 1971) and with rationalizations (Janis and Mann 1977). 2) The psychodynamic model stresses unconscious conflicts among instinctual, rational and ethical or moral determinants of behavior. Intervention consists of bringing these conflicts into awareness through individual or group therapy where they can be resolved. 3) Social learning theory holds that improper eating behavior has been learned, and that the same learning mechanisms can be used to replace faulty behavior patterns with sound ones. Interventions consist of identifying the rewards and punishments that are currently controlling the unwanted behavior and altering them so that more appropriate behavior will be supported by the new set of "reinforcing contingencies." Such theories now often include "modeling," which may lead to social imitation, reinforcement based on the confirmation of subjective expectations regarding one's own behavior ("self-control"), "vicarious reinforcement," based on the observation of rewards and punishments meted out to others, and reinforcement based on the expectation of future gratification. These and related elaborations of social learning theory make it possible to translate the propositions of rational theory and psychodynamic theory into the behavioral lexicon. The interventions of social learning theorists tend toward the management of rewards and punishments and the systematic recording of behavior. They focus specifically on the behavior to be changed, rather than providing information which *ought* to lead to a decision to change behavior or attempting to uncover the emotional and symbolic meanings of the clients' behavior.

Unfortunately, none of these interventions has proven highly effective in the treatment of obesity (Hall and Hall in press; Slawson 1965; Stunkard and McClaren-Hume 1959). Perhaps in part because its greater emphasis on the accurate recording of data has generated a greater quantity of objective data, the social learning approach can make the best case for at least a limited effectiveness (Abramson 1977; Stunkard and Penick 1979).

Substance abuse and the addictions   Many of the fundamental issues in the psychology of the abuse of alcohol, tobacco or other drugs are the same as those that have been discussed in the section on obesity, which can be considered to be the result of the abuse of food. The same questions can be asked about constitutional predispositions to the reinforcing effects of the abused substance, about lack of knowledge of the destructive consequences of the behavior, deep psychological needs that are somehow reduced by the behavioral patterns, and the failure to develop adequate skills of self-management. The same broad classes of interventions have been tried, with essentially similar results: while nothing works very well, the behavioral approaches seem to have a slight edge (Emrick 1975; Lichtenstein and Danaher 1976; National Institute on Drug Abuse 1979).

There are some differences in specific methods, to be sure. Aversion therapies, rarely employed for control of eating, were devised for use in the treatment of both alcoholism and smoking long before the term was introduced by the behavioral psychologists (see Voegtlin *et al.* 1940 for early history). Recent refinements in procedures and timing of punishments have increased both the acceptability and the effectiveness of these efforts to reduce self-destructive behavior. However, issues about obtaining the consent of the punished person are complex and require continuing thought and discussion (Lichtenstein and Danaher 1976).

In managing the abuse of opiates, the substitution of dependence on a drug that can be legally prescribed is the most widely used approach at the present time. This treatment can be seen as having psychological components relative both to the self-attributions of the addict and to the social acceptability of the treatment. Public opinion in this country has not supported the administration of morphine or heroin to addicts, but will tolerate the use of methadone, which is widely presumed to have little or no euphoriant effects. A more complex and psychologically sophisticated behavioral and pharmacological approach has been proposed by Goldstein (1976).

Mention should be made here of a substantially different approach to changing behavior that has just begun to engage the attention of applied social psychologists (Andrews and Debus 1978; deCharms and Muir 1978). In this approach, it is not the behavior itself that is the focus of the change effort, but self-attributions about the capacity for change. To date, the only application of this approach to health behaviors appears to be McClelland's "Power Motivation Training," which teaches alcoholics to attribute power to themselves rather than to drink out of frustration over their powerlessness (McClelland 1974). The effectiveness of McClelland's method has been questioned and defended (Cutter *et al.*

1977; McClelland 1978); the approach is complex and subtle, and much work will be needed in order to evaluate the efficacy of its various embodiments (deCharms and Muir 1978).

A relatively recent theme in the management of substance abuse is the investigation of moderate use rather than total abstinence as a treatment goal (Miller 1977). In the context of treatment, the reason for this shift in objectives is that it may be easier to secure long term maintenance of moderate usage than of cessation of use. Other important psychological issues are ripe for study in this area. There are some data suggesting that moderate use of alcohol may actually have physiologically (Yano, Rhoads, and Kagan 1977) as well as psychologically beneficial effects (Mishara *et al.* 1975). Justification of moderate use of tobacco, marijuana and even opiate drugs is sometimes made on the basis of the psychological costs to the individual of giving up these sources of gratification and the social costs of economic dislocations, in the case of tobacco, and law enforcement programs in the case of illegal drugs (Goldstein 1976).

Changing behavior in relation to risks   The material reviewed above leads to several generalizations about how people behave with respect to known risks and about efforts to modify such behavior. New questions arise in the context of these generalizations. Clearly, observable behavior often deviates radically from what experts consider healthful and from what people themselves say they want and intend to do. Faced with such discrepancies, psychologists may invoke hidden values (or reinforcers) to explain the continuation of unwanted behavior. When the behaving persons are confronted with the discrepancy, they may change their verbal descriptions of the situation by denying or distorting their estimate of risk, at least as these are applicable to them, they may discount the values they have previously espoused, or they may claim that they are helpless in the face of powerful and mysterious habits. A few people do change their behavior. We know relatively little about how such people differ from those who do not change, although a growing body of literature suggests that the belief that one is capable of change, and the valuing of such a capability are crucial factors (Bandura 1977).

It is very clear that simply informing people about risks will lead to changes in behavior only when the risks were previously unknown and the behavior to be changed is not supported by strong motivational structures. Change is especially likely to occur if the individual is also presented with clear guidelines for how to change. Attempts to dramatize risks and to present them graphically in order that they will be emotionally experienced as personally threatening – a technique known as "fear arousal" – have been unreliable and inconsistent in their effects. Methods of aversive conditioning that associate nausea, pain or other unpleasant physiological states with the unwanted behavior are somewhat more reliable. However, grave ethical problems are associated with their use without the consent of the person whose behavior is to be changed. Even when fully informed consent is given, such techniques may reinforce the belief that one is powerless to act on one's own behalf and prove less effective in the long run. Methods that demonstrate through graded steps and social support the possibility of becoming "responsible," of assuming control over one's behavior, seem to work most consistently and to be most compatible with a humanistic value system.

There are hazards associated even with this method of "self-control." As many critics have pointed out (Shapiro and Shapiro 1979; Eisenberg 1977), there is a danger that efforts to invoke personal responsibility will be used to divert our collective attention from needed changes in society and in the environment that it generates. There is a danger that, while the successful assumption of responsibility will lead to confidence and competence, unsuccessful efforts at self-control may lead to self-blame, guilt and depression, and may aggravate the health conditions they were intended to improve.

Psychological factors in the etiology of specific health problems

Several diseases have traditionally been acknowledged to have a psychological component. These "psychosomatic" diseases, including asthma, peptic ulcers, and colitis, have generated a vast literature on psychological determinants. More recently researchers have started to consider the contribution of psychological factors to the development of diseases that have traditionally been viewed as purely biological events. The research literature on two such diseases, coronary heart disease and cancer, is reviewed below. In addition, research on the role of psychological variables in obstetrical complications and in the creation of unwanted pregnancy will be examined.

Coronary heart disease An area that has attracted a great deal of recent attention and has entered public awareness, is research relating personality and life-style to coronary heart disease. A number of different psycho-social traits have been linked to heart disease, including anxiety, psychiatric problems, overwork, job dissatisfaction and conflicts regarding work, family or finances (Eastwood and Trevelyan 1971; Medalie *et al.* 1973; Theorell and Rahe 1972).

The strongest documentation for a link between personality and heart disease centers around the Type A/Type B differentiation (Friedman and Rosenman 1974; Rosenman *et al.* 1964). The Type A behavior pattern involves "a particular complex of personality traits, including excessive competitive drive, aggressiveness, impatience, and a harrying sense of time urgency. Individuals displaying this pattern seem to be engaged in a chronic, ceaseless, and often fruitless struggle with themselves, with others, with circumstances, with time and sometimes with life itself. They also frequently exhibit a free-floating but well-rationalized form of hostility, and almost always a deep-seated insecurity" (Friedman and Rosenman 1974: 4). In contrast, Type B individuals show no time urgency, harbor no free-floating hostility, can relax when appropriate, and speak in a less pressured manner. Prospective studies have established a link between the Type A behavior pattern and the likelihood of developing coronary heart disease (Jenkins *et al.* 1974a; Rosenman *et al.* 1964; Rosenman *et al.* 1970; Rosenman *et al.* 1975). In addition to the association between behavior style and coronary heart disease in general, researchers have identified specific patterns associated with myocardial infarction versus angina pectoris (Jenkins *et al.* 1974b; Jenkins *et al.* 1978; Ostfeld *et al.* 1964).

Researchers have attempted to identify biological mechanisms that could mediate the association between psychosocial variables and coronary heart disease. Cohen (1979) notes that most of the variables that have been shown to predict heart disease are closely tied to stress; the variables either reflect stressful life situations, or are personality traits or coping styles that foster stressful interactions with the environment. A number of studies have established an association between stress and risk factors such as serum cholesterol levels and blood pressure that in turn are tied to the likelihood of developing heart disease (Friedman *et al.* 1958; Kasl and Cobb 1970; Rahe *et al.* 1971; Rahe *et al.* 1974; Thomas and Murphy 1958). Other research has suggested that psychosocial variables could trigger specific biological mechanisms that increase the risk of heart disease. For example, Friedman and Rosenman (1974) suggest that Type A behavior is associated with increased secretion of epinephrine, norepinephrine and other hormones. A chronic excess discharge of these catecholamines can influence serum cholesterol level and the clotting mechanisms of the blood, increasing plaque build-up on artery walls and the possibility of forming a clot that would occlude a coronary artery. Weighing evidence from a thorough review of the literature, Cohen (1979: 104) concludes, "evidence supports the links between various psychological factors and biological changes, which, it has been shown, could increase the likelihood of coronary heart disease."

Cancer   As with research on the coronary-prone personality, research on cancer has attempted to discover if there is a cancer-prone personality type. A variety of variables have been studied, including both personality traits and the impact of stress on individuals: "it has . . . been suggested that those who develop cancer are unable to express hostile feelings and emotions (Renneker and Cutler 1952; Solomon 1969), are anally fixated (Mezei and Nemeth 1969), make extensive use of repressive and denying defenses (Bahnson and Bahnson 1966, 1969), are emotional and extroverted (Hagnell 1966), are introverted (McCoy 1976), report less closeness to parents (Thomas and Greenstreet 1973), or have suffered a significant loss or separation from a significant person (Greene 1954, 1966; Greene, Young, and Swisher 1956; LeShan and Worthington 1956; Schmale and Iker 1966, 1971)" (Cohen 1979: 105). Fox and Goldsmith (1976) posit a link between life stress and cancer through the effects of stress on hormone balance, with the resulting hormone disturbance possibly affecting immune suppression.

Studies have also explored the relationship of personality traits to the development of cancer at specific sites such as the lung or breast (Greer and Morris 1975; Kissen 1963, 1966; Kissen *et al.* 1969). However, Cohen (1979) notes that research on personality traits associated either with development of cancer in general or with cancer of specific sites is less strong than evidence of psychological determinants of heart disease. A major problem is that most of the research has been retrospective, using subjects who have already developed cancer. Retrospective designs preclude the possibility of making causal inferences about the contribution of psychological traits to the *development* of the disease. Fox (1978) notes that in studies in which comparisons are made between cancer patients and other patients, there is no control for possible precursors of cancer that could contribute to the subsequent pattern of psychosocial variables. Both cancer itself and the treatment of the disease may influence mood, feelings and capacities. Additional methodological problems of sample selection and operationalization of psychological variables add to the uncertainty about the links found between personality and cancer formation.

Obstetrical complications   In terms of numbers of individuals affected, perhaps the most significant area of health psychology is in research on psychological aspects of reproductive functioning. A number of authors have described the role that psychological variables can play in obstetrical complications, starting with problems of infertility and ranging through complications at each stage of pregnancy. Much of the evidence is based on clinical case observations by psychotherapists and awaits further verification. Other evidence, however, is based on more rigorous methodology and confirms some of the theoretical predictions.

Infertility is a common problem, affecting about 10% of married couples (Walker 1978). Problems of infertility of a couple can be due either to the male or female partner or to their interaction. It has been estimated that about a quarter of infertility problems derive from emotional factors. In males, spermatogenesis is sensitive to changes in constitutional and nervous energy (Ford *et al.* 1953). Psychological factors may affect the gonads and/or may cause spasms of the ductus deferens and seminal vesicles causing pseudoejaculation. Cases have been reported in which spermatazoa are plentiful in a man's masturbatory samples but cannot be found in his wife's cervix following intercourse (Fischer 1956).

Although male sexual dysfunction may play a significant role in infertility (Amelar *et al.* 1977), most of the writings on this problem have focused only on the role of the woman. Psychoanalytic writers tend to attribute infertility for which no organic bases can be found to a woman's defenses against fears of pregnancy (Deutsch 1945; Benedek 1952). Kroger (1952) noted that pseudocyesis (false pregnancy) graphically demonstrates the effect of psychological forces on the physiological mechanisms of pregnancy, and postulated that conflicts regarding conception could similarly upset endocrine balance and reproductive functions. Ford *et al.* (1953) speculated that psychological factors could affect ovulation or nonovulation through their effects on the pituitary and hypothalamus, and could play a role in nonpatent tubes due to chronic spasms, could contribute to the defective endometria, and could lead to "hostile" cervical secretions.

Deutsch (1945) noted that the relationship between psychological dynamics and reproductive outcomes is complex, and that the same guilt or fear that leads to sterility in one case may, in another, lead to "compulsive conceptions" with the possibility of later complications. A major problem of studies of psychogenic sterility is that the research focuses on couples who have already been identified as infertile. The retrospective nature of the research raises some serious questions. For example, Sturgis *et al.* (1957) studied 25 infertile couples, finding that only two were free of serious emotional conflicts. The couples had fears about such things as having a defective child, damage to the woman in delivery, being poor parents or the inadequacy of one or the other partner. However, with no control group, one cannot determine if such fears are more common in this group than in other couples who do conceive. In addition, such fears may be heightened by the experience of inability to conceive rather than (or in addition to) such fears contributing to fertility problems. To date no adequate longitudinal study of couples has been done that could permit more definitive statements about the extent to which particular personality dynamics or unconscious conflict affect one's fertility or infertility.

Once pregnancy occurs, psychological factors may play a significant role in the occurrence of complications (McDonald 1968). Hyperemesis gravidarum (excessive vomiting) has been linked to emotional stress and to anxiety (Caldwell 1958; Harvey and Sherfey 1954; Rosen 1955). Despite frequent theoretical assumptions linking excessive vomiting with rejection of the pregnancy, research has not demonstrated such a link (Bernstein 1952; Coppen 1959). Rather, it has been linked with ambivalence toward the pregnancy (Chertok *et al.* 1963).

Similar dynamics regarding unconscious conflicts about the pregnancy have been posited to account for habitual abortion (defined as the occurrence of three or more consecutive spontaneous abortions in the absence of an identifiable organic cause). Most studies of habitual abortion, investigating the effectiveness of supportive psychotherapy in enabling habitual aborters to carry to term, have reported success (Javert 1957; Rothman 1973; Weil and Stewart 1957). However, most of these studies have not used a control group. In a comparative study, Tupper and Weil (1962) reported that 16 of 19 patients who were randomly assigned to receive psychotherapy carried to term compared to only 5 out of 19 patients who were not treated. Stress, emotional immaturity and ambivalence about the pregnancy have also been related to premature delivery in both retrospective (Blau *et al.* 1963) and prospective studies (Gunter 1963).

Toxemia is one of the major complications of pregnancy. It is defined as the occurrence of excessive weight gain, significant proteinuria and hypertension. In a combination of prospective and retrospective design, Ringrose (1961a and b) found significantly more emotional disturbance among toxemia patients than among normal patients. Glick *et al.* (1965) found a number of variables that differentiated prenatal patients who subsequently developed preeclampsia (a type of toxemia) from those who did not: The preeclamptic group was significantly more likely to have childhood history reflecting emotional disorder; to be single, divorced, widowed or separated rather than be married; and to have a previous history of spontaneous abortion.

In addition to complications of pregnancy and delivery, researchers have been concerned with the delivery experience. A number of studies have investigated social and psychological variables that may predict ease or difficulty of labor, level of anaesthesia, etc. Key among the variables that have been studied is psychoprophylactic preparation for childbirth. Charles *et al.* (1978) note the inconsistent results of studies of the effectiveness of psychoprophylaxis, ranging from positive findings of shorter labors, fewer forceps deliveries, and improved condition of newborns (e.g., Laird and Hogan 1956; Toms and Karlovsky 1954; Tupper 1956) to findings of no difference between groups. Charles notes that it is often difficult to interpret differences since they could be attributed to the training itself or to the characteristics of women choosing to take the training (Davis and Curi 1968; Enkin *et al.* 1972; Scott and Rose 1976). Although there is mixed evidence, the data on the effect of preparation on amount of analgesia and anesthetic required is somewhat stronger, with a number of studies finding lower levels of each for prepared women (Charles *et al.* 1978; Davenport-Slack and Boylan 1974; Zax *et al.* 1975). In addition, lower levels of pain and more positive experiences are reported by women who have undergone preparation, including more positive reaction to their infant (Charles *et al.* 1978; Doering and Entwisle 1975).

Unwanted pregnancy Compared to research on psychological influences on the outcome of pregnancy, research demonstrating psychological influences on the etiology of unwanted pregnancy is much stronger. A number of personality variables have been linked to the occurrence of unwanted pregnancy, including lower feelings of competence, efficacy and a more external locus of control (Adler 1974; Keller *et al.* 1970;

MacDonald 1970; Meyerowitz and Malev 1973; Slage *et al.* 1974). Age and developmental status are particularly important influences on contraceptive use and reaction to pregnancy (Hatcher 1976; Zelnik and Kantner 1977, 1979; Schaffer and Pine 1972).

Unfortunately, most of the research in this area also has been retrospective with comparisons made between women who have experienced unwanted pregnancy and those who are currently using contraception. In a prospective study of adolescent contraceptive patients, Oskamp *et al.* (1978) found several characteristics that predicted subsequent unwanted pregnancy, including shorter future time perspective, poorer sexual knowledge, lower scores on the Socialization Scale of the Personal Values Abstract (Gough 1972), higher interviewer ratings of the clients' passivity and tendency to be masochistic, and lower socioeconomic status.

In addition to psychosocial characteristics of individual women, a few researchers have considered the broader context of their behavior. Several situational variables have been identified as being associated with the creation of an unwanted pregnancy: general life stress, the loss of significant others, and/or the loss of a mother, mother-surrogate or a real or fantasized loss of maternal interest (Downs and Clayson 1972; Patt *et al.* 1969; Schaffer and Pine 1972). The stage of one's sexual career and the nature of the relationship with one's partner are other important aspects of contraceptive behavior (Cvetkovich and Grote 1977; Miller 1973). In general, contraceptive use is likely to be less consistent at times of transition and crisis. Interaction with clinics and providers can also influence acceptance and use of contraceptives: Ager *et al.* (1973) found that dropouts from a family planning clinic perceived more barriers to obtaining clinic services than did those who continued. Unfortunately, a key influence, the male partner, has been virtually ignored. Little is known about male attitudes or use of contraception and the interaction of these with the attitudes and behavior of the female partner.

Psychological Factors in Response to Disease or the Threat of Disease

In the previous sections we considered behaviors that have harmful consequences to health and examined research on efforts to help people change these behaviors. Here we turn to behaviors that are directed toward improving or reestablishing health, and how such behavior can be supported by health professionals.

Psychologists have been much involved in both treatment and research on responses to the threat and occurrence of illness. Clinicians working in the health system have helped patients deal with the stresses associated with illness or injury and with treatment regimens that are in themselves threatening and upsetting. Researchers have also been interested in behaviors taken in response to health problems or the possibility of such problems and the relationship of these behaviors to the course of illness and recovery of health.

As Rosenstock and Kirscht (1979) note, there is not a clear differentiation between illness and health from either the providers' or patients' perspective. Nonetheless, researchers have tried to make some differentiations among behaviors that are more or less tied to states of health and illness. Kasl and Cobb (1966) identified three types of behavior: 1) *health behavior* which involves activities taken by people who consider themselves healthy in order to maintain that state (including preventive actions and detection of possible disease), 2) *illness behavior* which involves activities taken by people who believe themselves to be ill in order to define their illness and find appropriate treatment, and 3) *sick role behavior* which involves activities taken by people who believe themselves to be ill in order to reestablish a state of health. Baric (1969) added the concept of *at risk behavior* which involves activities of people who believe themselves to be at special risk of developing a health problem as they seek to reduce the potential of developing such a problem.

Psychological factors are important in each of these areas. The research reviewed below will examine how such factors play a role in 1) actions taken to avert or respond to the threat of disease, 2) adherence to therapeutic regimens prescribed to arrest or reverse the course of disease and 3) the course of the disease process itself.

Help-seeking behavior

Much of the research on health and illness behavior has focused on utilization of health services. While similar questions of determinants of help-seeking have been examined from other perspectives (for example, studies of cultural or demographic determinants of seeking care), psychologists have been particularly interested in the role of individual perceptions, beliefs, values, and personality characteristics in response to illness or potential illness.

A framework that has emerged to encompass much of the research on health behavior is the Health Belief Model (Becker 1974; Becker *et al.* 1977a; Rosenstock 1966, 1974). This model is a form of more generalized "value-expectancy" theory which posits that individuals act to maximize outcomes given their perception of the likelihood of various outcomes for any given choice and the value placed on those outcomes. The model identifies several classes of variables that relate to taking preventive health actions. These variables include "health-related motivations, subjective estimates of susceptibility to and severity of illness, and subjective estimates of the benefits or efficacy of any proposed regimens minus the perceived barriers to taking such action" (Rosenstock and Kirscht 1979: 171). The Health Belief Model, or aspects of it, has been found to relate to obtaining a chest x-ray to detect tuberculosis (Hochbaum 1958), participation in screening for the Tay-Sachs trait (Becker *et al.* 1975), use of preventive dental services in a prepaid dental care plan (Kegeles 1963), and taking preventive actions with regard to a threatened influenza epidemic (Leventhal *et al.* 1960). Evidence for the assumption of causality presented in the model (i.e. that the beliefs influence health behaviors) can be taken from the findings of Kegeles and of Leventhal cited above, since these were prospective studies in which beliefs measured at one time predicted subsequent behavior. Additional backing for the model is provided by Haefner and Kirscht (1970) who modified some of its components (perceived threat of a disease) through persuasive messages and found that the changes influenced subsequent behavior. However, a recent study (Taylor 1979), found that health beliefs measured at the outset of a program of medication for hypertension were less predictive of compliance than a measure of the same beliefs taken six months later. Results across studies have not been totally consistent in their findings of associations between all aspects of the model and health behaviors (Rosenstock 1966).

An alternative framework is being developed by Leventhal (Leventhal *et al.* in press) for describing illness behavior. In contrast to the Health Belief Model which has a strong emphasis on conceptual beliefs, the information-processing model proposed by these authors stresses the importance of an individual's experience of symptoms and the reactions to these sensory experiences. Using this model, Leventhal differentiates three different substages of illness behavior. Each substage has its own dynamic and shows a different pattern of correlations between delay and variables such as emotional reaction and negative imagery. Delay in one substage is unrelated to delay in another.

Delay in seeking care once the individual is aware of the possibility of a health problem is of particular interest since early initiation of treatment is a major variable in the prognosis for a number of diseases. Not surprisingly, most of the research on delay in seeking diagnosis and treatment has focused on cancer patients. Initial studies dealt mainly with the frequency and duration of delay (e.g., Gray and Ward 1952; Leach and Robbins 1947; Pack and Gallo 1938). Kutner et al. (1958) in their review of the literature noted that "despite a voluminous literature on delay in the diagnosis and treatment of cancer, little progress has been made in coming to terms with the central problem, namely, what is the nature of delay in cancer?" (1958:96). They differentiated unavoidable from avoidable delay. The former occurs between the time of biologic onset and the individual's recognition of symptoms, while the latter involves procrastination in seeking help once symptoms have been recognized. The literature they reviewed includes a number of psychological variables associated with delay, including defense mechanisms such as avoidance, suppression, denial and destiny neurosis (Shands et al. 1951); ignorance and fear (Aitken-Swan and Patterson 1955; Bates and Ariel 1948) and willingness or reticence to discuss one's symptoms with others (Goldsen 1953). However, as noted by Kutner et al. (1958) the interrelationships of these variables with each other and with the social, economic and biological variables that also impinge on delay have not been established.

Blackwell (1963), in her review of the area, identified fear as a major issue in delay. She found a number of fears associated with cancer: fear of death, fears related to the cancer site, to hospitalization, to the effects of the illness on one's family, and (for women with cancer of the breast or reproductive organs or men with prostate cancer) fears about adequate fulfillment of sex role expectations. Many individuals may defend against fear by the use of psychological defenses (Shands et al. 1951). However, there is a complex interplay of fear with individual predispositions. Cobb et al. (1954) noted significant differences between patients who had delayed seeking treatment for cancer beyond three months and those who had acted more promptly in the ways in which they coped with fear. The prompt patient controlled the fear and used it as an "organizing agent to institute steps toward counteracting the threat he felt (p. 923)." The delaying patient seemed to experience a more diffuse fear and became immobilized or channeled the awareness into a search for "miracle" cures. Similar to the description by Shands *et al.* (1951) of the destiny neurosis, some of the patients experienced the cancer as an inevitable punishment for past sins which they felt they had to accept.

In studies of cancer as well as other medical problems there is evidence that the individual's general strategy in coping with crises will affect the extent to which he or she delays or acts promptly in response to symptoms. Greer (1974) studied a sample of women undergoing breast biopsy. Those who had delayed more than three months following first discovery of a breast lump were found to be significantly more likely to use denial in relation to other life crises: "62% of delayers compared with only 24% of non-delayers were found to be habitual deniers (p. 472)." Even when they sought treatment, those who delayed were less likely to confront the possibility of cancer directly. The delayers were significantly more likely to present *other* symptoms or problems to the doctor when they did seek help. Andrew (1972) found personality characteristics related to delay of surgery for inguinal hernia. Using a sample of male veterans, she found repression versus sensitization and internal versus external locus of control both to relate to delay of surgery: delay was greater among neutrals compared to sensitizers or repressors and was greater among those with a more external compared to internal locus of control. The repression-sensitization dimension has also been related to treatment-seeking for emotional problems (Tempone and Lamb 1967; Thelen 1969) and for minor physical illnesses (Byrne *et al.* 1968).

Compliance

Once the patient has elected to seek professional health care, and has found a particular provider who will provide it, there begins a series of interactions between patient and provider to determine what services are indicated. Clearly, these interactions could be discussed in either this section, dealing with the behavior of the person whose health is at stake, or in a later section on the providers of health services. Since most of the research has focused on *patient* variables that affect adherence to medical regimens, the discussion is placed here. However, this should not imply that provider characteristics and attitudes are less important in affecting the outcome of the health transaction.

It seems best to consider the topic of patient compliance with the recommendations of health care providers by presenting a brief description of the structure of the patient-provider interaction (a fuller exposition is given in Stone 1979b). This will be treated in some detail since it is central to much of health care. The patient has identified some problem for which she or he believes professional help is required. The patient requests an appointment with a professional who considers herself or himself to be qualified to offer a range of services. At the moment of their first contact, they embark on a process that can be called a "problematic social situation." The situation is problematic because each of the parties has a set of goals that they are striving to achieve within it. It is social because the attainment of the goals by each is dependent upon the behavior of the other. Notice that there is not one set of goals but two. During the course of the interaction, some of these goals will be made explicit; others will not. Some will not be recognized as a part of the transaction even by the individual who holds them. Each party to the transaction embarks upon it with certain beliefs and expectations as to how it should proceed, what goals it may appropriately address and which ones it may not, who is responsible for knowing, deciding, and doing what. During the course of the transaction the participants communicate about the (more or less) agreed upon problem that brought the client to the professional. They communicate about the problem-solving process: "Have we reached an agreed upon diagnosis?" "Who is responsible for that decision?" And they communicate or withhold communication about the communication itself: "I did not understand what you said." "Your manner of addressing me is offensive."

The problematic social situation can be analyzed within the general framework that has been applied to the process of solving all types of problems, in which five phases are typically recognized: 1) formulation of the problem goal; 2) discovery or invention of feasible pathways to the goal; 3) deciding on an allocation of resources among the identified, alternative pathways; 4) implementation of the selected plan; and 5) evaluation of the results, with return to logically antecedent phases if necessary.

In the health transaction between health provider and client, the most typical pattern of activities has been for the provider to "interview" the client in order to gather information that will allow "diagnosis."

The diagnosis names the situation and allows a specification of likely outcomes (attainable goals), and of possible treatment approaches (legitimate pathways to a favorable outcome). The diagnosis may or may not be shared with the client. Treatment alternatives have, until recently, rarely been discussed with clients. Instead, the provider decides on the allocation of resources to alternatives, and communicates this decision to the client as a prescription. Implementation of this recommended set of actions, in outpatient care, is customarily left to the client. The client who succeeds in devising and executing a plan for carrying through the recommendations of the provider is "compliant."

Until quite recently, compliance was usually taken for granted by providers, and the evaluation of the patients' medical response to the treatment was based on the assumption that the recommendations were being followed (Charney 1972; Gordis 1979). If the problems did not clear up as anticipated, the provider would decide on a different treatment.

It seemed to come as a rude shock to the health care system that failures of compliance were widespread and extensive (Marston 1970; Sackett and Snow 1979). A trickle of studies of the problem that had been appearing since at least 1943 (Truesch and Krusen 1943) suddenly became a torrent. In the four years 1974–1977 more than 250 empirical reports were published (Haynes et al. 1976). At first, studies were mostly demonstrations of the extent of noncompliance (Allen et al. 1964; Curtis 1961; Dixon et al. 1957) followed by a variety of efforts to categorize the non-compliant patient in terms of demographic or personality characteristics (Haynes 1976). The upshot of these studies was the generalization that every patient should be recognized as potentially noncompliant (Blackwell 1976). Situational factors such as the duration and complexity of regimens (Haynes 1979) and factors in the interaction of patients and providers, including both the clarity (Hulka et al. 1976; Svarstad 1976) and quality (Davis 1971; Korsch et al. 1968) of the communications were recognized as influencing the degree of compliance achieved. As attention was directed to interactional factors, investigators began to note that the very term "compliance" was based on assumptions about the nature of the provider-patient relationship that might warrant re-evaluation (Stimson 1974). Alternative terms, including "adherence" (Caplan et al. 1976; Kasl 1975), "conformity" (Svarstad 1976), and "concordance" (Hulka et al. 1976) have been proposed. The phrase, "effective utilization of expert recommendations," although too awkward for regular use, appropriately captures the scope of the issue and indicates its generic relationships to problems of the teacher-student relationship, continuing education, dissemination of research results, and the adoption of social innovations.

Meanwhile, at a more practical level, information continues to accumulate: Functional degrees of compliance are achieved in anywhere from 5 to 95 percent of cases, depending on particulars of the situation. Typically, anywhere from a third to a half of all patients fail to follow recommendations sufficiently to achieve their full therapeutic benefits. Population and personality descriptors of the noncompliant suggest that they are more likely to be drawn from the less educated, from persons with chaotic living circumstances or lacking in social support, and from persons who have poorly developed skills of self control (Haynes 1976).

Interventions to increase compliance have sometimes been very successful. Simply providing patients with written instructions increased compliance markedly (Colcher and Bass 1972; Sharpe and Mikeal 1974). A simple device for presenting tablets against a calendar layout greatly increased the proportion of patients who maintained a therapeutically efficacious drug level (Linkewich et al. 1974). Training hypertensive patients to monitor their own blood pressures improved their cooperation with a treatment regimen and the clinical control of their blood pressures (Haynes et al. 1976). On the other side of the physician-patient dyad, Inui et al. (1976) gave physicians a two-hour tutorial on the problem of non-compliance in the treatment of hypertension with suggestions as to how improved compliance could be achieved. They demonstrated clinically significant improvements in the control of blood pressure for the patients of physicians who took part in the tutorial relative to patients treated by a control group of physicians who did not participate.

Research on this topic remains one of the most active areas for psychological investigation in the health care system.

Psychological issues in response to the occurrence of health problems

A key area of health psychology concerns reactions to the occurrence of illness or injury. The experience of a major health problem itself as well as the associated experiences such as hospitalization and invasive or painful treatments are stressful. Researchers have investigated the stress of illness, injury, and treatment, and modes of coping with these stresses. As will be seen below, some researchers have focused generally on the issue of stress and coping while others have examined psychological issues of specific health problems.

Stress and coping   Psychological models of stress and coping assume that events vary in the extent to which they pose challenges to individuals, and will not be experienced as equally stressful by all people. Two major stress researchers are Irving Janis and Richard Lazarus and their colleagues; their work is summarized below.

Janis (1958) conducted the first major study of stress and recovery from surgery. The research, examining experiences of surgery patients, included intensive interviews, behavioral ratings by hospital staff, and a larger scale questionnaire survey. The major hypotheses, which were based on psychoanalytic theory and case material, concerned the relationship between patients' levels of anticipatory fear and their subsequent adjustment to surgery. It was found that compared to patients who showed either low or high anticipatory fear, those who exhibited a moderate level were less likely to show emotional disturbance following surgery. Patients who showed very little fear beforehand and who did not anticipate problems were more likely to respond to the surgery with angry resentment, complaints, anxiety and depression. Those with high preoperative anxiety continued to show a high level of fear afterwards. Janis suggested that moderate anxiety prior to the surgery allowed for the "work of worrying" and the build-up of adequate defenses to deal with the stresses of surgery and the post-surgical period. The preoperative level of fear appeared to be a function of both the individual's disposition and situational variables in terms of information provided and preparation for surgery.

A different model of stress and coping has been developed by Lazarus and his colleagues (Cohen and Lazarus 1979; Coyne and Lazarus in press; Lazarus 1966; Lazarus and Launier 1978). This is a cognitive model which emphasizes the central role played by the individual's appraisal of stress. In a recent statement of the model, stress is seen as "a general rubric for somewhat different though related processes of person-environment transaction in which demands tax or exceed the resources of the person. It is neither simply an environmental stimulus, a characteristic of the person, nor a response, but a balance between demands and the power to deal with them without unreasonable or destructive costs" (Coyne and Lazarus in press: 1). Particular attention is paid to ways in which individuals cope with the stress to reduce the demands to a tolerable level. Coping attempts serve two functions. One is an instrumental or problem-solving function which serves to alter the stressful person-environment interaction itself. The second function is palliative, which serves to regulate stressful emotions within the individual (Coyne and Lazarus in press; Lazarus and Launier 1978). Cohen and Lazarus (1979) describe five modes of coping: 1) information-seeking to determine the nature of the problem and action possibilities, 2) direct actions, 3) inhibition of action, which can prevent impulsive or potentially dangerous or embarassing acts, 4) intrapsychic processes, and 5) turning to others for aid. Other investigators have also described common coping processes, both in general and in relation to health problems (e.g. Hamburg et al. 1953; Katz et al. 1970; Lipowski 1970; Moos and Tsu 1977; Weisman 1972). Cohen and Lazarus (1979) point out the usefulness of treating coping as a process rather than as a stable disposition. The individual may not only differ in coping strategies from one situation to another (Palmer 1968) but may also show different stages of coping (Hofer et al. 1972a and b; Horowitz 1976).

Cohen and Lazarus (1979), synthesizing the material of others, identified six types of threats that may occur with illness or injury: threat of death, threats to bodily integrity and comfort, threats to self-concept and future plans, threats to emotional equilibrium, threats to fulfillment of usual social roles and activities, and threats involving the necessity of adjusting to a new physical and social environment. Threats associated with the environment have been investigated by Taylor (1979) in her analysis of the hospital environment. She argues that the hospital depersonalizes patients and forces them into a situation of lack of control. Two possible reactions may occur. A person can become a "good patient" who complies with the demands but who may be in a "state of depressed or anxious helplessness" (p. 157) or become a "bad patient" who reacts against the lack of control with anger and lack of cooperation. Either reaction may have physiological correlates as well as direct effects complicating the patient's recovery.

Studies of stresses associated with illness and injury range from descriptive studies of patients with poliomyelitis, burns, myocardial infarction, cancer, stroke and physical disability, as well as those who are awaiting breast biopsy or undergoing hemodialysis, through studies investigating possible links between coping mechanisms and recovery, to studies of interventions to improve the effectiveness of coping attempts and facilitate recovery (an excellent review of these studies can be found in Cohen and Lazarus 1979).

The descriptive research generally agrees in reporting the frequent use of denial or avoidance by patients in the early stages of illness (e.g. Hamburg *et al.* 1953; Visotsky *et al.* 1961). There is greater inconsistency in the findings concerning the link between coping strategies and the actual course of illness and recovery. While there is ample evidence that both anxiety and the successful use of defenses can alter hormones, pain, and requests for pain medication (e.g. Bursten and Russ 1965; Drew *et al.* 1968; Weisenberg 1977; Wolff *et al.* 1964), the nature of the relationship between psychological state and recovery is not always clear. While Janis (1958) found a curvilinear relationship between preoperative anxiety and emotional reactions following surgery, others have reported a positive linear relationship between these variables (e.g. Cohen and Lazarus 1973; Johnson *et al.* 1971). Cohen and Lazarus (1979) note that research findings have been contradictory; for example, low fear patients have been shown to have both the most (Layne and Yudofsky 1971) and the least (Morse and Litin 1969) delirium following open-heart surgery. It appears that high preoperative anxiety is predictive of greater anxiety or emotional problems following surgery; low preoperative anxiety may be linked with either better or worse outcome than more moderate levels of worry. Thus, while anxiety seems important in terms of response to illness or surgery, its precise role has yet to be defined.

Other psychological variables have more consistently been related to outcome. A number of studies have shown depression to be linked with slower recovery from a variety of illnesses, including myocardial infarction, brucellosis, tuberculosis, and influenza. Similarly, an active, involved role has been found to be associated with more rapid recovery from severe burns and from reconstructive vascular surgery. Stresses in addition to those deriving from the illness itself have also been shown to relate to a more complicated or slower recovery (for review of all these areas see Cohen and Lazarus 1979).

A number of investigators have attempted psychosocial interventions with patients to affect recovery. Psychotherapeutic interventions have consistently brought about positive results; for example, reducing cardiac complications following myocardial infarction and reducing delirium following open-heart surgery. Other interventions, including provision of general or specific information about one's disease and treatment, encouragement of positive thinking, and systematic relaxation have been found in some studies to improve outcome but have not been found in others to relate to recovery (see Cohen and Lazarus 1979). In general, such interventions seem to be more effective in reducing use of pain medication and improving emotional reactions than in influencing length of hospital stay. There also appears to be an interaction between characteristics of patients and the effectiveness of the intervention. The timing and type of information presented may be more or less effective depending on individuals' general coping or defensive styles, such as their tendency to use an intellectualizing defense or their locus of control (Andrew 1970; Auerbach et al. 1976).

In summary, there is evidence that psychological variables can play a significant role in the course of and recovery from a disease or injury. However, the precise role played by such variables is not yet fully described and is likely to depend on the type of the health problem and the stage within it, the characteristics of the individual, the type of care received, and the level of outcome assessed.

Challenges of specific health problems   In addition to the stresses associated with illness and medical treatment in general, every health problem and intervention poses its own set of challenges. Psychologists have been interested in the nature of the problems faced by individuals who experience various health problems, the psychological meaning of these problems, and the interaction with the social environment in which the problems are met and dealt with. Examples of health problems that have been analyzed in this perspective are cancer and induced abortion which will be considered below. Others in which a good deal of work has been done but which we will not review here are coronary disease and heart surgery and renal dialysis (see for example, Abram 1970; Kimball 1969; Wishnie et al. 1971).

The psychological problems of cancer patients are of concern not only because of the seriousness of the disease itself, but because of the problematic nature of the interaction of the cancer patient with other people. Cancer is a chronic disease with an uncertain course. However, there are particular decision and crisis points within the typical span of the disease. As noted earlier, much of the research on delay in seeking treatment has focused on cancer, particularly on the roles of fear, anxiety and denial. Other areas that have received attention include 1) patients' awareness of their disease, 2) their response to diagnosis and their causal attributions concerning the etiology of the disease (e.g., Aitken-Swan and Easson 1959; Hinton 1973; McIntosh 1974; Moses and Cividali 1966), 3) reactions to surgery (especially mastectomy) for cancer (e.g., Bard and Sutherland 1955; Katz et al. 1970; Sutherland et al. 1952; Wirsching et al. 1975), 4) the effects of cancer (especially in children) on patients' families (e.g., Binger et al. 1969; Bozeman et al. 1955; Kaplan et al. 1973), and 5) treatment of the dying patient (e.g., Garfield 1978; Payne and Krant 1969; Schoenberg et al. 1972).

Much of the research on cancer has focused on the stresses associated with the disease and its treatment and patients' psychological and emotional responses. Using interviews with cancer patients, Hinton (1973) identified common sources of threat. These include pain, disfigurement from the disease or the treatment, concern over the future regarding treatment and death, loss of work role, dependency, and alienation. Holland (1976) presents a similar list. Evidence that these stresses take an emotional toll comes from the findings of frequent psychological symptoms among cancer patients. Depression is often reported. Craig and Abeloff (1974) found that half of the 30 patients studied reported depression on a self-report measure. Achte and Vauhkonen (1970) found that over half the cancer patients (58%) in an outpatient facility in Helsinki reported depression. Other emotional symptoms were also reported by these patients: 65% reported tenseness, 58% fear of death, 39% aggressiveness, 30% affect lability, 25% paranoid trends, 15% reduced interest in life, and 12% hypomania.

While cancer presents particular adaptive tasks to all patients, the particular challenges and the nature of the response will depend on the individual characteristics of the patient. Mages and Mendelsohn (1979) identify several variables that are likely to affect responses to the disease: age and stage of life, sex, and personal history. In their sample, cancer in young adults (age 18 to 35) seemed to disrupt the transition toward independence that generally occurs at this stage of life, making commitments more difficult and complicating the resolution of the crisis of "intimacy versus isolation" (Erikson 1950). Cancer in midlife (age 36 to 55) threatened the achievement of goals and tasks upon which individuals had already embarked. Patients in this stage showed the greatest variability in response. Older adults (age 56 to 75) tended to experience an acceleration of the aging process that generally occurs more slowly at this stage: they experienced a loss of capacities and a disengagement from the external world, frequently retiring early from their work even when physically able to continue. Perhaps because they had already begun to confront their own mortality, they showed much less anger and less active coping with the disease and treatment than did younger patients. Just as one's age has implications for responses to cancer, so does one's sex. In the sample studied by Mages and Mendelsohn women appeared to fare better emotionally than did men. Compared to the female patients, males were more fearful and irritable, were more likely to engage in self-destructive behaviors, blame others for their distress, and withdraw from social contacts, and more often showed a drop in self-regard as reflected in a diminishment of effectiveness, vigor and ambition. The authors note that "the few patients who used their experience with cancer in a clearly productive way were women, particularly younger women" (p. 278). Idiosyncratic individual variables are also likely to influence responses to cancer (for this reason Mages and Mendelsohn argue for the importance of in-depth case studies). Among these variables, prior psychiatric history and experience with cancer in others seem particularly important.

The social environment of the cancer patient is also crucial in affecting the person's response to the illness. Mages and Mendelsohn (1979) identify three basic modes of coping with cancer: techniques to minimize distress, active attempts to deal with problems associated with the disease, and turning to others for support and help. The effectiveness of this last technique is highly dependent on the responses of others. Wortman and Dunkel-Schetter (1979) analyzed the effect of interpersonal relationships on patients' adjustments to cancer. They note two consistent findings in the research literature: that cancer patients are likely to have problems in interpersonal relationships and that the quality of these relationships is related to the patient's ability to cope effectively with the illness (e.g., Carey 1974; Cobb 1956; Jamison *et al.* 1978; Kaplan *et al.* 1976; Parkes 1972; Sheldon *et al.* 1970). Wortman and Dunkel-Schetter (1979) provide a model of interpersonal relationships of cancer patients. Key elements of the model are the cancer patients' need for support and clarification of their feelings and experience, the responses of significant others to these needs, and the impact of the responses of others on the patient.

Wortman and Dunkel-Schetter point out that cancer patients are not only placed in a threatening and fear-arousing situation, but are required to make competent decisions under conditions of uncertainty. An important source of information and emotional support derives from other people, but there are obstacles to communication, among them being lack of access to others who are facing similar problems, patients' own inhibitions about disclosing their feelings to either family and friends or doctors, and the reactions of others which may discourage the patient. Because of the stigma attached to cancer in our society, a cancer patient may elicit feelings of fear and aversion as well as anger and sadness. One way that individuals may deal with these feelings is to derogate the patient, which allows them to maintain a belief in a "just world" (Lerner 1970, 1971) and to alleviate their guilt over not helping the patient. Others' ambivalence may lead to actual avoidance of patients, especially if they are perceived to be dying (Schulz 1978), to avoidance of open discussion of the disease and the patient's feelings (Jamison et al. 1978), or to discrepancies between verbal and nonverbal behaviors toward the patient. As a result of these dynamics, cancer patients find themselves in a dilemma: "either they can express their feelings and be themselves, thereby incurring others' avoidance and rejection, or they can enact a charade, pretending that everything is fine, and obtain at least some support from others (Wortman and Dunkel-Schetter 1979: 143)." Given that neither solution is satisfactory, patients may vacillate and this vacillation itself creates difficulties in interpersonal relationships. The authors make some specific suggestions for interventions with patients and family members and for medical personnel. Such interventions may be important not only in aiding the psychological adjustment of cancer patients and their families, but, insofar as psychological variables influence the course of the disease (Rogentine et al. in press; Stavraky and others 1968; Derogatis et al. 1979), better coping mechanisms may actually improve prognosis and survival.

We turn now to a very different health problem in which interpersonal relationships also play a significant role: induced abortion. More than any other medical procedure, it is embedded in a psycho-social context that influences the response of patients. While the procedure itself (especially for first trimester abortion) is relatively quick, safe and easy, the meaning of the procedure and the social norms surrounding it make it a potentially problematic experience. Research on psychological reactions to abortion has shown a dramatic shift from early research which concluded that abortion was likely to lead to significant psychological problems (see summary in Simon and Senturia 1966), to the recent research which has concluded that it is a fairly benign procedure (see below). The difference in the conclusions is in part due to actual changes in the nature of the procedure and the social context in which it is performed. Not only have better techniques been developed, but current research has studied women who have undergone safe, legal abortion, while earlier research more frequently studied women who had undergone illegal procedures. There have also been changes in the methods and perspectives of researchers.

The most consistent finding in recent literature is that the predominant response to abortion is relief and happiness but that women may experience periods of mild regret, depression and anxiety following the procedure, which diminish over time (e.g., Adler 1975; Ewing and Rouse 1973; Monsour and Stewart 1973; Osofsky and Osofsky 1972; Simon *et al.* 1967; Smith 1973).

A woman's response to abortion will be a function of her own characteristics, her social environment, and her actual experience in obtaining the procedure. There appear to be two major sources of stress associated with abortion (Adler 1975). One source derives from external, social conflicts occuring as a result of disapproval and stigmatization of abortion. The second source derives from the meaning of the abortion and from internal conflicts regarding loss of the pregnancy and potential child. The variables that have been found to correlate with more negative responses to abortion reflect these two aspects of the abortion experience. On average, younger women, single women, Catholic women, women with a history of psychiatric problems, women who are coerced into terminating their pregnancy either as a result of pressure from others or from medical problems, and women undergoing second trimester rather than first trimester abortion are more likely than other women to show negative after effects (Adler 1975; Bracken *et al.* 1974; Ewing and Rouse 1973; Kaltreider 1973; Niswander and Patterson 1967; Osofsky and Osofsky 1972; Payne *et al.* 1976; Senay 1970).

While most of the research has been addressed to the psychological responses of abortion patients, there is also concern about the emotional toll on providers of abortion services. Physicians who perform abortions have been found to experience depression, dread the days on which they are to do abortions and to engage in frequent rumination about the rights and wrongs of the procedure (Kane *et al.* 1973). The recent use of dilation and evacuation (d & e) in the second trimester has made for particular problems for physicians (Kaltreider *et al.* 1979; Rooks and Cates 1977). Nurses are also disturbed by their participation in abortion services. They tend to over-identify with the fetus and may suffer an identity crisis in relation to their medical role (Char and McDermott 1972; Kaltreider *et al.* 1979; Kane *et al.* 1973; Rosen *et al.* 1974). As with responses of abortion patients, the responses of providers seem to derive both from the nature of the procedure itself and from social stresses that occur as a result of their work. Kaltreider *et al.* (1979) note that doctors and nurses performing mid-trimester d & e procedures encounter hostility from their colleagues (for example, one nurse was nicknamed "killer" by other nurses) and may feel isolated. The responses of health professionals to the provision of abortion services is of concern in and of itself (see section on the stresses of health careers). It is of further concern since the attitudes of and stresses experienced by providers may influence their treatment of patients which in turn can have adverse effects on patients' responses to the procedure (Evans and Gusden 1973; Walter 1970; Wolff *et al.* 1971). Thus, research on abortion as well as on other diseases such as cancer continues to look not only at patients, but at the providers and at family members who are also affected by health problems and their treatment.

Psychological Factors in the Provision of Health Care Services

Provider issues

By virtue of their orientation to groups, organizations and systems, the other social and behavioral sciences have tended to come to the health system with a primary interest in those who provide health services. An early and continuing interest of medical sociologists has been in the socialization of health care providers; while medical anthropologists have placed a major emphasis on the role of the healer in traditional cultures (Fabrega 1972; Polgar 1962).

Psychologists, on the other hand, have tended to *be* providers of services rather than observers of others doing so, and have focused their attention much more on the behavior of patients than on that of providers. Much of what we know about some of the problems that arise in the providing of health care was therefore discovered by others before psychologists, in significant numbers, began to attend to this area.

Nevertheless, there is now beginning to appear a psychology of health care providers which can draw upon and supplement the knowledge gained by others. In reviewing this topic, we begin with a consideration of the characteristics of health care providers, the factors that lead them to select this field of endeavor and to find their way into a particular place in it. We then look at their experiences in health services careers, with particular emphasis on their stresses and strains. We conclude the section with a consideration of the psychological aspects of two major components of health care, clinical decision making, and the provider-patient interaction.

Characteristics of health care providers   What distinguishes those who enter the health care professions from the population at large? What are the factors that influence their choice of the field and the particular niche that they find in it? What impact does the engagement in health care have upon the further development of the individual? These are questions that psychologists have particularly addressed, in collaboration with those responsible for the selection and education of students of the health professions.

Gough (1971) summarized much of the data published up until about 1970, comparing the characteristics of applicants who were admitted to medical schools with those who were not selected. Few studies compared students to the population as a whole, but it is generally true that the factors that distinguish successful from unsuccessful applicants are the same as those which distinguish the applicant pool from the general population. Students admitted were younger, more frequently single, and came from families with high socio-economic status. In 1966, more than 90 percent were males and more than 95 percent Caucasian. (In the latest compilation of student characteristics for the entering classes of 1977, the corresponding figures were 75 percent male and 80 percent Caucasian [Gordon 1979].) Scores on the Medical College Admissions Test (MCAT) for admitted applicants average about .6 to .8 of a standard deviation unit higher than those of applicants who were not selected. The median IQ of admitted students from nine different studies was 127, corresponding almost exactly with a median value of 128 obtained from measures on 15,000 physicians. Gough did not report IQ values of rejected applicants. In one study of 405 applicants, premedical grades of those admitted averaged about .4 grade point units higher. It might be noted in this context that evidence that intellectual capacity or performance in premedical education is predictive of success in medical school or competence as a physician is very weak.

Personality measures made on medical students have found from 10 to 25 percent displaying "non-normal" or "other than favorable" test profiles. Using the Minnesota Multiphasic Personality Inventory, medical students were above average in "femininity" (true of highly educated students generally), "hysteria," "hypomania," and "psychopathic deviancy." Using tests designed for the study of normal personality medical students have been found to be high in needs for "achievement" and "endurance," low on needs for "change," "autonomy," "abasement," and "succorance." Gough found that students admitted were higher on scales of "socialization," "dominance," and "creating a good impression" than were rejected students. Medical students requested to select adjectives descriptive of themselves tended to choose those portraying high needs for "achievement," "dominance," "endurance," and "order" more than is true of the general population, and to avoid adjectives that would describe them as needing change, help or abasement. Thus, these self-descriptions agree well with the descriptions provided by the psychologists' tests.

Discussions of the salient characteristics of nursing students have tended to arise out of concerns about the high rate at which students drop out of schools and leave the profession (Hutcheson et al. 1973). This orientation leads naturally to the consideration of motives for entering the field and how these may be related to success and perseverance in it. A recent paper reviews and confirms earlier findings that student nurses place a high value on human welfare and describe the desire to help people as their primary reason for choosing to become nurses (Morris and Grassi-Russo 1979). High levels of this value differentiated students who remained in school from those who dropped out (Kibrick 1963). Also important to entering students are interests in science and medicine, in security and personal achievement, and in the excitement and glamor of the job. Kibrick's study found that those who emphasized glamor and excitement were more likely to drop out than were those who gave more weight to financial security and professional accomplishments. Morris and Grassi-Russo found that their respondents gave higher rank to excitement and glamor in describing their own motivations, and to financial reward and professional status in attributions about other students. They speculate that the more material values are seen as less humane and altruistic than those of excitement and challenge, and that some reality-oriented counselling might be of assistance to students.

In summarizing comparisons of dental students with medical students, Gershen and McCreary (1977) assert simply that "they have found remarkable similarity between the two groups and some minor differences" (p. 618). Differences cited in a major review of the characteristics of dental students (Fusillo and Metz 1971) include higher scores for dental students in measures of heterosexuality and economic values and lower on measures of theoretical and social or humanitarian interests and values. High school students who preferred dentistry to medicine tended to come from homes of lower economic and social status, to have lower class standings and lower scores on general ability measures. It needs to be reemphasized that these are *relative* differences, and that in most respects medical and dental students are closer to each other than either group is to the general population norms.

During the period when these studies of student characteristics were being carried out only about one percent of dental students were female, so it is not surprising that there are no comparisons of dental students with nursing students who were almost all female at that time.

Pharmacy students have been less studied than students of the other health professions. Manasse *et al.* (1977) reviewed the few earlier studies, and reported the usual pattern of varying results from different surveys. There did appear to be a consistent finding that pharmacy provides an avenue for bright students from lower income groups to enter a profession. These authors also describe a consistent trend based on three studies only, for students to demonstrate a negative shift in their attitudes toward the profession of pharmacy. This shift brought students' views closer to those of their faculty.

In attempting to understand the effects of the socialization process, Manasse *et al.* administered the Cattell "Sixteen Personality Factor Questionnaire" to students and faculty at the University of Minnesota in 1974, as well as to all who submitted applications to the School of Pharmacy that year. The profiles of students and faculty were similar, and there was no consistent tendency for more advanced students to be more like their faculty than the pre-pharmacy students who had never met them. Using test norms for comparison, Manasse *et al.* found that the pooled group of pharmacists and pharmacy students were distinguished from physicians and nurses in being somewhat more sober or serious, more trusting and accepting of conditions as they exist, and more self-assured and complacent. None of these differences was large, however.

As Gough has emphasized, these studies don't tell us much about the *individuals* entering or remaining in the professions. At best, these surveys provide only hints about the factors that lead individual students to choose and succeed in gaining access to education in the health professions. Research that studies individuals in depth will be needed to provide the basis for unambiguous interpretations of these data and to elaborate their policy implications.

Determinants of career choice   Funkenstein (1978) has provided a comprehensive study of the choice of medicine as a career and of the kind of specialization selected within the field, based primarily on data from Harvard University. He relates these choices to the fundamental values of students and their responses to questions about the world as well as to their entering characteristics, such as MCAT scores, and to their intellectual interests. Students with high scores in Science and Quantitative parts of the MCAT are likely to choose a "bioscientific" career as opposed to a "biosocial" career that emphasizes interpersonal and behavioral aspects of medicine. But this is only one of a host of factors that distinguish, for example, the students who enter full time academic medicine in a biologically oriented department from those who enter public health or psychiatry. Of particular interest is Funkenstein's tracing of changes in the patterning of interests over the years from 1958 to 1975. He distinguishes five distinct "eras" during this period, and presents evidence to support the view that it is large scale events in society as a whole, rather than policies with regard to medical education or faculty views and teaching methods, that give rise to major shifts in the orientation of students. In 1958, when his study began, the most common interest pattern was that of the "Clinical Specialist." In 1959, coincident with the launching of Sputnik, there was a very pronounced shift toward the bioscientific orientation. In 1969, there was a sharp swing toward the social sciences, giving rise to a period that Funkenstein labelled "Student Activism." This era was followed by briefer periods which he names "The Doldrums" (1971–74) and the era of "Primary Care and Increasing Governmental Control." While changing admission policies undoubtedly contributed to these changes, their synchrony among students at various stages of their education, including residency, argues for the major contribution of societal factors.

Much of the relevant literature on choice of occupation and its impact on those at different stages of their career has recently been summarized by Cartwright (1979) from the perspective of identifying factors relevant to the stress of health careers. She draws upon a number of studies to portray the development of the medical student's choice of a specialty area. A few enter medical school with a clear plan and persist in it throughout the many years of their training. Others have a plan when they enter, but modify it during their professional education. Surgeons and psychiatrists, for example, are likely to have had an early intention to enter these fields, while radiologists and dermatologists are likely to have chosen those specialties relatively late. Entering medical students have stereotypes of the personalities of the better known specialties, but faculty influence their views markedly, especially with regard to the less common or visible areas of specialization. There appears to be a match between the characteristics of the students and those of physicians in the field to which they aspire. Students see themselves as having personal characteristics similar to the positive traits of physicians in the specialty they choose. Psychological measures of personality and beliefs, demographic and biographic characteristics all depict significant differences among those who enter different specialties. Distinctions between those who choose psychiatry as opposed to surgery, for example, include the following: psychiatry residents, relative to those in surgery, are more likely to be low in authoritarianism, high in death anxiety, interested in interpersonal aspects of health care and disinterested in medical problem solving. Psychiatry residents are less likely to come from medical families and more likely to be female and to be Jewish. Although there are no reports of systematic efforts to influence choice of specialization, the amount and nature of the differences observed have led some observers to the conclusion that shifts in the distribution of specialists will more readily be changed through changes in selection criteria for entering students than by attempts to influence those who now enter medical schools.

A good deal of attention has been paid to the personal characteristics of those entering the health professions, and, as we shall see in the next section, there is now a developing literature on the stresses of these careers. However, apart from studies of stress, the impact of health careers on the adult development of those engaged has been little studied. One reason for this neglect, of course, is that the whole concept that adults continue to mature and change in important ways is quite new to the social and behavioral sciences. The general framework for such development, and the important transitions in it have been delineated only in the past decade (Chiriboga 1979; Fiske 1980), and the stage is now set for considering the variations from the modal pattern that arise out of such life circumstances as occupation. Sociologists (e.g., Freidson 1970) have provided us with descriptions of some relevant circumstances for the field of medicine, and several authors have reported on the satisfactions and dissatisfactions reported by health professionals (summarized in Cartwright 1979). These vary considerably from one profession to another. Physicians, for example, are generally satisfied with the work they do, but feel that it leaves them too little time for their families and for recreation, hobbies, and other interests. Other professionals report less job satisfaction. They have significant concerns about professional recognition and discrepancies between the roles they learned to play during their education and those they find they must fill in the real world of the health system. To date, there are no detailed studies of the ways in which these factors express themselves in the life patterns of the professionals outside of their work roles, except as they are manifest in stress indicators. It appears to be an area ripe for development.

Stresses of health care careers

A major review integrating data from six countries (King 1970), indicates that physicians show a higher incidence of coronary heart disease, diabetes, stroke and suicide than the general population, although they have lower mortality rates for other causes. Several studies (cited in Cartwright 1979) have also indicated that dentists may be excessively prone to coronary heart disease, and Russek (1962, 1965) demonstrated correlations of heart disease with the stressfulness of specialties within professions. Suicide has been shown to be more common among dentists and pharmacists than in the general population, in addition to the previously cited excess among physicians. Drug abuse is much greater among health professionals than in the general population. Nurses are involved in this particular kind of stress response, although they have not been reported to have high incidence of "stress diseases" or suicides. Data on mental illness and marital difficulties are less clear in their implications regarding stress. Some reviews have concluded that health professionals are more prone to such problems than the population as a whole, while others have questioned the validity of these conclusions (Rose and Rosow 1973; Vaillant et al. 1972).

Interpretation of these findings is complex. By now there are many indications of an interaction between personality and the kinds of illness and stress responses that one develops. In the research on health professionals the role of self-selection – who chooses to enter the stressful professions and the more stressful specialties within them – is difficult to separate from the role of stresses of the work. Also with regard to suicide and drug abuse, health professionals have greater knowledge and access to the means of such actions, and they are usually subject to less social surveillance. Despite these complications, it seems safe to conclude that the health care professions themselves are excessively stressful. We next consider some factors that have been identified as contributing to this stress.

The socialization processes of medical school and its stresses have been much studied, and with less attention paid to other health professional schools. Most of this work has been done by sociologists. However, the stressful impact of these processes on the students has attracted the attention of psychiatrists and psychologists (Canfield et al. 1976; Edwards and Zimet 1976; Goldstein 1979; Horowitz 1964; Lief 1971; Raskin 1972; Rosenberg 1971). Cartwright (1979) notes three sources of stress: the educational milieu itself, personality factors of the students, and patient-related experiences. In the first of these, it is the heavy curriculum that is the principal source of stated concern. Students feel overwhelmed and find that they have too little time for families and friends or for recreational activities. Another difficulty identified by some who observe the process is the conflict of values that emerges during the course of the education. One version of this issue emphasizes the confrontation between students' idealism on entry and the realities of the learning and treatment environments that students encounter. A marked increase in "cynicism" has been attributed to these discrepancies (Loupe et al. 1979), which may or may not diminish after the educational years are completed (Becker and Geer 1958). Dramatic temporal shifts in the values of medical students, paralleling major societal eras between 1958 and 1975, were mentioned in the previous section (Funkenstein 1978). Funkenstein calls attention to the disparity between faculty values and those of students, and although he has no data bearing on this, he speculates that these give rise to stresses for students.

Characteristics of the students themselves may interact with the medical school environment in a negative way. Studies of the personalities of medical students using the methods of depth psychology have found them to be predominantly of the obsessive-compulsive character structure and to rely on the associated defenses of isolation of affect, overcontrol of feelings, and intellectualization (Lief 1971). Tests developed for the study of normal personalities depict medical students as independent, dominant individuals with strong leadership potential (Cartwright 1972; Gough and Hall 1973). These traits may have strong survival value in some aspects of the environments of professional schools and careers. They do, however, portray individuals relatively low in flexibility, who may find it difficult to bend to the demands of interpersonal frustrations or to the changes in the social circumstances of medical practice that are now taking place.

The stresses of dealing with sick persons, particularly the severely injured and the terminally ill, affect all health care providers (Hay and Oken 1972; Maslach 1979). The particular stresses faced by providers of abortion services have already been mentioned. The phenomenon of "burn out," resulting from unremitting engagement with patients whose problems elicit a high degree of emotional arousal, has attracted increasing attention recently (Artiss and Levine 1973; Freudenberger 1974). Less dramatic, but more ubiquitous are the everyday stresses that arise in the interpersonal relationship between the provider of health care and the patient. For those who practice the model of health care in which responsibility resides primarily with the provider, the non-compliant patient, the patient with trivial complaints, and the person who cannot be helped all constitute continuing sources of irritation (Cartwright 1979; Kimmel 1973; Mechanic 1972). Shifts in the role definitions and expectations of health care providers may go far toward eliminating these problems as sources of stress in health careers (Blum 1974a; Burnum 1978; Stone 1979b).

Clinical decision making Psychology has made substantial progress toward understanding human thought processes during the past quarter of a century. The advent of the digital computer, with its demands for schemes for the representation and manipulation of information, brought to an end a period of several decades during which most psychologists excluded from their lexicons words like "ideas," "knowledge," and even "concepts." Although there has been a dramatic increase in attention to questions of how humans go about using information and information-processing algorithms to guide their behavior, until very recently almost no one attempted to use data from the health system in the development of the new models of human thought and decision making nor to apply the developing theories to the improvement of health care.

The material in this section is largely drawn from two significant publications by Elstein and his associates (Elstein and Bordage 1979; Elstein et al. 1978) that have begun to redress this situation. As these authors point out, health care providers make most of the decisions that determine how health care dollars, now approaching ten percent of our total expenditures, are spent. Yet their search of the literature turned up only a handful of empirical studies as to how these decisions were made. A moderate literature on the processes of diagnosis (which is only a part of the whole) was almost entirely *prescriptive*, advising how diagnosis should be done, rather than describing how it is done.

Elstein and his coauthors identify three major strands of cognitive theory relevant to clinical decision-making, which originated separately but now are beginning to converge. In their earlier publication (Elstein et al. 1978) these were labelled "process tracing," "judgment," and "decision-making models." In their later review (Elstein and Bordage 1979) they renamed and generalized the category of process-tracing as "information processing." In so doing, they incorporated the important demonstrations of limitations in human rationality (Kahneman and Tversky 1972, 1973; Leaper et al. 1972; Tversky and Kahneman 1973, 1974) with the earlier emphasis on analyses of problem solving processes.

Studies from three areas of early research demonstrated ways in which human thought deviated from the best that could be achieved by mathematical, statistical and computer algorithms. These studies led to the concept of "bounded rationality." According to this concept, humans are limited in their information processing by various constraints of the human nervous system, particularly those associated with the short term memory. With the recognition of these limitations, we can provide external support systems to circumvent them, and thus make better use of our long term memories and the enormously creative associations and innovations that arise from them, which no computer systems now in existence can begin to approximate.

Using this framework of psychological theory Elstein and others (Barrows et al. 1977, 1978; Slovic et al. 1971; Smedslund 1963; Wallsten 1978) have begun to mine the rich ore provided by the relatively constrained and crucial thought processes in which health care providers engage. While the work is only getting started, some outlines of significant patterns are already beginning to appear. Jason, in his foreword to the book by Elstein *et al.* (1978: x–xi), lists five generalizations, which are supported by the research to date. These generalizations are relevant to a basic framework which holds that the clinician engages in problem-solving much like that described first by Bartlett (1958) and later by Newell and Simon (1972). In this view, the clinician fills in the gaps between a set of givens and something to be proved or demonstrated. That is, the goal state is described at an early stage in the process, and a logical path from the starting point to that conclusion is the object of search. In the diagnostic process, the end state is represented in the form of alternative *hypotheses* as to what the diagnosis may be.

Jason's first three generalizations concern these hypotheses formulated by clinicians: 1) They are generated early in the problem-solving process, in spite of a widely taught precept that urges the deferral of conclusions until all data are in. 2) The number of alternative hypotheses considered is small, rarely more than five and almost never more than seven. 3) In an effort to simplify their task, clinicians "overinterpret" their data. They do so in three ways: disregarding new data that doesn't fit, regarding data as disconfirming of a hypothesis when it is not, and, most frequently, treating information as confirmatory when it is not. Jason's last two generalizations are: 4) Competence in reaching sound diagnoses varies according to the particular type of problem that is presented. We may need to think in terms of "*profiles* of competence" (italics in original, p. x), rather than of a single, highly generalized ability. 5) In spite of the limitations of generality just mentioned, competence does rest on information and experience. Having learned the necessary information is not sufficient; retaining it and mobilizing it when needed are capacities that depend on repetitive experience.

In their summation, Elstein and Bordage (1979) conclude, "the research reviewed offers a sobering perspective on clinical reasoning. The common thread running through all of it is the notion of our limited rationality and the consequence that clinical reasoning is a more error-prone and less perfect process than we have hoped or wished it be" (p. 366). Yet our recognition of its limitations is the first step in our overcoming them. Both the improvement of professional education and the development of cognitive prostheses offer real challenge to the field of health psychology. At the same time, the opportunity to study and understand clinical decision-making promises to make rich contributions to our developing theories of human cognition.

Provider–patient interaction No well-defined, psychological theories of provider–patient interaction are currently in view. A psychologist who confronts the chaotic literature that has developed in the fields of sociology (e.g. Parsons 1975; Svarstad 1976; Waitzkin and Stoeckle 1976), anthropology (Fabrega 1975; Hayes–Bautista 1976; Kleinman 1975), counselling (Anthony and Carkhuff 1976; Bernstein 1978; Kagan 1979), psychotherapy (Ruesch 1975), speech and communication (Vaughn and Burgoon 1976), medicine (Balint 1964; Bird, 1973; Charney 1972), nursing (Johnston 1976; Kalisch 1971), pharmacy (Davis *et al.* 1976; Ivey *et al.* 1975), and dentistry (Eijkman *et al.* 1977; Runyon and Cohen 1979) may well be overwhelmed by the complexity of the topic. There are documentations of problems (Ley and Spelman 1967), documentations of process (Korsch *et al.* 1968) and prescriptions both in general terms (Bird 1973) and as embodied in numerous courses on the teaching of the "skills" of communications and interpersonal relationships to students of the health professions (reviewed by Carroll and Monroe 1979; Kahn *et al.* 1979; Stone, Rowe, and Obedzinski 1979). As indicated earlier, much of the writing about provider–patient interactions is addressed primarily to the issue of the patient's "compliance" with the expert's recommendations. It seems more promising, however, to consider "compliance," or more appropriately, effective utilization of expert recommendations, as one aspect of a much larger transaction (Stone 1979b).

This transaction, which is focused in the face-to-face interaction of the health professional and the client, is greatly influenced by the preparations that each party has made for their direct engagement – preparations that are both explicit and implicit, conscious and unconscious. A number of different models have been proposed for describing the provider–patient interaction. Many are variants on the paradigm that the provider listens, then tells the client what to do (cf. Fletcher 1972: 7). In order to succeed in this task, it may be essential to be persuasive (Fishbein 1976), to arouse an appropriate amount of fear (Janis 1967; Leventhal 1970), or to trade upon the status of the provider's role to gain social influence (Rodin and Janis 1979; Janis and Rodin 1979). A more transactional model builds upon social exchange theory (Thibaut and Kelley 1959), recognizing that both providers and clients give and receive value in their interactions, and that the continuation of a relationship is gravely at risk if either party fails to receive satisfaction from it (Vaughn and Burgoon 1976).

A model proposed by some psychologists (D'Zurilla and Goldfried 1971; Stone 1979b) treats provider–patient interaction as joint problem-solving. (This was the model presented earlier in the description of the patient–provider interaction.) It views this problem-solving as one kind of transaction that proceeds within the more general processes of social learning and social exchange. By virtue of the mutual recognition by the participants that the client consults the provider because of an agreed upon difference in expertise, the expectation arises between them that the social exchange will result in the solution of a problem. Both the clinical decision-making discussed in the previous section and the question of compliance are components in the total transaction. From this perspective, the task of the provider–patient interaction is to exchange information in such a way that both parties to the transaction achieve their goals to a satisfactory degree. We should also note that there are other parties to the transaction, whose concerns about quality of care and health outcomes are currently regarded as legitimate constraints on its resolution.

It is characteristic of a psychological approach to the study of doctor–patient interactions to represent the contributions of past history and present social constraints in the situation in terms of their influence on the immediate expectations, goals, and internalized constraints of the active participants. There are substantial differences among psychologists in the extent to which they are willing to consider humans as *conscious* problem solvers who actively compare their own behaviour in the problem-situations with norms or algorithms for such behavior. While such differences have, in the past, been the basis for theoretical polemics, they are increasingly becoming a matter for empirical verification with full recognition of differences among individuals and cultures in the degree to which they engage in self-monitoring behavior. In our Western, middle-class, professionally-trained society – the one out of which health professionals operate – the problem solving model is sufficiently accepted as the norm to be made the reference basis from which deviations are described. Thus, we can approach the description and analysis of provider–patient interactions by asking in what way they deviate from an idealized process of joint problem-solving.

Ideally, there would be complete and explicit agreement between two parties as to which elements of their larger sets of goals were legitimate aspects of the current transaction. There would be full exchange of information at every stage of the problem-solving process, to which each party would contribute fully, appropriately, and in synchrony. Potential obstacles to this ideal process are numerous. Goals may not be fully cognized; covert or illegitimate "secondary agendas" may be brought to the transaction by either or both parties. Common and unprogrammed sources of such agendas are challenges to the self-esteem of either party and violations of their expectations regarding appropriate role behavior. The problem-solving process may not be well developed in the client. Providers are usually well-trained in individual problem-solving, but have rarely had explicit training in adapting it to the social, two-party context. The actual exchange of information may be obstructed by differences in language and vocabulary and in the cognitive representations of reality from which the two participants derive their messages. Obstruction may also arise from social conventions that limit the kinds of communications that are considered acceptable. For example, expression of negative feelings is usually proscribed. An obstacle to fuller communication often asserted by providers is that they lack the time to communicate more fully with patients.

No systematic appraisal has yet appeared documenting the relative contributions of the various kinds of obstacles cited as shortcomings in provider–patient interactions. Some indirect information is available in the literature on outcomes of transactions, especially those dealing with the satisfactions and frustrations of the participants. There are a good many reports on patients' satisfaction, based both on reactions to specific encounters (Ley et al. 1976; Francis et al. 1969) and on surveys of general opinions about health care providers (Congalton 1969; Ware and Snyder 1975). These studies are consistent in their findings that patients or clients place high value on receiving both competent treatment and respect from providers.

Most studies of the satisfaction and frustrations of providers of health care that arise during individual encounters with patients have come to us from sociologists and cannot gracefully be recounted in a summary about health psychology (Freidson 1970). The same could be said about evidence regarding the impact of secondary agendas reflected in struggles between provider and client for power in the clinical encounter (Waitzkin and Stoeckle 1976). Detailed study of the processes of interaction have also been mainly the province of sociologists and sociologically trained physicians (Davis 1971; Hulka et al. 1976; Korsch et al. 1968). Most of this work has been conducted within the broad outlines of the method of "interaction analysis" developed by Bales (1950, 1970). Recently, an entirely new method for recording interactions has been introduced (Stiles 1978) and has been applied to the description of physician–patient encounters with interesting results (Stiles *et al.* 1979). This method has, for example, demonstrated a temporal pattern of interaction, that reflects functionally the widely advocated technique of asking open-ended questions. Unlike most methods for demonstrating this behavior, which rely on observers' judgments of the form of the question, however, the technique of Stiles *et al.* (1979) makes use of a *pattern* of acts involving the behavior of both provider and patient. Working from typescripts, each utterance was assigned to one of eight categories of form and to one of the same categories with regard to the intent of the utterance. The numbers of occurrences of the predominant utterance types were factor-analyzed separately for three "segments" of the interaction – medical history, physical examination, and conclusion. "Closed questions" was a factor characterized by physician questions and patient acknowledgments with an intent to edify and disclose. The other major pattern for this segment of the interview was labelled "Exposition," which seemed to capture what is usually meant by open, exploratory types of questioning. In this pattern, which was positively associated with patient satisfaction, the patient engaged in edifying and informing forms of utterance, and the physician in acknowledgment. These inital results by Stiles *et al.* (1979) are the first to have demonstrated a significant association between the specific forms of utterances and patients' satisfactions with outcomes. Unfortunately, the method of Stiles *et al.* does not as yet provide a means for linking the behavior it observes to the sequences of the problem-solving model, since it makes no use of message content in its categorical scheme.

The method of Interpersonal Process Recall, developed by Kagan and colleagues for use in the training of counsellors and others in communication skills (Kagan 1979; Werner and Schneider 1974) has been used by Elstein *et al.* (1978) for their studies of clinical decision-making. This technique offers great promise for the study of communication processes. In essence, it engages the participants in an intensive review of their private thoughts during a transaction by replaying a videotape of the interaction. A person trained in a special form of non-evaluative inquiry facilitates the recall that is stimulated by the events on the tape. Remarkable detail can be recovered about intentions, alternatives considered, feelings aroused, and evaluations of the process. Vigorous exploitation of this method would seem to wait only on the development of a suitable set of categories for the recording of these elaborations.

Summary In concluding this section on psychological studies of health care providers, we are led to observe that the traditional themes of psychological theory have not directed the attention of psychologists toward the health care provider to the same extent as has been true in other social sciences. Except for the specialized field of psychotherapy research, there has been very little work until the past five years. One could speculate that the different emphases among the fields of social and behavioral science come about because of two characteristics that distinguish psychology: First, emphasis on the use of the experimental method as opposed to field studies for the gathering of basic knowledge has retarded our use of the phenomena of the health care system as substance for the development of theories. Second, the engagement of clinical psychologists in health care intervention has focused their attention on the problems of the patient or client. For them the psychology of the provider is the psychology of themselves. This reflexive study seems to come late in the development of a field. A final obstacle to the psychological study of health care providers may spring from the endemic status struggles of the health care system, in which psychologists have tended to occupy somewhat marginal and ambiguous positions. Being studied is very often found to be uncomfortable by those who are the subject of study, but may be more tolerable when it is done by frank outsiders than when proposed by members of a partially assimilated inside group.

Overview of Health Psychology

Relationships of health psychology to other health professions and disciplines

We reach the end of our summary of some of the topics currently under study by psychologists whom we would call health psychologists. As we have said earlier, much of the work cited was done by persons from other fields and disciplines, and others continue to contribute to our understanding of these topics. Thus, we cannot define the field without reference to these others. Separation from the other basic disciplines of the behavioral and social sciences, particularly medical sociology and medical anthropology, may be made (with difficulty sometimes) on the basis of the different methods of gathering data and the different theoretical structures into which these data are fit that are used by the several disciplines. We feel no need to undertake this separation, since we believe the disciplines to be complementary rather than competitive.

The field of health psychology is in principle very broad, but it is so new as a self-conscious enterprise that its researchers and professionals have hardly sighted many of its regions, let alone begun to work in them. It finds itself in a social environment where established disciplines and professions already flourish, and where other approaches to similar problems have been developing concurrently with health psychology. In this section, we will examine the relationships with a few of the more salient of these – clinical psychology, medical psychology, pediatric psychology, rehabilitation psychology and behavioral medicine.

A scheme for defining the attributes demarcating the issues within the realm of health psychology was offered by Stone (1977). The framework comprised a cube defined by three dimensions relative to the study and amelioration of health problems (see Figure 1): 1) The *level* of the

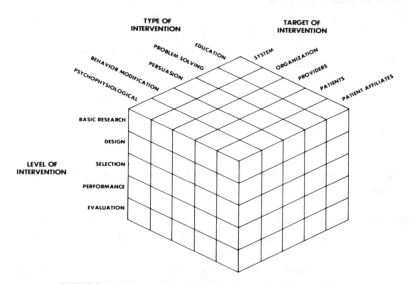

FIGURE 1.1 The psychological dimensions of health psychology

behavioral scientist's intervention in the system, ranging from basic research that describes phenomena without any consideration about changing them, to evaluation of one's own interventions or those made by others. Intermediate steps in this dimension involve designing, selecting and recommending, or performing interventions. 2) The second dimension concerns the *type* of intervention involved. It ranges from the modification of physiological or psychophysiological states (as by administration of drugs or by biofeedback) to providing of information without any consideration of the mechanisms whereby that information is assimilated (educational lectures). Intermediate stages address mechanisms of stress management, clarification of values and motivations and modification of cognitive structures such as attitudes, beliefs and skills. Thus, this dimension has to do with a range from physiological to purely informational. 3) The third dimension has to do with the *target* of the information. It ranges from the patient and those who are significantly related to this person to the health system as a whole. We can address health problems by attending to the person who has such a problem, or by looking at the people, organizations, and institutions that are attempting to assist the person with a problem.

It is possible, using this cube, to discuss what various subgroupings of health professionals and scientists do. Behavioral medicine is concerned (according to our view) with the application of psychophysiological, stress management, and behavior modification techniques to the health problems of identified patients, and, in fact, its types of interventions extend beyond the boundaries of the cube to be continuous with medicine in general. Behavioral medicine includes limited intervention with families of patients and with educational interventions directed at providers, although its primary targets are patients. The levels at which behavioral medicine intervenes extend all the way from basic research to performance of the interventions with patients and, in the best situations, into the level of evaluation of its own work, although the field known as program evaluation appears not to be a part of behavioral medicine, according to most present usages. With these specifications, it is possible to demarcate a region within the cube that is the province of behavioral medicine.

"Medical psychology" is a term that, in the United States, usually refers to the application of clinical psychological methods of assessment, behavior change (or psychotherapy) and consultation to the problems of individual patients. Traditionally it has not emphasized psychophysiological methods, nor has it used purely educational methods, but it has placed considerable stress on the families of patients. Pediatric psychology is a subspecialty within medical psychology that limits its attention to a particular group of patients, and rehabilitation psychology limits its concern to a particular phase of the patient's interaction with the health system. In fact, it would be possible to add a fourth dimension to the cube to reflect this issue of the stage in the health problem at which the intervention is directed.

Clinical psychology has traditionally concerned itself almost entirely with problems in the area of mental health. With a membership almost as large as the combined memberships of the other 39 divisions of the American Psychological Association, the Division of Clinical Psychology might think it presumptuous of us to claim that their field is a subspecialty within the subspecialty we have here called "Medical Psychology." We would, in fact, prefer the term "Clinical Psychology" for that whole region of health psychology, here termed "Medical Psychology," allowing for specialization within the field as to classes of illness and methods of approach in the same way that the field of medicine recognizes specialties such as cardiology and urology, surgery and radiology and psychiatry. A clinical psychology, thus defined as the clinical arm of health psychology, would obviously overlap extensively with behavioral medicine, even as clinical psychology, as it is now defined, overlaps with psychiatry. Boundaries within and between these domains of practice will no doubt be set along lines of clinical privilege.

The field of psychosomatic medicine as it was first defined by its originators confined its attention mainly to the role of psychodynamic conflicts in the etiology of certain diseases (Stone 1979c). In the past ten years, the topics included in reviews of psychosomatic medicine are almost indistinguishable from those covered by the definition of behavioral medicine.

What is the significance of these distinctions among fields? Surely, there are many issues of professional jurisdiction and clinical competence that will be debated along the interior boundaries of the occupied regions of our cube. What is striking to us are the large spaces within the cube that remain almost totally devoid of psychological research or practice. Psychologists are only beginning to turn their attention to attitudes of health care providers, to the stress in the organizations of the health system, to the implications of psychophysiological limits on human capabilities for the operation of the health system as a whole.

Members of other social and behavioral sciences have long been at work in some of these regions, using their own types of approaches and interventions (Adler and Stone 1979). By conceiving of health psychology in this comprehensive way, in which the current activities of the workers in clinical psychology and behavioral medicine are recognized as but a part of the whole, we may be able to encourage psychologists to join their concepts and methods with those of their colleagues in other disciplines in the farther reaches of the health system.

REFERENCES CITED

Abram, H.S., 1970. Survival by machine: The psychological stress of hemodialysis, *Psychiatry in Medicine* **1**: 37–51.

Abramson, E.E., 1977. Behavioral approaches to weight control: An updated review, *Behavior Research and Therapy* **15**: 355–363.

Achte, K, and M. Vauhkonen, 1970. *Cancer and Psyche*, Monographs from the Psychiatric Clinic of the Helsinki University Central Hospital.

Ackerknecht, E.A., 1968. *A Short History of Medicine*, New York: Ronald Press.

Adler, N.E., 1974. Factors affecting contraceptive use. Paper delivered at 82nd Annual Convention of the American Psychological Association, New Orleans, LA.

Adler, N.E., 1975. Emotional responses of women following therapeutic abortion, *American Journal of Orthopsychiatry* **45**: 446–454.

Adler, N.E., and A. Milstein, 1979. Psychological perspectives on health system planning, in *Health Psychology*, G.C. Stone, F. Cohen, N.E. Adler, and Associates (eds.), pp. 395–418, San Francisco: Jossey-Bass.

Adler, N.E., and G.C. Stone, 1979. Social science perspectives on the health system, in *Health Psychology*, G.C. Stone, F. Cohen, and N.E. Adler, and Associates (eds.), pp. 19–46, San Francisco: Jossey-Bass.

Ager, J.W., H.H. Werley, and F. Shea, 1973. Correlates of continuance in a family planning program, *JOGN Nursing* **2**: 15–23.

Aitken-Swan, J., and E.C. Easson, 1959. Reactions of cancer patients on being told their diagnosis, *British Medical Journal* **1**: 779–783.

Aitken-Swan, J., and R. Patterson, 1955. The cancer patient: Delay in seeking advice, *British Medical Journal* **1**: 623–627.

Allen, E.A., M. Stewart, and P. Jeney, 1964. The efficiency of post-sanitarium management of tuberculosis, *Canadian Journal of Public Health* **55**: 323–333.

Amelar, R.D., L. Dubin, and P.C. Walsh, 1977. *Male Infertility*, Philadelphia: W.B. Saunders.

American Psychological Association, Task Force on Health Research, 1976. Contributions of psychology to health research: Patterns, problems, and potentials, *American Psychologist* **31**: 263–274.

Andrew, J.M., 1970. Recovery from surgery, with and without preparatory instruction, for three coping styles, *Journal of Personality and Social Psychology* **15**: 223–226.

Andrew, J.M., 1972. Delay of surgery, *Psychosomatic Medicine* **34**: 345–354.

Andrews, G.R., and R.L. Debus, 1978. Persistence and the causal perception of failure: Modifying cognitive attributions, *Journal of Educational Psychology* **70**: 154–166.

Anthony, W., and R. Carkhuff, 1976. *The Art of Health Care: Handbook of Psychological First Aid Skills*, Amherst, Mass.: Human Resources Development Press, Inc.

Artiss, K.L., and A.S. Levine, 1973. Doctor–patient relation in severe illness, *New England Journal of Medicine* **288**: 1210–1214.

Attkisson, C., W. Hargreaves, M. Horowitz, and J.E. Sorensen (eds.), 1978. *Evaluation of Human Service Programs*, New York: Academic Press.

Auerbach, S.M., P.C. Kendall, H.F. Cuttler, and N.R. Levitt, 1976. Anxiety, locus of control, type of preparatory information, and adjustment to dental surgery, *Journal of Consulting and Clinical Psychology* **44**: 809–818.

Bahnson, C.B., and M.B. Bahnson, 1966. Role of the ego defenses: Denial and repression in the etiology of malignant neoplasm, *Annals of the New York Academy of Sciences* **125** (Art. 3): 827–845.

Bahnson, M.B., and C.B. Bahnson, 1969. Ego defenses in cancer patients, *Annals of the New York Academy of Sciences* **164**(Art. 2): 546–557.

Bales, R.F., 1950. *Interaction Process Analysis*, Cambridge, Mass.: Addison-Wesley.

Bales, B.F., 1970. *Personality and Interpersonal Behavior*, New York: Holt.

Balint, M., 1964. *The Doctor, His Patient, and the Illness* (Second Edition), London: Pitman.

Bandura, A., 1969. *Principles of Behavior Modification*, New York: Holt, Rinehart and Winston.

Bandura, A., 1977. Self-efficacy: Toward a unifying theory of behavior change, *Psychological Review* **84**: 191–215.

Bard, M., and A.M. Sutherland, 1955. Psychological impact of cancer and its treatment, IV. Adaptation of radical mastectomy, *Cancer* **8**: 656–672.

Baric, L., 1969. Recognition of the "at risk" role – a means to influence health behavior, *International Journal of Health Education* **12**: 24–34.

Barrows, H.S., J.W. Feightner, V.R. Neufeld, and G.R. Norman, 1978. *Analysis of the Clinical Methods of Medical Students and Physicians*, Hamilton, Ontario: School of Medicine, McMaster University.

Barrows, H.S., G.R. Norman, V.R. Neufeld, and J.W. Feightner, 1977. Studies of the clinical reasoning process of medical students and physicians, in *Proceedings of the Sixteenth Annual Conference on Research in Medical Education*, pp. 351–355, Washington, D.C.: Association of American Medical Colleges.

Bartlett, F.C., 1958. *Thinking*, New York: Basic Books.

Bates, F.E., and I.M. Ariel, 1948. Delay in treatment of cancer, *Illinois Medical Journal* **94**: 361–365.

Becker, H.S., and B. Geer, 1958. The fate of idealism in medical school, *American Sociological Review* **23**: 50–60.

Becker, M.H. (ed.), 1974. The health belief model and personal health behavior, *Health Education Monographs* **2** (# 4): 324–473.

Becker, M.H., D.P. Haefner, S.V. Kasl, J.P. Kirscht, L.A. Maiman, and I.M. Rosenstock, 1977a. Selected psychosocial methods and correlates of individual health-related behaviors, *Medical Care* **15**: 27–48.

Becker, M.H., M. Kaback, I.M. Rosenstock, and M. Ruth, 1975. Some influences on public participation in a genetic screening program, *Journal of Community Health* **1**: 3–14.

Becker, M.H., L.A. Maiman, J.P. Kirscht, D.P. Haefner, and R.H. Drachman, 1977b. The health belief model and dietary compliance: A field experiment, *Journal of Health and Social Behavior* **18**: 348–366.

Benedek, T., 1952. Infertility as a psychosomatic defense, *Fertility and Sterility* **3** (# 6): 527–541.

Bernstein, I.C., 1952. An investigation into the etiology of nausea and vomiting of pregnancy, *Minnesota Medicine* **35**: 34–38.

Bernstein, L., 1978. Teaching counselling skills to medical students, *Patient Counselling and Health Education*, Spring Issue: 30–33.

Binger, C.M., A.R. Arlin, R.C. Feuerstein, J.H. Kushner, S. Zoger, and C. Mikkelsen,

1969. Childhood leukemia, *New England Journal of Medicine* **238**: 414–418.

Bird, B., 1973. *Talking with Patients*, Philadelphia: J.B. Lippencott.

Blackwell, Barbara, 1963. The literature of delay in seeking medical care for chronic illnesses, *Health Education Monographs* **16**(# 3): 3–31.

Blackwell, Barry, 1976. Treatment adherence, *British Journal of Psychiatry* **129**: 513–531.

Blau, A., B. Slaff, K. Easton, J. Welkowitz, J. Springarn, and J. Cohen, 1963. The psychogenic etiology of premature births, *Psychosomatic Medicine* **25**: 201–211.

Blaug, S.M., B. Gold, G. Sonnedecker, B. Suarstad, D.E. Knapp, L.A. Morris, D.A. Knapp, and F.B. Paulumbo, 1975. Interdisciplinary panel discussion: A realistic appraisal of the potential contribution of the social and behavioral sciences to professional education in pharmacy, *American Journal of Pharmaceutical Education* **39**: 593–595.

Bloom, B., 1976. The use of social indicators in the estimation of health needs, in *Need Assessment in Health and Human Services: Proceedings of the Louisville National Conference, University of Louisville, Louisville*, Ky. R.A. Bell, M. Sundel, J.F. Aponte, and S.A. Murrel (eds.), pp. 155–171, (Expanded version to be published by Human Sciences Press, 1981.)

Blum, H.L., 1974a. Evaluating health care, *Medical Care* **12**(12): 999–1011.

Blum, H.L., 1974b. *Planning for Health*, New York: Human Services Press.

Bott, E.A., 1928. Teaching of psychology in the medical course, *Bulletin of the Association of American Medical Colleges* **3**: 289–304.

Bozeman, M.F., C.E. Orbach, and A.M. Sutherland, 1955. Psychological impact of cancer and its treatment, III, *The Adaptation of Mothers to the Threatened Loss of their Children through Leukemia*, Part I **8**: 1–20.

Bracken, M.B., M. Hachamovitch, and G. Grossman, 1974. The decision to abort and psychological sequelae, *Journal of Nervous and Mental Disease* **158** (2): 154–162.

Brownell, K.D., and A.J. Stunkard, 1978. Behavioral treatment of obesity in children, *American Journal of Diseases of Children* **132**: 403–412.

Burnum, J.F., 1978. The worried sick, *Annals of Internal Medicine* **88**: 572.

Bursten, B., and J.J. Russ, 1965. Preoperative psychological state and corticosteroid levels of surgical patients, *Psychosomatic Medicine* **27**: 309–316.

Byrne, D., M.A. Steinberg, and M.S. Schwartz, 1968. Relationship between repression-sensitization and physical illness, *Journal of Abnormal Psychology* **73**: 154–155.

Caldwell, J., 1958. Personality in pregnancy and labor, *Southern Medical Journal* **51**: 1026–1029.

Canfield, R.C., G.L. Powell, and P. Weinstein, 1976. Facilitating the transition to dental school, *Journal of Dental Education* **40**: 269–271.

Caplan, R., E.A.R. Robinson, J.R.P. French, Jr., J.R. Caldwell, and M. Shinn, 1976. *Adhering to Medical Regimens*, Ann Arbor: Institute for Social Research, University of Michigan.

Carey, R.C., 1974. Emotional adjustment in terminal patients: A quantitative approach, *Journal of Counseling Psychology* **21**: 433–439.

Carroll, J.G., and J. Monroe, 1979. Teaching medical interviewing: A critique of educational research and practice, *Journal of Medical Education* **54**: 498–499.

Cartwright, A., 1979. *Patients and their Doctors*, London: Routledge and Kegan Paul.

Cartwright, L.K., 1972. Personality differences in male and female medical students, *Psychiatry in Medicine* **3**: 213–218.

Cartwright, L.K., 1979. Sources and effects of stress in health careers, in *Health Psychology*. G.C. Stone, F. Cohen, and N.E. Adler, and Associates (eds.), pp. 419–445, San Francisco: Jossey-Bass.

Char, W.F., and J.F. McDermott, 1972. Abortions and acute identity crisis in nurses, *American Journal of Psychiatry* **238** (8): 952–957.

Charles, A.G., K.L. Norr, C.R. Block, S. Meyering, and E. Meyers, 1978. Obstetric and psychological effects of psycho-prophylactic preparation for childbirth, *American Journal of Obstetrics and Gynecology* **131**: 44–52.

Charney, E., 1972. Patient–doctor communication: Implications for the clinician, *Pediatric Clinics of North America* **19**: 263–279.

Chertok, L., M.L. Mondzain, and M. Bonnaud, 1963. Vomiting and the wish to have a child, *Psychosomatic Medicine* **25**: 13–18.

Chiriboga, D.A., 1979. Conceptualizing adult transitions: A new look at an old subject, *Generations* **4** (# 1): 4–6.

Cobb, B., 1956. Nurse–patient relationships, *Journal of the American Geriatric Society* **4**: 690–698.

Cobb, B., R.L. Clark, C. McGuire, and C.D. Howe, 1954. Patient-responsible delay of treatment in cancer, *Cancer* **7**: 920–926.

Cohen, F., 1979. Personality, stress, and the development of physical illness, in *Health Psychology*, G.C. Stone, F. Cohen, and N.E. Adler, and Associates (eds.), pp. 77–111, San Francisco: Jossey-Bass.

Cohen, F., and R.S. Lazarus, 1973. Active coping process, coping dispositions, and recovery from surgery, *Psychosomatic Medicine* **35**: 375–389.

Cohen, F., and R.S. Lazarus, 1979. Coping with the stresses of illness, in *Health psychology*, G.C. Stone, F. Cohen, and N.E. Adler, and Associates, pp. 217–254, San Francisco: Jossey-Bass.

Colcher, I.S., and J.W. Bass, 1972. Penicillin treatment of streptococcal pharyngitis: A comparison of schedules and the role of specific counseling, *Journal of the American Medical Association* **222**: 657–659.

Congalton, A.A., 1969. Public evaluation of medical care, *The Medical Journal of Australia* **2**: 1165–1171.

Coppen, A.J., 1959. Vomiting of early pregnancy: Psychological factors and body build, *Lancet* **24**: 172–173.

Coyne, J.C., and R.S. Lazarus, (In press) Cognition, stress and coping: A transactional perspective, in *Pressure Point: Perspectives on Stress and Anxiety*, I.L. Kutash and L.B. Schlesinger (eds.), San Francisco: Jossey-Bass.

Craig, T., and M. Abeloff, 1974. Psychiatric symptomatology among hospitalized cancer patients, *American Journal of Psychiatry* **131**(12): 1323–1327.

Craig, T.J., G.W. Comstock, and P.B. Geiser, 1974. The quality of survival in breast cancer: A case-control comparison, *Cancer* **33**: 1451–1457.

Cullen, J.W., B.H. Fox, and R.N. Isom, 1976. *Cancer: The Behavioral Dimensions*, New York: Raven.

Cummings, N.A., and W.T. Follette, 1976. Brief Psychotherapy and Medical Utilization, in *The Professional Psychologist Today*, H. Dorken and Associates (eds.), pp. 165–174, San Francisco: Jossey-Bass.

Curtis, E.B., 1961. Medication errors made by patients, *Nursing Out-look* **9**: 290–291.

Cutter, H.S., R.E. Boyatzis, and D.D. Clancy, 1977. The effectiveness of power motivation training in rehabilitating alcoholics, *Journal of Studies on Alcohol* **38**: 131–141.

Cvetkovich, G., and B. Grote, 1977. Current research on adolescence and its program implications. Paper presented at joint meeting of the Washington State Council on Family Planning and Washington Alliance Concerned with School Age Parents, Olympia, Washington.

Davenport-Slack, B., and C.H. Boylan, 1974. Psychological correlates of childbirth pain, *Psychosomatic Medicine* **36**: 215–223.

Davis, C.D., and J.F.J. Curi, 1968. A comparative clinical study of a prepared child-birth program, *Connecticut Medicine* **32**: 113–121.

Davis, L.G., J.P. Gagnon, and C.K. Bryan, 1976. Pharmacist–patient communication: Its effect on pharmacy's image, *American Journal of Pharmacy* **148**: 168–179.

Davıs, M.S., 1971. Variations in patients' compliance with doctors' orders: medical practice and doctor–patient interaction, *Psychiatry in Medicine* **2**: 31–54.

deCharms, R., and M.S. Muir, 1978. Motivation: Social approaches, *Annual Review of Psychology* **29**: 91–113.

Delbecq, A.L., 1976. The use of the nominal group method in the assessment of community needs, in *Need Assessment in Health and Human Services: Proceedings of the Louisville National Conference*, University of Louisville, Louisville, Ky. R.A. Bell, M. Sundel, J.F. Aponte, and S.A. Murrel (eds.), pp. 217–230, (Expanded version to be published by Human Sciences Press, 1981.)

Dennis, W., 1950. *Current Trends in the Relation of Psychology to Medicine*, Pittsburgh: University of Pittsburgh Press.

Derogatis, L.R., M.D. Abeloff, and N. Melisaratos, 1979. Psychological coping mechanisms and survival time in metastatic breast cancer, *Journal of the American Medical Association* **242**: 1304–1308.

Deutsch, H., 1945. *The Psychology of Women, Volume 2*, New York: Grune and Stratton.

DeWatteville, H., 1957. Psychologic factors in sterility, *Fertility and Sterility* **8**: 12–24.

Dixon, W.M., P. Stradling, and I.D. Wooton, 1957. Outpatient PAS therapy, *Lancet* **2**: 871–872.

Doering, S.G., and D.R. Entwisle, 1975. Preparation during pregnancy and ability to cope with labor and delivery, *American Journal of Orthopsychiatry* **45**(5): 825–837.

Dorken, H., and Associates, 1976. *The Professional Psychologist Today*, San Francisco: Jossey-Bass.

Downs, L.A., and D. Clayson, 1972. Unwanted pregnancy: A clinical syndrome defined by the similarities of preceding stressful events in the lives of women with particular personality characteristics. Paper presented at the 20th Annual Meeting of the American College of Obstetricians and Gynecologists, Chicago, Illinois.

Drew, F.L., R.W. Moriarty, and A.P. Shapiro, 1968. An approach to the measurement of the pain and anxiety responses of surgical patients, *Psychosomatic Medicine* **30**: 826–836.

Drotar, D., 1977. Clinical psychological practice in a pediatric hospital, *Professional Psychology* **8**: 72–80.

D'Zurilla, T.J., and M.R. Goldfried, 1971. Problem-solving and behavior modification, *Journal of Abnormal Psychology* **78**: 197–226.

Eastwood, M.R., and M.H. Trevelyan, 1971. Stress and coronary heart disease, *Journal of Psychosomatic Research* **15**: 289–292.

Edwards, M.T., and C.N. Zimet, 1976. Problems and concerns among medical students, *Journal of Medical Education* **51**: 619–625.

Eijkman, M.A., N.E. Karsdorp, Boeke, and E.H.L.M. Karsdorp-Bimmerman, 1977. Experiences with a training course in patient counselling, *Journal of Dental Education* **41**: 623–625.

Eisenberg, L., 1977. The social imperative of medical research, *Science* **198**: 1105–1110.

Elstein, A.S., and G. Bordage, 1979. Psychology of clinical reasoning, in *Health Psychology*, G.C. Stone, F. Cohen, and N.E. Adler, and Associates (eds.), pp. 333–367, San Francisco: Jossey-Bass.

Elstein, A.S., L.S. Shulman, and S.A. Sprafka, 1978. *Medical Problem Solving: An Analysis of Clinical Reasoning*, Cambridge: Harvard University Press.

Emrick, C.D., 1975. A review of psychologically oriented treatment of alcoholism: II. The relative effectiveness of different treatment approaches and the effectiveness of treatment versus no treatment, *Journal of Studies on Alcohol* **36**: 88–108.

Enkin, M.W., S.L. Smith, S.W. Dermer, and J.O. Emmett, 1972. An adequately controlled study of effectiveness of PPM training, in *Psychosomatic Medicine in Obstetrics and Gynecology*, N. Morris (ed.), Basel: Karger, S.

Erikson, E.H., 1950. *Childhood and Society*, New York: Norton.

Evans, D.A., and J.P. Gusden, 1973. Postabortion attitudes, *North Carolina Medical Journal* 34: 271–273.

Ewing, J.A., and B.A. Rouse, 1973. Therapeutic abortion and a prior psychiatric history, *Journal of Psychiatry* 130(1): 37–40.

Fabrega, H., Jr., 1972. Medical anthropology, in *Biennial Review of Anthropology*, 1971. B.J. Siegel (ed.), pp. 167–229, Stanford, California: Stanford University Press.

Fabrega, H., Jr., 1975. The need for an ethnomedical science, *Science* 189: 969–975.

Fischer, I., 1956. Psychogenic aspects of infertility, *Fertility and Sterility* 6: 465–471.

Fishbein, M., 1976. Persuasive communication, in *Communication between Doctors and Patients*, A.E. Bennett (ed.), pp. 101–127, London: Oxford University Press for the Nuffield Provincial Hospitals Trust.

Fiske, M., 1980. Tasks and crises of the second half of life: The interrelationship of commitment, coping, and adaptation, in *Handbook of Mental Health and Aging*, J.F. Birren and R.B. Sloane (eds.), pp. 337–373, Englewood Cliffs, N.J.: Prentice Hall.

Fletcher, C.M., 1972. *Communication in Medicine*, Abingdon, Berkshire, England: Burgess and Son for the Nuffield Provincial Hospitals Trust.

Follette, W., and N.A. Cummings, 1967. Psychiatric services and medical utilization in a prepaid health plan setting, *Medical Care* 5: 25–35.

Ford, E.S.C., I. Forman, J.R. Willson, W. Char, W.T. Mixson, and C. Shcolz, 1953. A psychodynamic approach to the study of infertility, *Fertility and Sterility* 4: 456–465.

Fox, B.H., 1978. Premorbid psychological factors as related to cancer incidence, *Journal of Behavioral Medicine* 1: 45–133

Fox, B.H., and J.R. Goldsmith, 1976. Behavioral issues in prevention of cancer, *Preventive Medicine* 5: 106–121.

Francis, V., B. Korsch, and M. Morris, 1969. Gaps in doctor–patient communication: Patients' response to medical advice. *New England Journal of Medicine* 280: 535–540.

Franz, S.I., 1913. On psychology and medical education, *Science* 37: 555–566.

Freidson, E., 1970. *The Profession of Medicine*, New York: Harper and Row.

Freudenberger, H.J., 1974. Staff burn-out, *Journal of Social Issues* 30: 159–165.

Friedman, M., and R.H. Rosenman, 1974. *Type A Behavior and Your Heart*, New York: Knopf.

Friedman, M., R.H. Rosenman, and V. Carroll, 1958. Changes in the serum cholesterol and blood clotting time in men subjected to cyclic variation of occupational stress, *Circulation* 17: 852–861.

Funkenstein, D.R., 1978. *Medical Students, Medical Schools and Society during Five Eras: Factors Affecting the Career Choices of Physicians*, Cambridge, Mass.: Ballinger

Fusillo, A.E., and A.S. Metz, 1971. Social science research on the dental student, in *Social Sciences and Dentistry: A Critical Bibliography*, N.D. Richards and L.K. Cohen (eds.), pp. 15–67, The Hague: Fedération Dentaire Internationale.

Gambrill, E.D., 1977. *Behavioral Modification: Handbook of Assessment, Intervention, and Evaluation*, San Francisco: Jossey-Bass.

Garfield, C.A. (ed.), 1978. *Psychosocial Care of the Dying Patient*, New York: McGraw-Hill.

Garfield, C.A. (ed.), 1979. *Stress and Survival: The Emotional Realities of Life Threatening Disease*, St. Louis: Mosby.

Garrow, J.S., 1975. The regulation of body weight, in *Obesity: Its Pathogenesis and Management*, T. Silverston (ed.), pp. 1–28, Lancaster, England: Medical Technical Publishing Co.

Gershen, J.A., and C.P. McCreary, 1977. Comparing personality traits of male and female dental students: A study of two freshman classes, *Journal of Dental Education* 41: 618–622.

Glick, I.D., L.J. Salerno, and J.R. Royce, 1965. Psychophysiologic factors in the etiology of preeclampsia, *Archives of General Psychiatry* **12**: 260–266.

Glover, E., 1934. Medical psychology or academic (normal) psychology: A problem in orientation, *British Journal of Medical Psychology* **14**: 31–49.

Goldberg, I.D., G. Krantz, and B.Z. Locke, 1970. Effects of a short-term outpatient psychiatric therapy benefit on utilization of medical services in a prepaid group practice medical program, *Medical Care* **8**: 419–427.

Goldsen, R.K., 1953. *Factors Related to Delay in Seeking Diagnosis for the Danger Signals of Cancer*, Ithaca. N.Y. : Social Science Research Center, Cornell University.

Goldstein, A.M., 1976. Denial and external locus of control as mechanisms of adjustment in chronic medical illness, *Essence* **1**: 5–22.

Goldstein, M.B., 1979. Sources of stress and interpersonal support among first year dental students, *Journal of Dental Education* **43**: 625–629.

Gordis, L., 1979. Conceptual and methodological problems in measuring patient compliance, in *Compliance in Health Care*, R.B. Haynes, D.W. Taylor, and D.L. Sachett (eds.), pp. 23–45, Baltimore: Johns Hopkins University Press.

Gordon, T.L., 1979. Study of U.S. medical school applicants, 1977–1978, *Journal of Medical Education* **54**: 677–702.

Gough, H.G., 1971. The recruitment and selection of medical students, in *Psychological Aspects of Medical Training*, R.H. Coombs and C.E. Vincent (eds.), pp. 5–43, Springfield, Ill: Thomas.

Gough, H.G., 1972. *Manual for the Personal Values Abstract*, Palo Alto, Ca.: Consulting Psychologists Press.

Gough, H.G., and W.B. Hall, 1973. A prospective study of personality changes in students of medicine, dentistry, and nursing, *Research in Higher Education* **1**: 127–140.

Gray, D.B., and G.E. Ward, 1952. Delay in diagnosis of carcinoma of the stomach, *American Journal of Surgery* **83**: 524–526.

Greene, W.A., 1954. Psychological factors and reticuloendothelial disease: I. Preliminary observations on a group of males with lymphomas and leukemias, *Psychosomatic Medicine* **16**: 220–230.

Greene, W.A., 1966. The psychosocial setting of the development of leukemia and lymphoma, *Annals of the New York Academy of Sciences* **125** (Art. 3): 794–801.

Greene, W.A., L.E. Young, and S.N. Swisher, 1956. Psychological factors and reticuloendothelial disease: II Observations on a group of women with lymphomas and leukemias, *Psychosomatic Medicine* **18**: 284–303.

Greer, S., 1974. Psychological aspects: delay in the treatment of breast cancer, *Proceedings of the Royal Society of Medicine* **67**: 470–473.

Greer, S., and T. Morris, 1975. Psychological attributes of women who develop breast cancer: A controlled study, *Journal of Psychosomatic Research* **19**: 147–153.

Gunter, L., 1963. Psychopathology and stress in the life experience of mothers of premature infants, *American Journal of Obstetrics and Gynecology* **86**: 333–340.

Haefner, D.P., and J.P. Kirscht, 1970. Motivational and behavioral effects of modifying health beliefs, *Public Health Reports* **85**: 478–484.

Hagnell, L., 1966. The premorbid personality of persons who develop cancer in a total population investigated in 1947 and 1957, *Annals of the New York Academy of Sciences* **125** (Art. 3): 846–855.

Hall, S.M., and R.G. Hall, (In press),Maintaining change, in *Comprehensive Handbook of Behavioral Medicine*, J. Fergusen and C.B. Taylor (eds.), New York: Spectrum.

Hamburg, D.A., B. Hamburg, and S. deGoza, 1953. Adaptive problems and mechanisms in severely burned patients, *Psychiatry* **16**: 1–20.

Harvey, W.A., and M.J. Sherfey, 1954. Vomiting in pregnancy: A psychiatric study, *Psychosomatic Medicine* **16**: 1–9.

Hatcher, S., 1976. Understanding adolescent pregnancy and abortion, *Primary Care* **3**(3): 407–425.

Hay, D., D. Oken, 1972. The psychological stresses of intensive care unit nursing, *Psychosomatic Medicine* **34**: 109–118.

Hayes-Bautista, D.E., 1976. Modifying the treatment: Patient compliance, patient control, and medical care, *Social Science and Medicine* **10**: 233–238.

Haynes, R.B., 1976. A critical review of the 'determinants' of patient compliance with therapeutic regimens, in *Compliance with Therapeutic Regimens*, D.L. Sackett and R.B. Haynes (eds.), pp. 26–39, Baltimore: Johns Hopkins University Press.

Haynes, R.B., 1979. Determinants of compliance: The disease and the mechanics of treatment, in *Compliance in Health Care*, R.B. Haynes, D.W. Taylor, and D.L. Sackett (eds.), pp. 49–62, Baltimore: Johns Hopkins University Press.

Haynes, R.B., D.L. Sackett, E.S. Gibson, D.W. Taylor, B.C. Hackett, R.S. Roberts, and A.L. Johnson, 1976. Improvement of medication compliance in uncontrolled hypertension, *Lancet* **1**: 1265–1268.

Henderson, J.B., S.M. Hall, and H.L. Lipton, 1979. Changing self-destructive behaviors, in *Health Psychology*, G.C. Stone, F. Cohen, and N.E. Adler, and Associates (eds.), pp. 141–160, San Francisco: Jossey-Bass.

Hinton, J.M., 1973. Bearing cancer, *British Journal of Medical Psychology* **46**: 105–113.

Hochbaum, G., 1958. *Public Participation in Medical Screening Programs: A Sociopsychological Study*, Public Health Service Publication No. 572, Washington, D.C.: Superintendent of Public Documents.

Hofer, M.A., C.T. Wolff, S.B. Friedman, and J.W. Mason, 1972a. A psychoendocrine study of bereavement: Part I. 17-hydroxy-corticosteroid excretion rates of parents following death of their children from leukemia, *Psychosomatic Medicine* **34**: 481–491.

Hofer, M.A., C.T. Wolff, S.B. Friedman, and J.W. Mason, 1972b. A psychoendocrine study of bereavement: Part II. Observations on the process of mourning in relation to adrenocortical function, *Psychosomatic Medicine* **34**: 492–504.

Holland, J.C.B., 1976. Coping with cancer: A challenge to the behavioral sciences, in *Cancer: The Behavioral Dimensions*, J.W. Cullen, B.H. Fox, and R.N. Isom (eds.), pp. 263–268, New York: Raven Press.

Horowitz, M.J., 1964. *Educating Tomorrow's Doctors*, New York: Appleton-Century-Crofts.

Horowitz, M.J., 1976. *Stress Response Syndromes*, New York: Aronson.

Hulka, B.S., J.C. Cassel, L. Kupper, and J. Burdette, 1976. Communication, compliance, and concordance between physicians and patients with prescribed medications, *American Journal of Public Health* **66**: 847–853.

Hutcheson, J.D., L.M. Garland, and J.E. Prather, 1973. Toward reducing attrition in baccalaureate degree nursing programs: An exploratory study, *Nursing Research* **22**: 530–533.

Insel, P.M., and R.H. Moos, 1974. *Health and the Social Environment*, Lexington, Massachusetts: D.C. Heath and Company.

Inui, T., E. Yourtee, and J. Williamson, 1976. Improved outcomes in hypertension after physician tutorials, *Annals of Internal Medicine* **84**: 646–651.

Ivey, M., Y. Tso, and K. Stamm, 1975. Communication techniques for patient instruction, *American Journal of Hospital Pharmacy* **32**: 828–831.

Jamison, K.R., D.K. Wellisch, and R.O. Pasnau, 1978. Psychosocial aspects of mastectomy: I. The woman's perspective, *American Journal of Psychiatry* **134** (4): 432–436.

Janis, I.L., 1958. *Psychological Stress: Psychoanalytic and Behavioral Studies of Surgical Patients*, New York: Wiley.

Janis, I.L., 1967. Effect of fear arousal on attitude change: Recent developments in theory and research, in *Advances in Experimental Social Psychology*, Volume 3. L. Berkowitz (ed.), pp. 167–224, New York: Academic Press.

Janis, I.L., and L. Mann, 1977. *Decision Making: A Psychological Analysis of Conflict, Choice, and Commitment*, New York: Free Press.

Janis, I.L., and J. Rodin, 1979. Attribution, control, and decision making: Social psychology and health care, in *Health Psychology*, G.C. Stone, F. Cohen, and N.E. Adler, and Associates (eds.), pp. 487–521, San Francisco: Jossey-Bass.

Javert, C.T., 1957. *Spontaneous and Habitual Abortion*, New York: McGraw-Hill.

Jenkins, C.D., R.H. Rosenman, and S.J. Zyzanski, 1974a. Letter to the editor, *Journal of the American Medical Association* 229: 1284.

Jenkins, C.D., R.H. Rosenman, and S.J. Zyzanski 1974b. Prediction of clinical coronary heart disease by a test for the coronary-prone behavior pattern, *New England Journal of Medicine* 290: 1271–1275.

Jenkins, C.D., S.J. Zyzanski, and R.H. Rosenman, 1978. Coronary-prone behavior: One pattern or several? *Psychosomatic Medicine* 40: 25–43.

Johansson, B.G., and P. Nilsson-Ehle, 1978. Alcohol consumption and high density lipoprotein, *New England Journal of Medicine* 298: 633–634.

Johnson, J.E., H. Leventhal, and J. Dabbs, 1971. Contribution of emotional and instrumental response processes in adaptation to surgery, *Journal of Personality and Social Psychology* 20: 55–64.

Johnston, M., 1976. Communication of patients' feelings in hospital, in *Communications Between Doctors and Patients*, A.E. Bennett (ed.), pp. 31–43, London: Oxford University Press for the Nuffield Provincial Hospitals Trust.

Kagan, N., 1979. Counseling psychology, interpersonal skills, and health care, in *Health Psychology*, G.C. Stone, F. Cohen, and N.E. Adler, and Associates (eds.), pp. 465–486, San Francisco: Jossey-Bass.

Kahn, A., 1969. *Theory and Practice of Social Planning*, New York: Russell Sage Foundation.

Kahn, G.S., B. Cohen, and H. Jason, 1979. The teaching of interpersonal skills in U.S. medical schools, *Journal of Medical Education* 54: 29–35.

Kahneman, D., and A. Tversky, 1972. Subjective probability: A judgment of representativeness, *Cognitive Psychology* 3: 430–454.

Kahneman, D., and A. Tversky, 1973. On the psychology of prediction, *Psychological Review* 80: 237–251.

Kalisch, B., 1971. An experiment in the development of empathy in nursing students, *Nursing Research* 20: 202–211.

Kaltreider, N., 1973. Emotional patterns related to delay in decision to seek legal abortion: A pilot study, *California Medicine* 118: 23–27.

Kaltreider, N., S. Goldsmith, and A.J. Margolis, 1979. The impact of midtrimester abortion techniques on patients and staff, *American Journal of Obstetrics and Gynecology* 135: 235–238.

Kane, F.J., P.A. Lachenbruch, M.A. Lipton, and D. Baram, 1973. Motivational factors in abortion patients, *American Journal of Psychiatry* 130: 290–293.

Kaplan, D.M., R. Grobstein, and A. Smith, 1976. Severe illness in families, *Health and Social Work* 1: 72–81.

Kaplan, D.M., A. Smith, R. Grobstein, and S.E. Fischman, 1973. Family mediation of stress, *Social Work* 18: 60–69.

Kaplan, R.M., J.W. Bush, and C.C. Berry, 1976. Health status: Types of validity for an index of well-being, *Health Services Research* 11: 478–507.

Kasl, S.V., 1975. Issues in patient adherence to health care regimens, *Journal of Human Stress* 1(3): 5–17.

Kasl, S.V., and S. Cobb, 1966. Health behavior, illness behavior, and sick role behavior, *Archives of Environmental Health* 12: 246–266 and 531–541.

Kasl, S.V., and S. Cobb, 1970. Blood pressure changes in men undergoing job loss: A preliminary report, *Psychosomatic Medicine* 32: 19–38.

Katz, J.L., H. Weiner, T.G. Gallagher, and L. Hellman, 1970. Stress, distress, and ego defenses, *Archives of General Psychiatry* **23**: 131–142.

Kegeles, S.S., 1963. Some motives for seeking preventive dental care, *Journal of the American Dental Association* **67**: 90–98.

Keller, A.B., J.H. Sims, W. Henry, and T.J. Crawford, 1970. Psychological sources of "resistance" to family planning, *Merrill–Palmer Quarterly of Behavior and Development* **16**: 286–302.

Kibrick, A.K., 1963. Dropouts in schools of nursing: The effect of self and role perception, *Nursing Research* **12**: 140–149.

Kimball, C.P., 1969. Psychological responses to the experience of open-heart surgery: I., *American Journal of Psychiatry* **126**: 348–359.

Kimmel, K., 1973. Stress situation in dental practice, *Quintessence International* **11**: 77–82.

King, H., 1970. Health in the medical and other learned professions, *Journal of Chronic Diseases* **23**: 257–281.

Kissen, D.M., 1963. Personality characteristics in males conducive to lung cancer, *British Journal of Medical Psychology* **36**: 27–36.

Kissen, D.M., 1966. The significance of personality in lung cancer in men, *Annals of the New York Academy of Sciences* **125** (Art. 3): 820–826.

Kissen, D.M., R.I.F. Brown, and M. Kissen, 1969. A further report on personality and psychosocial factors in lung cancer, *Annals of the New York Academy of Sciences* **164** (Art. 2): 535–544.

Kleinknecht, R.A., R.K. Klepac, and D.A. Berstein, 1976. Psychology and dentistry: Potential benefits from a health care liaison, *Professional Psychology* **7**: 585–592.

Kleinman, A.M., 1975. Explanatory model transactions in health care relationships, in *Health of the Family: 1974 International Health Conference*, pp. 159, Washington, D.C.: National Council for International Health.

Knecht, B.H., 1978. Experience with gastric bypass for massive obesity, *American Surgeon* **44**: 496–504.

Korsch, B.M., E.K. Gozzi, and V. Francis, 1968. Gaps in doctor–patient communication: I. Doctor–patient interaction and patient satisfaction, *Pediatrics* **42**: 855–871.

Kroger, W.S., 1952. Evaluation of personality factors in the treatment of infertility, *Fertility and Sterility* **3**(#6): 542–553.

Kutner, B., 1958. Surgeons and their patients: A study in social perception, in *Patients, Physicians, and Illness*, E.G. Jaco (ed.), pp. 384–397, New York: Free Press.

Kutner, B., H.B. Makover, and A. Oppenheim, 1958. Delay in the diagnosis and treatment of cancer: A critical analysis of the literature, *Journal of Chronic Disease* **7**: 95–120.

Laird, M.D., and M. Hogan, 1956. An elective program on preparation for childbirth at the Sloane hospital for women, *American Journal of Obstetrics and Gynecology* **72**: 641–647.

Layne, B.L., Jr., and S.C. Yudofsky, 1971. Postoperative psychosis in cardiotomy patients, *New England Journal of Medicine* **284**: 518–520.

Lazarus, H.R., and J.H. Hagens, 1968. Prevention of psychosis following open-heart surgery, *American Journal of Psychiatry* **124**: 1190–1195.

Lazarus, R.S., 1966. *Psychological Stress and the Coping Process*, New York: McGraw-Hill.

Lazarus, R.S., and R. Launier, 1978. Stress-related transactions between person and environment, in *Perspectives in Interactional Psychology*, L.A. Pervin and M. Lewis (eds.), pp. 287–327, New York: Plenum Press.

Leach, J.E., and G.F. Robbins, 1947. Delay in the diagnosis of cancer, *Journal of the American Medical Association* **135**: 5–8.

Leaper, D.J., J.C. Horrocks, J.R. Staniland, and F.T. de Dombal, 1972. Computer-assisted diagnosis of abdominal pain using 'estimates' provided by clinicians, *British Medical Journal* **2**: 350–354.

LeBow, M.D., 1975. Operant conditioning-based behavior modification: One approach to treating somatic disorders, *International Journal of Psychiatry in Medicine* **6**: 241–254.

Lerner, M.J., 1970. The desire for justice and reactions to victims, in *Altruism and Helping Behavior*, J. Macaulay and L. Berkowitz (eds.), pp. 205–229, New York: Academic Press.

Lerner, M.J., 1971. Observer's evaluation of a victim: Justice, guilt and veridical perception, *Journal of Personality and Social Psychology* **20**: 127–135.

LeShan, L.L., and R.E. Worthington, 1956. Personality as a factor in pathogenesis of cancer: A review of the literature, *British Journal of Medical Psychology* **29**: 49–56.

Leventhal, H., 1970. Findings and theory in the study of fear communications, *Advances in Experimental Social Psychology* **5**: 119–186.

Leventhal, H., D. Meyer, and D. Nerenz, (In Press). The common sense representation of illness danger, in *Medical Psychology*, Volume II. S. Rachman (ed.), New York: Pergamon Press.

Leventhal, H., I.M. Rosenstock, G.M. Hochbaum, and B. Carriger, 1960. Epidemic impact on the general population in two cities, in *The Impact of Asia Influenza on Community Life: A Study in Five Cities*, I.M. Rosentock, G.M. Hochbaum, H. Leventhal, *et al.* (eds.), pp. 53–77, Washington, D.C.: United States Department of Health, Education and Welfare, Public Health Service, Publication Number 766.

Ley, P., R.W. Bradshaw, J.A. Kincey, and S.T. Atherton, 1976. Increasing patients' satisfaction with communication, *British Journal of Social and Clinical Psychology* **15**: 403–413.

Ley, P., and M.S. Spelman, 1967. *Communicating with the Patient*, St. Louis, Mo.: Green.

Lichtenstein, E., and B.G. Danaher, 1976. Modification of smoking behavior: A critical analysis of theory, research, and practice, in *Progress in Behavior Modification*, Volume 3. M. Hersen, R.M. Eisler, and P.M. Miller (eds.), New York: Academic Press.

Lief, H.I., 1971. Personality characteristics of medical students, in *Psychosocial Aspects of Medical Training*, R.H. Coombs and C.E. Vincent (eds.), pp. 44–87, Springfield, Ill.: Thomas.

Linkewich, J.A., R.B. Catalano, and H.L. Flack, 1974. The effect of packaging and instruction on outpatient compliance with medication regimens, *Drug Intelligence and Clinical Pharmacy* **8**: 10–15.

Lipowski, Z.J., 1970. Physical illness, the individual, and the coping process, *Psychiatry in Medicine* **1**: 91–102.

Loupe, M.J., L.H. Meskin, and T.A. Mast, 1979. Changes in the values of dental students and dentists over a ten year period, *Journal of Dental Education* **43**: 170–175.

Lubin, B., R.G. Nathan, and J.D. Matarazzo, 1978. Psychologists in medical education: 1976, *American Psychologist* **33**: 339–343.

MacDonald, A.P., Jr., 1970. Internal-external locus of control and the practice of birth control, *Psychological Reports* **27**: 206.

Mages, N.L., and G.A. Mendelsohn, 1979. Effects of cancer on patients' lives: A personological approach, in *Health Psychology*, G.C. Stone, F. Cohen, and N.E. Adler, and Associates (eds.), pp. 255–284, San Francisco: Jossey–Bass.

Manasse, H.R., Jr., H.F. Kabat, and A.I. Wertheimer, 1977. Professional socialization in pharmacy: A cross-sectional analysis of dominant value characteristics of agents and objects of socialization, *Social Science and Medicine* **11**: 653–659.

Marston, M.V., 1970. Compliance with medical regimens. A review of the literature, *Nursing Research* **19**: 312–323.

Maslach, C., 1979. The burn-out syndrome and patient care, in *Stress and Survival: The Emotional Realities of Life-Threatening Illness*, C. Garfield (ed.), pp. 111–120. St. Louis: Mosby.

Matarazzo, J.D., 1955. The role of the psychologist in medical education and practice, *Human Organization* 14(2): 9–14.

Matarazzo, J.D., 1979. Health psychology: APA's newest division, *The Health Psychologist* 1(1): 1.

Matarazzo, J.D., 1980. Behavioral health and behavioral medicine: Frontiers for a new health psychology, *American Psychologist* 35(9): 807–817.

Matarazzo, J.D., and R.S. Daniel, 1957. The teaching of psychology by psychologists in medical schools, *Journal of Medical Education* 32: 410–415.

McClelland, D.C., 1974. Drinking as a response to power needs in man, *Psychopharmacology Bulletin, NIMH* 10(4): 5–6.

McClelland, D.C., 1978. The impact of power motivation training on alcoholics, *Journal of Studies on Alcohol* 38: 142–144.

McCoy, J.W., 1976. Psychological variables and onset of cancer. Unpublished doctoral dissertation, Oklahoma State University.

McDonald, R., 1968. The role of emotional factors in obstetric complications: A review, *Psychosomatic Medicine* 30(#2): 222–237.

McIntosh, J., 1974. Processes of communication, information seeking, and control associated with cancer: A selective review of the literature, *Social Science and Medicine* 8: 167–187.

McNamara, J.R. (ed.), 1979. *Behavioral Approaches to Medicine*, New York: Plenum Press.

Mechanic, D., 1972. *Public Expectations and Health Care*, New York: Wiley.

Medalie, J.H., M. Snyder, J.J. Groen, H.N. Neufeld, U. Goldbourt, and E. Riss, 1973. Angina pectoris among 10,000 men: 5-year incidence and univariate analysis, *American Journal of Medicine* 55: 583–594.

Meyerowitz, S.H., and J.S. Malev, 1973. Pubescent attitudinal correlates antecedent to adolescent illegitimate pregnancy, *Journal of Youth and Adolescence* 2: 251–258.

Mezei, A., and G. Nemeth, 1969. Regression as an intervening mechanism: A system-theoretical approach, *Annals of the New York Academy of Sciences* 164(Art. 2): 560–567.

Miller, W.B. 1973. Psychological vulnerability to unwanted pregnancy, *Family Planning Perspectives* 5: 199–201.

Miller, W.R., 1977. Behavioral self-control: Training in the treatment of problem drinkers, in *Behavioral Self-Management: Strategies, Techniques, and Outcomes*, R.B. Stuart (ed.), pp. 154–175, New York: Brunner/Mazel.

Millman, M., 1980. *Such a Pretty Face*, New York: Norton.

Mishara, B.L., R. Kastenbaum, F. Baker, and R.D. Patterson, 1975. Alcohol effects in old age: An experimental investigation, *Social Science and Medicine* 9: 535–547.

Monsour, K., and B. Stewart, 1973. Abortion and sexual behavior in college women, *American Journal of Orthopsychiatry* 43: 804–813.

Moos, R.H. (ed.), 1977. *Coping with Physical Illness*, New York: Plenum Press.

Moos, R.H., and V. Tsu, 1977. The crisis of physical illness: An overview, in *Coping with Physical Illness*, R.H. Moos (ed.), pp. 3–21, New York: Plenum Press.

Morris, P.B. and N. Grassi-Russo, 1979. Motives of beginning students for choosing nursing school, *Journal of Nursing Education* 18: 34–40.

Morse, R.M., and E.M. Litin, 1969. Postoperative delirium: A study of etiologic factors, *American Journal of Psychiatry* 126: 388–395.

Moses, R., and M. Cividali, 1966. Differential levels of awareness of illness: Their relation to some salient features in cancer patients, *Annals of the New York Academy of Sciences* 125: 984–994.

Nathan, R.G., B. Lubin, J.D. Matarazzo, and G.W. Persely, 1979. Psychologists in schools of medicine: 1955, 1964, 1977, *American Psychologist* **34**: 622–627.

National Institute on Drug Abuse, 1979. *Behavioral Analysis and Treatment of Substance Abuse* (edited by N.A. Krasnegor), Rockville, MD.: National Institute on Drug Abuse.

Newell, A., J.C. Shaw, and H.A. Simon, 1960. Report on a general problem-solving program, in *Proceedings of the International Conference on Information Processing*, pp. 256–264, Paris: UNESCO.

Newell, A., and H.A. Simon, 1972. *Human Problem Solving*, Englewood Cliffs, N.J.: Prentice-Hall.

Nguyen, T.D., C.C. Attkisson, and M.J. Bottino, 1976. Definition and identification of human service need in a community context, in *Need Assessment in Health and Human Services: Proceedings of the Louisville National Conference*, University of Louisville, KY. R.A. Bell, M. Sundel, J.F. Aponte, and S.A. Murrel (eds.), pp. 30–39, (Expanded version to be published by Human Sciences Press, 1981.)

Niswander, K., and R. Patterson, 1967. Psychological reaction to therapeutic abortion. *Obstetrics and Gynecology* **29**: 702–706.

Oskamp, S., B. Mindick, D. Berger, and E. Motta, 1978. A longitudinal study of success versus failure in contraceptive planning, *Journal of Population* **1**: 69–83.

Osofsky, J.D., and H.J. Osofsky, 1972. The psychological reaction of patients to legalized abortion, *American Journal of Orthopsychiatry* **42**(1): 48–60.

Ostfeld, A.M., B.Z. LeBovits, R.B. Shekelle, and P. Pual, 1964. A prospective study of the relationship between personality and coronary heart disease, *Journal of Chronic Diseases* **17**: 265–276.

Pack, G.T., and J.S. Gallo, 1938. Culpability for delay in treatment of cancer, *American Journal of Cancer* **33**: 443–462.

Palmer, R.D., 1968. Patterns of defensive response to threatening stimuli, *Journal of Abnormal Psychology* **73**: 30–36.

Parker, B.R., and V. Srinivasan, 1976. A consumer preference approach to the planning of rural primary health-care facilities, *Operations Research* **24**: 991–1025.

Parkes, C.M., 1972. The emotional impact of cancer on patients and their families, *Journal of Laryngology and Utology* **89**: 1271–1279.

Parsons, T., 1975. The sick role and role of the physician reconsidered, *Millbank Memorial Fund Quarterly* **53**: 257–278.

Patt, S.L., R.G. Rappaport, and P. Barglow, 1969. Follow-up of therapeutic interruption of pregnancy, *Archives of General Psychiatry* **20**: 408–414.

Payne, E.C., A.R. Kravitz, M.T. Notman, and J.V. Anderson, 1976. Outcome following therapeutic abortion, *Archives of General Psychiatry* **33**: 725–733.

Payne, E.D., and M.J. Krant, 1969. The psychosocial aspects of advanced cancer, *Journal of the American Medical Association* **210**: 1238–1242.

Polgar, S., 1962. Health and human behavior: Areas of interest common to the social and medical sciences, *Current Anthropology* **3**: 159–205.

Pomerleau, O.F., 1979. Behavioral medicine: The contribution of the experimental analysis of behavior to medical care, *American Psychologist* **34**: 654–663.

Rahe, R.H., R.T. Rubin, and R.J. Arthur, 1974. The three investigators study: Serum uric acid, cholesterol, and cortisol variability during stresses of everyday life, *Psychosomatic Medicine* **36**: 258–268.

Rahe, R.H., R.T. Rubin, E.K.E. Gunderson, R.J. Arthur, 1971. Psychologic correlates of serum cholesterol in man: A longitudinal study, *Psychosomatic Medicine* **33**: 399–410.

Raskin, M., 1972. Psychiatric crises of medical students and the implications for subsequent adjustments, *Journal of Medical Education* **47**: 210–215.

Renneker, R., and M. Cutler, 1952. Psychological problems of adjustment to cancer of the breast, *Journal of the American Medical Association* **148**: 833–838.

Rezler, A.G., H.R. Manasse, Jr., and J.M. Buckley, 1977. Comparative study of the personality types attracted to pharmacy and medical school, *American Journal of Pharmaceutical Education* **41**: 7–10.

Ringrose, C.A.D., 1961a. Psychosomatic influences in the genesis of toxemia of pregnancy, *Canadian Medical Association Journal* **84**: 647–650.

Ringrose, C.A.D., 1961b. Further observations on the psychosomatic character of toxemia of pregnancy, *Canadian Medical Association Journal* **84**: 1064–1065.

Rodin, J., and I.L. Janis, 1979. The social power of health-care practitioners as agents of change, *Journal of Social Issues* **35**: 60–81.

Rogentine, S.N., D.P. van Kammen, B.H. Fox, J.P. Dorherty, J.E. Rosenblatt, S.C. Boyd, and W.E. Bunney, (In Press). Psychological Factors in the Prognosis of Malignant Melanoma, *Psychosomatic Medicine*.

Rokeach, M., 1971. Long-range experimental modification of values, attitudes, and behavior, *American Psychologist* **26**: 453–459.

Rooks, J.B., and W. Cates, 1977. Emotional impact of D & E vs. instillation, *Family Planning Perspectives* **9**: 276–277.

Rose, K.D., and I. Rosow, 1973. Physicians who kill themselves, *Archives of General Psychiatry* **29**: 800–805.

Rosen, R.A., H.H. Weley, J.W. Ager, and F.P. Shea, 1974. Health professionals' attitudes toward abortion, *Public Opinion Quarterly* **38**(2): 159–173.

Rosen, S., 1955. Emotional factors in nausea and vomiting of pregnancy, *Psychiatric Quarterly* **29**: 621–633.

Rosenberg, P.P., 1971. Students' perceptions and concerns during their first year in medical school, *Journal of Medical Education* **46**: 211–218.

Rosenman, R.H., F.J. Brand, C.D. Jenkins, M. Friedman, R. Straus, and M. Wurm, 1975. Coronary heart disease in the western collaborative group study: Final follow-up experience 8.5 years, *Journal of the American Medical Association* **233**: 872–877.

Rosenman, R.H., M. Friedman, R. Straus, C.D. Jenkins, S.H. Zyzanski, and M. Wurm, 1970. Coronary heart disease in the western collaborative group study, *Journal of Chronic Disease* **23**: 173–190.

Rosenman, R.H., M. Friedman, R. Straus, M. Wurm, R. Kositchek, W. Hahn, and N.T. Werthessen, 1964. A predictive study of coronary heart disease: The western collaborative group study, *Journal of the American Medical Association* **189**: 15–22.

Rosenstock, I.M., 1966. Why people use health services, *Millbank Memorial Fund Quarterly* **44**: 94–124.

Rosenstock, I.M., 1974. The health belief model and preventive health behavior, *Health Education Monographs* **2**(4): 354–386.

Rosenstock, I.M., and J.P. Kirscht, 1979. Why people seek health care, in *Health Psychology* G.C. Stone, F. Cohen and N.E. Adler, and Associates (eds.), pp. 161–188, San Francisco: Jossey-Bass.

Rothman, D., 1973. Habitual abortion and sexual conflict, *Medical Aspects of Human Sexuality* **7**: 56–67.

Routh, D.K., 1977. Postdoctoral training in pediatric psychology, *Professional Psychology* **8**: 245–250.

Ruesch, J., 1961. *Therapeutic Communication*, New York: W.W. Norton.

Ruesch, J., 1975. Communication and psychiatry, in *Comprehensive Text-book of Psychiatry-II*, Vol. I. A.M. Freedman, H.I. Kaplan, and B.J. Saddock (eds.), pp. 336–349, Baltimore: Williams and Witkins.

Runyon, H.L., and L.A. Cohen, 1979. The effects of systematic human relations training on freshman dental students, *Journal of the American Dental Association* **98**: 196–201.

Russek, H.I., 1962. Emotional stress and coronary heart disease in American physicians, dentists, and lawyers, *American Journal of the Medical Sciences* **243**: 716–726.

Russek, H.I., 1965. Stress, tobacco, and coronary heart disease, *Journal of the American Medical Association* **192**: 89–94.

Sackett, D.L., and J.C. Snow, 1979. The magnitude of compliance and noncompliance, in *Compliance in Health Care*, R.B. Haynes, D.W. Taylor, and D.L. Sackett (eds.), pp. 11–22, Baltimore: Johns Hopkins University Press.

Schaffer, C., and F. Pine, 1972. Pregnancy, abortion and the developmental tasks of adolescence, *The Journal of the American Academy of Child Psychiatry* **11**: 511–536.

Schiebel, D., and P. Castelnuovo-Tedesco, 1977. Studies of superobesity III: Body image changes after jejunoileal bypass surgery, *International Journal of Psychiatry in Medicine* **8**: 117–123.

Schmale, A.H., Jr., and H.P. Iker, 1966. The affect of hopelessness and the development of cancer: I. Identification of uterine cervical cancer in women with atypical cytology, *Psychosomatic Medicine* **28**: 714–721.

Schmale, A.H., Jr., and H.P. Iker, 1971. Hopelessness as a predictor of cervical cancer, *Social Science and Medicine* **5**: 95–100.

Schoenberg, B., A.C. Carr, D. Peretz, and A. Kutscher, 1972. *Psychosocial Aspects of Terminal Care*, New York: Columbia University Press.

Schofield, W., 1969. The role of psychology in the delivery of health services, *American Psychologist* **24**: 565–584.

Schulz, R., 1978. *The Psychology of Death, Dying and Bereavement*, Reading, MA.: Addison–Wesley Publishing Co.

Schwartz, G., 1979. The brain as a health care system, in *Health Psychology*, G.C. Stone, F. Cohen, and N.E. Adler, and Associates (eds.), pp. 549–571, San Francisco: Jossey-Bass.

Schwartz, R., 1973. Follow-up by phone or by mail, *Evaluation* **1**: 25–26.

Scott, J.R., and N.B. Rose, 1976. Effect of psychoprophylaxis (Lamaze Preparation) on labor and delivery in primiparas, *New England Journal of Medicine* **294**: 1205–1207.

Sechrest, L., and R.Y. Cohen, 1979. Evaluating outcomes in health care, in *Health Psychology*, G.C. Stone, F. Cohen, N.E. Adler, and Associates (eds.), pp. 369–394, San Francisco: Jossey-Bass.

Senay, E.C., 1970. Therapeutic abortion: clinical aspects, *Archives of General Psychiatry* **23**: 408–415.

Shands, H.C., J.E. Finesinger, S. Cobb, and R.D. Abrams, 1951. Psychological mechanisms in patients with cancer, *Cancer* **4**: 1159–1170.

Shapiro, J., and D.H. Shapiro, Jr., 1979. The psychology of responsibility: Some second thoughts on wholistic medicine, *New England Journal of Medicine* **301**: 211–212.

Sharpe, T.R., and R.L. Mikeal, 1974. Patient compliance with antibiotic regimens, *American Journal of Hospital Pharmacy* **31**: 479–484.

Sheldon, A., B. Chir, C.P. Ryser, and M.J. Krant, 1970. An integrated family oriented cancer care program: The report of a pilot project in the socio-emotional management of chronic disease, *Journal of Chronic Diseases* **22**: 743–755.

Simon, N., and A. Senturia, 1966. Psychiatric sequelae of abortion: A review of the literature, 1935–64, *Archives of General Psychiatry* **15**(4): 378–389.

Simon, N., A. Senturia, and D. Rothman, 1967. Psychiatric illness following therapeutic abortion, *American Journal of Psychiatry* **124**: 97–103.

Skinner, B.F., 1953. *Science and Human Behaviour*, New York: Macmillan.

Slage, S.J., C.B. Arnold, and E. Glascock, 1974. Self-competence: A measure of relative risk of unwanted pregnancy? Paper presented at the 82nd Annual Meeting of the American Psychological Association, New Orleans, LA.

Slawson, P.F., 1965. Group psychotherapy with obese women, *Psychosomatics* **6**: 206–209.

Slovic P., L.G. Rorer, and P.J. Hoffman, 1971. Analyzing use of diagnostic signs, *Investigative Radiology* **6**: 18–26.

Smedslund, J., 1963. The concept of correlation in adults, *Scandinavian Journal of Psychology* **4**: 165–173.

Smith, E.M., 1973. A follow-up study of women who request abortion, *American Journal of Orthopsychiatry* **43**: 574–585.

Solomon, G.F., 1969. Emotions, stress, the central nervous system, and immunity, *Annals of the New York Academy of Sciences* **164** (Art. 2): 335–343.

Stavraky, K.M., and others, 1968. Psychological factors in the outcome of human cancer, *Journal of Psychosomatic Research* **12**: 251–259.

Stiles, W.B., 1978. Verbal response modes and dimensions of interpersonal roles: A method of discourse analysis, *Journal of Personality and Social Psychology* **36**: 693–703.

Stiles, W.B., M. Putnam, M.H. Wolf, and S.A. James, 1979. Interaction exchange structure and patient satisfaction with medical interviews, *Medical Care* **17**: 667–681.

Stimson, G., 1974. Obeying doctors' orders: A view from the other side, *Social Science and Medicine* **8**: 97–104.

Stone, G.C., 1977. Health and behavior. Paper presented at American Psychological Association Meetings, San Francisco, Ca.

Stone, G.C., 1979a. Health and the health system: A historical overview and a conceptual framework, in *Health Psychology*, G.C. Stone, F. Cohen, and N.E. Adler, and Associates (eds.), pp. 1–17, San Francisco: Jossey-Bass.

Stone, G.C., 1979b. Patient compliance and the role of the expert, *Journal of Social Issues* **35**(1): 34–59.

Stone, G.C., 1979c. Psychology and the health system, in *Health Psychology*, G.C. Stone, F. Cohen, and N.E. Adler, and Associates (eds.), pp. 47–75, San Francisco: Jossey-Bass.

Stone, G.C., F. Cohen, N. Adler, and Associates, 1979. *Health Psychology*, San Francisco: Jossey-Bass.

Stone, G.C., D.S. Rowe, and J.E. Obedzinski, 1979. Objectives and evaluation criteria in the teaching of communication skills. Paper presented at the annual meetings of the American Psychological Association. New York, N.Y.

Stunkard, A.J., and M. McClaren-Hume, 1959. The results of treatment of obesity: A review of the literature and report of a series. *Archives of Internal Medicine* **103**: 79–85.

Stunkard, A.J., and S.B. Penick, 1979. Behavior modification in the treatment of obesity: Problem of maintaining weight loss, *Archives of General Psychiatry* **36**: 801–806.

Sturgis, S.H., M.L. Taymor, and T. Morris, 1957. Routine psychiatric interviews in a sterility investigation, *Fertility and Sterility* **8**: 521–526.

Sutherland, A.M., C.E. Orbach, R.B. Dyk, and M. Bard, 1952. The psychological impact of cancer and cancer surgery: I. Adaptation to dry colostomy: Preliminary report and summary of findings, *Cancer* **5**: 857–872.

Svarstad, B., 1976. Physician- patient communication and patient conformity with medical advice, in *Growth of Bureaucratic Medicine*, D. Mechanic (ed.), pp. 220–238. New York: Wiley.

Taylor, D.W., 1979. Health beliefs and compliance with antihypertensive regimens: A test of the belief model in hypertension, in *Compliance in Health Care*, R.B. Haynes, D.W. Taylor, and D.L. Sackett (eds.), pp. 103–109. Baltimore: Johns Hopkins University Press.

Taylor, S., 1979. Hospital patient behavior: Reactance, helplessness, or control? *Journal of Social Issues* **35**: 156–184.

Tempone, V.J., and W. Lamb, 1967. Repression-sensitization and its relation to measures of adjustment and conflict, *Journal of Consulting and Clinical Psychology* **31**: 131–136.

Thelen, M.H., 1969. Repression-sensitization: Its relation to adjustment and seeking psychotherapy among college students, *Journal of Consulting and Clinical Psychology* **33**: 161–165.

Theorell, T., and R.H. Rahe, 1972. Behavior and life satisfactions characteristics of Swedish subjects with myocardial infarction, *Journal of Chronic Diseases* **25**: 139–147.

Thibaut, J.W., and H.H. Kelley, 1959. *The Social Psychology of Groups*, New York: Wiley.

Thomas, C.B., and R.L. Greenstreet, 1973. Psychobiological characteristics in youth as predictors of five disease states: Suicide, mental illness, hypertension, coronary heart disease, and tumor, *Johns Hopkins Medical Journal* **132**: 16–43.

Thomas, C.B., and E.A. Murphy, 1958. Further studies on cholesterol levels in the Johns Hopkins medical students: The effect of stress at examinations, *Journal of Chronic Diseases* **8**: 661–668.

Toms, H., and E. Karlovsky, 1954. 2000 deliveries under a training for childbirth program, *American Journal of Obstetrics and Gynecology* **68**: 279–284.

Truesch, J.V., and F.H. Krusen, 1943. Physical therapy applied at home for arthritis: A follow-up study with a supplementary summary of the sedimentation rate of erythrocytes in 229 cases of arthritis, *Archives of Internal Medicine* **72**: 231–238.

Tupper, C., 1956. Conditioning for childbirth, *American Journal of Obstetrics and Gynecology* **71**: 733–740.

Tupper, C., and R.J. Weil, 1962. The problem of spontaneous abortion. IX. The treatment of habitual aborters by psychotherapy, *American Journal of Obstetrics and Gynecology* **83**: 421–424.

Tversky, A., and D. Kahneman, 1973. Availability: A heuristic for judging frequency and probability, *Cognitive Psychology* **5**: 207–232.

Tversky, A., and D. Kahneman, 1974. Judgment under uncertainty: Heuristics and biases, *Science* **185**: 1124–1131.

Vaillant, G.E., N.C. Sobowale, and C. McArthur, 1972. Some psychologic vulnerabilities of physicians, *New England Journal of Medicine* **287**: 372–375.

Vaughn, D.R., and M. Burgoon, 1976. Interpersonal communication in therapeutic setting: Mariah or messiah? in *Explorations in Interpersonal Communication*, G.R. Miller (ed.), pp. 255–274, Beverly Hills, California: Sage.

Visotsky, H.M., D.A. Hamburg, M.E. Goss, and B.A. Lebovitz, 1961. Coping under extreme stress: Observations of patients with severe poliomyelitis, *Archives of General Psychiatry* **5**: 423–448.

Voegtlin, W.L., F. Lemere, W.R. Broz, and P. O'Hollaren, 1940. The treatment of alcoholism by establishing a conditioned reflex, *American Journal of Mental Science* **199**: 802–809.

Waitzkin, H., J.D. Stoeckle, 1976. Information control and the micropolitics of health care: A summary of an ongoing research project, *Social Science and Medicine* **10**: 263–276.

Walker, H.E., 1978. Sexual problems and infertility, *Psychosomatics* **19**: 477–484.

Wallsten, T.S., 1978. Three biases in the cognitive processing of diagnostic information. Unpublished paper, Psychometric Laboratory, University of North Carolina, Chapel Hill.

Walter, G., 1970. Psychologic and emotional consequences of elective abortion, *Obstetrics and Gynecology* **36**: 482–487.

Ware, J.E., Jr., and M.K. Snyder, 1975. Dimensions of patient attitudes regarding doctors and medical care services, *Medical Care* **13**: 669–682.

Warheit, G.J., 1976. The use of the field survey to estimate health needs in the general population, in *Need Assessment in Health and Human Services: Proceedings of the Louisville National Conference, University of Louisville*, Louisville, KY. R.A. Bell, M. Sundel, J.F. Aponte, and S.A. Murrel (eds.), pp. 189–197. (Expanded version to be published by Human Sciences Press, 1981.)

Webster, T.G., 1971. The behavioral sciences in medical education and practice, in *Psy-*

chosocial Aspects of Medical Training, R.H. Coombs and E.V. Clark (eds.), pp. 285–348. Springfield, Ill.: Thomas.

Weil, R.J., and L.C. Stewart, 1957. The problem of spontaneous abortion: III. Psychosomatic and interpersonal aspects of habitual abortion, *American Journal of Obstetrics and Gynecology* **73**: 322–327.

Weisenberg, M., 1977. Pain and pain control, *Psychological Bulletin* **84**: 1008–1044.

Weisman, A.D., 1972. *On dying and denying: A psychiatric study of terminality*, New York: Behavioral Publications.

Werner, A., and J.M. Schneider, 1974. Teaching medical students interactional skills: Research-based course in the doctor–patient relationship, *New England Journal of Medicine* **290**: 1232–1237.

Wirsching, M., H.V. Druner, and G. Herrmann, 1975. Results of psychosocial adjustment to long-term colostomy, *Psychotherapy and Psychosomatics* **26**: 245–256.

Wishnie, H.A., T.P. Hackett, and N.H. Cassem, 1971. Psychological hazards of convalescence following myocardial infarction, *Journal of the American Medical Association* **215**: 1292–1296.

Wolff, C.T., S.G. Friedman, M.A. Hofer, and J.W. Mason, 1964. Relationship between psychological defenses and mean urinary 17-hydroxycoricosteroid excretion rates: I. A predictive study of parents of fatally ill children, *Psychosomatic Medicine* **26**: 576–591.

Wolff, J.R., P.E. Nielson, and P.J. Schiller, 1971. Therapeutic abortion: Attitudes of medical personnel leading to complication in patient care, *American Journal of Obstetrics and Gynecology* **110**: 730–733.

Wortman, C.B., and C. Dunkel-Schetter, 1979. Interpersonal relationships and cancer: A theoretical analysis, *Journal of Social Issues* **35**: 120–155.

Yano, K., G.G. Rhoads, and A. Kagan, 1977. Coffee, alcohol and risk of coronary heart disease in Japanese Americans, *New England Journal of Medicine* **297**(8): 405–409.

Zax, M., A.J. Sameroff, and J.E. Farnum, 1975. Childbirth education, maternal attitudes, and delivery, *American Journal of Obstetrics and Gynecology* **123**: 185–190.

Zelnik, M., and J.F. Kantner, 1977. Sexual and contraceptive experience of young, unmarried women in the United States, 1976 and 1971, *Family Planning Perspectives* **9**(2): 55–74.

Zelnik, M., and J.F. Kantner, 1979. Reasons for nonuse of contraception by sexually active women aged 15–19, *Family Planning Perspectives* **11**(5): 289–296.

2 Trends and Developments in the Sociology of Medicine

Samuel W. Bloom and Ruth E. Zambrana

Introduction

Although barely thirty-five years old as a distinct field, medical sociology is today one of sociology's most active subspecialties. The Medical Sociology Section of the American Sociological Association (ASA) contains over 1200 members, the largest number of any section. The *Journal of Health and Social Behavior*, originally published privately under the section's auspices, is now an official journal of the ASA in its twenty-second volume. Special activities of the section have attracted financial support from The Milbank Memorial Fund and the Carnegie Foundation. The National Institute of Mental Health (NIMH), in order to recruit and train sociologists for health-related research, has committed large sums of money to doctoral training programs continuously since 1957 (Lutterman 1975:310).[1] Even larger fiscal support to sociologists was granted by both NIMH and the National Center for Health Services Research (NCHSR) for individually conceived research studies (Williams 1972).[2] It is also clear from a spate of recent textbooks

1. As this paper is being written, financial support for training medical sociologists is being reduced, and severe pressure exists to eliminate it entirely. Such forces, however, do not single out medical sociology but are being applied to the social sciences generally, and even to other previously sacred areas of higher education, such as medicine. Cf. USDHEW, *Forward Plan for Health*, 1976: pp. 89–92; National Research Council, Study of National Needs for Biomedical and Behavioral Research Personnel, Commission on Human Resources, "Personnel Needs and Training for Biomedical and Behavioral Research," 1976. Early indications of the policies of the Reagan administration suggest focused cuts in social science manpower training and research support. See *Science*, March 27, 1981: p. 1397 (Vol. 211, No. 4489).

2. Research support also shows a downward trend pattern. See National Research Council, 1976, op. cit., and *Science*, 1981, op. cit.

that the teaching of medical sociology is established as part of the standard undergraduate college curriculum (Rosengren 1980; Cockerham 1978; Twaddle and Hessler 1977; Mechanic 1978b). By all the major criteria that Shils describes for the institutionalization of an intellectual activity, therefore, medical sociology qualifies (Shils 1970).

Another important feature of this rapid expansion is the dual character of medical sociology's development as both a basic and applied social science (Bloom 1976). Early contributors in the United States, where the first and strongest institutionalization occurred, were established scholars in the mainstream of sociology, each pursuing some intrinsic theoretical problem, seeking in medicine only the data to demonstrate propositions about more general social phenomena (Faris and Dunham 1939; Parsons 1951; Merton et al. 1957; Hollingshead and Redlich 1958). Very quickly, however, sociologists were accepted into active roles in medicine (Straus 1957), where, as the collaborators of a profession that was accustomed to use its basic science partners, they joined the effort to translate knowledge into policy, and policy into practice (Rosengren 1980: 95–96; Bloom 1978).

Against this background of diversity and rapid expansion, any attempt to review the full scope of activity now attributed to medical sociology would be too great for a single paper. Fortunately for the field, excellent special reviews have been spaced throughout its history (Caudill 1953; Clausen 1956; Freeman and Reeder 1957; Reader and Goss 1959; Reader 1963; Suchman 1964; Graham 1964; Bloom 1965; Hyman 1967; Kendall and Reader 1979; McKinlay 1972; Mechanic 1975b; Fox 1976). Our approach here, therefore, will be limited first to a discussion of the development of knowledge in medical sociology; in other words, to what is generally called the "sociology of medicine." Second, we acknowledge at the start the selective bias of our own particular work, which has focused on the sociology of medical education, the doctor–patient relationship, and the organization of health care delivery. Where unequal depth of treatment occurs, these special interests are likely to be reflected. We also limit this discussion to the United States.[3]

The assigned general goal of this paper will be to review the literature

---

3. Although relevant contributions to the field, historically, have occurred elsewhere, especially in England and Germany, medical sociology as an organized field did not develop in other countries until more recently. The international growth is now proceeding rapidly, with the newly published British journal, *Sociology of Health and Illness*, as just one example.

of medical sociology in order to identify major trends and developments. More specific goals are incorporated in the following questions:

1) What are the major trends and developments in the field over the past quarter century?

2) What have been the landmark studies – studies which are responsible for new research directions?

3) What are the major current trends?

We begin with a historical view, tracing the developmental sequence chronologically. The discussion then turns to the analysis of current trends, with an attempt to find an organizing principle that clarifies the patterns and achievements of this field of knowledge.

I. A Historical Overview

Medical sociology emerged as an identifiable field only after World War II. There were, however, important antecedents between the two World Wars. Much of the early work anticipated the major trends which were to develop later. Some grew in straight cumulative fashion while others appear as research episodes. Four such fields will be identified according to their scholarly origins, and discussed:

a) social histories of medicine;

b) the social psychology of interpersonal relations in therapeutic institutions;

c) social epidemiology;

d) the sociology of the professions.

(a) Social histories of medicine

Bernhard J. Stern (1927) set an early model for the use of the historical method in the study of American medicine. His work was strong in its analysis of institutions related to the organization of medical care, especially the economic and political. Sigerist (1934) and Davis (1927, 1941) also wrote about the organization of medicine, with reference to the significance of social and economic determinants. Each of these achievements, however, stands essentially alone. When the main thrust of medical sociology's development occurred soon after World War II, there is no evidence of a trend of analysis developing out of any of these individually excellent studies. Instead, each individual historical scholar was left to continue work that was not fully recognized by the field until almost three decades later.

Stern, for example, continued his work, publishing three important books at the end of World War II (1945, 1946a, and 1946b). Described as "the first American sociologist to work seriously and intensively in the field of the sociology of medicine" (Stern 1959: viii), Stern wrote six books (1927a, 1927b, 1941, 1945, 1946a, 1946b) and many papers in medical sociology. Moreover, his scholarly achievements were broad, including a research monograph based on his own fieldwork among the Lummi Indians of the northwest United States (1934), a study of Lewis Henry Morgan (1931), and a basic anthropology text (with Melville Jacobs, 1947). He was also a founder and a key editor of the journal *Science and Society*. Yet, soon after he died in 1956, his influence in medical sociology rapidly dissipated, and for young scholars entering the growing field that he pioneered, he was virtually unknown. There is then a special irony in the eulogy written by Robert K. Merton shortly after Stern's death:

The many now at work in the sociology of medicine are all the beneficiaries of his pioneering studies begun only twenty years ago .... We sociologists have taken particular pride in having Bernhard Stern represent us to disciplines which otherwise knew little or nothing of our work or of our capabilities (Stern 1959: xi).

At the time of his death, Stern's formal academic status did not match the acknowledged excellence and extent of his scholarly achievements. The irony deepens against the vigorous revival today of precisely those issues that were central in Stern's work: the influence of economic and political structural factors on the segmented nature and inefficiency of health care delivery in the United States and especially on the inequalities that have resulted for racial minorities and lower socioeconomic groups.

Stern was, of course, an outspoken Marxist. That the prime of his working life coincided with the McCarthy Era is one explanation for the apparent neglect of his work. However, this does not explain the failure of contemporary Marxist spokesmen to give Stern even a single mention (Navarro 1978; Waitzkin and Waterman 1974). Moreover, others, not so labelled, suffered an equal fate. Erwin Ackerknecht is such an example.

Ackerknecht, after receiving his M.D. in Germany in the late twenties, studied for his Ph.D. in anthropology at the Sorbonne. A protege of Sigerist, and later his successor as Professor of History of Medicine at the University of Zurich, Ackerknecht developed as his specialty the history of primitive medicine (Ackerknecht 1942a, 1942b, 1943). Brought to the United States in the late thirties, Ackerknecht filled a Chair in the History of Medicine at the University of Wisconsin for almost two decades, writing a series of articles on primitive medicine and three books on more general medical subjects (1953, 1955, 1959). Throughout his work, there is a highly developed sociological frame of reference. Yet beyond a small circle of historical scholars, he is relatively little known, at least within medical sociology. Among the field's best-known textbooks, for example, Ackerknecht, like Stern, typically receives not a single mention (Mechanic 1978b; Rosengren 1980).

There are other social historians (Shryock 1947; Deutsch 1949) who began their work in the period between the World Wars. In spite of the excellence of their work, however, the social history of medicine did not grow into a distinctive sub-field until very recently. After World War II, they (Shryock and Deutsch) and other individual scholars, including Sigerist (1948), Rosen (1947, 1979), and Brian Abel-Smith (1960, 1964) continued their work, and at Yale University and Johns Hopkins, long-standing traditions in the history of medicine were sustained. Thus, what appears at first to be a trough in the curve of development was not entirely barren.

Recently, however, there are strong signs of a revival in the use of the historical method in the social analysis of American medicine. Freidson's very important study of the professions (1970) draws heavily on historical materials and methods. Stevens, a student of Abel-Smith, has completed important studies of the impact of specialization and state medicine on medical practice in England (Stevens 1966), of American medicine (1971), and of Medicaid (Stevens and Stevens 1974). George Rosen has continued research that dates to the early 1940s on public health in the United States and Europe (Rosen 1968, 1974, 1979). Historical scholarship has contributed also to two very current social problems as they relate to health care, the poverty of minority groups (Bullough and Bullough 1972) and the social and ethical implications of advanced technology (Fox and Swazey 1974). Along the same lines of direct address to current health-policy issues, Reverby and Rosner (1979) have collected a remarkable group of essays in social history.

In sum, working mainly in the traditions of individual scholarship and with much less financial support for their work than those who use quantitative methodologies, the social historians of medicine, in our judgment, have made unusually significant contributions to the sociology of medicine which, at the same time, are strikingly articulate in their relevance for public policy. Stevens' analysis of the legislative history of American law as it affects health care is a good example. Her criticism of what she calls the "categorical approach" to public support for health services continues a line of critical judgment developed by Stern and by Michael Davis before him. By "categorical" she means the policy of public support that makes access to services contingent upon the recipient falling into a category, "as a veteran, a crippled child, an Indian, a merchant seaman, a migrant, an Appalachian, a pre-school or school-aged child" (Stevens 1971: 522). Nowhere that we know of has this aspect of American health care policy been more clearly and cogently called to task.

Also notable is the style of collaboration between sociologists and historians exemplified by the Bulloughs and Fox and Swazey. The result is a blending of methodologies binding the data of records with direct empirical inquiry. The results have contributed to our understanding – particularly of health care delivery systems, health care legislation, interinstitutional relations, the power structures of health care systems, and the ethical implications of medical technology.

(b) Interpersonal relations in therapeutic situations

At the same time as sociologists like Bernhard Stern and Michael Davis were studying the history of the social and economic organization of medical care, a different type of sociological perspective was applied to mental illness, psychiatric practice, and psychiatric illness. Particularly from the work in psychiatry of Harry Stack Sullivan, a social psychology of therapeutic situations emerged. Two papers by Sullivan, published in 1931, are generally cited as the beginning of a movement toward a therapeutic orientation – as opposed to the custodial – to hospital care for the chronically ill, especially the mentally ill (Sullivan 1931a and 1931b). The conception of the hospital as a "therapeutic community" grew from these origins to become one of the most active substantive areas for sociological study immediately following and very much influenced by the war.

This was but one facet of a more general social psychology of inter-personal relations in therapeutic situations (Di Matteo and Friedman 1979). The work of Lawrence J. Henderson on the doctor–patient relationship, for example, can be argued to be a close kin given that both share a functionalist theoretical perspective. For purposes of simplicity and, hopefully, increased clarity, we discuss them separately, interpreting Henderson (below in section Id, "The Sociology of the Professions") as the fountainhead of a group of studies that focuses on the distinctive qualities of medicine as a profession and the implications particularly for the social role structure and function of practitioners and their clients.

During the half century preceding Sullivan, "hospital care" came to be synonymous with "doctor's care." In effect, the hospital functioned as an expanded waiting and examining room, a special accommodation for the physician. Therapy was conceived of as the time spent with the doctor, or under the specific orders of the doctor. All else was secondary. Even the nurse was an instrument, more or less, primarily designed to carry out the doctor's orders. For the patient, the hospital was a place for two distinctly different experiences: there was the doctor's "therapy," and lumped together, all the rest. For the hospital staff, the dichotomy was similar. There was the specifically therapeutic part of their job, and the rest was "custodial."

The attitudes associated with the therapy-custody dichotomy may have been appropriate for the acute and dramatic types of illness which dominated the general hospital until the last thirty-five years. However, when medical science gained control over the most dangerous elements of acute infections, such attitudes became outdated. The reaction of the health professions since World War II has been to shift the view of the patient into a new perspective. The twenty-three or more "other" hours of the patient's day, the nondoctor hours, so to speak, are being regarded as important in their own right. The patient's total experience in the hospital has come into the focus of therapeutic concern, replacing the preoccupation with the doctor's fraction alone. This observation applies to the hospital care of all types of illness; chronic illness, however and particularly psychiatric illness, were affected to a greater degree than others.

The period since World War II has witnessed a remarkable effort to understand the contributions to therapy that adhere to the hospital as a *total* social experience. The groundwork for this effort, however, is almost a separate chapter in itself. Although, as noted above, the origins are usually attributed to the work of Sullivan, some credit must also be given to a remarkable series of personal documents, autobiographical writings which were used as the data, at least in a preliminary sense, for early conceptions of the therapeutic community. Probably the best known of these is Clifford Beers (1907). Others which deserve mention include Packard (1873), Seabrook (1935), Kerkhoff (1952), Ward (1955), and Frame (1961).

The conception of the hospital as a small society is vividly portrayed in these personal documents. They form a rich background of illustration for the ethnographic approach which was to appear later. "One of the greatest secret societies in the world," said Beers, "is the psychiatric hospital," and he proceeded to record a patient's view of the culture of this society, its structure and content. Sullivan's observations are closely parallel, forming the basis of his interpretation that psychosis itself is "disordered interpersonal relations nucleating ... in a particular person." Differentiating "social recovery" from "personal recovery," Sullivan weighed heavily the importance of social environment in the therapeutic process.

By turning the spotlight away from intrapsychic aspects of mental disorder and toward the interpersonal, Sullivan inspired a generation of ethnographic studies of the mental hospital as a small society. Rowland (1938, 1939) and Devereux (1944) provided lengthy descriptions of patient culture in hospitals, based upon participant observation before World War II. Maxwell Jones (1953) and Eli Ginzberg and his associates (1959) were stimulated to similar conceptions and interpretations on the basis of experiences with mental illness during the war itself. Jones, working in England, is credited with organizing, in a systematic way, the therapeutic community approach in hospital care for the mentally ill. To understand the patterns of behavior that were underlying to Jones' approach, however, it was important to gain an inside patient-view, a need that was met by the participant observation studies of Barrabee (1951), Belknap (1956), Caudill (1958), and Goffman (1957, 1959, 1961). Moreover, supplementing the intensive institutional case studies were a variety of more focused and smaller scale researches dealing with particular aspects of the dialogue between custodial and therapeutic approaches to the hospitalized mental patient (Greenblatt, York, and Brown 1955; and Greenblatt, Levinson, and Williams 1957).

The mental hospital, in these studies, was conceived as a social system or small society; the focus was on the internal hospital environment, seen as essentially total and self-contained. The generalizations that emerged rested on assumptions of universal social process. Goffman's conception of "total institutions" expressed an underlying assumption common to most of these studies, namely that institutions like prisons, hospitals and certain types of schools develop analogous social systems to provide for the requirement that "inmate populations" frame the whole of their lives within a community. Similarly, the analogy was extended to industrial communities. Largely left out of this analysis was the influence of the larger societal context within which hospitals operate, what has been called the external environment.

Within this generally shared approach, however, three separate theoretical positions may be differentiated. These have been called (1) the human relations approach, (2) the power-structure argument, and (3) social remotivation (Etzioni 1960; Bloom 1965).

The *human relations* approach derives from the work of Kurt Lewin and his students. It is represented in industrial sociology by a movement generally associated with Harvard University, strongly influenced by the pioneer work of Roethlisberger and Dickson (1939). This school underscores the importance of two-way communication among the individuals. Conflicts, it is asserted, may be resolved by the clarification of views, and the freeing of access by one point of view to the other.

The power-structure argument, on the other hand, places more importance on group loyalties and differences. To all extents and purposes, this is conflict theory, as it is usually referred to, with origins in the University of Chicago. Between workers and managers, for example, it is argued that there are real differences which cannot be resolved simply by opening up channels of communication. These differences are basic, it is contended, to the distinctive character of each group and can be solved only by bargaining and compromise. Moreover, the concentration of authority in one group tends to drive the other underground and thus to a life of duplicity. The work of Sullivan, Rowland, Stanton and Schwartz (1954), and Caudill clearly fits into the human relations approach. Belknap and Goffman, on the other hand, take the second approach, emphasizing status differences among structured groups and the resultant power structure conflicts.

A third theoretical approach appears in the works of Greenblatt and his associates and von Mering and King (1957). This approach focuses on the value system that dominates a given hospital community. It is in the values, or the ideology of treatment, they argue, that the fate

of the client population is determined. Certain myths are found to dominate institutions for the treatment of the chronically ill. This conception
describes a "Legend of Chronicity" which preconceives a pessimistic
result for mental illness and thereby produces custodialism in treatment
regardless of the structure of the hospital. To counteract such legends,
a vigorous and aggressive therapeutic approach is recommended that is
called "social remotivation."

There are two observations which all sociological observers of mental
hospitals have noted, irrespective of theoretical orientations. The first
is the change of objective status in society that occurs with admission to
a mental hospital. The patient loses civil rights, social class position,
economic power, and neighborhood and community esteem. It is about
the *meaning* of this change of status that the theoretical views differ.
The human relations approach generally finds that the seriously disordered patient needs a radically changed and protective situation such as that
provided by a hospital. It is in the attitude of the hospital staff that they
see the major source of risk to the goals of therapy. Goffman, on the other
hand, saw a serious psychological loss which occurred as part of the
loss of objective social status. He and others from the Chicago school
see the hospital as an institution which strips self-esteem, stigmatizes,
and drives the patient into a double life, inevitably to work against therapeutic goals.

The second observation that, virtually without exception, sociological
observers have noted in mental hospitals, is the boundary line between
staff and patients. "The patients and employees live in two entirely
separate worlds," Rowland observed, "yet these two groups live in the
closest proximity." Almost word for word, the same observation appears
in the works of Stanton and Schwartz, Belknap, Caudill, and Goffman.
Again, however, the significance of this fact is interpreted very differently,
according to the theoretical orientation. The human relations group
sees in the hospital a situation where a consensus of purpose between
staff and patient world is both possible and strongly inherent in the nature
of the institution. In other words, there is a pressure towards common
purpose. Breakdowns occur in communication between separate but
inherently congenial groups. The problem is mainly to release a basic
commonality of purpose, to keep lines of communication open and thus
to promote a cooperative relationship of therapeutic concern.

For Goffman, however, the "staff-inmate split" is a fundamental conflict. The two worlds, he believes, are *not* united in purpose; the har-

monious balance they strive for is *not* homeostatic as assumed by the human relations approach. On the contrary, Goffman argues, balance is only used to describe a truce between superordinate (staff) and subordinate (patient) groups. It is an arrangement whereby the subordinate group "plays the game" in order to preserve harmony and, more importantly, to prevent punishment or the withdrawal of privileges and to protect against the "assault upon the self" which exists in the social structure of the institution as an inherent threat to the inmate.

The theoretical differences among these several points of view have provided a rich seedbed for discourse among researchers over the past thirty-five years. Although the mental hospital tended to be the main focus in the early stages, increasingly one notes the expansion of effort to include other types of specialty hospitals and the general medical and surgical hospital. An example of the former is the study of a tuberculosis hospital by Roth (1963) and the comparative study of the social organization and dynamics of a medical and surgical ward by Coser (1962). Studies of the general hospital which have been of special influence in this field include Burling, Lentz, and Wilson (1956), Wessen (1958), Duff and Hollingshead (1968), Rosengren and Lefton (1969), and Mumford (1970). Out of these studies there comes an expanded view theoretically, attempting to account for the influence of the hospital's external environment. Mumford, for example, presents a reference group analysis which shows a high degree of significance for the behavior of physicians in hospitals according to the orientation of their major reward systems. Hospitals which are dominated by a dependence upon academic medicine are contrasted with hospitals where the orientation is directed to the community of health consumers being served, the so-called community hospital. Duff and Hollingshead document one part of this dichotomy, the academic hospitals, and reach conclusions very similar to those of Mumford.

Another approach to the study of hospitals uses the frame of reference of complex organizational analysis, especially focused on bureaucratic structure and technology. Goss (1963), Perrow (1963, 1965), Rosengren and Lefton (1969), Georgopoulos (1962, 1975) and Heydebrand (1973) are examples. This perspective focuses on the internal structure of the hospital, the definition and degree of codification of roles, the arrangement of authority and responsibility, the divisions of labor, and the flow of communication. Technology is seen as the major determinant of behavior, and with expanding modernized medical technology, the outcome is increased rationalization of behavior. Obviously, classic Weberian concepts of bureaucratization are basic to the approach, but the unique variations, especially those caused by the resistance of the physician's role to the standard bureaucratic hierarchy, are the subject of intense theoretical concern. Is the hospital a subtype of the classically defined ideal-type of bureaucracy? Or, does the manner of adaptation between technology and the hospital's service function create a distinctive variant? Depersonalization and alienation are also scrutinized as outcome variables within this framework.

Paralleling the concern about the depersonalization of the hospital's internal structure have been two decades of intensified study of the effects on hospital patients of factors in the external environment. For example, the therapeutic community conception, despite its humanizing influence upon the staff in mental hospitals, appears to have been so alien to the patient in terms of his/her outside environment that success within the institution has little relationship to effective adjustment in the community (Stuart 1970: 27). This is especially the case for patients from poverty backgrounds and racial minorities. This contradiction between the cultures of health institutions and the real worlds of the greater part of their client constituency gave a theoretical rationale to the consumer partisanship that emerged from the social movements of the 1960s. The therapeutic community concept was, after all, designed to counteract the depersonalization of bureaucratic hospital organization, and its efficacy as a solution was called to question by "opportunity theory" (Cloward and Ohlin 1966). Similar depersonalization of care also was described in other types of health care settings (Mechanic 1976; Navarro 1976; Taylor 1979), again seen as related to organizational characteristics, and to the lack of opportunity to participate by the patient/consumer in the process of care.

Organizationally, several changes occurred in apparent response to both social scientific interpretations and to the political activism of new constituent groups representing patients. Interprofessional teams were incorporated into in-patient units, and night hospitals, day hospitals, day-care centers, halfway houses, and family care settings. Community mental health centers became a significant part of the psychiatric institutional network. Simultaneously neighborhood health centers, primary care providers and health maintenance organizations emerged as organizational modalities designed to provide accessible, comprehensive personalized care (Lewis, Fein and Mechanic 1976). Characteristically, these new organizational forms were community-based. Their physicians and allied personnel were more aware of the sociocultural context of care, and their clients had some choice in the selection and/or termination of care. Nevertheless, the role of the majority of patients in the actual interpersonal process has continued to be both passive and quite limited. This has been attributed to the patient's definition of the sick role as passive, and to absence of information regarding illness and treatment in hospital settings (Taylor 1979: 167). The role as passive recipient of care has been of particular importance in identifying and analyzing the role of women within the health care system.

On the whole, this channel of inquiry has been one of the most active and varied. Intensive analysis of the social psychology of interpersonal relations within medical organizations, particularly the hospital, has attempted in various ways to interpret and document a social system frame of reference which heavily underscores processes of socialization and the importance of value systems and their effect on the doctor–patient relationship. Recent studies have more critically examined the impact of values on poor populations in general (Antonovsky 1979) and on women (Notman 1978) and on how best to deliver primary care in ambulatory care settings, HMO's and group practices. Furthermore, the role of the hospital in regionalization processes, the role of the consumer in the planning of health services, and the relationship between use of new technology, quality of care, and hospital costs all represent important and promising research areas to be explored. Theoretically, there seems a need to expand complex organizational theory to apply the internal component parts of the general hospital (such as ambulatory services, in-patient services, and research) with external forces, especially the new planning and regulatory groups such as the Health Systems Agency, government and private third party payers, and PSRO-medical audit requirements.

The diversity of approaches and interpretations by these sociological studies is judged by some as a sign of research vitality but by others as quite the opposite. Especially in assessments of social psychiatry, the major studies of interpersonal relations in therapeutic situations have been criticized for their lack of relevance both to sociological knowledge (Clausen 1956; Schatzman and Strauss 1966) and to psychiatric practice (Bell and Spiegel 1966). Most accurately, however, these criticisms are of the field called "social psychiatry," and therefore will be discussed in the next section, since social epidemiology is one of the most important contributing types of research to social psychiatry.

(c) Social epidemiology

Social epidemiology is another research area that has a well-defined set of studies conducted before World War II. Sociologists played a significant part especially in studies of the incidence and prevalence of mental illness.

Probably the most influential program of research on what came to be known as the social ecology of mental illness was conducted by Faris and Dunham in the thirties, based upon the urban sociology of Burgess (Faris and Dunham 1939). Actually, however, their work comes not so much at the beginning as at the mid-point of a developing series of studies using the epidemiological method to document and interpret the nature and scope of mental disorder. There were several related propositions which were at the foundation of this research field:

1) There has been a substantial increase in the rate of mental illness in the United States over the past century.

2) The increase in mental illness is associated directly with increased industrialization and urbanization; therefore, it can be concluded that the causes of serious mental disorder, in significant part, include factors of life-style, particularly the stress and pressure of modern society.

3) There is, beyond the increase in the rate of diagnosed cases of mental illness, a significant amount of undetected and consequently untreated mental illness in the society.

Much of the epidemiological research on mental illness of the past half century has been concerned with the documentation and analysis of these three basic propositions. Concerning the first, a large amount of data have been collected which challenge the correctness of the statement that mental illness has indeed increased over the past century. The second proposition has also been seriously challenged: that is, urbanization and industrialization as such, especially compared with rural life style, has not been shown to correlate with increased psychotic illness. The third proposition has been supported by those studies which are available: that is, a considerable amount of undetected mental disorder has been found. The latter finding, however, is preliminary and based upon a difficult type of study which, although excellent examples are now available, needs to be further pursued before any final answer can be given.

The amount of "recognizable" mental illness indeed has been large enough to cause legitimate concern. In 1960, for example, it could be stated with reasonable accuracy that as many as 1,814,000 cases of mental illness each year were "recognizable" as severe enough "to warrant treatment." (Plunkett and Gordon 1960). However, as Malzberg and others have been gradually documenting since the early thirties (Malzberg 1936; as reviewed in Leacock 1957), the increasing rate is more apparent than real. Probably the most thorough analysis of this question that is available to date was presented by Goldhamer and Marshall (1949) who concluded that no "long term increase during the last century in the incidence of the psychoses in early middle life" is indicated by the available data.

These studies demonstrated that the correct interpretation of long-term trends in mental disorder must include age and life expectancy. The substantial increases of gross rates of mental illness which have been reported are accurate in themselves, but they do not necessarily signify that psychiatric illness has become a greater hazard in modern America than in other historical periods and in other cultures. Hidden by the gross figure is the uneven distribution according to age. It would appear that proportionately large amounts of mental illness are being reported at both ends of the life cycle, while in the "prime" age periods of early and middle adulthood, the rates of serious mental disturbance have remained stable.

The very young show a substantial increase in serious mental illness largely, it is now believed, because of better diagnostic procedures for children. The elderly, merely on the basis of the greater number of persons who now reach ages above 55 compared with a century or even a half century ago would be expected to become a larger source of psychiatric cases. It is estimated that about one-third of the first admissions are over 55 years old (Plunkett and Gordon 1960; Monroe, Klee, and Brody 1967). In mental hospitals themselves, chronic patients live longer and thus increase the figures of prevalence. Important methodological advances were made in the process of answering this general proposition. Even as the methods of study became more refined, the results were qualified by the increased awareness, from preliminary studies, of the possibility that a significant amount of untreated and therefore unreported mental illness existed in the society and required documentation before any firm final conclusions about rates of mental disorder could be reached. Epidemiologically, this question is at the base of studies of "total prevalance" as opposed to studies which, implicitly or explicitly, are based only on reported prevalence (i.e., diagnosed cases extant at a given time).

In their report to the Joint Commission on Mental Illness and Health, Plunkett and Gordon (1960) cite eleven community studies which included among their research goals the calculation of the total prevalence of mental illness. Since the publication of that report, at least two additional community surveys have been published, The Midtown Manhattan Study (Srole and associates 1962) and the Stirling County Studies of Nova Scotia (Leighton and associates 1959, 1963, Hughes *et al.* 1960), both containing very careful efforts to estimate total prevalence.

In all of these studies, the ratio of untreated to treated mental illness is very high, but the variation of rates, on all counts, is bewilderingly diverse. What, if any, common thread of meaning do they contain?

The Midtown Manhattan Study is, in several respects, a landmark research. On this particular question, the findings of Srole and his associates have attracted considerable public attention precisely because the extent of estimated – and untreated – mental impairment is so high. Fully 80 percent of their sample contains some degree of the symptoms of psychiatric illness. The methodology of total prevalence study was reviewed exhaustively by Srole, leading to the choice of a combination of psychiatric with sociological techniques. A strenuous effort was made to avoid the errors of preceding research. What, then, does the calculation mean that only 1 out of 5 persons in central New York City qualify (in the judgement of the Midtown Study's team of mental health professionals) for the designation "essentially well"?

A close study of the Midtown Manhattan research indicates that the picture is not quite as bleak as suggested by the ratio of "essentially well" to "psychiatrically disabled." Only 1 out of 5 in the sample was totally free of significant psychiatric symptoms, but, of the remainder, almost 60 percent were judged to be reasonably well-adjusted to their life circumstances in spite of some degree of emotional difficulty. Thus the percentage which is judged to be "impaired" is 23.5, and only half of these were judged to be severely impaired or incapacitated. Thus, of the total sample, 1 in 10 are "severely impaired."

The Leightons, in their study of Nova Scotia, and using methods similar to those of Srole, found a notably smaller total prevalence, 57 percent, but the amount of "psychiatric disorder with significant impairment" was virtually identical, 20 percent. Thus, although more individuals in the rural and small town environment of Stirling County were judged to be "essentially well" in comparison with Midtown Manhattan's urban community, the same proportion – 1 out of 5 – were judged to be notably handicapped in their life adjustment because of symptoms of mental illness, and less than that suffered from severe disorder.

The next question was how many of the total were treated? On this question Pasaminick's (1961) study of Baltimore is often cited. Also a total prevalence study, there were reported by Pasaminick twenty cases of untreated mental illness for every one treated psychiatric patient.

Various questions have been raised about the Pasaminick data. In spite of its weaknesses, the core of its results are difficult to refute. For example, the data had been tested for the possibility that a large proportion of untreated psychiatric illness may be explained simply by the severity of symptoms. That is, those with severe symptoms tend to fall into the treated category while those with the less severe symptoms constitute the bulk of the untreated. Indeed, when those who were diagnosed as seriously disturbed are analyzed separately, the proportion of untreated is dramatically reduced. Nevertheless, about 1 out of every 2 diagnosed as psychotic were untreated.

On close comparison, therefore, the results of Pasaminick (1961), Leighton (1959, 1963), and Srole (1962) show a similar hard core of severely impaired individuals. Allowing for error, something like 1 out of 5 in the population studied were notably impaired, and of these about half, or 1 out of 10 in the total sample, were severely impaired. The number of these who were treated cannot be generalized, but from the Baltimore Study there is indication that the amount of serious psychiatric illness which is untreated is considerable.

Threaded throughout these studies, at least two basic conclusions consistently reappear. First, there is a tendency for the rate of severe mental illness, the so-called psychoses, to be stable when computed on an age-specific basis. This is the category, of course, about which there is the most agreement concerning identifying symptoms. The second conclusion raises important questions about the first. No matter how it is calculated, the ratio of untreated to treated mental illness appears to be very high. When one finds further that the untreated category includes a high proportion of the most seriously ill, how can one explain the fact that so many individuals who, it is reasonable to assume, are very visible in their disturbance, remain, nevertheless, outside of the range of the methods provided by modern society for their identification and care?

In seeking to answer this question, one finds that there are useful data from some of the earliest studies of the epidemiology of mental illness, particularly the work done at Chicago University (Faris and Dunham) over forty years ago. On a more conceptual level, important analysis has appeared only recently by a number of investigators, both sociologists and psychiatrists, who challenge the very premises upon which the officially accepted definitions of mental illness rest (Szasz 1961; Goffman 1961; Ernest Becker 1962; Scheff 1966; and Howard Becker 1963). The core of the latter work is the assertion that mental illness is a highly relative descriptive category into which individuals are placed more because of their social origins and environmental situations than they are because of a specific illness that can be diagnosed exclusive of social factors.

Actually, beginning with the Chicago Study, a considerable amount of epidemiological research has been conducted on this question of the possible correlations between different ways of life (as sociologically defined) and different forms and degrees of mental illness. The data of these studies have produced some of the major hypotheses about the relation between social conditions and mental disorder. Leacock (1957) provides an excellent summary of these inquiries. She concludes that the social epidemiology of mental illness has developed around three closely related but theoretically separable areas: the question of rural versus urban living, the importance of nationality (or the cultural factor) and the significance of socioeconomic variables. Mobility is also discussed by Leacock "as an important situational factor which operates in all three." A large body of research has developed in the effort to answer the question of what significance, if any, these variables possess as determinants of mental illness.

Concerning the "urbanism hypothesis of mental illness," the research literature provides a story with all the fascination of a detective whodunit. There are the false leads and unexpected findings, the unfolding of precise details to fill in the early general suspicions, and inevitably a new set of hypothetical formulations with which to start the cycle of search all over again (cf. Leacock 1957; Milbank Memorial Annual Conference Proceedings 1950 and 1953; Dunham 1959).

It becomes more and more clear that the urban hypothesis has been an expression, at least in part, of a "rural bias" which runs strong in the values of Western culture. One of its basic assumptions has been that the rural and urban environments represent coherent, mutually exclusive types of human experience which have differential effect upon the personality organization of their participants. The "bias" in this hypothesis prejudges the adjustment and integration challenges that adhere to these two differing life experiences, arguing that "complex, heterogenous, value-conflicting urban cultures produce intra-personal organizations which are correspondingly heterogenous and unintegrated," whereas simpler folk (or rural) cultures "produce simpler, unified personality integrations" (Seeman 1946).

As the epidemiological data accumulated, so did the doubts about the validity of the urban hypothesis. There were no consistently higher urban rates of mental disorder found either for general categories such as the "psychoses" or specific types of disease. Greater differences were found from one city to another than between urban and rural settings. As it became clear that some rural areas had very high rates of mental disorder, a revision of the hypothesis was suggested in which "urbanization" was separated conceptually from "social integration." Whereas previously the degree of social integration was belived to be a direct function of urbanization, the relation between these two variables became itself a focus of study rather than an assumption.

As revised, the question for investigation became not what degree of urbanization was associated with the incidence of mental disorder but instead what type of rural area was involved or what type of section of the city. The special distribution or "ecology" of mental disorder replaced urbanization as the major concern for epidemiological inquiry about mental illness.

It was just this type of ecological frame of reference that characterized the major study by Faris and Dunham forty years earlier. They anticipated the major directions of research in this field. It can be stated without any question that *this is a major, landmark study* in medical sociology generally and in social epidemiology specifically. Their findings that schizophrenia was distributed *indirectly* according to socioeconomic status in Chicago and that manic depression was not so distributed became the basis of questions that influenced most of the research which followed. The research of Hollingshead and Redlich (1958) is perhaps the best known of the large-scale efforts to test the earlier Chicago findings about socioeconomic status.

As can be seen the significance of the urbanism hypothesis and the relationship between socioeconomic status and mental disorder are not always separable in the review of research in this field. The two are closely connected and have been frequently studied at the same time. The same may be said for the study of the significance of cultural variables. Faris and Dunham included cultural and racial variables in their study. (For a full review of research in this area, Leacock 1957 is an excellent source.) Mention of particular studies should include, however, Eaton and Weil (1955), another landmark research. One important generalization which follows from its findings is that the perception and definition of mental illness varies by culture; the basic symptoms of severe disorder do not. Similarly, the treatment of mental disorder is very different according to culture and the outcomes (improvement and cure) vary, but in terms that are not clearly understood.

To summarize, the social epidemiology of mental disorder has been one of the most active areas of research in medical sociology, with one of the earliest historical beginnings. As Clausen (1979) has concluded, however, such studies have revealed more about differences in life patterns and the ways in which persons with emotional problems come to the attention or treatment of psychiatric facilities than they have revealed about the etiology of mental disorder. Although government agencies continue to collect basic statistics about incidence and prevalence of mental disorder, the commitment of teams of scholars to intensive programs of research in this area seems to have slowed down in favor of efforts to clarify issues of application in the field of social psychiatry and community mental health.

As important as the study of mental illness has been, social epidemiology should not be regarded as limited to or even mainly concerned with mental illness. As far back as 1755, Sir Percival Pott (Pott 1775 cited in Graham and Reeder 1972) used this method to link an occupation, chimney sweep, with scrotal cancer, pointing to the etiological significance of soot in that disease. The epidemiological method has been used with special effectiveness to study diseases that may be classified "by the social groups evincing them or the behavior patterns associated with them" (Graham and Reeder 1972: 75). These include the diseases that occur more frequently in lower socioeconomic classes and those associated with particular racial or ethnic backgrounds. They also include smoking-related diseases: coronary disease, peptic ulcers, and cancer of the bladder, mouth and lung.

Perhaps the most important lesson of the history of social epidemiology and the successful application of its findings in preventive medicine has been that disease is produced by a multi-factorial process, a chain of events. It is possible, with only a partial knowledge of the exact operation of every factor, to interrupt the chain and effectively stop the process. Thus was Percival Pott able to reduce the incidence of scrotal cancer even though he possessed no knowledge of the exact agent that caused the disease or the nature of the disease as such. It was enough for him to know the patterns of behavior associated with the disease and to change them (he prescribed bathing).

The success of some epidemiological findings, however, raised expectations that, when they were frustrated, have produced strong, sometimes bitter criticism. It is one thing to identify behavior patterns that are associated with disease; it is quite another to change them. Smoking, for example, does not yield to knowledge about its pathogenic qualities so readily as the cleanliness of chimney sweeps. Nor do eating habits, the use of alcohol, or "Type A" personalities. Polluted water can be purified but pathogenic human behavior cannot be so directly controlled.

One result has been a shift from the focus of inquiry on finding "causes" to an attempt to develop and test new sociological hypotheses in the areas of innovation and behavioral and attitude change (Graham and Reeder 1972). Quite explicitly, this is a move away from the orientation of basic science toward applied science. It is, for social epidemiology generally, the same research trend which we traced for the social epidemiology of mental illness.

Against this background, the major criticisms of social psychiatry are not, in our judgment, valid. Sociological research in both interpersonal relations in therapeutic situations and social epidemiology have not, as critics charge, been identified so closely with dominant medical values that they have failed to challenge the role of the physician. On the contrary, sociologists like Schwartz (Stanton and Schwartz), Goffman, Caudill, Belknap and others contributed substantially to radical changes in psychiatric hospitals. Similarly, the works of Srole and associates, the Leightons, and other social epidemiologists helped to open the delivery of psychiatric care to the poor through new types of institutions like the community mental health centres.

(d) The sociology of the profession[4]

Sociologists have studied the professions largely within definitions originally conceived by Carr-Saunders and Wilson (1933). Based on per-

---

4. This section adapts a substantial amount of material from the paper by Bloom and Wilson (1979).

spectives of the division of labor in society, they identified a set of characteristics which separated professions from other occupations and placed the existence of professionalism distinctively in modern Western society, dating from the late Middle Ages in association with the appearance of the university. Those individuals who represented such occupations as medicine and law in previous ages were seen not as professionals but more as craftsmen-spiritualists until the thirteenth century. This definitional framework was the point of departure for the development of the sociology of the professions as an active field of inquiry, and medicine, as the prototypical profession, has been the subject of much of the modern work in this field.[5]

Two core characteristics were conceived by Carr-Saunders and Wilson as being, in combination, the distinctive properties of a profession. The first was the extended formal training required for qualification which began with the medieval doctor (only in the medieval university was the present title of "doctor" created), lawyer or priest. Such formal training was not required in earlier times and today it remains a core characteristic of the professions. A second basic attribute of a profession, according to this definition, is an orientation toward service to the community. Thus a profession is "a vocation in which a professed knowledge of some department of learning or science is used in its application to the affairs of others or in the practice of an art founded upon it" (Oxford English Dictionary, Unabridged 1933). A further set of characteristics were derivative: the practitioners of a profession form a distinct social group, classified as such both by the practitioners themselves and by the society in which they operate. The basis of this social group is in their professional activity and not some other social or economic attribute. The social group itself – or "community," as recent scholars prefer (see Larson 1977) – is organized into an association which establishes formal rules and informal practices of behavior. The association disciplines its own members, maintaining an ethical standard by its own means, and thus preserving the independence of its members in the practice of the profession.

Talcott Parsons, beginning in the 1930s, is the sociologist who is usually credited with the beginnings of the sociology of medicine as a profession. His work, in turn, owes much to his colleague-mentor at

---

5. The distinction between "modern" work and the general history of the field is important to make clear. In the sociology of the professions, the sociology of law is much the older, especially in European sociology. Medicine emerges as a focus coincident with the Carr-Saunders and Wilson writings, and subsequently attracts most of the substantive inquiry.

Harvard, L.J. Henderson (1935, 1936, 1937; see also Barber 1970 and Bloom and Wilson 1979).

It was not until after World War II, however, that the full development of this area of work occurred. In 1951, Parsons produced the most complete and articulate enunciation of his sociology of medicine (Parsons 1951: 428–479), and, as though to prove the dictum, "an industrializing society is a professionalizing society" (Goode 1960), the scholarly interest in the professions during the next thirty years has been intense (Freidson 1970; Johnson 1972; Larson 1977).

Almost from the start, two distinct perspectives dominated inquiry about the professions: the ideal-typical construction of professions as "functional" social systems, and the "Chicago school" view – represented by Everett C. Hughes and his students – that looks at what professions actually do in everyday life (Larson 1977). Although both approaches were active, functionalism was the dominant paradigm until the challenge of Freidson (1961, 1970).

The essence of the social system formulation is that human social relationships can be described as patterns, rooted in cultural expectations about the social roles of group members; that the fundamental process of behavior is communication; and that the integrity of the system is maintained by homeostasis. In science generally, functional system theory was developed to meet the inadequacies of linear causality: the whole was not the sum of its parts, for change in any part alters simultaneously the character of the whole system. This formulation was by Henderson who, in turn, built upon both Pareto and his own theoretical analysis of physiological systems, with the doctor–patient relationship as the illustrative case. Parsons expanded the perspective to a more institutional approach, viewing medicine as an important sub-system of Western society.

The premises of the Parsonian model include the following:

1) The problem of health is "intimately involved in the *functional prerequisites* of the social system." Too low a general level of health, too high an incidence of illness, is *dysfunctional*.

2) Sickness and health are, because of their importance, part of the culture.

3) Health care is a social role relationship between a helping agent and a person needing help.

4) The social roles of the health care relationship are a patterned sector of culture, and thus learned sequences of behavior.

From these premises, Parsons constructs ideal types of sick role and professional role. The former is a form of social deviance which, though involuntary in cause, must be controlled to prevent the abuse that is an inherent threat because of the psychological rewards of the legitimized dependency of illness. The professional role combines healing the patient and social control as the agent of the society. Within this framework, the sick role is temporary, undesirable, and socially disruptive. The professional is a technical expert who legitimizes the claim to illness and is responsible for returning the sick person to his normal role in society.

Critics have focused on two aspects of the relationship: (1) Parsons' emphasis on the asymmetry in the therapeutic situation, and (2) the "distancing" effect of the role attributes of the professional. Parsons is interpreted as a defender of the technical elitism of the modern professional. Patients must be "controlled" lest they take advantage of the privileges of the sick role to prolong dependency; physicians must be "protected" from emotional overinvolvement with their patients. Role asymmetry, critics charge, is based not only on achieved technical expertise but on labeling the patient passive and dependent and the doctor expert, the one needing control and the other protection. Moreover, the Parsonian model is criticized as an ideal type model that so emphasizes rationality that other factors which are culturally and situationally derived receive only token significance. The theoretical problem is centered first in the question about what is the major determining variable – culture or situation – and second, in the question of what is the guiding behavioral process – homeostatic adaptation or encounter bargaining. Feminists, for example, challenge the applicability of this model in the medical proscriptions for pregnancy and childbirth. Furthermore, the sociological assumption that the patient is a deviant raises serious issues regarding the participation of a patient in the recovery process, perhaps most dramatically in the encounter between physician and patient in the situational context of birth.

Challenge by the "Chicago school" to the Parsonian functional approach is most thoroughly developed in Freidson, although Mechanic (1968), Zola (1966) and Davis (1964) have contributed significantly.

In brief, Freidson's differences with social system analysis can be stated in the following terms:

1) The Parsons model sees the doctor–patient relationship from too limited a perspective, most essentially the physician's. It ignores the varying expectations of all members of the "role set" (Merton 1957),

including those of the patient (or more inclusively his lay associates) and other health-related personnel (such as nurses) who are significant in treatment process.

2) Expectations are presented by Parsons as though they are the primary influence on actual behavior. In fact, they are only an ideal standard against which actual behavior is judged.

3) Influence does not inhere in the expectation but in the position of the person holding it. Only from the structure of the situation and its intrinsic limits can one weigh the possibility of an expectation being met.

4) Most important, the functional model ignores the necessity of conflict in human relationships. If the professional and the patient each seeks his own terms from the other, there is conflict.

The doctor–patient relationship, Freidson concluded, is most effectively analyzed within a framework of *a clash of perspectives* – an encounter between two distinct social systems, not a functionally contained, homeostatic system in itself: "the professional expects patients to accept what he recommends on his terms; patients seek services on their own terms. In that each seeks to gain his own terms, there is conflict" (Freidson 1961).

It was Freidson's analysis of *authority* in the professional role that influenced other scholars most. The terms "monopoly" and "autonomy," as applied to professions, were given fresh meaning in his analysis. Again, Parsons is his point of reference.

For Parsons, illness is most essentially a biological state with social implications and consequences; the sick role involves a separate motivational step. In this conception, there is choice and variable behavior in the sick role; in illness, substantially there is none. Thus Parsons argues for the legitimacy of the physician's authority as the agent of social control over *illness*, by his (the physician's) achieved expertise (functional specificity) in judging what the valid connections are between illness and sick-role behavior. Freidson, however, asserts that medicine is a monopoly with the right to create illness as an official social role.

Unlike Parsons, I do not argue merely that medicine has the power to legitimize one's acting sick by conceding that he really is sick. My argument goes further than that. I argue here that by virtue of being the authority on what illness "really" is, medicine creates the social possibilities for acting sick. In this sense, medicine's monopoly includes the right to create illness as an official social role .... It is part of being a profession to be given the official power to define and therefore create the shape of problematic segments of social behavior: the judge determines what is legal and who is guilty, the priest what is holy and who is profane, the physician what is normal and who is sick (Freidson 1970).

In these terms, Freidson articulates the basic sociological position underlying the "labeling theory" of Szasz (1961), Scheff (1966), and Goffman (1961) in their analyses of mental illness, and extends it to chronic illness (1965).

More than for labeling theory, however, Freidson supplied the basis for the critical challenge to Parsons' theory of the inherent authority of the professional role. Autonomy, Freidson argued, is not a consequence of technical and scientific knowledge – as Parsons believed it is and should be; rather, it is the source of power and therefore something the profession seeks to preserve with or without benefit of expertise. Professional autonomy, thus, is seen as a method for keeping the knowledge base of a profession secret, and the mystification of such knowledge is a most effective means for institutionalizing authority. Moreover, professional autonomy has dysfunctional aspects. It "provides an order similar to that of bureaucracy and seems to be as responsible for the pathologies of the system as is bureaucracy" (Freidson 1970; see also Leyerle 1981).

Freidson's conflict model was timely in that it coincided with the dramatic social events of the "sixties." Indeed, for subsequent scholarship in this field, attention to social change and ideology were expanded. As Larson wrote:

The ideal-typical approach seldom takes account of the concrete historical conditions in which groups of specialists have attempted to establish a monopoly over specific areas of the division of labor. The class context in which authority is delegated and privileges are granted to these particular occupations tends to be neglected. Thus, while Freidson's analysis emphasizes that a profession must gain support from strategic social or political groups, the institutional approach suffers from a tendency to present professions as categories which emerge from the division of labor in unmediated connection with society as a whole (Larson 1977: xiii).

This was the takeoff position for the Marxist critique that developed in the 1970s. As represented by Waitzkin and Waterman (1974) and Navarro (1975), the doctor–patient relationship is a "typical collectivity" within the institution of medicine. That social institution, in turn, is only comprehensible as part of the sociopolitical structure of the society. In their own words:

The sick do not suffer in isolation from the broad sociopolitical structures of the societies in which they live . . . . In all societies, health care is a service provided by one group of people (health workers) to another (patients). Societies differ greatly, however, in the ways they organize this service (Waitzkin and Waterman 1974: 8).

They argue that in American society medicine is organized essentially for profit, reflecting the normative principles of capitalism. Therefore, although the need for good health to maintain the system creates a certain "ambiguity" about the right to health, the tension between profit and good health has persisted. One group exploits the other. Only in this way can the persistent maldistribution of health services favoring wealthy patients be explained. They document the structure of the growing industries which provide health services and produce medical products, together with the increasingly concentrated distribution of profits among certain small groups of physicians.

Most recently, the sociology of the medical profession has been absorbed into a more general theoretical analysis of the role of professions in society. Gouldner (1979) and Konrad and Szelenyi (1979) have introduced intriguing arguments about the growth of a new class in modern industrial society. Larson (1977) has integrated a wide range of literature into the effort to construct a comprehensive sociology of the professions. Without a question, this has been a rich intellectual vein and medical sociology has provided many of the miners.

II. The Sociology of Medical Education[6]

As we have shown, the early intellectual roots of the sociology of medicine were strong. Although medical sociology was not established as a field until after 1945, the pattern of its substantive concerns was set during the two prior decades. One outstanding exception was the sociology of medical education.

Unlike the other major substantive problems that medical sociologists studied, medical education was approached in a style that broke sharply from its antecedents. To be sure, especially in the hands of Merton (Merton et al. 1957) and Hughes (Becker et al. 1961), the conception of

6. This section condenses material originally published by one of the authors, Samuel W. Bloom, "Socialization for the Physician's Role: A Review of Some Contributions of Research to Theory," in Eileen L. Shapiro and L. M. Lowenstein (editors), Becoming a Physician, Cambridge, Mass.: Ballinger, 1979, pp. 3–52.

research was continuous with long-established theory, in this case with those processes of human development called "socialization." The application of socialization theory to professional education, however, was new and the medical school was chosen as the first site for a major effort to describe and interpret the professional school as a social system, the major roles of the participants (especially the student and faculty member), and the direct and indirect ways in which the attitudes and values of future professional role behavior are learned.

Prior to World War II, studies of medical education were confined, for the most part, to psychological research. The pattern of these earlier studies had been set by the Flexner "doorkeeper" dictum: "It is necessary to install a doorkeeper (in the medical school) who will . . . ascertain the fitness of the applicant" (Flexner 1910:72). Flexner's influence was reflected in the massive effort, between the two World Wars, to develop effective methods of selection to medical school. The result was the intensive work by psychologists to find objective measures of cognitive intellectual factors. The Moss Test, followed by the Medical College Admissions Test (MCAT) were the direct consequences (Gough 1971).

The interest in a more detailed description of the actual experience of medical students came with the spirit of educational reform that characterized the immediate post-War period. From that point on inquiry focused on the school as the social environment of learning, unlike earlier research in which the school was conceived as secondary to the student. *Student culture* came into its own as a study variable.

Critical interpretations have been written about the sociology of medical education specifically (Becker and Geer 1963; Becker et al. 1972; Bloom 1965 and 1979) and about its contributions to theories of adult socialization more generally (Mortimer and Simmons 1978; Levinson 1967; Van Maanen 1977; Light 1980). They chart the following steps in the postwar history of this field:

1) Selection studies, based on Flexner's "doorkeeper" premises, were continued, but as a kind of research ritual. The focus of attention shifted to the proposition that medical schools function as social environments to change their students with reference to future behavior in the physician's role, i.e., to socialization research.

2) Another research dimension developed, more from educational psychology than from sociology, concerned with *how* to teach more effectively for specific educational goals.

3) Associated with radicalization of the university in the late 1960s, studies of power, involving analysis of the organizational structure of the medical school and the profession, appeared for the first time as a pattern of research effort and not just the interest of isolated individuals (Bucher 1970; Bloom 1973). Socialization studies shifted, in close association with this trend, toward an emphasis on the later stages of professional training, internship and residency (Mumford 1970; Miller 1970; Bucher and Stelling 1977; Coser 1979; Light 1980). There was also the beginning of comparative socialization studies, both of collaborating health professions and across cultures (Kelner *et al.* 1980; Olesen and Whittaker 1968).

4) Finally, there are signs of organized educational concern about the ethical values that medical students acquire as part of professional education (Simmons and DiCanio 1979; Fox 1976). For some, this is seen as the logical consequence of the ethical dilemmas uncovered by the technology of modern medicine. Others see it as a digression from the still incomplete discourse that emerged from studies of organization structure and power in the medical school.

Within this broad outline, we will sketch here only very briefly the highlights of three decades of research in this field.

The new focus on the student and his social environment was closely associated with a revived sense of the importance of the patient and his social environment. The educational experiments, that proliferated in so many varieties and in so many places in American medical education thirty years ago, were joined together in their motivation as much toward the improvement of medical care as they were toward the improvement of medical education. More precisely, the intent was to assure the patient a type of medical care which, in addition to the best scientific techniques, would include concern about the emotional and social factors in his illness. They were designated as experiments in teaching both attitudes and skills in the "human" side of medicine.

This dual interest in the student and the patient, especially at its beginning, was expressed in programs of comprehensive care which experimented with both the implementation of a concept of medical practice and how it should be taught. This was the particular innovation which, in retrospect, appears to be the most important "precipitating factor" (Merton *et al.* 1957) for the development of a sociology of medical education. In keeping with the general spirit of the "climate of change," the question which was asked of the behavioral scientist was: Do our new programs for the teaching of comprehensive care achieve the effects on student attitudes and skills that are intended? Two outstanding examples are the Cornell Comprehensive Care and Teaching Program (CC & TP) and the General Medical Clinic (GMC) program at the University of Colorado School of Medicine (Reader 1954; Reader and Goss 1967; Hammond and Kern 1959).

Both the Cornell CC & TP and the Colorado GMC began as efforts to apply the experimental method to the complex problem of evaluating educational practice. However, especially in the Cornell research, a before-and-after study of experimental and control groups of students was reassigned from its early prominence as the primary research design to a position of only equal importance with others. The Cornell CC & TP, it was decided soon after the study began, was more likely to be understood in the full context of the school as a four-year experience than as a disconnected six-month program. Consequently, although the carefully constructed experimental design was continued as one step in the evaluation of the program, there were added observational, interviewing, and questionnaire studies of the school as a social system, covering all four years of student experience. Among the widely ranging research styles which have developed as part of the continuing studies of medical education at Cornell are the analysis of the teaching hospital as a special type of bureaucracy (Goss 1959, 1963), the intensive scrutiny of particular aspects of professional socialization such as "training for uncertainty" or "detached concern," (Fox 1957; Lief and Fox 1963), and selected conceptions of the student's attitudinal development studied by panel questionnaire (Merton *et al.* 1957).

At about the same time, early in the 1950s, interest in the study of the whole four-year student experience crystallized at two other medical schools, Western Reserve and Kansas. At Western Reserve, the impetus again came from an educational experiment but, in this case, the entire four-year curriculum was revised. Under such circumstances, interest in the whole of the student's experience would seem to follow logically. At the University of Kansas Medical School, on the other hand, no particularly novel change was being attempted at the time when the research was started. Nevertheless, the Kansas study became one of the most ambitious – a detailed case study of a social institution based on extensive participant-observation and interviewing (Becker *et al.* 1961).

At Western Reserve, a different type of case method became the major tool of research. Under the direction of Milton Horowitz, a psychologist on the medical school's faculty, 20 students were selected on the basis of sociometric ratings. A detailed analysis of data on these students, focused on the four years at Western Reserve but including follow-up studies five years after graduation, was published (Horowitz 1964). Data on medical student experiences at Western Reserve were also collected by the Bureau of Applied Social Research of Columbia University. However, these data for the most part have not been published with specific reference to the Western Reserve experiment, but have instead been incorporated in comparative studies of more specific and limited questions about the process of becoming a doctor (Merton, Rogoff, Bloom 1956; Rogoff 1957; Huntington 1957).

Another variant of the effort to look at the medical school as a total four-year experience began in the early 1950s at the University of Buffalo School of Medicine. The Buffalo Project in Medical Education, as it was called, became a large-scale self-study, in which nearly 100 faculty members actively participated (Miller 1961). The frame of reference for this work was derived from educational psychology. The School of Education of Buffalo University worked in close collaboration with the project. Nathaniel Cantor, a professor of sociology in the University's Liberal Arts College, was a primary source of inspiration and direction.

Reflecting the influence of the education specialists, the Buffalo project became essentially a study of teaching techniques. The summary publication is both a critical appraisal of the prevailing methods of medical education and a statement of recommendations for improvement. The student is the focus. The assumptions emphasize how teaching can and frequently does "get in the way of students who want to learn, rather than help them in learning."

The five research programs that have been discussed up to this point were all organized and conducted by research teams, and were focused on a single institution. The Columbia studies could be considered an exception because they were conducted in three medical schools, Cornell, the University of Pennsylvania, and Western Reserve. However, Cornell was the central focus of study, and the Cornell CC&TP the point of departure for all of the Columbia group's research.

These early researches barely had time to gather their full momentum when a shift toward large-scale surveys occurred in new research on medical education. The Association of American Medical Colleges (AAMC) initiated a series of inquiries on national samples of students and faculty members. Specifically, these surveys were instituted for the collection of information to be used at annual teaching institutes sponsored by the AAMC (Comroe 1962; Gee and Cowles 1957; Gee and Glaser 1958). Some were designed to study the different disciplines and phases of the medical curriculum. Others studied the major problems which, it was agreed, were at the source of the trends toward change which followed the war. Among the latter, one study represented the continuing interest in the type of applicant and the growing concern over apparent changes in the quality of applicants to the medical school (Gee and Cowles 1957). Another survey was concerned with the medical school's social environment (Gee and Glaser 1957). This direction of interest was sustained by the creation of a permanent staff of research personnel in the AAMC which has engaged in continuing studies (Sanazaro 1966; Hutchins 1964), including a longitudinal study of a national cohort of students who entered medical schools in 1956 (Yancik and Bartholomew 1975; Erdman *et al.* 1978).

Another example of this interest in large sample surveys is the work of a group of behavioral scientists at the University of North Carolina School of Public Health. Choice of specialties was the focal problem of this group's research based on a sample drawn from nine medical schools. Most particularly, they studied the attitudes toward public health as a career, but a variety of other questions were included (Coker *et al.* 1959, 1960a, 1960b).

More experiments in medical education, in the meantime, continued to be started. Among them were programs of comprehensive care teaching, but, almost as though they were content to await the results of the Cornell and Colorado studies, they did not include research on their effects (Lee 1961). Toward the end of the 1950s another shift occurred in the type of teaching experiments; they expressed a renewed and revised relationship between the professional school and the university. At Johns Hopkins, Northwestern, and Boston universities, the premedical and medical courses were integrated; early acceptance (in Boston's case, from the time of high school graduation) and the possibilities of a shortened total period of higher education were included (Lee 1961).

Lief, at Tulane University College of Medicine, added still another dimension. Lief and a group of psychiatric colleagues had been conducting longitudinal studies of the emotional development of medical students (Lief *et al.* 1960). The subjects included both "normals" – that is, students who do not ask for and are not referred for psychiatric treatment – and students who have emotional problems severe enough to bring them into psychiatric treatment. Unlike similar studies, the Tulane project has always included in its field of concern the school as a social environment, and, to a degree, collaboration with sociological consultants was an important adjunct to the research procedure.

The thrust of sociological research on medical education diminished notably during the early 1960s. The commitment of teams of researchers on the scale of the previous decade seemed ended. For at least a half dozen years, the sociological effort receded.

On the other hand, the trend of development in medical education itself continued much along the lines that had been established at the beginning of the twenty-five-year period, shifting only into a more radical phase. Especially the trend toward integration, both across disciplines and between the preclinical and clinical studies, expanded from a few test cases to embrace virtually the whole national scene. After almost two decades of watchful waiting, during which the Western Reserve curriculum revision was looked at, discussed, and cautiously tested in bits and pieces, suddenly many medical schools acted. The basic curriculum reform that Western Reserve had pioneered was widely adopted and, at the same time, striking revisions in the use of electives and the behavioral sciences occurred.

From the trends of curriculum change, it would appear that the moratorium in sociological studies of medical education in the early sixties was balanced by educational reforms that reflected, at least to some degree, the research findings of the preceding decade. Such influence is difficult to demonstrate, but what is certain is the change of mood among educators: they became more action-oriented, and instead of continuing to pursue questions about basic behavioral process in education, their requests were for methods and principles of policy change and implementation.

The educational research that did occur during this period (roughly between 1958 and 1968) centered on the evalution of styles of teaching, and on the attempt to answer specific questions about how to teach. This brought educational specialists, especially educational psychologists, into the effort in strength. New departments of medical education were formed in many schools of medicine, but sociologists were essentially peripheral to this development. George Miller, as the Chairman of the Department of Medical Education at the University of Illinois

School of Medicine, and his previous associates at Buffalo, Hilliard Jason and Steve Abrahamson, emerged as leaders of this movement which continues to be strong to this day.

The context for all these developments was an expanding society, and the rapid development of medical technology within general industrial growth and related social change. Service functions increased dramatically, with unanticipated consequences for the economy as the balance of manpower shifted toward service industries, including a vastly expanded health sector (Fuchs 1974). Medical education, stimulated and supported by various federal financing programs, accepted a mandate to increase the ratio of physicians to the population by creating 47 new medical schools between 1950 and 1979 (from 79 to 126), and by more than doubling its admissions from 7,177 in 1950 to 17,014 in 1979 (JAMA 1980, 244: 2813–2814).

By 1970, however, it began to be clear that the expansion of the quantity of physicians available to society was not checking the specialization trend. Nor were the reforms in medical education affecting the patterns of career choice. "Comprehensive medicine," the approach that was designed to brake runaway tendencies to specialization, went out of fashion, even though its principles were incorporated into the Medicare amendments to the Social Security Act in terms of setting levels of care appropriate to patient needs, and also in the Office of Economic Opportunity plans for neighborhood health centers (Reader and Soave 1976). In their place, "primary care" and "family practice" were installed.

Most important, financial incentives by the government were withdrawn from programs of medical school expansion. Manpower distribution has become the central theme. The belief that future physicians could be persuaded to fill the evident social need by a more self-consciously social and humanistic minded education has been dropped.

The reaction of sociologists has been to renew their interest in medical education, but with a change of focus from the social psychology of individual development to scrutiny of the bureaucratic nature of the organization of the modern medical center. Especially questions about power in the medical school – the analysis of power structure, decision-making, and inter-organizational relations in the expanded medical center – have engaged sociological researchers (cf. Duff and Hollingshead 1968; Bucher and Stelling 1977; Bucher 1970; Mumford 1970; Miller 1970; Bloom 1973). In other words, the socializing agency, as a social institution, has become the center of inquiry rather than the socializee.

There remains the important question of what the research findings of this field were during these three decades.

One result was an elaborate updating of the descriptive picture of recruits to the profession. At the beginning of the thirty-year period, medical students were intelligent, curious, largely from the middle class, and basically practical in their orientation toward their future careers. They were already interested in large numbers in specialty practice. Thirty years later, although the demographic background of the students is essentially the same and the already high intellectual qualifications are, if anything, somewhat better, there is some evidence that the motivation of at least a large and visible minority has shifted toward a social-minded service and community emphasis (Funkenstein 1971). One major change in the social profile of medical students is its sex composition: 28 percent of the entering class of 1979 were women compared to 9 percent in 1969, and less than 5 percent in 1950. Efforts to expand racial minorities have not been as successful (Shapiro and Lowenstein 1979).

What also emerges in the evidence is the suggestion of a change in the orientation of medical students toward the educational process itself. From general compliance with faculty standards and even a sense of pride in "making it" as an elite group, students show evidence of increasing restiveness and even boredom (Funkenstein 1957, 1978). The improved methods of teaching the sciences in secondary schools and college were not matched in quick order by much medical school teaching. The best students (and the selection is such that the distance between best and worst is very narrow indeed), having experienced a very different and exciting approach to learning, encountered the ramrod memorization demands of many medical schools with consternation and then frustration. The "revolution" of the late sixties built upon such student dissatisfaction as well as on the change in the general social climate of the university. More recently, medical students have been observed by some to have reverted to earlier, more passive and compliant type, but the evidence is only impressionistic.

A quite different type of result emerges from the studies dealing specifically with the process of professionalization. In our judgment, the major achievement of sociologists has been to construct a set of clear research questions from the series of intensive case studies of medical schools in combination with quantitative survey data about medical students. These are process questions, guided by but also pointing the way to theoretical interpretation of adult socialization. Three such questions are illustrative:

1) Concerning the status of the student in the medical school, is he/she most essentially a student, required to survive a rite-of-passage that emphasizes a trial by intellectual ordeal? Or is he/she a physician-in-training, a junior colleague to the medical professional and therefore already the partial beneficiary of rights and privileges of membership in the profession, which are gradually increased to full measure on a graduated scale? It is assumed that such status contains elements that potentially can influence significantly the outcomes of medical school experience.

2) Concerning student values, what are the characteristic beliefs of the medical student when he/she enters medical school, and what happens to these beliefs while the student moves through the school? Does he/she, as one group of studies contends, change from an idealist to a cynic? Or does the student, as another group of studies proposes, go through a process of social maturation that is more of a developmental process than a change of specific attitudes? If it is a developmental growth experience, is it in the nature of the correction of naive stereotyped motivation to more specific and realistic conceptions of the doctor's role? Or is it a complex and often indirect learning of functional attitudes and behavioral attributes that relate directly to the special demands of behavior in the professional role?

3) Concerning continuity (or discontinuity) between the medical school and the medical profession, does the student receive a professional education in medical school that represents directly the standards and realities of his future professional role? Or is the school mainly a step which is limited in its function to establishing a groundwork of knowledge and skill, to be succeeded later by some form of training by profession of its new members in the standards of professional behavior?

This is not the place for a full discussion of the accumulating knowledge that pertains to these questions. Clearly, however, much active research has clustered around each of these questions. The results feed into the recent focus on the study of middle life experience, within the framework of a social psychology of "adult development" (Levinson 1978; Vaillant 1977; Cox 1970). Most current is the conception of work and family as intersecting systems (Kanter 1977), and here again the medical profession has been the target of specially intense scrutiny. Adult socialization shows every evidence of attracting continued research activity. Even sharply critical appraisals of the field's approach and achievement, such as the most recent by Light (1980), agree.

III. Major Trends in the Sociology of Medicine

Thirty-five years ago, the major assignment to medical sociology was to develop knowledge about social behavior as it relates to health and illness. A second assignment was always present; that is, to join in collaborative work with medicine and the other health professions. However, especially in the medical school (their main entry point), medical sociologists began as behavioral scientists in a pattern similar to the basic biomedical sciences seventy-five years earlier.[7] The pressure was typical of the scholarly, academic professions. They were expected to inquire, to develop knowledge, and, in the process, to demonstrate their legitimacy to scientific peers.

Speaking only to these patterns of knowledge development, this review uncovered the following trends of research emphasis:

FROM	TO
a social psychological frame of reference	institutional analysis
small-scale social relations as subject of research	large social systems
role analysis in specifically limited settings	complex organizational analysis
basic theoretical concerns with classic social analysis of behavior	policy science directed toward systematic translation of basic knowledge into decision-making
a perspective of human relations and communication	power structure analysis

7. For more detailed discussion, see S.W. Bloom, "The Profession of Medical Sociologist in the Future: Implications for Training Programs," in Y. Nuyens and J. Vansteenkiste (editors), *Teaching Medical Sociology*, Leiden, the Netherlands: M. Nijhoff, 1978.

At the outset, such sociological research developed often from the investigators' intrinsic theoretical interests, and medicine was itself secondary to the more generic problems of study. Rapidly, however, these basic interests were shaded toward issues that were visibly relevant to application. In Table 1, Williams shows how readily the basic and applied were joined in medical sociology.

TABLE 1
Sociomedical knowledge: its applications[8]

STUDIES OF	FOCUSED ON	
	Behavioral or psychological function as such ('basic') and viability of the action system of individual actors ('applied')	Social, social-psychological, and sociocultural factors in other aspects of health and disease 'basic' and their management ('applied')
Biology and ecology of disease and health	1. Ecology of mental disorders; production and reproduction of successful or unsuccessful coping behavior in families; basic studies of motivation, learning perception, etc.	2. Social factors in the epidemiology of cancer, rheumatoid arthritis, etc.
Response to health and disease	3. Communication of mental health concepts; social-psychological careers of mental patients during and after hospitalization; emotional factors and coping behavior in relation to leukemia, death and other stressful situations	4. Factors affecting acceptance of fluoridation or other public health programs; the impact of influenza on a community
Organization of medical facilities and other groups affecting health	5. Social structures and functioning of a mental hospital; mental health in schools and industry (i.e., impact of schools or industries as sociocultural systems on the viability of the action systems of their members)	6. Social structure and functioning of the general hospital, health departments, group practice of medicine, etc.
Education, career development, and professionalization as a social process	7. Career development in all the 'mental health' professions (i.e., all those whose primary concern is with helping other achieve a more viable action system); development of new roles in the field of mental health (e.g., the mental health worker)	8. The development of student physicians; choice of public health as a career; social factors in revising education

Source: Richard H. Williams, 'The Strategy of Sociomedical Research,' in Freeman, et. al., 1972: 463.

8. This table is reproduced as it was adapted in Bloom, 1978, p. 41.

For three decades, research activities in the sociology of medicine expanded and with it grew the role of sociologists *in* medicine (Straus 1957). From 1957, when the National Institute of Mental Health began to fund the research training of sociologists, the training budget grew from $84,916 for programs supporting 14 predoctoral students to $5 million for 626 students in 1969. In 1968, a second research training program was begun, focused specifically on social scientists to work in medicine, by the National Center for Health Services Research (NCHSR). The latter grew rapidly to $5 million in 1971.

By 1973, however, the climate changed for social science. The Office of Management and the Budget (OMB) decided to suspend the training program of NCHSR, and by 1978, all its training programs were ended. Research training at NIMH continued, but at steadily reduced levels. From 77 programs supporting 626 predoctoral students in 1969, NIMH was forced to reduce its training program to 33 program grants in 1980, supporting 99 predoctoral and 97 postdoctoral students, based on expenditure of $3 million. As this article is being completed, NIMH training funds are frozen, and *Science* (March 27, 1981) reports that all institutional support for training in social science will be eliminated by the OMB. More significant to this discussion in which discussion has been focused on the development of knowledge in medical sociology, the same *Science* article reports that all research on "social problems" will be cut from the federal HHS budget by OMB.

Because these policies have been initiated during Republican Party administrations (Nixon in 1973, Reagan in 1981), it is all too tempting to see the current negative climate toward biomedical and sociomedical training as the result of political ideological change. In the United States, the Republican Party is, after all, the conservative party, in favor of economies of government activities and, in its attitude toward the university, more suspicious and anti-intellectual than the Democrats. The facts are, however, that there are similarities between the parties as well as differences. In their attitudes toward research, some important conclusions are shared. For example, *Science* reported in 1976:

Senator Edward M. Kennedy (Democrat, Massachusetts), as Chairman of the Senate Health Subcommittee, has just begun what he describes as a yearlong process of review and examination of public policy in the areas of biomedical and behavioral research. Out of this may come legislation that substantially reshapes the National Institutes of Health (NIH), by mandating a new emphasis on clinical research and the assessment of new biomedical technology.

'. . . Our committee does not come to these hearings with any deep distrust or disillusionment with biomedical and behavioral research,' Kennedy declared at the outset of the first day's session. But as the morning wore on, it became apparent that though 'disillusionment' may be too strong a term to express his feelings, 'dissatisfaction' certainly is not. For more than a year now, Kennedy has been challenging the research community to throw itself into activities that would show it is responsive to its social obligations (*Science*, 20 June 1975) and he leaned on that theme as heavily as ever. His subcommittee colleague Richard S. Schweiker (R-Pa.) was even more persistent, indeed, strident, in asking scientists to tell him why they have not done more for him (the public) lately. *It is going to be a rough, and extremely important, year* [our italics] (Culliton 1976).

That prediction, in retrospect, looks optimistic. It *was* rough for both the biomedical and behavioral sciences for more than just one year. Moreover, Schweiker, the "strident" critic, is the new Secretary of the Department of Health and Human Services.

Medical sociology, in our view, should be studied as a case example of the effects of the increased fiscal control by the federal government of the professions. In this case, we see a discipline, small but increasingly visible, among the university-based professions: these are most essentially *scholarly* professions, oriented toward the increased understanding of human behavior, and engaged mainly in roles of study and teaching. Because its subject and methods are defined as relevant to problems of health and illness, medical sociology found itself increasingly drawn into new roles first as research collaborator, then as educator, in medical education. In the process, it has been caught in the tides of medical manpower development, sharing the experience of institutional changes which were occuring in medicine. Only part of the path traversed by the biomedical sciences has been trodden by medical sociology: It followed the same path to full-time teaching in medical schools, and to virtually total dependence upon federal subsidy, but its legitimacy as an essential part of medical training is not yet so secure.

The withdrawal of federal funds from both training and basic research in medical sociology is the current reality. The question is: what does this mean for the future?

To attempt to answer this question is beyond the scope of this discussion. What can be said is that medical sociology, as a field of developing knowledge, has experienced a rich period of development. The evidence is in the use of social science knowledge to frame important health policies such as the Neighborhood Health Center program of the "War on Poverty." Within medicine itself, social science knowledge was basic to the conception of the therapeutic community approach of mental hospitals, to the development of community mental health centers and the deinstitutionalization of a large proportion of hospitalized mental patients. In the past decade, the identification of consumers as particular ethnic, racial or gender groups, and the conception of the neighborhood as the natural environment of urban life have been particularly useful in the development of a more responsive health movement and have provided part of the impetus for the expansion of environmental and occupational health.

In the final analysis, however, we do not believe that medical sociology, as a field of knowledge, should be judged by the evidence of its utility. At heart, sociology is a scholarly profession and, as such, requires a work environment that protects and nurtures free, intellectual inquiry. There is a natural tension between independent intellectual analysis and the controlled knowledge enterprise of "targeted" research. The latter increasingly is demanded of medical sociology in the form of evaluation research. The threat is that, to survive in the current climate created by scarce resources for an expanded high-skill social science manpower, we will become the "hired guns" (Britell 1980) of government agencies and special interest groups, charged with producing research results that fit preconceived policies. In the process, we may lose the traditional heart of our enterprise.

REFERENCES CITED

Abel-Smith, Brian, 1960. *A History of the Nursing Profession*, London: William Heinemann.
Abel-Smith, Brian, 1964. *The Hospitals, 1800–1948*, London: William Heinemann.
Ackerknecht, Erwin H., 1942a. Problems of primitive medicine, *Bulletin of the History of Medicine* **11**: 503–521.
Ackerknecht, Erwin H., 1942b. Primitive medicine and culture patterns, *Bulletin of the History of Medicine* **12**: 545–574.
Ackerknecht, Erwin H., 1943. Psychopathology, primitive medicine, and primitive culture, *Bulletin of the History of Medicine* **14**: 30–67.
Ackerknecht, Erwin H., 1953. *Rudolf Virchow: Doctor, Statesman, Anthropologist*, Madison, Wisconsin: University of Wisconsin Press.
Ackerknecht, Erwin H., 1955. *A Short History of Medicine*, New York: The Ronald Press Company.
Ackerknecht, Erwin H., 1959. *A Short History of Psychiatry*, New York and London: Hefner Publishing Company.
Antonovsky, Aaron, 1979. *Health, Stress and Coping: New Perspectives on Mental and Physical Well-Being*, San Francisco, California: Jossey-Bass.
Barber, Bernard, 1970. *L.J. Henderson on the Social System*, Chicago, Illinois: University of Chicago Press.

Barrabee, Paul S., 1951. A study of a mental hospital: The effects of its social structure on its function. Unpublished Ph.D. dissertation, Harvard University.

Becker, Ernest, 1962. *The Birth and Death of Meaning: A Perspective in Psychiatry and Anthropology*, New York: The Free Press of Glencoe.

Becker, Howard S., 1963. *Outsiders: Studies in the Sociology of Deviance*, New York: The Free Press.

Becker, Howard S., and Blanche Geer, 1963. Medical education, in *Handbook of Medical Sociology* (1st ed.), Howard E. Freeman, Sol Levine, and Leo G. Reeder (eds.), pp. 169–186, Englewood Cliffs, New Jersey: Prentice-Hall.

Becker, Howard S., Blanche Geer, Everett C. Hughes, and Anselm L. Strauss, 1961. *Boys in White: Student Culture in Medical School*, Chicago: University of Chicago Press.

Becker, Howard S., Blanche Geer, and Stephen Miller, 1972. Medical education, in *Handbook of Medical Sociology* (2nd ed.), Howard E. Freeman, Sol Levine, and Leo G. Reeder (eds.), pp. 191–205, Englewood Cliffs, New Jersey: Prentice-Hall.

Beers, Clifford W. 1907. *A Mind that Found Itself*, American Foundation for Mental Hygiene. (Reprinted 1956, New York: Doubleday and Co.)

Belknap, Ivan, 1956. *Human Problems of a State Mental Hospital*, New York: McGraw-Hill Book Co.

Bell, Norman W., and John P. Spiegel, 1966. Social psychiatry–vagaries of a term, *Archives of General Psychiatry* **14**: 337–345.

Bloom, Samuel W., 1963. *The Doctor and His Patient: A Sociological Interpretation*, New York: Russell Sage Foundation.

Bloom, Samuel W., 1965. Sociology of medical education: Some comments on the state of a field, *The Milbank Memorial Fund Quarterly* (April), Vol. XLIII, No. 2: 143–184.

Bloom, Samuel W., 1971. The medical school as a social system: A case study of faculty–student relationships. Monograph published as part 2, *Milbank Memorial Fund Quarterly*, Vol. XLIX (April).

Bloom, Samuel W., 1973. *Power and Dissent in the Medical School*, New York: The Free Press of Macmillan.

Bloom, Samuel W., 1976. From learned profession to policy science: A trend analysis of sociology in medical education in the United States, in *Health and Society*, Magda Aokolowski (ed.), pp. 435–447, Dordrecht, Holland: D. Reidel Publishing Co.

Bloom, Samuel W., 1978. The profession of medical sociologist in the future: Implications for training programs, in *Teaching Medical Sociology*, Y. Nuyens and J. Vansteenkiste (eds.), pp. 38–60, Leiden, the Netherlands: Martinus Nijhoff Social Sciences Division.

Bloom, Samuel W., and Robert N. Wilson, 1979. Patient–practitioner relationships, in *Handbook of Medical Sociology* (3rd ed.), Howard E. Freeman, Sol Levine, and Leo G. Reeder (eds.), pp. 275–296, Englewood Cliffs, New Jersey: Prentice-Hall.

Bosk, Charles L., 1978. *Forgive and Remember: Managing Medical Failure*, Chicago: University of Chicago Press.

Britell, Jenne K. 1980. *Hazards in Social Research*, The New York Times, September 7.

Bucher, Rue, 1970. Social process and power in a medical school, in *Power in Organizations*, M.N. Zald (ed.), pp. 3–48, Nashville: Vanderbilt University Press.

Bucher, Rue, and John E. Stelling, 1977, *Becoming Professional*, Beverly Hills, California: Sage Publications, Inc.

Bullough, Bonnie, and Vern L. Bullough, 1972. *Poverty, Ethnic Identity, and Health Care*, New York: Appleton-Century-Crofts.

Burling, Temple, Edith M. Lentz, and Robert N. Wilson, 1956. *The Give and Take in Hospitals: A Study of Human Organiation in Hospitals*, New York: G.P. Putnam's Sons.

Carr-Saunders, A.M., and P.A. Wilson, 1933, *The Professions*, London: Oxford University Press.

Caudill, William, 1953. Applied anthropology in medicine, in *Anthropology Today*, A.L.

Kroeber (ed.), pp. 771–806, Chicago: University of Chicago Press.

Caudill, William, 1958. *The Psychiatric Hospital as a Small Society*, Cambridge, Massachusetts: Harvard University Press (for the Commonwealth Fund).

Clausen, John A., 1956. *Sociology and the Field of Mental Health*, New York: Russell Sage Foundation.

Clausen, John A., 1979. Mental disorders, in *Handbook of Medical Sociology* (3rd ed.), Howard E. Freeman, Sol Levine, and Leo G. Reeder (eds.), pp. 97–112, Englewood Cliffs, New Jersey: Prentice-Hall.

Cloward, Richard A., and Lloyd E. Ohlin, 1966. *Delinquency and Opportunity: A Theory of Delinquent Gangs*, New York: Free Press.

Cockerham, William C. 1978. *Medical Sociology*, Englewood Cliffs, New Jersey: Prentice-Hall.

Coker, Robert E., Jr., Kurt W. Back, Thomas G. Donnelly, Norman Miller, and Bernard S. Phillips, 1959. Public health as viewed by the medical student. *American Journal of Public Health* **49** (May): 601–609.

Coker, Robert E., Jr., Norman Miller, Kurt W. Back, and Thomas G. Donnelly, 1960a. The medical student: Specialization and general practice, *North Carolina Medical Journal* **21** (March): 96–101.

Coker, Robert E., Jr., Kurt W. Back, Thomas G. Donnelly and Norman Miller, 1960b. Patterns of influence: Medical school faculty members and the values and specialty interests of medical students, *Journal of Medical Education* **35** (June): 518–527.

Comroe, J.H. (ed.), 1962. Research and medical education, *Journal of Medical Education* **37** (December), Part 2.

Coser, Rose Laub, 1962. *Life on the Ward*, East Lansing, Michigan: Michigan State University Press.

Coser, Rose Laub, 1979. *Training in Ambiguity*, New York: Free Press.

Cox, Rachel D., 1970. *Youth Into Maturity*, New York: Mental Health Material Center.

Culliton, B.J., 1976. Kennedy hearings: Year long probe of biomedical research begins, *Science* **193** (2 July): 32–35.

Davis, Fred, 1964. Deviance disavowal: The management of strained interaction by the visibly physically handicapped, in *The Other Side*, H. Becker (ed.), pp. 119–137, New York: The Free Press.

Davis, Karen, and Cathy Schoen, 1978. *Health and the War on Poverty*, Washington, D.C.: The Brookings Institution.

Davis, Michael M., 1927. *Clinics, Hospitals and Health Centers*, New York: Harper.

Davis, Michael M., 1941. *America Organizes Medicine*, New York: Harper.

D'Costa, Ayres, and R. Yancik, 1974. *AAMC Longitudinal Study of Medical Students of the Class of 1960. Follow-up Project*, Washington, D.C.: AAMC.

Deutsch, Albert, 1949. *The Mentally Ill in America: A History of Their Care and Treatment from Colonial Times*, New York: Columbia University Press.

Devereux, George, 1944. The social structure of a schizophrenic ward and its therapeutic fitness, *Journal of Clinical Psychopathology and Psychotherapy*, Vol. **VI** (October): 231–265.

DiMatteo, M. Robin, and Howard S. Friedman (eds.), 1979. *Journal of Social Issues*, Vol. **35**, No. 1.

Duff, Raymond S., and August B. Hollingshead, 1968. *Sickness and Society*, New York: Harper & Row.

Dunham, Warren H., 1959. *Sociological Theory and Mental Disorder*, Detroit: Wayne State University Press.

Eaton, Joseph W., and Robert J. Weil, 1955. *Culture and Mental Disorders*, Glencoe, Illinois: The Free Press.

Erdman, James B., *et al.* 1978. *The AAMC Longitudinal Study of Medical School Graduates of*

1960, Washington, D.C.: AAMC Division of Educational Measurement and Research.

Etzioni, Amitai, 1960. Interpersonal and structural factors in the study of mental hospitals, *Psychiatry*, Vol. **XXIII** (February): 13–22.

Faris, Robert E.L., and H. Warren Dunham, 1939. *Mental Disorders in Urban Areas*, Chicago: University of Chicago Press.

Flexner, Abraham, 1910. *Medical Education in the United States and Canada: A Report to the Carnegie Foundation for the Advancement of Teaching. Bulletin No. 4*, New York: Carnegie Foundation.

Fox, Renee C., 1957. Training for uncertainty, in *The Student-Physician: Introductory Studies in the Sociology of Medical Education*, Robert K. Merton, George G. Reader, and Patricia L. Kendall (eds.), pp. 207–241, Cambridge, Massachusetts: Harvard University Press (for the Commonwealth Fund).

Fox, Renee C., 1976. Advanced medical technology – Social and ethical implications, in *Annual Review of Sociology*, Vol. 2. A. Inkeles (ed.), pp. 231–268, Palo Alto, California: Annual Reviews.

Fox, Renee C., and Judith P. Swazey, 1974. *The Courage to Fail: A Social View of Organ Transplants and Dialysis*, Chicago: The University of Chicago Press.

Frame, Janet, 1961. *Faces in the Water*, New York: George Braziller, Inc.

Freeman, Howard E., and Leo G. Reeder, 1957. Medical sociology: A review of the literature, *American Sociological Review*, Vol. 22 (February): 73–81.

Freeman, Howard E., Sol Levine, and Leo G. Reeder, 1979. *Handbook of Medical Sociology* (3rd ed.), Englewood Cliffs, New Jersey: Prentice-Hall.

Freidson, Eliot, 1961. *Patients' Views Toward Medical Practice*, New York: Russell Sage Foundation.

Freidson, Eliot, 1965. Disability as social deviance, in *Sociology and Rehabilitation*, Marvin B. Sussman (ed.), pp. 71–99, Washington, D.C.: American Sociological Association.

Freidson, Eliot, 1970. *Profession of Medicine*. New York: Dodd, Mead and Co.

Fuchs, Victor R., 1974. *Who Shall Live?* New York:Basic Books.

Funkenstein, Daniel H., 1957. Possible contributions of psychological testing of the non-intellectual characteristics of medical school applicants. in *The Appraisal of Applicants to Medical School*, Helen H. Gee and John T. Cowles (eds.), pp. 88–112, Evanston, Illinois: The Association of American Colleges.

Funkenstein, Daniel H., 1971. Medical students, medical schools, and society during three eras, in *Psychosocial Aspects of Medical Training*, Robert H. Coombs and Clark E. Vincent, (eds.), pp. 229–281, Springfield, Illinois: Charles C. Thomas Publisher.

Funkenstein, Daniel H., 1978. *Medical Students, Medical Schools, and Society During Five Eras*, Cambridge, Massachusetts: Ballinger Publishing Co.

Gee, Helen H., and John T. Cowles (eds.), 1957. The appraisal of applicants to medical schools, *Journal of Medical Education* **32** (October), Part 2.

Gee, Helen H., and Robert J. Glaser (eds.), 1958. The ecology of the medical student, *Journal of Medical Education* **33** (October), Part 2: 3–11.

Georgopoulous, Basil S., 1975. *Hospital Organization Research: Review and Sourcebook*, Philadelphia: W.B. Saunders.

Georgopoulous, Basil S., and Floyd Mann, 1962. *The Community General Hospital*, New York: Macmillan Co.

Ginzberg, Eli, J.B. Miner, J.K. Anderson, Sol W. Ginsburg, and John L. Herma, 1959. *The Ineffective Soldier: Breakdown and Recovery*, New York: Columbia University Press.

Goffman, Erving, 1957. Characteristics of total institutions, in *Symposium on Preventive and Social Psychiatry*, pp. 43–84, Washington, D.C.: Walter Reed Army Institute of Research, Walter Reed Army Medical Center.

Goffman, Erving, 1959. The moral career of mental patients, *Psychiatry*, Vol. 22 (May): 123–142.

Goffman, Erving, 1961. *Asylums*, Garden City, New York: Doubleday Anchor Books.

Goldhamer, Herbert, and Andrew W. Marshall, 1949. *The Frequency of Mental Disease: Long-Term Trends and Present Status*, Santa Monica, California: The Rand Corporation.

Goode, William J., 1960. Encroachment, charlatanism, and the emerging professions: Psychology, sociology, and medicine, *American Sociological Review* 25: 902–914.

Goss, Mary E.W., 1959. Physicians in bureaucracy: A case study of professional pressures in organizational roles. Unpublished doctoral dissertation, Columbia University.

Goss, Mary E.W., 1963. Patterns of bureaucracy among hospital staff physicians, in *The Hospital in Modern Society*, Eliot Freidson (ed.), pp. 170–194, New York: The Free Press of Glencoe.

Gough, Harrison G., 1971. The recruitment and selection of medical students, in *Psychosocial Aspects of Medical Training*, Robert H. Coombs and Clark E. Vincent (eds.), pp. 5–43, Springfield, Illinois: Charles C. Thomas Publisher.

Gouldner, Alvin W., 1979. *The Future of Intellectuals and the Rise of the New Class*, New York: The Seabury Press.

Graham, Saxon, 1964. Sociological aspects of health and illness, in *Handbook of Modern Sociology*, Robert E.L. Faris (ed.), pp. 310–347, Chicago: Rand McNally and Co.

Graham, Saxon, and Leo G. Reeder, 1972. Social factors in the chronic illnesses, in *Handbook of Medical Sociology* (2nd ed.), Howard E. Freeman, Sol Levine, and Leo G. Reeder (eds.), pp. 63–107, Englewood Cliffs, New Jersey: Prentice-Hall.

Greenblatt, Milton, Richard H. York, and Esther Lucile Brown, 1955. *From Custodial to Therapeutic Patient Care in Mental Hospitals*, pp. 407–416, New York: Russell Sage Foundation.

Greenblatt, Milton, Daniel J. Levinson, and Richard H. Williams (eds.), 1957. *The Patient and the Mental Hospital*, Glencoe, Illinois: The Free Press.

Hammond, Kenneth R., and Fred J. Kern, Jr., 1959. *Teaching Comprehensive Medical Care*, Cambridge, Massachusetts: Harvard University Press (for the Commonwealth Fund).

Henderson, Lawrence J., 1935. Physician and patient as a social system, *New England Journal of Medicine* 212: 819–823.

Henderson, Lawrence J., 1936. The practice of medicine as applied sociology, *Transactions of the Association of American Physicians*, Vol. 51: 8–22.

Henderson, Lawrence J., 1937. *Pareto's General Sociology: A Physiologist's Interpretation*, Cambridge, Massachusetts: Harvard University Press.

Heydebrand, Wolf U., 1973. *Hospital Bureaucracy*, New York: Dunellen Publishing Co., Inc.

Hollingshead, August B., and Frederick C. Redlich, 1958. *Social Class and Mental Illness*, New York: John Wiley Sons, Inc.

Horowitz, Milton J., 1964. *Educating Tomorrow's Doctors*, New York: Appleton-Century-Crofts.

Hughes, Charles C., Marc-Adelard Tremblay, Robert N. Rapaport, and Alexander H. Leighton, 1960. *People of Cove and Woodlot*, New York: Basic Books, Inc.

Huntington, Mary Jean, 1957. The development of a professional image, in *The Student-Physician*, Robert K. Merton, George G. Reader, and Patricia L. Kendall (eds.), pp. 179–187, Cambridge, Massachusetts: Harvard University Press (for the Commonwealth Fund).

Hutchins, Edwin B., 1964. The AHMC longitudinal study: implications for medical education, *Journal of Medical Education* **39**: 265–277.
Hyman, Martin, 1967. Medicine, in *The Uses of Sociology*, Paul F. Lazarsfeld, William H. Sewell, Harold L. Wilensky (eds.), pp. 119–155, New York: Basic Books.
Illich, Ivan, 1975. *Medical Nemesis: The Expropriation of Health*, London: Calder and Boyars Ltd.
Irigoyen, Matilde, and Ruth E. Zambrana, 1979. Foreign medical school graduates: Determining their role in the U.S. health system, *Social Science and Medicine* **13A**: 775–783.
Johnson, Terence, 1972. *Professions and Power*, London: Macmillan.
Jones, Maxwell, 1953. *The Therapeutic Community*, New York: Basic Books, Inc. (This book was first published a few years earlier in England under the title *Social Psychiatry*.)
Journal of the American Medical Association, 1980. December 26, p. 2813.
Kanter, Rosabeth Moss, 1977. *Work and Family in the United States*, New York: Russell Sage.
Kelman, Sander, 1971. Toward the political economy of health care, *Inquiry* VIII (3): 31–38.
Kelner, Merrijoy, Oswald Hall, and Ian Coulter, 1980. *Chiropractors: Do They Help?* Toronto: Fitzhenry and Whiteside.
Kendall, Patricia L., and George G. Reader, 1979. Contributions of sociology to medicine, in *Handbook of Medical Sociology* (3rd ed.), Howard E. Freeman, Sol Levine, and Leo G. Reeder (eds.), pp. 1–22, Englewood Cliffs, New Jersey: Prentice-Hall, Inc.
Kerkhoff, J.D., 1952. *How Thin the Veil: A Newspaperman's Story of His Own Mental Crackup and Recovery*, New York: Chilton Books.
King, Stanley H., 1972. Social-psychological factors in illness, in *Handbook of Medical Sociology* (2nd ed.), Howard E. Freeman, Sol Levine, and Leo G. Reeder (eds.), pp. 129–147, Englewood Cliffs, N.J.: Prentice-Hall, Inc.
Konrad, George, and Ivan Szelenyi, 1979. *The Intellectuals on the Road to Class Power: A Sociological Study of the Role of the Intelligentsia in Socialism*, New York: Harcourt, Brace Jovanovich Inc.
Larson, Magali Sarfatti, 1977. *The Rise of Professionalism*, Berkeley: University of California Press.
Leacock, Eleanor, 1957. Three social variables and the occurrence of mental disorder, in *Explorations in Social Psychiatry*, Alexander H. Leighton, John A. Clausen, Robert N. Wilson (eds.), pp. 308–340, New York: Basic Books, Inc.
Lee, Peter V., 1961. Medical schools and the changing times: Nine case reports on experimentation in medical education, 1950–1960, *Journal of Medical Education* **36** (December), Part 2: 45–46.
Leighton, Alexander., 1959. *My Name is Legion*, New York: Basic Books.
Leighton, Dorothea C., John C. Harding, David B. Macklin, Alistair M. Macmillan, and Alexander H. Leighton, 1963. *Character of Danger: Psychiatric Symptoms in Selected Communities*, New York: Basic Books.
Levinson, Daniel J., 1967. Medical education and the theory of adult socialization, *Journal of Health and Social Behavior* **8**: 253–65.
Levinson, Daniel J., 1978. *The Seasons of a Man's Life*, New York: Alfred A. Knopf.
Lewis, Charles, Rashi Fein, and David Mechanic, 1976. *Right to Health: The Problems of Access to Primary Medical Care*, New York: Wiley.
Leyerle, Betty, 1981. Authority and change in the American health care system. Unpublished Ph.D. dissertation, City University of New York, Graduate School Library.
Lief, Harold I., Kathleen Young, Vann Spruiell, Robert Lancaster, and Victor F. Lief, 1960. A psychodynamic study of medical students and their adaptational problems: A preliminary report, *Journal of Medical Education* **35** (July): 695–704.
Lief, Harold I., and Renee C. Fox, 1963. Training for detached concern, in *The Psycho-*

logical Basis of Medical Practice, H.I., V.F., and N.R. Lief (eds.), pp. 12–35, New York: Harper and Row.

Light, Donald, 1980. *Becoming Psychiatrists*, New York: Norton Publishing Company.

Lutterman, Kenneth G., 1975. Research training from the perspective of government funding, in *Social Policy and Sociology*, N.J. Demerath, Otto Larson, and K.F. Schuessler (eds.), pp. 307–320, New York: Academic Press, Inc.

McKinlay, John B., 1972. Some approaches and problems in the study of the use of services — An overview, *Journal of Health and Social Behavior* 13: 115–152.

Mechanic, David, 1968. *Medical Sociology: A Selective View*, New York: The Free Press.

Mechanic, David, 1975a. The organization of medical practice and practice orientations among physicians in prepaid and nonprepaid primary care settings, *Medical Care* 13 (March): 189–204.

Mechanic, David, 1975b. The comparative study of health care delivery systems, in *Annual Review of Sociology*, Vol. I. A. Inkeles (ed.), pp. 43–66, Palo Alto, California: Annual Reviews.

Mechanic, David, 1976. *The Growth of Bureaucratic Medicine: An Inquiry into the Dynamics of Patient Behavior and the Organization of Medical Care*, New York: John Wiley and Sons.

Mechanic, David, 1978a. Approaches to controlling the costs of medical care: Short-range and long-range alternatives, *The New England Journal of Medicine* 298 (February): 294–254.

Mechanic, David, 1978b. *Medical Sociology* (2nd ed.)., New York: Free Press.

Merton, Robert K., Natalie Rogoff, and Samuel W. Bloom, 1956. Studies in the sociology of medical education. *Journal of Medical Education* 31 (August): 552–565.

Merton, Robert K., George G. Reader, and Patricia L. Kendall (eds.), 1957. *The Student-Physician*, Cambridge, Massachusetts: Harvard University Press (for the Commonwealth Fund).

Milbank Memorial Fund, 1950. *Proceedings of the Annual Conference*, Epidemiology of mental disorder, New York: Milbank Memorial Fund.

Milbank Memorial Fund, 1953. *Interrelations Between the Social Environment and Psychiatric Disorder*, New York: Milbank Memorial Fund.

Miller, George E. (ed.), 1961. *Teaching and Learning in Medical School*, pp. 22–23, 31–33, 34–35, Cambridge, Massachusetts: Harvard University Press.

Miller, Stephen J., 1970. *Prescription for Leadership: Training for the Medical Elite*, Chicago: Aldine Publishing Co.

Monroe, Russell R., Gerald D. Klee, and Eugene B. Brody (eds.), 1967. *Psychiatric Epidemiology and Mental Health Planning*, pp. 1–63, Washington, D.C.: The American Psychiatric Association.

Mortimer, Jeylan T., and Roberta G. Simmons, 1978. Adult socialization, in *Annual Review of Sociology*, R.H. Turner (ed.), pp. 421–454, Palo Alto, California: Annual Reviews.

Mumford, Emily, 1970. *Interns: From Students to Physicians*, Cambridge, Massachusetts: Harvard University Press.

Navarro, Vicente, 1975. Social policy issues: An explanation of the composition, nature and functions of the present health sector of the United States, *Bulletin of the New York Academy of Medicine* 57: 199–234.

Navarro, Vicente, 1976. Social class, political power and the state and their implications in medicine, *Social Science and Medicine* 10 (9/10): 437–457.

Navarro, Vicente, 1978. *Class Struggle, the State and Medicine*, New York: Prodist.

Notman, Malkah T., and Carol C. Nadelson (eds.), 1978. *The Woman Patient*, New York: Plenum. Vol. I.

Olesen, Virginia L. (ed.), 1977. *Women and Their Health: Research Implications for a New Era*, Springfield, Virginia: NTIS (Publication No. (HRA) 77–3138).

Olesen, Virginia L., and Elvi W. Whittaker, 1968. *The Silent Dialogue*, San Francisco: Jossey Bass.

Packard, Mrs. E.P.W., 1873. *Modern Persecution or Insane Asylums Unveiled*, Chicago: published privately.

Parsons, Talcott, 1951. *The Social System*, Chapter X, pp. 428–479, Glencoe, Illinois: The Free Press.

Pasaminick, Benjamin, 1961. A survey of mental disease in an urban population: IV. An approach to total prevalence rates, *Archives of General Psychiatry*, Vol. 5 (August): 151–155.

Perrow, Charles, 1963. Goals and power structures: A historical case study, in *The Hospital in Modern Society*, Eliot Freidson (ed.), pp. 112–146, New York: The Free Press.

Perrow, Charles, 1965. Hospitals: Technology, structure, and goals, in *The Handbook of Organizations*, James G. March (ed.), pp. 910–971. Skokie, Illinois: Rand McNally & Co.

Plunkett, Richard J., and John E. Gordon, 1960. *Epidemiology and Mental Illness*, New York: Basic Books.

Prewitt, Kenneth, 1981. *Usefulness of the Social Sciences*, Science, Vol. 211, No. 4483 (Feb. 13): 659.

Reader, George G., 1954. Organization and development of a comprehensive care program, *American Journal of Public Health* 44 (June): 760–765.

Reader, George G., 1963. Contributions of sociology to medicine, in *Handbook of Medical Sociology*, Howard E. Freeman, Sol Levine, and Leo G. Reeder (eds.), pp. 1–6, Englewood Cliffs, New Jersey: Prentice-Hall, Inc.

Reader, George G., and Mary E.W. Goss, 1959. The sociology of medicine, in *Sociology Today*, Robert K. Merton, Leonard Broom, and L.S. Cottrell, Jr. (eds.), pp. 229–248, New York: Basic Books, Inc.

Reader, George G., and Mary E.W. Goss (eds.), 1967. *Comprehensive Medical Care and Teaching*, Ithaca, New York: Cornell University Press.

Reader, George G., and Rosemary Soave, 1976. Comprehensive care revisited. *The Milbank Memorial Fund Quarterly* 54 (Fall): 391–414.

Reverby, Susan, and David Rosner, 1979. *Health Care in America* (Essays in Social History), Philadelphia, Pennsylvania: Temple University Press.

Roethlisberger, Fritz J., and William J. Dickson, 1939. *Management and the Worker*, Cambridge, Massachusetts: Harvard University Press.

Rogoff, Natalie, 1957. The decision to study medicine, in *The Student Physician*, Robert K. Merton, George G. Reader, and Patricia L. Kendall (eds.), pp. 109–129, Cambridge, Massachusetts: Harvard University Press (for the Commonwealth Fund).

Rosen, George, 1947. What is social medicine: A genetic analysis of the concept, *Bulletin of the History of Medicine* 21 (July–August): 674–733.

Rosen, George, 1968. *Madness in Society: Chapters in the Historical Sociology of Mental Illness*, Chicago: University of Chicago Press.

Rosen, George, 1974. *From Medical Police to Social Police to Social Medicine*, New York: Neale Watson Academic Publications, Inc.

Rosen, George, 1979. The evolution of social medicine, in *Handbook of Medical Sociology*, Howard E. Freeman, Sol Levine, and Leo G. Reeder (eds.), pp. 23–50, Englewood Cliffs, New Jersey: Prentice-Hall, Inc.

Rosengren, William R., 1980. *Sociology of Medicine* (Diversity, Conflict, and Change), New York: Harper and Row.

Rosengren, William R., and Mark Lefton, 1969. *Hospitals and Patients*, New York: Atherton Press.

Roth, Julius A., 1963. *Timetables: Structuring the Passage of Time in Hospital Treatment and Other Careers*, Indianapolis: The Bobbs-Merrill Co., Inc.

Rowland, Howard, 1938. Interaction processes in a state mental hospital. *Psychiatry.* Vol. 1 (August): 323–337.

Rowland, Howard, 1939. Friendship patterns in a state mental hospital, *Psychiatry*, Vol. 2 (August): 363–373.

Sanazaro, Paul V., 1966. An agenda for research on medical education, *Journal of the American Medical Association*, Vol. 197: 979–984.

Schatzman, Leonard, and Anselm Strauss, 1966. A sociology of psychiatry: A perspective and some organizing foci, *Social Problems* **14**(1): 3–16.

Scheff, Thomas J., 1966. *Being Mentally Ill: A Sociological Theory*, Chicago: Aldine Publishing Co.

Science, 1981. *Dark Days for Social Science*, Vol. 211, No. 4489, March 27: pp. 1397–1398.

Seabrook, William, 1935. *Asylum*, New York: Harcourt, Brace & Co.

Seeman, Melvin, 1946. An evaluation of current approaches to personality differences in folk and urban societies, *Social Forces*, Vol. 25, No. 2: 160–165.

Shapiro, Eileen L., and L.M. Lowenstein (eds.), 1979. *Becoming a Physician*, Cambridge, Massachusetts: Ballinger.

Shaw, Nancy Stoller, 1974. *Forced Labor*, New York: Pergamon.

Shils, Edward, 1970. Tradition, ecology and institution in the history of sociology, *Daedalus, Fall 1970*, Vol. 99: 760–825.

Shryock, Richard H., 1947. *The Development of Modern Medicine*, New York: Alfred A. Knopf, Inc.

Sigerist, Henry E., 1934. *American Medicine* (1st ed.), New York: W.W. Norton Co.

Sigerist, Henry E., 1948. Medical history in the United States, *Bulletin of the History of Medicine*, Vol. 22 (January–February): 47–63.

Simmons, Roberta G., and M. DiCanio, 1979. Biology, technology and health, in *Handbook of Medical Sociology*, (3rd ed.). Howard E. Freeman, Sol Levine, and Leo G. Reeder (eds.), pp. 150–173, Englewood Cliffs, New Jersey: Prentice-Hall, Inc.

Srole, Leo, Thomas S. Langner, Stanley T. Michaels, Marvin K. Opler, and Thomas A.C. Rennie, 1962. *Mental Health in the Metropolis: The Midtown-Manhattan Study*, Vol. I. New York: McGraw-Hill Book Co., Inc.

Stanton, Alfred H., and Morris S. Schwartz, 1954. *The Mental Hospital*, New York: Basic Books, Inc.

Stern, Bernhard J., 1927a. *Should We Be Vaccinated?* A survey of the controversy in its historical and scientific aspects, New York: Harper and Bros.

Stern, Bernhard J., 1927b. *Social Factors in Medical Progress*, New York: Columbia University Press.

Stern, Bernhard J., 1931. *Lewis Henry Morgan, Social Evolutionist*, Chicago: University of Chicago Press.

Stern, Bernhard J., 1934. *The Lummi Indians of Northwest Washington*, New York: Columbia University Press.

Stern, Bernhard J., 1941. *Society and Medical Progress*, Princeton: Princeton University Press.

Stern, Bernhard J., 1945. *American Medical Practice in the Perspectives of a Century*, New York: Commonwealth Fund.

Stern, Bernhard J., 1946a. *Medical Services by Government: Local, State and Federal*, New York: Commonwealth Fund.

Stern, Bernhard J., 1946b. *Medicine in Industry*, New York: Commonwealth Fund.

Stern, Bernhard J., 1959. *Historical Sociology: The Selected Papers of Bernhard J. Stern*, New York: Citadel Press.

Stern, Bernhard J., and M. Jacobs, 1947. *Introduction to Anthropology*, New York: Barnes and Noble.

Stevens, Rosemary, 1966. *Medical Practice in Modern England*, New Haven: Yale University Press.

Stevens, Rosemary, 1971. *American Medicine and the Public Interest*, New Haven: Yale University Press.

Stevens, Robert, and Rosemary Stevens, 1974. *Welfare Medicine in America: A Case Study of Medicaid*, New York: The Free Press.

Straus, Robert, 1957. The nature and status of medical sociology, *American Sociological Review* **22**: 200–204.

Stuart, Richard B., 1970. *Trick or Treatment: How and When Psychotherapy Fails*, Champaign, Illinois: Research Press.

Suchman, Edward A., 1964. *Sociology and the Field of Public Health*, New York: Russell Sage Foundation.

Sullivan, Harry Stack, 1931a. Socio-psychiatric research: Its implications for the schizophrenia problem and for mental hygiene, *American Journal of Psychiatry*, Vol. 10 (May): 977–991.

Sullivan, Harry Stack, 1931b. The modified psychoanalytic treatment of schizophrenia, *American Journal of Psychiatry*, Vol. 11 (November): 519–540.

Szasz, Thomas S., 1961. *The Myth of Mental Illness*, New York: Hoeber–Harper.

Taylor, Shelley E., 1979. Hospital patient behavior: Reactance, helplessness or control? *The Journal of Social Issues*, Vol. 35 (1): 156–184, M. Robin Dimatteo and Howard S. Friedman (eds.)

Twaddle, Andrew C., and Richard M. Hessler, 1977. *A Sociology of Health*, St. Louis: C.V. Mosby Co.

Vaillant, George E., 1977. *Adaptation to Life*, Waltham, Massachusetts: Little Brown.

Van Maanen, John (ed.), 1977. *Organizational Careers: Some New Perspectives*, New York: Wiley.

von Mering, Otto, and Stanley H. King, 1957. *Remotivating the Mental Patient*, New York: Russell Sage Foundation.

Waitzkin, Howard B., and Barbara Waterman, 1974. *The Exploitation of Illness in Capitalist Society*, Indianapolis and New York: Bobbs-Merrill.

Ward, Mary Jane, 1955. *The Snakepit*, New York: Signet Books.

Wessen, Albert F., 1958. Hospital ideology and communication between ward personnel, in *Patients, Physicians and Illness*, E. Gartly Jaco (ed.), pp. 448–468, Glencoe, Illinois: The Free Press.

Williams, Richard H., 1972. The strategy of sociomedical research, in *Handbook of Medical Sociology* (2nd ed.), Howard E. Freeman, Sol Levine, and Leo G. Reeder (eds.), pp. 459–482. Englewood Cliffs, New Jersey: Prentice-Hall.

Yancik, Rosemary, and Susan Bartholomew, 1975. *AAMC Longitudinal Study Project. Status Report*, Washington: Association of American Medical Colleges.

Zola, Irving K., 1966. Culture and symptoms – An analysis of patients presenting complaints, *American Sociological Review* **31**: 615–630.

3 Power, Health, and Service

Elliott A. Krause

POWER IS the ability of one individual or group to make another individual or group do what the possessor of power wishes, whether the target wishes to do so or not. Power is closely related to the control of resources, or, in the vernacular of the hill country, "them that has, gets." Power in complex societies has a shape, a structure. And the analysis of the nature of power structures, especially in advanced capitalist societies such as our own, is critically important if we are to understand the *why* behind levels of health, the nature of professional and interprofessional relations, the shape of the service system, and the changing relationships between the state and the health service system. In this critique of research to date, we will review the relevant issues. We will note only a few of the landmark studies, for our main purpose is to show what the issues are which demand further research.

The areas we have chosen for discussion are: power and the level of health, the politics of health professions, the political shaping of service systems, and the role of the state in controlling service. We will conclude with a summary of needed research and an analysis of why such research is not likely to be funded by those who ought to do so.

Power and the Level of Health

In studies of the field of health and service, it is often forgotten that the ultimate aim of service is to restore or preserve health. But the social context, at any period in history, is often far more effective as a creator of illness or a preserver of health, than the comparatively feeble actions of the health care workers in that historical period. Indeed, until quite

123

recently, the actions of the service professions had little or no concrete, measurable effect.

It is critical to understand, in historical perspective, the ways that changes in social and political power structures affected the everyday subsistence (and thus nutrition and life span) of the population. Several studies stand out in the literature as providing major insights into this phenomenon. Ullmann (1966), in his classic analysis of the individual and society in the Middle Ages, explains that two theoretical principles for organizing society were at war in this era. The first he calls "descending order," rule from the top down from the King to nobles and subjects, legitimated by the Church, which crowned the King. Simultaneously, there grew a second and opposite principle, the "ascending order" – the slow growth of local rights, citizen participation and self-rule. The power structure of medieval times legitimated the exploitation and near-starvation of millions, but simultaneously the Church, at the apex of this power structure, provided the "welfare," the orphanages, homes for the aged, and hospices, as well as food for the unattached poor. The break-down of the medieval order, then, can be seen as a long-term opportunity for a higher standard of living, but it created in the interim a mass deprivation of services. Especially in nations where Church power was successfully challenged and smashed suddenly, such as in England under Henry VIII, the monasteries and orphanages were burned and people turned out to wander the streets until they died.

The Renaissance brought new opportunities, especially in science and public health. New and important work on public health in the Renaissance in Italy by Cipolla (1976) indicates that the new individualism and self-consciousness concerning government extended to social planning in the area of public health, with area-wide health plans in existence as well as an understanding of the need for proper health manpower distribution across the map. A caution, however, is in order, for Italy was the home at the time of some of the world's most progressive medical schools, such as Padua. Again, though, this illustrates our point on the relation of the social context to the level of health. The same intellectual revolution that led in science to the publishing of the work of the anatomist Vesalius led to the creation of one of the world's first public health services at the community level. This may have led in turn to greater public sanitation and a rise in the level of health.

Another illustration of this principle takes us far closer to the present – the level of health of the industrial working class during the early years of the industrial revolution. For example, the ground-breaking work of Villermé (1840) indicates that the level of health among the cotton workers of France in the early 1800's demonstrated the close relationship between ownership of the factories, the profit motive, and both the near-starvation wages paid to workers and the tremendously unhealthy working conditions in the factories themselves. Together, these factors created a short and brutal life for a growing mass of citizens. More recent scholarship by Rosenkrantz (1972) makes essentially the same point for our own industrial revolution, on the banks of the Merrimac River north of Boston, in the new industrial mills of Lowell and Lawrence, Massachusetts. Rosenkrantz shows how the first generation of public health reformers carried on a moral and political campaign to clean the streets of sewage and the mills of bad drinking water and killing working conditions. She documents as well the bitter opposition to the reformers by both the industrialists of the time and the medical profession. Both groups used the free market or *laissez faire* ideology which claimed that state intervention, even to protect health and deliver service, was a bad idea. The opposition, as she, I, and many others see it, was actually on economic grounds. Rosenkrantz notes that by the end of her study period (the early Thirties of the present century) public health had been professionalized and narrowed in its scope. Occupational health and safety inspection was almost non-existent, and health services publicly delivered were restricted to epidemiologic measures and service to the poor. Industrialists had sharply limited the scope of protection in factories, while the American medical profession had cancelled any attempt to create a general system of public services for the delivery of health care to all.

Another area of importance here lies in the history of hospitals, such as in the work of Knowles (1966). Here the clear class stratification of services is preserved while hospital-based medicine grows in scope. Charity medicine gradually is replaced by welfare medicine, but the class stratification of services within hospitals remains, with separate wards for the Blue Cross, middle class patients, and for the Welfare/ Medicaid patients, given a different degree of staffing and care. A related issue is the history of health insurance politics, given that funds for services in such places as hospitals are necessary for maintaining the system. Landmark studies have been done on the 1930's attempt by Roosevelt's staff to attach National Health Insurance ("Health Security") onto the Social Security legislation, by Hirshfield (1970) and of the

AMA's fight against the Medicare program, by a number of researchers.

Each of the above themes was reviewed at great length by the present author in his recent sociological study of power and health (Krause 1977), in an introductory section titled "The Political Context of Health." A new issue has been heating up about the future of these phenomena, one that will bear much further inspection in the years to come: who is responsible for the level of health? Two opposing positions, both of which should be consulted, are the self-care, cut-back-the-service-system position of Ivan Illich, in *Medical Nemesis* (1976), and the neo-Marxian all-services-should-be-public position of Vicente Navarro in *Medicine Under Capitalism* (1976). I tend to agree with Illich that the medical profession is too powerful and has some tendency to *create* illness through diagnosis and overtreatment, as well as needlessly technologizing the end of life. Illich also says individuals, not societies, are primarily responsible for illness. But, I ask, for poverty and malnutrition? For cancer developed at work? I strongly agree as well with Navarro's critique of Illich that Illich's argument is presently being found useful by the state and the corporations, jointly interested in cutting costs through a cutback in services to those in need. We will return to this last issue in our discussion of the role of the state in health care.

The Politics of the Health Professions

A political-sociological approach to the occupations involved in health work must deal with a series of complex questions. First, what is the existing nature of power relations *within* the field of health work? Second, how does that existing set of power relations relate to a truer, and more basic, division of labor? Third, how are the health professions – individually and en masse – able to affect the political dynamics of the wider society? Fourth, how has that wider society, especially but not only the mechanisms of the state, *responded* to the attempts by health professions and other organizations of health workers to influence the social process?

Within health work itself, a historical perspective reveals a picture somewhat at variance with the present, where there appears to be a clear dominance of the medical profession over the other workers in health care. While licensing laws and a theoretical monopoly over practice existed in the early years of the American colonies, during the

Jacksonian era these laws were repealed. From this point until licensing monopolies over practice were reinstituted in the late 1800's, anyone who wished could practice medicine. (The same held for law.) With the onset of modern science and the formation of the research-oriented medical schools the power and prestige of medicine grew. By the 1950's, Freidson (1970) notes that the medical profession had "professional dominance" over all other health workers, except for the "deviant" practitioners such as chiropractors. Partly this was due to accreditation politics – the process by which the AMA began to control the university and professional accreditation, not only of its *own* profession, but also that of many others.

Yet the underlying *division of labor* is in itself a socio-political issue. Conflicts within the division of labor are as common as cooperation across the lines of work within an area of endeavor. For example, a certain amount of work must get done in the hospital setting. Whether it is presently done by a physician, a nurse practitioner, or by a nurse or a nurse's aide, will depend on several considerations: who is *legally allowed* to do the work (or is legally able to accept delegation of tasks from above), who is *actually on site* at a given moment, how the *informal division of labor* has been set up in a given setting, legal or not, and the extent to which the occupational group *shares responsibility* (clinical and legal) for work done or fights with other groups over the right to do it alone. Each of these bear discussion, with the observation that needed research is just beginning in most of these areas.

The legal issue is a reflection of the politics of credentialling. The state statutes vary at this time not only in terms of scope of practice (who can do what to whom) but also in terms of delegation of authority (who can legally hand off what kind of work to whom, and under what conditions). For example, it is possible to demonstrate, as Lobene (1979) did with dental hygienists and technicians, that they can more effectively fill teeth under general dental supervision than can a random sample of dentists themselves. But it is quite another thing for dental hygienists to have the political clout in a state legislature to make this practice legal, even if it is the very same state (Massachusetts) in which the experiment took place. The *de facto*, actually observed division of labor may also clearly deviate from the official, or even the legal, division of labor. A now classic study was carried out by Goldstein and Horowitz (1977) on who *actually* did what, with a list of more than fifty health care tasks involving registered nurses, licensed practical nurses, and aides or "candy stripers." In spite of clear occupational, status, prestige, and legal differences between these different occupational roles, in spite of the hospital's official statement that they did "different work" from one another, and *also* in spite of the statements from the three groups themselves that their work was widely different and clearly structured in a hierarchical fashion, these investigators found a wide overlap in tasks – more than fifty percent from rank to rank. Conclusion – there is a true spectrum of tasks, and *not* a clear division of labor in the real health work world.

New organizational forms for delivering health care, such as the HMO, have arrangements for division of work which place both the power to assign work and the legal responsibility for it into the hands of the organization, rather than the individual service worker. This allows greater flexibility in use of manpower, taking direct advantage of the actual state of affairs concerning overlap of work. But it is not necessarily acceptable to many professionals, who prefer their mythology of exclusiveness of work tasks to any reality. This is one factor working against greater acceptance of physician assistants, as Schneller (1978) points out, though there are others as well in that particular case. Changing the division of labor puts one up against organized occupational resistance, cultural barriers, and expectations on "who is expected to do what medical/service procedure on me."

A third general area within the research area of "politics of the professions" lies in their action vis-à-vis the wider society. This area is often conceptually oversimplified to mean the study of organized medicine lobbying against the passage of Medicare and similar programs. Actually, however, the action of the professions, quite remote from medicine, is complex and the targets toward which action is directed are varied. Legislative action is of course paramount. Here the work of Strickland (1972) on cancer politics, and Redman (1973) on legislation for the Health Service Corps, stand out as landmark studies. Both show the ways the complexities of the legislative process do indeed include the professions acting in their own interest in the legislative arena. But these studies show as well, and in detail, how other equally powerful interests intervene to shape the final legislation, and thus shape a new program that will directly affect practicing professionals in the community.

Conversely, the society has responded to the attempts on the part of the profession to influence it. Thus the work of Navarro (1976) and the present author on new attempts to rationalize the medical profession in the service of cost-cutting by a threatened capitalist order. This work tends to indicate that the petit-bourgeois or "storekeeper" role that physicians have played in our society may be succeeded by a more bureaucratic role, already common in Western Europe and also in the socialist world. In the case of the capitalist orbit, it may simply be cheaper for the great corporations (who pay half the bill for service) to organize the health services into "inhouse HMOs" for their employees and families of employees. Japan has actually proceeded far down this route, especially with the giant firms such as Mitsubishi and Sony. The issue, however, is *corporate control of medicine* (not necessarily in consumers' interest) being the successor of *medical profession control* over service, cost, and availability (also not necessarily in consumers' interest). The research has only just begun, but it tends to indicate that most past and present arrangements of service tend to downplay or make nearly impossible any consumer control of policy concerning health care.

It is in this context that the women's health movement appears so important conceptually, even if not yet that strong politically. Wertz and Wertz's critique (1977) of medical dominance over childbirth (the anti-midwife movement) provides us with a needed revisionist approach, as does the clear record of joint consumer/provider action in the Boston Women's Health Book Collective's modern classic, *Our Bodies, Ourselves* (1976). Here counter-institutions are not only described, they are recommended for the future, to work against the twin dangers of excessive professional dominance of health service (past and present) or corporate dominance (a potential future). Basic comparative research on the varied outcomes for patient care and patient satisfaction is in its infancy at present. It thus constitutes an overwhelmingly important area for comparing how the type of control of the service relates to the health outcome and satisfaction with the service.

Finally, the politics of professions increasingly involve the element Haug and Sussman (1969) call "the revolt of the client." Studies such as Piven and Cloward (1972) on regulating the poor, or the same authors (Piven and Cloward 1979) on poor peoples' political movements, show the demand for service may have to become violent before the present society even begins to recognize the need. Yet the study of this phenomenon and problem is only in its infancy. Much important historical, economic, and political sociological work on the power and consequences of client movements remains to be done. There is no question, however, that these movements *do* affect, in some way, decisions made about provision of services and the shape of the service system. Yet the shape of this system is of critical importance in its own right, and constitutes an area of study we can turn to next.

The Political Shaping of Service Systems

On the west coast, near Big Sur, stands a famous and often photographed tree. Bent by the prevailing wind from the west, the branches, gnarled and knobby, stretch almost horizontally to the east, high on a cliff above the sea. The *shape* of the tree was not predetermined in its genes – it was bent that way by the forces of nature. It can serve as a visual metaphor for the health care system of any nation. Consider the needed functions of health service delivery as the genes, and the political field of forces the wind which blows upon the system.

Chile provides an example. Before Allende in Chile, as Navarro (1976) noted, the poor starved in the slums and in the mountains. Allende's attempts at reform included the development of community health centers and free milk to the infants among the poor. After his defeat (at least in part sponsored by the American government through the CIA) the nurses in the community health centers were rounded up. Many were tortured and shot by the junta that took over, as were professors of public health who had worked for reforms. The free milk ended. History records that at the day and hour of the storming of the presidential palace, the Chilean Medical Association toasted the junta with champagne. They too had helped to finance the coup.

In a sense, the social and power structure of a society has a clear reflection in its health service system. The American system, for example, is characteristically a two-class one, with one class of care for the upper and middle class (who pay with private wealth or employer-connected health insurance) and another class of care for the poor, old, and unemployed, especially those of racial and linguistic minorities. In a recent analysis (1977), I have noted that the dynamics of politics and policy work toward *preserving the two-class system even when demonstration projects are created to change it.* The example I chose was the Medicare-Medicaid funding system, with service delivery primarily through public hospitals. A massive rise in costs of the program led to long periods between service delivery by the providers and payment by the government for those services. Private practitioners began to avoid the program, and the poor, with almost the same energy as most had done so in the past. This left the poor to return to the only place that was left – the public system. Thus, a "voucher system" strategy, which was the theoretical model for payment, collapsed and led to the continuation of the existing two-class system. Note that the society would have to pay far more for the services to these people than it presently does to give them the care they need. Yet their increased health will have no clear immediate return in productivity, since they are unemployed. The power structure sees this and limits the funds accordingly – my hypothesis at least. What we need is a series of research studies on the fate of a whole series of attempts to change the present shape of the system, using a wide variety of strategies.

A second illustration of the way political dynamics can work against change is the area of attempts to change the distribution of health manpower in the United States. Similar studies are available for other nations, especially for Britain (Watkin 1978). A generation of American studies has indicated that the American system is seriously deficient in manpower in urban ghetto and in rural areas. For the past decade, various scholarship and direct tuition schemes have been created, the aim of which is to require scholarship holders to practice in rural or ghetto areas after graduation. Since this proved somewhat ineffective, the Bureau of Health Manpower at H.E.W. initiated, more than five years ago, a program of capitation grants to medical schools – money provided "per head" with no strings attached. In 1977 a string appeared – the schools taking the capitation money (nearly all did) were required to create 50% of their post-graduate training slots as internships and residencies in general practice or family practice. The idea was simple – get the schools hooked on H.E.W. money, then call the shots about how the students should be trained.

But it hasn't worked out that way. Infighting and lobbying by the medical profession within the bureaucracy have so effectively widened H.E.W.'s definition of what a "general practice" or "primary care" residency is that the true proportion of grads going into these areas has not changed appreciably.

Another related program, the Area Health Education Centers program of the Bureau of Health Manpower, attempted to build "networks of education" between major medical centers and outlying community hospitals, the idea being the creation of a richer intellectual atmosphere in the rural areas, one more attractive to new family practitioners.

But local medical associations fought against those AHEC programs in many areas, viewing them as a form of medical school "empire-building." Then, before the program could even be evaluated, national political forces within and outside of the health field killed the program for further funding. Far more research should be done in these two areas: the twisting of existing and continuing experiments in a conservative, preserve-the-system direction, and the political squashing of any new programs that threaten existing interests and patterns in the health field.

We will need much more research as well in the relationships between *general* community power structure, as in the works of Hunter (1953), Dahl (1961), Banfield and Wilson (1963), and Caro (1975), and the specific community power structure of the health field. A beginning has been made by Alford, who writes (1975: 165), in an analysis of health planning in New York City:

All agencies, whether directly "political" or not, have to justify their existence by new and better programs, and the question of how these programs will be integrated with existing ones is quite low on the priority list. In fact, from the point of view of the organizational incentives involved, it may be that the *less* integrated and more autonomous, isolated, and dependent the new staff and agency are upon the administrative or political officials which sponsored them, the more likely the agency is to provide legitimacy for the sponsoring agency or officials and thus to become part of the resources of their political and organizational base.

Thus the ultimate interconnection between community health politics and *general* community politics is in fact even closer. That is, community *health* politics are simply one expression of the general fight for power and control over resources at the community, state, or national level. The resulting shape of the system is the outcome of who wins and who loses these battles, over time.

The State and the Control of Services

In the Middle Ages, the modern state as we know it today did not exist. Tuchman (1978: 5–6) observes:

Political balance among the competing groups was unstable because the king had no permanent armed force at his command. He had to rely on the feudal obligation of his vassals to perform limited military service, later supplemented by paid service. Rule was still personal, deriving from the fief of land and oath of homage. Not citizen to state but vassal to lord was the bond that underlay political structure. The state was struggling to be born.

When the modern state did rise, it appeared at the same time as early capitalism. Consequently, the growth of nationalism, economic expansion and colonialism, and the interconnection of the economic world and the world of statecraft have a centuries-long history. Poggi, in his excellent review (1978), suggests the following four eras: the feudal system of rule, the Ständestaat, the absolutist system of rule, and the nineteenth century constitutional state. We live in a late version of the last.

In our modern era, in the advanced capitalist nations of the west, the *political role of economic technocrats and planners*, working within the executive branches of central governments, and in close coordination with the giant international corporations, is central to understanding the relations of the state to health care. Miliband (1969), in his critically important analysis of the problem, reminds us that in a capitalist nation, the state *must* function to keep "the economy" on its tracks. But if the economy is capitalist in nature, no government policy that drastically affects corporate profits can long be held by government, for the corporations can legitimately complain – given the basic system – that "workers will be laid off." Elections, with candidates all basically supporting the capitalist ideology, never change this power situation. But both he and Gough (1979) note the rising "fiscal crisis of the state" within the broader crisis of capitalism itself. In a world economy which increasingly is being affected by Third World politics and its rejection of economic colonialism by American and European corporations, American corporations find themselves squeezed concerning profitability. Finding more strongly organized unions at home which prevent wage cutbacks, and no longer able to exploit wage-wise elsewhere in the world at the old rates, and paying more for energy in Third World hands, they look for a place to cut costs and find the tax system – especially funds they pay for services to the poor. A "fiscal crisis" is pronounced – a need to cut back on public services in general.

The role of the state, in this situation, is to be the acting partner in the close relationship between the corporate sector and the state, vis-à-vis the world of service providers and clients in need of service. In health, this political-economic cutback dynamic lies behind the following phenomena in present-day health and service in America: the continuation of malnutrition among the poor, the outrageous and continuing toll in occupational disease, the changes in the politics of licensure in health service occupations, the growing role of central health planning, the rise in regulatory cost control programs, and the politics of national health insurance. Each can be briefly mentioned, primarily as an area for further research to test out this overall theory and refine it with more extensive data than are presently available.

Continuation of malnutrition among the poor

To effectively deal with poverty and the malnutrition, disease and infant mortality that accompany it, this society must spend vastly more than it presently does in support of the poor. To do so means voting the money for it and seeing that the programs are adequately supported. The corporate control of Congress, especially when it comes to voting increased expenditures for welfare and support of the poor, is fought out on grounds that are both ideological and economic. The neo-conservative ideology of "cutting back on government" is pushed by right-wing politicians, and the squeezed middle class, caught between levelled-off wages and rising inflation, buys the argument and supports the corporate-inspired policies. Consequently, the infant mortality rate and malnutrition rate, high before the "anti-poverty" efforts of the mid-Sixties, are higher still today. Piven and Cloward (1979) suggest that the only known remedy to this drastic situation is the violent rebellion of the poor, who then sue for support as a condition of a return to peace. Even when food is provided, as Kotz shows (1971), there is often a monumental cynicism on the part of local bureaucrats and even, in some areas, the use of the food as a bargaining chip to force the poor to work at near-starvation wages, especially when a political machine is in control of the food supplements and coupon systems in a state or metropolitan area.

Continuation of occupational disease and death

Page and O'Brien's (1973) social history of the passage and early implementation of the Occupational Health and Safety Act of 1970, shows clearly that the state does *not* act neutrally vis-à-vis labor and management in the enforcement of the rules. Costs of true safety are pleaded as excuses for inaction by the corporations and *accepted* as excuses by the state. An H.E.W. (1973) study showed 100,000 deaths per year, and the figure is probably inflated beyond that by now. Ashford's (1976) study indicates that the economic theory behind such a non-enforcement policy makes the assumption that cost-benefit equations can be applied to the loss of life in the factory, and *is*, in fact, by OSHA itself. A study of the few successful actions by unions to get the state to enforce its own laws in this area has shown that the usual result is temporary enforcement and then backsliding. Yet there is also some evidence, especially from the plastics industry, that costs can be reduced in the long run (because of avoidance of disease and thus lower health insurance costs) if the barrier of high costs for the equipment can be surmounted. Much more research is in order here.

Rationalization of health care through governmental and semi-governmental planning mechanisms

The late 1960's were characterized by two attempts to rationalize the fragmented and chaotic American health care system: the Comprehensive Health Planning Program and the Regional Medical Program. Both used the classic pluralist model of competing interest groups, and applied to different segments of the system. RMP attempted to base planning around the medical school and CHP to base it in the community physician/ hospital/agency world *without* medical school participation. (Both bills passed within months of one another, in 1967.) Their combination, in PL. 93–641, the National Health Planning Resources and Development Act of 1974, was and continues to be an experiment in both greater central authority over planning (H.E.W. funds the professional planning staffs at state and community levels) and control over health system expansion. The motives behind the new planning act have clearly been cost-control inspired, but little research exists to date to prove whether the service systems have been more systematized under 93–641, or whether the program acts instead simply as a phase-out of small hospitals and other community programs, which may in fact have been more cost-efficient.

Far more research needs to be done on the politics of health planning. Work by Alford referred to above is a start here. But we need far more work on the way the context of health planning (especially corporate pressures on H.E.W. and on local health system agencies) aids or hinders the rationalization process. Also, more basic questions need to be asked about whether rationalization per se is the necessarily best goal for such action. Comparisons of this project with programs with a greater community-control dimension than the somewhat passive Health Systems Agency provider/consumer boards, should be made.

Given the centrality of cost problems in health at present, *regulation for cost control* is a growth industry, a major area for inspecting the complex relationships between the state, the service deliverers, and the consumer. Much narrow and *ad hoc* research has been done recently on three programs of this type: Professional Standards Review Organizations (PSRO's), the Determination of Need (DON) program which is now administered in each state as part of state-wide health planning responsibilities, and rate-setting commissions, in the dozen or so states that have them. The last are state bodies with legal control over the price of hospital beds and nursing home day charges, as well as some other aspects of health care. In each area, the results to date indicate that the political sociological approach is absolutely necessary in understanding why a given program of this type does or does not work.

For example, Decker and Bonner (1973) have shown that the PSRO program intends to have a group of health professionals, supervised by physicians, review other physicians' decisions to hospitalize, extend the stay of, and discharge patients who are on public funds. The PSRO program thus by its very construction creates a double standard for justifying a little extra care – if a patient is on private funds or private insurance, the physician does *not* have to justify expense to the PSRO. But if it's a welfare mother's hospital stay, he/she does. This either leads to shorter hospital stays for the poor or an organized attempt by community physicians to challenge the PSRO program, or to feed it what it wants to hear by way of information. Staffed at the center by health care practitioners, the program has seldom used its potential to oversee and improve the quality of care; many have doubts whether the program has any aims beyond cost-saving (a goal which it has *not* reached to date, incidentally). Here the politics of maltreatment and undertreatment of the poor structure the program and the professional politics of resistance to government oversight nullify the experiment as a cost-saver with these same people. Should one cheer or sob? The same pattern, where the socio-political dynamics really explain what does or does not happen, applies to the Determination of Need program; there is proposed research on rate-setting commissions which systematically slights the importance of political factors in a very political regulatory program.

In general, we point here to the need for a greater political-sociological understanding of the complex interface between state mechanisms and the wider society, including the role of professional action groups, health care anti-establishment activists, and consumers. This topic, as each of the other major research topics reviewed thus far, is highly controversial. The nature of the controversy, and its impact on further research in these areas, is our final concern.

The Politics of Further Research

In each of the areas we have reviewed – power and the level of health, the politics of health professions, the shaping of service systems, and the role of the state – further research has been suggested. Basic studies need to be done in order to determine effective strategies for changing our existing health care system. *Yet the needed research itself is a political issue.* Specifically, to do this research requires resources. This brings up the question of who has them at present. The research could also lead to findings embarrassing if not threatening to the status quo, and thus to those who benefit from it. The problem can be discussed in three of its dimensions: the politics of research funding, the conceptualization of these problems, and the relationship between research and action.

Funding in the health service research area is primarily at present from federal research bureaucracies, the best known of which are the Public Health Service, the Health Care Financing Administration, the National Center for Health Services Research, and the National Institute of Mental Health. While the ideal of research into the problems of the health care system is an interdisciplinary one, in practice Congress (which funds these agencies) and the Office of the President primarily have been pushing for research directed to lowering the costs of the existing system, not for research directed at basically changing such a system, or proposing alternatives such as a National Health Service. Note that broader research, and funded experimental action, along these lines is defined as part of the political sphere proper, and therefore not a "professionally acceptable" (read fundable) area for research. Furthermore, each particular bureau has its own research priorities, increasingly presented through the *contract* rather than the free proposal route, a method for handing out research funds which often guarantees a focus on the problem so narrow that the social and political field of forces cannot be studied with the funds. This has the effect of so defining the research that it can narrowly describe *what* is happening without telling *why*.

This does not make the true research problem any less real, especially if your research focus is on the political sociology of health and service. For example, the baccalaureate nursing programs of the Bureau of Health Manpower are presently under evaluation by a research contract, and great effort will be taken to trace the relationship between career choice (and job placement) with previous socialization and training in nursing school. As with physicians, the best-trained nurses appear to be absent where they are most needed – in rural areas and urban poverty areas, as well as nursing homes. On the other hand, the profit motive of settings such as private nursing homes leads them to refuse the hiring of expensive baccalaureate nurses when aides "will do." Also, the absence of developed health care systems which could hire nurses in the community means they often have no place to go except the traditional setting.

Problem: even if the true explanation of the post-graduate pattern of nurses lies in studying the community, can the Division of Nursing within the Bureau of Health Manpower do a controversial study of hiring practices in nursing homes and cost-cutting shortcuts (some illegal in the narrow sense) in the private and public sectors – even if these drastically affect where college-trained nurses go? Very probably not, in spite of the real desire of some staff of such a bureau to do such a study. Other competing bureaus such as the National Center for Health Services Research might say that the issue was *their* turf. Or, even more likely, nursing associations might get wind of the idea before the formal contract proposals were let, and might act against the idea, on the grounds that the idea that *hirers* rather than nurses control the fate of a profession might be damaging to the aspirations of this occupational group for higher prestige. Or, given the focus of the potential funding agency on *training*, the proposal could be ruled as too far out of bounds by others within H.E.W. at higher levels. Regardless of these potential scenarios, or others that I haven't mentioned, the result is a narrowing of focus, an elimination of focus on the context, and thus a drastic limitation in the true explanatory function of the research.

A second problem can be called *the politics of conceptualization*. More bluntly, in the Seventies and Eighties, I propose to describe this as the rule of an "economist Mafia," a rule by these particular social science professionals within decision-making areas in the federal research world. Since Congress persists in defining the problem almost exclusively in terms of costs (not, for example, quality, accessibility, and degree of system organization, though lip service is given to all), the economists rise in the federal research power structure.

They do the defining of the problems. We are experts on costs, they crow; they mean experts on building econometric mathematical models and cost graphs which go up and down, without ever understanding *why* the phenomena behave as they do. To share the research funds with sociologists and political scientists (who may also have a good working knowledge of applied economics in health) offends their sense of disciplinary purity, and might also disturb the flow of funds to colleagues in the same profession in the world of the university.

I recently received a request for proposals from the National Institute of Mental Health to study "the community system of services and its implications for the mentally ill." It noted that all were welcome to apply – sociologists, political scientists, systems analysts, and economists. Then the magic phrase: "those proposals which deal with describing and analyzing *costs* will receive top priority for funding in the first year." As Bob and Ray used to say, "Hang by your thumbs, and write if you get work!"

The first dimension of the problem – the narrowness of research focus – and the second – a too-narrow conceptualization of the problem – frequently lead to a situation where the research contracted and paid for by the government is so restricted that it cannot really *have* any practical used in action, whether by the state or anyone else. Abt summarizes this problem in an article titled "Social Science Research and the Modern State" (1979: 95):

The *contractor* completes the research and delivers a conclusive report to the agency within a year. The *agency* then provides the legislators with a decisive summary and a briefing. The legislators consider the best interest of the nation and decide whether to expand, maintain, modify, contract, or terminate the policy or program.

This model is violated most of the time and all along the line. More often than not it is the executive agency's appointed research, planning, and evaluation "shops" that propose the funding of information collection, not legislative committees . . . . The legislature is generally interested in who gets what – a type of equity concern – and how much it costs. Its concern is the budget even more than efficiency.

Finally, there is a basic question about the relationship between research and action. It is not an accident that research in controversial areas is stifled or underfunded by government while those who might be forced to change conditions point to the absence of reliable research –

research they have had an active hand in preventing. Take, for example, the cases of cigarette/cancer relationships, occupational disease, and the problem of dangerous drugs. For years research with very strong findings had to fight for crumbs, for an all-out research effort to confirm these findings could threaten a whole industry. For this reason, many action groups such as Nader organizations and the Environmental Defense Fund fund their own research. Opponents combat their findings by claiming they are not neutral, all the while ensuring that the state will not start to pay for such research, through political pressure on the research bureaucracies and on the funding committees of Congress that ultimately frame research priorities.

What, then, is to be done? I would not give up pressuring the relevant research shops within the government, and insisting that someone besides economists should be making decisions on the way problems are approached, but for the reasons I have given above I am not very optimistic here, even if the results become so irrelevant that even the government research funders begin to complain themselves. Rather, I would strongly suggest that we go ahead and *do* the research, without funding if necessary, and publish the results in the newer and more interdisciplinary journals such as *Advances in Medical Social Science, Journal of Health Politics, Policy and Law*, and the *International Journal of Health Services*. Documentation, data, and interviews can be achieved without the large grants and restrictive contracts that often invalidate such efforts even as they handsomely reward the makework that avoids a true investigation. We need far more research on power, health, and service. It is my profound hope that many others will take up this task, in the years to come, as a first step in building a better health care system for us all.

REFERENCES CITED

Abt, Clark C., 1979. Social science research and the modern state, *Daedalus* **108**: 89–100.
Alford, Robert, 1975. *Health Care Politics: Ideological and Interest Group Barriers to Reform*, Chicago: University of Chicago Press.
Ashford, Nicholas, 1976. *Crisis in the Workplace: Occupational Disease and Injury*, Cambridge: M.I.T. Press.
Banfield, Edward C., and James Q. Wilson, 1963. *City Politics*, Cambridge: Harvard University Press.

Boston Women's Health Book Collective, 1976. *Our Bodies, Ourselves,* New York: Simon and Schuster.

Caro, Robert, 1975. *The Power Broker: Robert Moses and the Fall of New York,* New York: Random House.

Cipolla, Carlo M., 1976. *Public Health and the Medical Profession in the Renaissance,* Cambridge, England: Cambridge University Press.

Dahl, Robert, 1961. *Who Governs? Democracy and Power in an American City,* New Haven: Yale University Press.

Decker, Barry, and Paul Bonner, 1973. *PSRO: Organization for Regional Peer Review,* Cambridge: Ballinger.

Freidson, Eliot, 1970. *Profession of Medicine: A Study of the Sociology of Applied Knowledge,* New York: Harper and Row.

Goldstein, Harold M., and Morris A. Horowitz, 1977. *Entry-Level Health Occupations: Development and Future,* Baltimore: Johns Hopkins Press.

Gough, Ian, 1979. *The Political Economy of the Welfare State,* London: MacMillan.

Haug, Marie, and Marvin B. Sussman, 1969. Professional autonomy and the revolt of the client, *Social Problems* **17**: 153–161.

Health, Education and Welfare (U.S. Department of), 1973. *Work in America,* Cambridge: M.I.T. Press.

Hirshfield, Daniel, 1970. *The Lost Reform: The Campaign for Compulsory Health Insurance in the United States from 1932 to 1943,* Cambridge: Harvard University Press.

Hunter, Floyd, 1953. *Community Power Structure,* Chapel Hill: University of North Carolina Press.

Illich, Ivan, 1976. *Medical Nemesis: The Expropriation of Health,* New York: Pantheon.

Knowles, John H., 1966. *Teaching Hospital: Evolution and Contemporary Issues,* Cambridge: Harvard University Press.

Kotz, Nick, 1971. *Let Them Eat Promises: The Politics of Hunger in America,* New York: Doubleday.

Krause, Elliott A., 1977. *Power and Illness: The Political Sociology of Health and Medical Care,* New York: Elsevier.

Lobene, Ralph R., with Alix Kerr, 1979. *The Forsyth Experiment: An Alternative System for Dental Care,* Cambridge: Harvard University Press.

Miliband, Ralph, 1969. *The State in Capitalist Society: An Analysis of the Western System of Power,* New York: Basic Books.

Navarro, Vicente, 1976. *Medicine Under Capitalism,* New York: Prodist.

Page, Joseph A., and Mary-Win O'Brien, 1973. *Bitter Wages,* New York: Grossman.

Piven, Frances Fox, and Richard A. Cloward, 1972. *Regulating the Poor: The Functions of Public Relief,* New York: Vintage.

Piven, Frances Fox, and Richard A. Cloward, 1979. *Poor People's Movements: How They Succeed, Why They Fail,* New York: Vintage.

Poggi, Gianfranco, 1978. *The Development of the Modern State. A Sociological Introduction,* Stanford: Stanford University Press.

Redman, Eric, 1973. *The Dance of Legislation,* New York: Simon and Schuster.

Rosenkrantz, Barbara G., 1972. *Public Health and the State: Changing Views in Massachusetts, 1842–1936,* Cambridge: Harvard University Press.

Schneller, Eugene, 1978. *The Physician's Assistant,* Cambridge: Lexington Books.

Strickland, Stephen P., 1972. *Politics, Science, and Dread Disease: A Short History of the United States' Medical Research Policy,* Cambridge: Harvard University Press.

Tuchman, Barbara, 1978. *A Distant Mirror: The Calamitous Fourteenth Century,* New York: Knopf.

Ullmann, Walter, 1966. *Individual and Society in the Middle Ages*, Baltimore: Johns Hopkins Press.

Villermé, Louis René, 1840. *Tableau de l'état physique et moral des ouvriers employés dans les manufactures de soie, de coton, et de laine*, Paris: Academy of Moral Sciences.

Watkin, Brian, 1978. *The National Health Service: The First Phase*, London: Allen and Unwin.

Wertz, Richard W., and Dorothy C. Wertz, 1977. *Lying-in: A History of Childbirth in America*, New York: Free Press.

4 Health: An Economist's Perspective

Douglas J. McCready

There is a fundamental conflict which has gone on through almost all of recorded history between the heroic and the economic, between greatness and prudence, between extravagance and sobriety, and between glory and common sense. Economics is the good, gray, rational science. After the charge of the Light Brigade, economics asked the reason why. Byronic frenzy may inspire us to say, "Let joy be unconfined"; the economist says: "You will have to pay for this tomorrow." Even when St. Francis urges us to give and not to count the cost, the economist says that somebody has to count the cost; and when somebody wants a Great Society, the economist says: "Who is going to pay for it?" It is no wonder that the economist is not very popular (Boulding 1968).

Boulding's writing may, in this instance, be rather more in line with the concept of economics as a "dismal" science, but economists have done much that is more cheerful and hopeful. It is in other ways that this quotation is appropriate here. Boulding talks of prudence, sobriety, rationality, and common sense as being measures of economics. In a sense, this article does not claim great advances for medical science just because economists have been examining and probing the health care system, nor does it allege the presence of a complete fund of knowledge about the health care system from the vantage point of economics. Rather, this article will deal with the roots and foundations on which the economist's understanding of the health care system is based and detail some of the developmental aspects of that understanding.

It is important to understand that while research is faddish, the attention by economists to the health care system is not simply a fad. History ensures that.

Since this paper is intended to examine the development and interests of health economists, it will not look at the development of health care *per se* which has been done elsewhere (Hartwell 1974; Helleiner 1957; and Perlman 1974) except to note that until the nineteenth century health was regarded as a private good. Private goods were dealt with in the

143

literature as being allocated according to demand, which depended on the marginal utility (the additional utility obtained from *one* additional unit of a good), and supply, which depended on a producer calculating how best to maximize net income by minimizing costs for any level of output. Obviously, the free services provided by the physician to those too poor to pay were regarded as transfer payments (payments that do not arise out of current productive activities) from the physician to the patient and were grounded in the realm of ethics as represented by the Hipprocratic Oath.

Health economics is not solely a question of money even though for many uninitiated that is what a health economist should have as his concern. Indeed, the journal *Medical Economics* is essentially a journal dealing with office practice for physicians. The June 25, 1979 issue contains articles entitled "What the I.R.S. Hunts for in Doctor Corporation Audits," "Are you Chasing Tax Savings Down the Investment Tube?", "New Quality Controls on Your Practice: How Soon, How Tough?", and eight other similar-type articles. However, most economists would not be health economists if all they were dealing with were office practice. The primary concern of the health economist is the optimal use of scarce economic resources to care for the ill and to prevent illness, always aware that there are competing uses for these resources. Allocating resources in the health field is not a simple private market exercise since there are external (effects on parties who did not initiate the economic action) benefits attached to such things as "flu shots"; if an individual has such protection from "flu" his neighbors are also less likely to contract the disease. Economists have known for some time that where such externalities exist, individual decisions will undervalue the good and thus result in underproduction unless supplemented by government or other such agencies or unless a private market develops in the externalities which is very unlikely in the case of health care (Coase 1960; Herber 1979).

It is important that the economist's role as it is seen in this paper is clearly understood. First, we are dealing with individual decisions. While health care has some role in the macro-economy (for instance, the effect on Gross National Product [GNP] of the health care system reducing morbidity), the major interests of health economists have been in micro-decisions (decisions affecting the allocation of resources and/or the distribution of income), and this is reflected in this paper. Secondly, as we have just indicated in the last paragraph, the primary concern is to make optimal use of scarce resources to improve the level of health of individuals. That implied that the health economist is going to be interested in the allocation of resources both to and within health care; physician remuneration; access and equity in health care; and hospital economics. Each topic will be dealt with in turn within the paper.

History of Economists' Involvement in Medical Care

Until the late 1950's economists had little to say about either the market organization of health services or the yield of investment in health. Partly, this lack of attention was a general phenomenon related to the lack of attention to human factors with a greater attention to physical or material production, and, partly, it resulted from the special characteristics of the health system (Mushkin 1958).

However, some early economists provided the basis upon which the massive explosion of interest in health economics of the last twenty years has been built. Sir William Petty included in his estimate of national wealth, a measure of labor although not differentiated according to health (Hall 1899). Indeed, labor, in Petty's analysis, is the source and measure of wealth. Malthus also paid attention to human capital. His well-known *Essay on the Principle of Population*, published in 1798, led to a series of economic postulates, most important of which was his insistence that wages would tend to subsistence (the "iron law of wages").

It was Alfred Marshall (1920), widely considered the originator of modern economics, who first dwelt on health as a part of production. In Book 4 of his *Principles of Economics*, Marshall devotes a chapter to the "conditions on which depend health and strength, physical, mental and moral" (p. 193). According to Marshall the production process and industrial efficiency depended on health and strength but in turn, material wealth when wisely used could lead to increases in health and strength, physical, mental and moral.

This concept of the capital value of man as seen in Petty and Marshall is summarized along with the thinking of others of that era in Dublin and Lotka's *The Money Value of a Man* (1946). Ultimately, they take into account the costs of birth as well as maintenance costs (including health care costs) in calculating man's capital value.

Another aspect of health economics which has its basis in the writings of early economists is cost-benefit analysis. Early writings on the topic even included one article on the health care field (Fisher 1908). However, it has only been in recent times that economists have become truly involved in carrying out cost-benefit studies of health programs (Mushkin 1958; Ruchlin and Rogers 1973). The first major attention to cost-benefit analysis of the health care system in modern economic writings is that of Weisbrod (1960), who attempted to estimate the benefits of a death avoided by calculating the present value of that person's future production. Others (Klarman 1965; and Mushkin 1962) added useful surveys of techniques involved and that led to a lengthy list of output by economists on the cost and benefits, one of the most recent being a paper entitled: "Treating the Mentally Ill: Benefits and Costs of Alternative Approaches," which was presented by Burton Weisbrod and Margaret Helming at the 1979 Eastern Economic Association meetings.

In a recent article (Frenzel and McCready 1979) the growth of health economics has been documented in terms of the numbers involved in the sub-discipline, the amount of research (theses, articles, and grants), and the factors that accommodated the growth. In that article the initial development of health economics as a sub-discipline is shown to be in the late 1950's and the substantial growth and achievement of sub-discipline status is found to be in the mid-1960's. Growth is attributed to such factors as rising incomes, proverty awareness (Harrington 1962), the Kefauver Hearings on the drug industry, (U.S. Congress 1960), the introduction of government medical schemes world-wide, as well as examinations of new forms of financing and organizing medical services (Andreano and Weisbrod 1975).

Thus, it might be said that economists have had an interest in health economics for centuries but it is only in the last two decades that real development has occurred. It is now time to turn to some of those developments as they relate to health economics.

Resource Allocation and Health Care

Somewhere near the beginning of any textbook in economics there is usually a discussion of resource allocation as an economic problem. Basically, the economics student is told to consider such questions as "What commodities are being produced and in what quantities?" and "By what methods are the commodities produced and are those methods efficient?" In this section of the paper, these questions as they relate to health care, are explored.

Most economists relate the quantity of a good being produced to the demand and supply of that good. When there is a divisible good the demand for a commodity relates the price which people are willing to pay for given quantities to the value they derive from that quantity. Similarly, suppliers are willing to supply a given quantity so long as it contributes to revenues more than to costs. The system is simple and direct. Any change in costs or perceived benefits will lead to a change in the amount supplied or demanded respectively and that will precipitate a new equilibrium.

Health care is not always a divisible good. We have already noted the external effect of innoculation and when there are externalities, resource allocation does not occur optimally in the same way as it does when there are divisible goods without externalities. Another problem associated with the allocation of resources to health care is the private market assumption that both the consumer and producer have perfect knowledge. In the case of medical care, the consumer is comparatively ignorant about the utility of a particular product or service. The patient's demand for a service is, in at least a portion of cases, determined by the supplier who thus can change the demand/supply equilibrium to suit. While it is true that consumers may initiate the demand, who is going to argue if a physician prescribes medicine, surgery, or another visit? Thus, the special conditions attaching to the demand and supply of medical services make the question of the optimum quantity of health care an important one for the economist.

To further complicate matters, the economist who tries to unravel the mysteries as to the optimum quantity of health services will find some rather alarming problems facing him. First, the incidence of illness seems to be very uneven. Countries experience quite different patterns of infant mortality and morbidity, for instance. The United States, which has larger expenditures per capita and as a percentage of GNP than most other countries and more doctors per 100,000 population, continues to have lower life expectancies for males and females. The United Nations reports that countries such as Sweden, Norway, Netherlands, Denmark, Switzerland, New Zealand, Canada, United Kingdom, and Australia have life expectancies longer than those for the United States even though these same countries have fewer doctors or spend less as a percentage of GNP than does the United States (United Nations 1979).

This kind of information is of little help in determining the optimum quantity of services.

Let us suppose that the question economists are trying to answer is how much medical care there should be. Let us go even further and suppose that the answer has been found. There is a further question to be asked and that is: How is it determined which services should be provided? Who decides whether there should be another dialysis unit or whether there should be a community-oriented psychiatric group home (Reiser 1977)?

Obviously, the economist would answer the question by saying that the programs should be selected so as to maximize a "welfare function" (including health production and costs) subject to constraints (Klarman 1977). Difficulties abound in achieving this ideal. Much of the work of medical economics, though, has been directed at improving measures of health improvement and costs so that realistic maximization of a health "welfare function" can occur. One of the earliest surveys in this area was the classic "Health as an Investment" (Mushkin 1962) and others have followed (Grossman 1972). The gist of these studies is that health is an investment in human capital, that the benefits of health care lie in increased productivity resulting from a lower mortality rate or improvements in the morbidity rate, and that costs can be measured.

However, there is some evidence that while this methodology is helpful when applied to specific diseases, it misses some of the intricacies of the health sector. Indeed, the nature of the work on human capital as we noted in the introduction was applicable to several types of economic study besides health care. The Dublin and Lotka work cited earlier along with another article (Fein 1971) survey the early literature. In bibliographies of health economics (Culyer *et al.* 1977) reference is made to Becker (1964), which is not considered to be in the area of health but rather the economics of education. However, the economics of health and education economics have had similar growth patterns.

The technical aspect of health care is not the only one. In fact, the patient may benefit in many ways from treatment that is not always technical or productive and this creates even greater measurement problems.

Work on the allocation of resources can be characterized as being of two types. There is the whole question of macro (aggregate) decisions whereby the "medical outcome" for a region is related to the aggregate services of that region. There has been at least one major attempt to quantify the "state-of-health" by taking into account intensity of pain and/or disability (measured on a ten-point scale from normality to death) by the expected period of duration (until recovery or death) (Culyer *et al.* 1971). This measure allows both preventive and therapeutic medical activity to be incorporated into any analysis. Obviously, no one is able to measure, with any degree of rigor, the level of pain, and economists have been no more successful than have other health professionals.

Until economists can agree on some measure of "state-of-health" however, studies can not be conclusive. Morbidity data are often considered unreliable when aggregated because there is no clear cut reporting requirement. Neonatal, stillbirth, perinatal, and infantile mortality, for instance, may describe genetic and/or socio-economic status rather than health status although the latter clearly must take into account the former. Thus, reported outcomes are not very helpful either. Surveys and sickness benefit reporting tend to be unreliable in time-series (data collected for successive periods of time and analyzed as such). For instance, the incidence of tuberculosis (or, for that matter, any disease which has decreased or been eliminated) has decreased but the incidence of more trivial disabilities has increased at an even faster rate. Is the net effect of observed morbidity a real increase in sickness, or does it represent an excuse to remain away from employment or does it represent an increased income-related propensity to report minor ailments?

Rationing of scarce resources also implies a micro decision. Most of the work of this nature has been done on individual diseases using methods originating in the cost-benefit literature. One person very much connected with this type of literature is Burton Weisbrod (1960 and 1971). The real advantage of cost-benefit analysis (expediting comparisons among several programs which have different objectives) and cost-effectiveness analysis (comparisons among different programs which have the same objective) lies in drawing attention to the alternative (Van Matré and Miller 1974) as well as in making the decision-making process a rational one (Schneider and Twiggs 1972). However, there are legitimate concerns about basing decisions on those factors for which data are readily available to the exclusion of non-measurable ones and in the health area the latter are many. It is important, then, that the decision-making include political and social factors which economists have difficulty including in their models. For instance, fluoridation was known to have the highest benefit-cost ratio but was rejected by the Johnson Administration in the United States in favor of a less effective but more expensive treatment for political reasons (Sorkin 1975).

What is important to note in this section is that we have been reviewing the process by which investment in health care is made. We have rejected the private sector as an allocator although it is useful in some very important respects (Blomqvist 1979), because the health sector demonstrates some very real "public good" characteristics. Economists have made very real gains in measuring the output of health programs but there is much to be learned yet. Furthermore, there is much to be done in cooperation with other social scientists in the art of decision-making. The careful reader will also note that the remaining sections of the paper each relates in some way to resource allocation which underlies the economist's involvement in all health topics.

Physician Remuneration

One of the initial reasons for the lack of interest that economists displayed in the health care system was the fact that physicians seemed to be guided by non-economic motives. Physicians were seen to be providing care without any guarantee of remuneration. Yet, it is in the very way in which physicians and/or governments control supply that they are able to control their remuneration and that has been going on for some significant time (Eu 1978).

Modern economists who have worked on the question of manpower have been concerned with a number of different questions. Obviously, one area of concern has been the optimal number of physicians, nurses, etc., along with the whole question of substitution between occupations. Also, the question of service location is important. There is the further question of methods of remuneration which is both connected to the question of supply and demand and to the structure of the health care industry.

A classic look at physician remuneration of the modern era is that by Friedman and Kuznets (1945). The physician, it was concluded, was receiving higher than market rates of return (in other words, the return to being a physician was higher than the requisite amount to induce the same numbers to become physicians) which could only be explained by limitations being placed on the numbers of physicians. Although the study by Friedman and Kuznets was published prior to the majority of the large number of items which constitute the literature of health economics, there has been little real advance made in the area.

The question of the optimal number of physicians has often been expressed in terms of a "shortage" of physicians. For some economists and politicians it is the income differential between physicians and other professions which leads them to believe there is a shortage (Hansen 1964). On the other hand, there are those who deny a shortage because of the productivity increases that have occurred (Dickinson 1951). Yet the consensus seems to be that the "physician supply situation will not be loose enough to fill the gaps that now exist in supply of physicians' services available in some areas and to some parts of the population" (Fein 1967). In other words, economists have not been able to determine an exact number of physicians, nurses, dentists, or whatever that is optimal in terms of equating the benefits derived with the costs. For instance, in Canada, the population per physician varied from 780.5:1 to 2636.8:1 in the provinces while that for dentists varied from 2801.0:1 to 14502.9:1, (Marr et al. 1980), but without specific information about the health status, productivity levels, etc., it is impossible to judge which province is optimally supplied with a given health occupation.

What does become evident is that physician and/or health professional location is extremely important. Not only does the location affect the services provided and the costs, it represents for many economists a real misallocation in resources. Since many health services are provided in urban areas, there tend to be large gaps in available services in rural areas which the statistics are unable to portray, even when the aggregation level is that of a state or province.

The literature on health manpower location indicates that there are a number of factors which influence physicians and/or dentists to locate in a given area. These include income, barriers to entry, prior exposure, environmental factors, medical environment, and demand determinants (Hambleton 1971; Marr et al. 1980; and McFarland 1973). Of these, environmental (cultural and social) and economic (income, distance) factors are invariably the most significant in one's choice of practice location.

Economists are aware that an increase in the number of physicians in total or in one location can lead to increased costs to government and/or to private consumers. For instance, in Canada, where physicians receive payment on a fee-for-service basis from the government, the costs have not just been for the added visits paid to physicians. Complementary services such as hospital, laboratory work, and drugs all add up to an increase in societal cost with no attendant proof that there is an improvement in mortality or morbidity rates (McCready and Winn 1978; and Vayda 1973). One alternative that has been looked into is increasing the productivity of physicians who are already practising. This is important in that a 4 percent increase in physician productivity would increase total supply of health services as much as one year's graduation of U.S. medical schools (Sorkin 1975).

Productivity increases can arise from the form of medical care organization, as well as from the greater use of auxiliary medical personnel. The organization of health services into solo practice which is the predominate system makes it highly unlikely that an optimum combination of personnel and capital equipment will be achieved. The inflexibility that exists in solo practice undoubtedly causes the physician to operate below potential efficiency. However, those economists who have empirically examined the productivity of group practitioners as against solo practitioners find little difference in the level of output (Bailey 1970; and Newhouse 1973) although there is some evidence peer consultation in groups may improve quality (Peterson et al. 1956).

One type of group practice that has been of particular interest to economists has been the Health Maintenance Organization ("any organization that provides and assures the delivery of comprehensive health maintenance and treatment services for an enrolled group of persons under a prepaid, fixed capitation arrangement ... designed to emphasize preventative medicine by providing incentives for cost consciousness and for increasing the productivity of available resources" [Hepner and Hepner 1973:275]). Their basic attraction lies in the change of emphasis from "episodic" care to prevention with its attendant perceived advantages in so far as total health costs (over a life-time) are concerned. However, the success of such plans has itself been the subject of recent debate (Roemer and Shonick 1973). Although there tends to be a lower hospitalization rate for enrollees, Soderstrom claims that does not imply lower total health costs or better quality care (Soderstrom 1978:61). Enrollment targets have been difficult to achieve and there are difficulties developing and maintaining a commonality of purpose.

Groups tend to increase the possibility of substitution between physician and allied health workers. Allied health manpower covers all health occupations below the doctoral level and includes technologists, technicians, therapists, and assistants in patient care, community health, public health, and environmental health. Those with baccalaureate degrees are considered "allied health professionals." The potential lies in having lower cost inputs into the production function (Reinhardt and Smith 1974) but there is a degree of concern about how far substitution can go since there is evidence that supervision of these paraprofessionals tends to decrease the efficiency and quality of service after a certain proportion is attained (Ginzberg 1977:91). What is unclear is the proportion that is optimal and that is still very much unsettled.

The method of payment used for physicians can, as any economist knows, have dramatic effect on the incentives as well as the type of treatment. Not much in the way of research was conducted on this question prior to 1960 because physicians provided many free services to those unable to pay their fees and although their incomes were high, their hours were long and public opinion was generally positive. In 1950, 85 per cent of all spending for physicians' services was in the form of direct payment from patients, but by 1975, less than 40 per cent were direct payments (Ginzberg 1977:100). Private insurance and government payments increased dramatically so that physicians no longer had to forego some of their fees. The result of this switch, and the jump in the expenditure per capita on physicians' services from $18 to $105 in the same period was to cause economists to look at systems of remuneration (Ginzberg 1977:100).

Basically, there are three systems of remuneration. The most common is known as "fee-for-service." Because third parties pay the majority of these fees, there is an incentive to the physician to cause the number of services to increase – particularly after the first contact has been made (Evans 1974). Alternatives such as capitation and salary are being looked at with more vigor to determine whether they provide greater incentives for physicians to improve efficiency and, thereby, ultimately cut costs (Ruderman 1976). It would appear, for instance, that the Kaiser Plans, whereby the physician group contracts ahead of time to provide health care to an individual, do have incentives built into them. The physician's leisure time and income depend on him practicing preventive care (U.S. Department of Health, Education, and Welfare 1967).

The reader will have noted in this section of the paper that a variety of topics have been surveyed. Specifically, the question of physician remuneration is related clearly to the supply and demand for physicians in total and in a narrower geographical area. The remuneration is also closely related to the type of practice (solo vs. group) and the method of payment (Kaiser, capitation, and fee-for-service). Because the income of medical practitioners affects the quantity and quality of care globally, as well as by geographic region, the question of physician remuneration is directly related to resource allocation.

Access to Medical Care

Perhaps because of its political currency, many economists have devoted a great deal of energy to examining the payments system for medical care both in the United States and other countries. U.S. economists argue quite correctly that a great deal can be learned from the comprehensive medicare schemes which operate in Canada, the United Kingdom, and other Western industrialized nations. The basic issue remains access to medical care.

Supposedly, the introduction of a payments scheme whereby the government pays physicians out of funds raised from taxes or income-geared premiums makes access to medical care possible for those who could not previously afford the care. This is unassailable. In Canada, where a comprehensive medicare scheme was introduced in 1969, and a comprehensive hospitalization plan has been in operation since 1958, however, the question has been examined by economists and others and the increased access to medical care is not as clear cut as it at first appears (Beck 1973; Enterline et al. 1973; Manga 1978; and McCready and Winn 1975). While the poor and the elderly no longer have to pay for services, and, therefore, are able to use the system, there are other factors keeping their usage from rising to the same extent as those in higher income brackets. These other factors include the costs of complementary goods such as transportation and drugs as well as sociodemographic factors including an education barrier which inhibits those who are less educated from seeking help from highly educated professionals (Manga 1978: 57–137).

If there is disagreement about the Canadian medical care system and whether it provides a greater equity, there has been disagreement in the United States about whether or not medicare and medicaid should be changed into a universal medical insurance program and if so, what should be the essential features of the new systems. Although it has become a political issue (Carter 1979; and Kennedy 1979), economists have also been addressing the issue (Fein 1976; Klarman 1974; and

Somers and Somers 1967 and 1972). The concerns of the latter have been the cost on the public treasury but perhaps of greater importance is the question of access as represented by the distribution of health facilities and personnel (Ginzberg 1977, ch. 12).

The basic problem is one of attracting physicians to rural and poor urban localities. Economists have studied the factors which effectively can move physicians towards these underserviced areas and have found student aid to be somewhat helpful (Mason 1971). However, if one remembers that health care is a complex of multiple products and multiple inputs, then one will note that the distribution of hospitals will also affect the distribution of physicians. Most physicians have admission privileges at one or two hospitals at most and are interested in establishing a practice where the complementary hospital services are present. Thus, sometimes hospitals will overexpand or build in certain areas to attract physicians. A recent phenomenon has been the closing of inner city hospitals and the attendant shift of resources (Rule 1979). Finally, the presence of physicians attracts related medical personnel such as nurses and pharmacists.

While a great deal of the recent literature on access deals with medicare and medicaid, there is a movement away from these solutions by economists. It is felt that private insurance coupled with changes in the tax-subsidy system could make access more equitable than even medicare and medicaid (Blomqvist 1979 and Olendzki *et al.* 1972). However, further work on the incidence of health care (in economics, incidence refers to statistics relating usage to some other variable, usually income) under U.S. programs is continuing and will be useful.

Again, the reader will have noted that the discussion of access to medical care is a question of resource allocation almost more than a question of equity. While the latter, with its strong political implications, has become a major current interest, it is important that the economist continue to consider the implications of various schemes on resource allocation both as they relate to the total allocation between one public good and another and as they affect allocation of resources within the health sector.

The Hospital Sector

The largest sector, when we consider health economics, is the hospital sector. Approximately 40 percent of current national health expenditures are accounted for by hospitals and if capital and research costs are included, that figure jumps to 47 percent (Sorkin 1975:75). That makes them a subject for a great deal of study by economists.

Like many of the topics in the health sector, economists showed little concern so long as the voluntary non-profit hospital was predominant and charity patients were readily cared for. More recently, as state and local as well as proprietary hospitals have increased in numbers and as costs per patient day have risen (574 per cent between 1950 and 1972) more interest has been shown (Sorkin 1975: 76).

Some of the questions which have been of most interest to economists have been the optimal size of a hospital, the question of costs and reimbursements, the effect hospitals have on the question of access and equity, and the allocation of resources within and between hospitals. These are weighty questions and except for the question of access and equity which is dealt with in another section of this paper, each will be dealt with here.

On the question of scale, it is generally agreed that many hospital services depend on "lumpy" inputs. For instance, it is probably impossible to construct one-half of an operating room. On the other hand, countervailing administrative costs arise from the inability of a management team to effectively observe and control the hospital as it gets larger and this would be consistent with a U-shaped long-run average cost curve (a U-shaped cost curve implies that economies of scale cause a decrease in the per diem per bed cost but that at some number of beds additional administration or whatever will cause the per bed cost per diem to rise). Some people have hypothesized that the cost curve is L-shaped, meaning that the first bed has extremely high costs per day and as the number of beds increase, the per bed cost per diem decreases, ultimately levelling out at a constant marginal cost per bed. In the latter case, it is not possible to find an optimum size because there is no single number of beds where the per bed per diem cost is lowest but in the case of U-shaped cost curves, there is a lowest per bed per diem cost.

A significant amount of research has been conducted on the óptimum hospital size. To date, there is no consensus on the measure of output except that for empirical research the number of adult and pediatric patient days has been almost always used. This ignores outpatient services and also differences in the quality and type of care. Since these are significant factors, to ignore them makes the results of the research suspect. There is some indication but no conclusion that the long-run average cost curve is U-shaped and that the minimum costs occur at a higher level of output than is the current average output of U.S. hospitals. The current level of output of U.S. non-profit general hospitals is approximately 135 beds, and empirical studies (Hefty 1969) show a minimum cost at anywhere from 190 beds to 300 beds. This is an active interest which economists are still pursuing with vigor.

On the question of costs and reimbursement, there seems to be a general interest in cost containment (Zubkoff and Raskin 1977). Moreover, this becomes important when there are third-parties involved in payment. In Canada, the government pays for hospitalization in all but a few cases and in the United States Blue Cross and Medicare provide a significant portion of the reimbursement. Here the basis of reimbursement is a reasonable cost plus arrangement where costs include direct costs plus such indirect expenses as loan interest, bad accounts, certain non-recoupable research costs, and nursing school operation.

In the United States, the unit operating cost per patient day in public general hospitals is some $32 greater than in Canada (Blomqvist 1979: 127). Part of the explanation for this difference, as well as for the rapid increase in hospital costs over the last decade is attributable to ancillary services which are becoming technologically sophisticated and expensive. Examples of these ancillary services which have expanded most rapidly in the United States include coronary care units, intensive care units, dialysis machines, radiology departments, and the new "computerized axial tomography" (CAT) diagnostic scanners. Economists have not argued that these innovations are not welcome but have been anxious to determine the factors influencing the purchase of these items (for instance, the degree to which the demand for these goods is responsive to income change) and the systems of planning which could be adopted to avoid unnecessary duplication.

A further factor in the higher cost in the United States over Canada appears to be the shorter duration of stay in United States hospitals. The increased stay in Canada, 11.3 days versus 8.7 in the United States (Blomqvist 1979: 126), tends to increase costs per treated case and lower costs per day (Evans and Walker 1972). That raises, of course, the question of which figure economists are most interested in. The cost per treated case is the only figure which can be used to measure effectiveness and from the point of view of resource allocation is the most relevant. It is only when the industry as a whole is being examined that the cost per day become relevant. Perhaps, the greatest contribution economists, as opposed to hospital administrators and politicians, make to the debate on hospital costs, is in the area of what is relevant and what is not.

A number of studies implicate insurance coverage as a factor in hospital inflation (Feldstein 1971 a and b; Salkever 1972). However, reimbursement on the basis of costs does not appear to induce higher prices (Davis 1973; and Pauly and Drake 1970) rather, overall increases in insurance coverage tended to increase demand with a consequent increase in price (and costs). This is just the regular market mechanism which occurs when demand increases while supply remains constant or increases by a smaller degree than demand.

While there are many suggested solutions to the spiralling costs of hospitals, some of the more sensible include developing lower-cost alternatives such as outpatient care and emphasizing preventive rather than curative care (Davis and Russell 1972). Allowing hospitals to establish fees for services (as is the case in some U.S. States) may cause hospitals to compete, whereas, in the present situation of costplus financing, there are few incentives for efficiency (Blomqvist 1979: 177).

The question of allocation of resources within a hospital or between two constituent hospitals, brings us to the problems of multiproduct firms and competition. The idea that a hospital is a multiproduct firm has been around for some time but data have not been readily available to those economists wishing to do empirical work. That has not stopped the development of models to help in predicting the effects of changing case-mix or mean stays by diagnosis (Granfield 1975; Goldfarb et al. 1977; and Joseph 1976). For instance, Goldfarb et al., using a non-linear programming approach, showed that a move to make outpatient services less costly and more used would weight the patient-mix toward the longer-staying types, reduce admissions, and reduce net revenue per patient (Goldfarb et al. 1977: 30). What could be learned about resource allocation is immense, yet to have its ultimate impact, it would be necessary for economists to have both program and functional accounts for a large number of hospitals along with diagnosis and outcome data.

Other Developments in Health Care Economics

Economists writing on health care are each year devoting a larger portion of their words to the other factors which influence the health care system. For instance, it has long been recognized that increasing health care itself can have a negative return in terms of morbidity and/or mortality rates. The infant mortality rate in countries like the Netherlands, where a substantial percentage of births occur in the home under the supervision of a midwife, is lower than in countries where the pregnant woman consults an obstetrical specialist in early pregnancy, delivers in a hospital with a full range of facilities and personnel, and follows up with post-natal visits. Economists are beginning to recognize that there may be clues in these figures. For instance, the return on medical care facilities may be extremely high when applied to high risk populations – in the case of pregnancy the risk is high for the very young, for those of low socio-economic status, and the older woman. On the other hand, the return on medical care may be almost zero when applied to other types of pregnancy. Herein, lies another truth that economists, along with other social scientists, are learning and that is that most disease, morbidity, and mortality stems from the environment and/or age of the patient and resources can be allocated to counteract these factors without changing the basic structure of the medical sector. Such a transfer of priorities towards the environment would leave more funds within the health sector available for the care of the aged. Even here economists are quickly rediscovering the importance of nutrition, and the absence of toxic substances in producing healthy geriatrics (Fuchs 1974). Moreover, as there appears to be a correlation between schooling and health, economists have begun to suggest that an increase in schooling costs, to educate the population about their environment and health, could have significant cost-saving features in the longer-run.

Economists along with other social scientists have also begun the search for occupational-related diseases and here the emphasis is on prevention. A disease that is occupation-specific may be controlled by eliminating the source (toxic chemical or the technology of carrying out certain functions) but at some point the economist has to weigh the benefits gained from eliminating the source of particular disease against the costs of doing so. For instance, none of us would be willing to forego the pleasures of having electricity in our homes and offices. Yet the generation of electricity by coal, gas or nuclear reaction is unsafe to somebody's health and the benefits of eliminating coal, gas, and nuclear reaction generated electricity are positive. Here, somebody has to determine what health risks we are prepared to make in order to have electricity. Clearly, the same problem of resource allocation arises for each and every production process. Clearly, economists should be working on lowering risk (and ultimate costs) as much as on eliminating them.

Although not related to occupational health problems, the United States, which lowered speed limits to 55 mph and Ontario, Canada, which lowered speed limits to 100 km/hr. and required the use of seatbelts, both found unexpected benefits. Accidents decreased and health costs (which in Ontario are paid by the government) dropped significantly. It becomes clear then that medical costs are related to a large number of government policies and therefore, the whole topic of medical social science is broad. Since economists are involved in resource allocation problems, economists have to take this broad view of the question.

Economists have also become involved in the discussions on the drug industry. The macroeconomic importance of the industry (Fuchs 1974: 106) inevitably attracts attention to such questions as drug abuse, drug prices, and profits from drugs. The opportunities for misallocation of resources are immense. Many individuals are dealing with more than one medical practitioner with the potential of dangerous drug combinations beings administered. Some physicians may use prescriptions as a substitute for taking time with a patient. Others may want to appear to be healing an ailment where in the long-run the person's immunity to the ailment may be increased by no treatment.

The interest that economists have in the drug industry is an interest that they also have in other industries. One of these interests is in the degree of concentration [the fraction of market purchases supplied by the largest supplier(s)] and here it is crucial that the concentration ratio be calculated by drug category because of the high degree of specialization. A further question which has received some very specific attention is the question of generic versus brand name drugs. Pharmacists are not legally permitted to substitute generic or lower-priced drugs in all jurisdictions and until a true marketplace can operate, the prices of drugs will be higher than they otherwise would be.

Certainly, there has not been a significant shift of interest on the part of economists towards examination of the drug industry. The shift towards environmental questions and occupational health has been of much larger proportions although both questions involve allocating resources so as to more efficiently produce "good health."

Conclusion

Perhaps it is trite to suggest that there is no consensus amongst economists about the importance of health economics but there is a significant amount of truth in such a statement. Moreover, when one tries to discern the important topics, there are almost as many answers as there are economists. In this paper, resources have had to be allocated (not every possible topic could be discussed) with the result that the microeconomic decisions affecting individuals were stressed. Furthermore, major attention was directed at the market for physician-related aspects of health care.

The result is that many questions that are very much a part of health economics have been ignored. Questions such as "the effect of a change in morbidity on GNP" are important but not dealt with here. In the same way, the questions of dentist, pharmacist, and nurse allocation and remuneration are not dealt with in this paper although there have been many significant contributions (e.g., Yett 1970).

It is significant that the number of economists interested in health questions has grown so greatly over the last twenty years. Undoubtedly, it would have been impossible to write a great deal about resource allocation in the health field in the early 1960's whereas now it is impossible to even scratch the surface of knowledge about hospitals, physician remuneration, and access to services as these relate to individual health care. More significant than the advances being made on these questions, there is the rapid and recent development of a new interest on the part of economists in questions of environmental health as well as occupational health.

Health economics like all economics is allocating resources to achieve consumer satisfaction in an efficient and least expensive manner. All the questions dealt with here relate to allocating resources whether that be allocating funds to nutritional education or granting medical doctors' licenses to only those willing to practice in certain geographical locations. Thus, this paper is a survey of some of the recent work of this nature as well as the developments leading up to those advances. The need for further work has been indicated in almost every section of the paper but in many instances the really major advances await the development of new measures and new statistics. The need for further advances should not overshadow the fact that health economists have been active in researching the whole question of producing "good health" efficiently in the broadest sense.

Acknowledgements

Financial assistance for bibliographic search by Wilfrid Laurier University is gratefully acknowledged. Comments on an earlier draft by

K.A. Frenzel; D.J. Grant; P. Manga; F. Millerd; and C. Pierce were extremely helpful but the responsibility for remaining errors or problems remains with the author.

REFERENCES CITED

Andreano, Ralph L., and Burton A. Weisbrod, 1975. *American Health Policy*, Chicago: Rand McNally College Publishing Co.
Bailey, R., 1970. Economies of scale in medical practice, in *Empirical Studies in Health Economics*, H.E. Klarman (ed.), pp. 255–273, Baltimore: Johns Hopkins Press.
Beck, R.G., 1973. Economic class and access to physician services under public medical care insurance, *International Journal of Health Services* 3: 341–355.
Becker, Gary S., 1964. *Human Capital*, New York: National Bureau of Economic Research.
Blomqvist, Ake, 1979. *The Health Care Business*, Vancouver, B.C.: Fraser Institute.
Boulding, Kenneth E., 1968. Is scarcity dead? in *A Great Society*, Bertram M. Gross (ed.), pp. 209–226, New York: Basic Books Inc.
Carter, Jimmy, 1979. National health plan legislation, *Challenge* 22: 11–16.
Coase, R.H., 1960. The problem of social cost, *Journal of Law and Economics* 3: 1–44.
Culyer, A.J., R.J. Lavers, and A. Williams, 1971. Health indicators, *Social Trends* 2: 31–42.
Culyer, A.J., J. Wiseman, and A. Walker, 1977. *An Annotated Bibliography of Health Economics*, London: Martin Robertson & Company.
Davis, Karen, 1973. Theories of hospital inflation: Some empirical evidence, *Journal of Human Resources* 8: 181–201.
Davis, Karen, and L.B. Russell, 1972. The substitution of hospital outpatient care for inpatient care, *Review of Economics and Statistics* 54: 109–120.
Dickinson, Frank G., 1951. *Supply of Physicians Services*, Chicago: Bureau of Medical Economic Research, American Medical Association.
Dublin, L.I., and A.J. Lotka, 1946. *The Money Value of A Man*, Rev. ed., New York: Ronald Press Co.
Enterline, P.E., V. Salter, A.D. McDonald, and J.C. McDonald, 1973. The distribution of medical services before and after 'free' medical care – The Quebec experience, *New England Journal of Medicine* 228: 1174–1178.
Eu. Stephen R., 1978. Governmental regulation of medicine in late medieval Venice, *Fifteenth Century Studies* 2: 83–89.
Evans, R., 1974. *Beyond the Medical Market Place: Expenditure, Utilization, and Pricing of Insured Health Care in Canada*, Vancouver, B.C.: Department of Economics, University of British Columbia.
Evans, R.G., and H.D. Walker, 1972. Information theory and the analysis of hospital cost structure, *Canadian Journal of Economics* 5: 398–418.
Fein, Rashi, 1967. *The Doctor Shortage*, Washington, D.C.: The Brookings Institution.
Fein, Rashi, 1971. On measuring economic benefits of health programmes, in *Medical History and Medical Care*. G. MacLachland and T. McKeown (eds.), pp. 181–220, London: Oxford University Press.
Fein, Rashi, 1976. Access and equity in health care, in *Health Economics Symposium*, R.D. Fraser (ed.), pp. 156–163, Kingston, Ontario: Industrial Relations Centre, Queen's University.
Feldstein, Martin S., 1971a. Hospital cost inflation: A study of non-profit price dynamics, *American Economic Review* 61: 853–872.

Feldstein, Martin S., 1971b. *The Rising Cost of Hospital Care*, Washington D.C.: Information Resources Press.

Fisher, Irving, 1908. Report on national vitality: Its wastes and conservation, 1923 in *Committee of One Hundred on Public Health*, Washington: Government Printing Office.

Frenzel, K. Arnold, and Douglas J. McCready, 1979. Health economics: A sub-discipline?, *Economic Development and Cultural Change* **27**: 267–282.

Friedman, Milton, and S. Kuznets, 1945. *Income from Independent Professional Practice*, New York: Columbia University Press for the National Bureau of Economic Research.

Fuchs, Victor R., 1974. *Who Shall Live?*, New York: Basic Books.

Ginzberg, Eli, 1977. *The Limits of Health Reform*, New York: Basic Books.

Goldfarb, M., M. Hornbrook, and J. Rafferty, 1977. Behavior of the multi-product firm: A model of the non-profit hospital system. Paper delivered to the European Meeting of the Econometric Society, Vienna, Austria.

Granfield, Michael E., 1975. Resource allocation within hospitals: An unambiguous analytical test of the A-J hypothesis, *Applied Economics* **7**: 241–249.

Grossman, Michael, 1972. *The Demand for Health: A Theoretical and Empirical Investigation*, New York: National Bureau of Economic Research.

Hall, C. (ed.), 1899. *The Economic Writings of Sir William Petty*, Cambridge: Cambridge University Press.

Hambleton, J.W., 1971. *Main Currents in the Analysis of Physician Location*, Madison, Wisconsin: Department of Economics, Health Economics Research Center, University of Wisconsin.

Hansen, W. Lee, 1964. Shortages and investment in health manpower, in *The economics of Health and Medical Care*, W. Lee Hansen (ed.), pp. 75–91, Ann Arbor, Michigan: Bureau of Public Health Economics and Department of Economics, University of Michigan.

Harrington, Michael, 1962. *The Other America: Poverty in the United States*, New York: Macmillan Co.

Hartwell, R.M., 1974. The economic history of medical care. in *The Economics of Health and Medical Care*, Mark Perlman (ed.), pp. 3–20, London: The Macmillan Press Ltd.

Hefty, T.R., 1969. Returns to scale in hospitals: A critical review of recent research, *Health Services Research* **4**: 267–280.

Helleiner, K.F., 1957. The vital revolution reconsidered, *Canadian Journal of Economics and Political Science* **23**: 1–9.

Hepner, James O., and Donna M. Hepner, 1973. *The Health Strategy Game: A Challenge for Reorganization and Management*, St. Louis: The C.B. Mosby Co.

Herber, Bernard P., 1979. *Modern Finance*, Fourth ed., Homewood, Illinois: Richard D. Irwin, Inc.

Joseph, Hyman, 1976. On interdepartment pricing of not-for-profit hospitals, *Quarterly Review of Economics and Business* **16**: 33–44.

Kennedy, Edward M., 1979. Health care for all Americans act, *Challenge* **22**: 5–10.

Klarman, Herbert E., 1965. Syphilis control programs, in *Measuring Benefits of Government Investments*, Robert Dorfman (ed.), pp. 367–410, Washington, D.C.: Brookings Institution.

Klarman, Herbert E., 1974. Major public initiative in health care, *The Public Interest* **34**: 106–123.

Klarman, Herbert E., 1977. The financing of health care, in *Doing Better and Feeling Worse: Health in the United States*, John H. Knowles (ed.), pp. 215–234, New York: W.W. Norton & Company Inc.

Manga, Pran, 1978. *The Income Distribution Effect of Medical Insurance in Ontario*, Toronto: Ontario Economic Council.

Marr, W.L., D.J. McCready, and F.W. Millerd, 1980. Canadian internal migration of medical personnel. *Growth and Change*, forthcoming.

Marshall, Alfred, 1920. *Principles of Economics*, Eighth ed., London: Macmillan and Company.

Mason, H.R., 1971. Effectiveness of student aid programs tied to a service commitment, *Journal of Medical Education* **46**: 580–581.

McCready, Douglas J., and Conrad J. Winn, 1975. *Social Class and Health Care Benefits Among Consumers in Ontario: A Pilot Study of Some Problems of Research*. Mimeographed for Ontario Economic Council.

McCready, Douglas J., and Conrad J. Winn, 1978. A note on regional differences in health care usage in Ontario, *Growth and Change* **9**: 8–14.

McFarland, J., 1973. The physicians' location decision, in *Profile of Medical Practice*, 1973, pp. 89–97, Chicago: American Medical Association.

Mushkin, Selma J., 1958. Toward a definition of health economics, *Public Health Reports* **73**: 785–793.

Mushkin, Selma J., 1962. Health as an investment, *Journal of Political Economy* 70, 5, Pt. **2**: 129–157.

Newhouse, J., 1973. The economics of group practice, *Journal of Human Resources* **8**: 37–56.

Olendzki, M.C., R.P. Gramm, and C.H. Goodrich, 1972. The impact of medicaid on private care for the urban poor, *Medical Care* **10**: 201–206.

Pauly, M.V., and Drake, D.F., 1970. Effect of third party methods of reimbursement on hospital performance, in *Empirical Studies in Health Economics*, H.E. Klarman (ed.), pp. 297–314, Baltimore: The Johns Hopkins Press.

Perlman, Mark, 1974. Economic history and health care in industrialized nations, in *The Economics of Health and Medical Care*, Mark Perlman (ed.), pp. 21–33, London: The Macmillan Press Ltd.

Peterson, O.L., L.P. Andrews, R.S. Spain, and B.G. Greenberg, 1956. An analytical study of North Carolina general practice 1953–1954, *Journal of Medical Education* **31**: 1–165.

Reinhardt, U.E., and K.R. Smith, 1974. Manpower substitution in ambulatory care, in *Health Manpower and Productivity*, John Rafferty (ed.), pp. 3–37, Lexington, Mass.: Lexington Books.

Reiser, Stanley Joel, 1977. Therapeutic choice and moral doubt in a technological age, in *Doing Better and Feeling Worse: Health in the United States*, John J. Knowles, (ed.), pp. 47–56, New York: W.W. Norton & Company.

Roemer, M.I., and Shonick, W., 1973. HMO performance: The recent evidence, *Health and Society* **51**: 271–318.

Ruchlin, Hirsch S., and Daniel C. Rogers 1973. *Economics and Health Care*, Springfield, Illinois: Charles C. Thomas.

Ruderman, P., 1976. The political economy of fee-setting and the future of fee-for-service, in *Health Economics Symposium*, R.D. Fraser (ed.), pp. 75–90, Kingston, Ontario: Industrial Relations Centre, Queen's University.

Rule, Sheila, 1979. *Inner Cities' Hospitals Vanishing in Wake of Sharply Rising Costs*, New York Times, Sept. 2, p. 1.

Salkever, David, 1972. A microeconomic study of hospital cost inflation, *Journal of Political Economy* **80**: 1160–1161.

Schneider, J., and L.B. Twiggs, 1972. The costs of carcinoma of the cervix, *Obstetrics and Gynecology* **40**: 851–859.

Soderstorm, Lee, 1978. *The Canadian Health System*, London: Croom–Helm.

Somers, H.M., and A.R. Somers, 1967. *Medicare and the Hospitals, Issues and Prospects*, Washington, D.C.: The Brookings Institution.

Somers, H.M., and A.R. Somers, 1972. Major issues in national health insurance, *Millbank Memorial Fund Quarterly* **50**: 177–210.

Sorkin, Alan L., 1975. *Health Economics*, Lexington, Mass.: Lexington Books.

United Nations, 1979. *United Nations Demographic Yearbook, 1978*, New York: United Nations.

U.S. Congress, Senate, Subcommittee on Antitrust and Monopoly of the Committee on the Judiciary, 1960. *Hearings on Administered Prices in the Drug Industry*, Washington D.C.: Government Printing Office.

United States Department of Health Education and Welfare 1967. Report of the national advisory commission on health manpower, Vol. II, Appendix 4. The Kaiser Foundation Medical Care Program. Washington D.C.: Government Printing Office.

Van Matre, J.G., and J.M. Miller, 1974. Spinal cord injury – A cost-benefit analysis of alternative treatment modals, *Paraplegia* 12: 222–231.

Vayda, Eugene, 1973. A comparison of surgical rates in Canada and in England and Wales, *The New England Journal of Medicine* 289: 135–144.

Weisbrod, Burton A., 1960. *Economics of Public Health: Measuring the Economic Impact of Diseases*, Philadelphia: University of Pennsylvannia Press.

Weisbrod, Burton A., 1971. Costs and benefits of medical research: A case study of poliomyelitis, *Journal of Political Economy* 80: 527–544.

Yett, Donald E., 1970. The nursing shortage, in *Empirical Studies in Health Economics*, H.E. Klarman (ed.), pp. 357–389, Baltimore: Johns Hopkins Press. 1973 in *Health Economics: Selected Readings*, M.H. Cooper and A.J. Culyer (eds.), pp. 172–209, Harmondsworth, England: Penguin Books, Ltd.

Zubkoff, Michael, and Ira E. Raskin, 1977. *Hospital Cost Containment: Selected Notes for Future Policy*, New York: Millbank Memorial Fund.

5 Medical Geography

R. W. Armstrong

MEDICAL GEOGRAPHY has been a focus of study for centuries. Its basic principle is that the things that condition human health, like all other phenomena on the earth's surface, are subject to a universal geographical variable. Geographical variations in matters of health and disease, like temporal variations, are fundamental facts and of common interest to many scientific disciplines. Each discipline brings to bear its own concepts and methodologies in attempting to explain geographical variations so that there has been a wealth of ideas as to the nature and purpose of medical geography. At the same time there has been considerable sharing of concepts and methods and the emergence of interdisciplinary ideas. On the principle itself there is little disagreement: medical geography is a field of study because matters of health and disease exhibit geographical variation.

History

In a recently published textbook, one of the first in many years in medical geography, Gerald F. Pyle (1979: 3) suggests that an understanding of medical geography is best developed within an evolutionary context. A brief historical perspective is certainly essential to an explanation of the current status of the subject. We begin with the writings of Greek scholars in the fifth and fourth centuries B.C. in which are found the earliest recorded observations of geographical variations in the health of populations and the diseases that affected them. At about this time, many Greek thinkers were rejecting belief in the supernatural as the cause of disease and accepting the idea that natural factors in the environment

167

might have a relationship to disease. Scholars such as Herodotus and Hippocrates applied knowledge of the geography of illnesses, weather, topography, water, agriculture, and social behavior to the practice of medicine. Illnesses of people were found to differ from place to place almost as soon as physicians began to travel. Some places were recognized as being healthier than others and these variations were ascribed to the nature of the local people, their environment, and their behavior.

Medical geography became part of the Greek philosophy and teaching of medicine, and a diagnostic and therapeutic tool for physicians. Patients were questioned about where and how they lived for information useful to diagnosis, and they might be advised to seek remedy for their illness by changing some pattern of their lifestyle or their environment as by moving to a different climate. Medical geography become part of Western medical teaching and practice until late in the nineteenth century.

Barkhuus (1945a), in an excellent history of medical geography, recognizes the early descriptions of places, such as towns, cities, districts or entire countries, written by physicians as being "medical surveys." They were descriptions of people and places, the known diseases that afflicted them, the local methods of treatment, and beliefs as to cause. They lacked precision as to location or time of events, or any systematic collection of data. These medical surveys became more voluminous as Europeans began to travel to Asia, the Americas, and Africa. The diaries of travellers in the sixteenth and seventeenth centuries contain a wealth of descriptive information on the geography of medicine that had been observed in different places. It was not until the eighteenth century and the beginning of systematic collection of data in tabular form, of mapping, and of measurement that knowledge of medical geography was subjected to systematic and comprehensive study.

The systematic description of the geography of disease began with "medical topography." Medical topographies were included with the sanitary reports of medical officers of the eighteenth century in Europe. They were detailed descriptions of particular towns, cities, or districts under the medical officer's charge which dealt with "health conditions, meteorologic and hydrographic data, plants, and the mode of life of the inhabitants" (Rosen 1953: 187). They incorporated data on the demography and vital statistics of their communities including morbidity and mortality, and measurements of geographical factors such as weather, soil, landforms and vegetation. Medical topographies were recognized at the time as being important in official evaluation of laws and regulations made for the protection of health in different countries (Barkhuus 1945b: 1998). They varied considerably in their consistency of detail, in their critical evaluation of sources, and their reference to time. There was a static quality to the writings as though people, places and disease were fixed in time, and the authors had little apparent concern for change.

One of the first major attempts to describe the medical geography of many places in a single work was that of Finke who drew primarily on published medical topographies and on the journals of travellers to assemble in 1792, a three volume encyclopedia that was global in its treatment. Finke was concerned with principles to guide the writing of geographical medicine as illustrated in the following passage:

It must from the nature of the soil, the air, from the habits of the people, etc., understand the origin, development, increase and decrease of disease. It must show why in one country this, in another that disease is prevalent. It must further show what means are used in the different countries against disease. For that reason, all medicines, hospitals, etc., must be described. Obviously, a good topography is absolutely necessary. We must go further than Hippocrates and describe the foods, clothes, habits, and education of the people. Numbers of births and deaths are important . . . .

(Barkhuus, 1945b, p. 2001)

Finke had considerable influence on the work that followed in the nineteenth century. Among the more important writers of this time were Schnurrer, Boudin, Fuchs, Meuhry, Drake, and Hirsch, all of whom became increasingly concerned with tabulation and comparative analysis of physiological, pathological, and environmental data. Daniel Drake, a Cincinnati physician and medical educator, wrote a distinctive two-volume medical topography of the Ohio Valley (Drake 1850) which remains a classic of its kind. August Hirsch, also a physician and professor, in Berlin, wrote a textbook (Hirsch 1883–1886) that became a classic in medicine. From the time of its first appearance in 1860, his *Handbook of Geographical and Historical Pathology* was a major text in Western schools of medicine and remained so for 25 years. It was the last such work in medical geography to serve as a major component in the education of physicians. Written in the Hippocratic tradition, the text used a geographical analysis of the natural history of disease as the framework for presentation of content. The approach was holistic and forced a comprehensive view of the likely causes of disease in the physical, biological and cultural environments of human beings, and in their individual physiology and behavior. There was reference to microparasites but in non-specific ways. Although in broad concept the work was an anticipation of the ecological approaches to come, it lacked synthesis that might have led to principles or sharp concepts. The theories of evolution, genetics, bacteriology, chemistry, and physics that were about to transform medicine were entirely lacking in the essentially descriptive work of Hirsch.

The revolution in medicine that came with the science of bacteriology saw the demise of medical geography as a substantive part of modern Western medical curricula. Geography gradually disappeared as a subject of direct concern in the training of physicians and by 1940 it could be said that: "the very concept of a geography of diseases had been virtually erased from the memory of the practicing physician" (Ackerknecht 1965:1). In the first half of the twentieth century it was geographers, epidemiologists, and pathologists who did most to develop concepts, methods, and applications in medical geography.

Emerging Concepts

Geographers were chiefly concerned with environmental factors as causes of disease, especially weather and climate. The concept of environmental determinism dominated geographers' thinking in the early part of the century forcing an emphasis on the elements of the physical environment as "factors" in "determining" geographical distributions and relations. Huntington (1924) and McKinley (1935) are representative in their emphases on climate as a cause of geographical variations in disease. Perhaps the most important contribution by geographers at this time was in the development of cartography and the mapping of geographical distributions. For the first time precise and detailed topographical maps of large areas were being produced by national land survey agencies, and thematic atlases of environmental elements were being prepared by geographers, both of which were essential to the mapping of disease and the study of environmental associations.

Epidemiologists continued to be concerned with the geography of disease because spatial distributions are often important in the analysis of an epidemiological problem. Snow's famous map of cholera cases in London in 1854 is still cited as an example (MacMahon and Pugh 1970: 149); but mapping of the incidence of disease cases quickly became an established epidemiological routine. In 1900, cancer was a disease for which bacteriology did not have an obvious etiological explanation, and its geographical distribution of cases continued to be studied in terms of possible relations to geological formations and soils (Haviland 1892); and to "cancer houses," residences where multiple cases occurred (Brand 1902), until it was shown that such clusterings were a function of the age of the residents (Stocks 1935). Other examples at this time of epidemiological interest in the medical geography of disease were the studies of the spread of successive epidemics of cholera and plague in Asia, and the mapping in the 1930's of iodine deficient soils in relation to the occurrence of goitre.

The Second World War with its massive movements of troops throughout Europe, North Africa, Asia, and the Pacific sparked considerable work in the geography of those diseases likely to be encountered by armies. The Nazi military made use of an atlas of endemic diseases of the Balkans that was expanded after the war into a world atlas (Rodenwalt and Jusatz 1952 – 61). Allied forces relied more on written reports, some of which were later published (Simmons et al. 1944).

Pathologists have long recognized the value of comparative study of pathological conditions in different parts of the world. Reference collections of pathological specimens from different cultures and environments were developed in several countries after 1900. The museum of the Armed Forces Institute of Pathology in association with the Smithsonian Institution in Washington, D.C., is an example. Geographical pathology is almost a synonym for medical geography except that its chief interest is in the pathology of disease, and it is carried out by pathologists (Doll 1959; Hopps 1977). Beginning in 1931, the International Society of Geographical Pathology served as a forum for scientific papers and a series of international conferences, each focused on a specific disease topic. The subjects of these conferences emphasized chronic diseases such as cancers, cerebrovascular disease, and heart disease. Most attention at this time was given to geographical variations in pathological and clinical conditions, and less to physical, biological, and cultural environments or to human behaviors in geographical association with disease. By 1960, however, there was more interest in a broader perspective for geographical pathology (Armstrong 1965), as seen in the work of the Subcommittee on Geographic Pathology of the U.S. National Academy of Sciences which functioned from 1962 to 1965.

An important advance in concept in medical geography took place after 1930 with the introduction of ecological perspectives chiefly by geographers and epidemiologists. Sorre (1947 – 52), a French geographer, incorporated early concepts of human ecology in his presentation of principles and a regional analysis of medical geography, which formed part of a major text in geography. Pavlovsky and other epidemiologists in the Soviet Union, working both before and after World War II, developed a field technique for rapid survey and mapping of potential zoonotic disease habitats. These maps were used in the selection of virgin lands in Soviet Central Asia for agricultural development with least risk of human disease. Based on ecological principles that viewed disease habitats as systems with natural foci in certain environments, the technique used geographical variables that could be easily surveyed, such as terrain, vegetation, climate, surface water, and insect and small animal populations. These variables were measured and mapped using criteria known to reflect characteristics of particular disease habitats. The method came to be called "landscape epidemiology" because in effect it recognized certain landscape as the likely habitats for disease, and was most successful for vector-born diseases such as relapsing fever and encephalitides where the habitats favorable for mosquitoes and ticks became the focus of study (Pavlovsky 1966).

A more sophisticated approach came from the work of Audy who was initially concerned with the ecology of scrub typhus in India, Burma and Malaysia, and later with assemblages of several diseases in particular communities and environments. Those diseases caused by microorganisms were seen to form part of general parasite patterns, and the variations in these parasite patterns were largely determined by geographical environment. Differences in parasite patterns were seen by Audy as being related to small scale geographical differences (Audy 1954).

A basic problem in medical geography is to find a practical method of sorting out from the complexities of particular places those geographical variations that are relevant to a disease study. Audy's suggestion was to use specific disease parasites as "ecological labels" of the assemblages of parasites and host animals which live in distinctive places, or habitats. Different populations of the same host species have different disease patterns and these variations are in large part a reflection of differences in environment and organism behavior from place to place. Audy found that the distribution patterns of his "ecological labels" were sufficiently specific and sensitive to detect subtle geographical variations in the assemblages of parasites and hosts (Audy 1958).

Audy's approach has seen little practical application because it requires a great deal of basic information about the natural history of disease parasites in particular places before the "ecological labels" can be drawn up. The fieldwork for this has not been done for most places in the world.

Modern Medical Geography

Since 1950 there has been a considerable resurgence in interest in medical geography involving an increasing number of scientists and with consequent advance in concepts, methodologies, and applications. There are many reasons for this, but among them must be the foresight of earlier workers in pointing directions, the rising interest in environment and behavior as major factors in disease etiology, the revolution in data availability and computer processing, and the development of scientific associations and outlets for regular publication.

Among the people who promoted medical geography in the 1950's, almost single-handedly in their respective countries, were Jacques May in the United States, Maximilien Sorre in France, and Andrew Learmonth and Melvyn Howe in the United Kingdom. A larger cadre of scientists was working in the Soviet Union (Markovin 1962). Through their publications they kept the field alive, particularly for geographers, and gave the encouragement and direction needed for younger scholars to join them. In 1964, L. Dudley Stamp, a distinguished British geographer, did much to give wider appeal to medical geography in Europe and America through a series of public lectures and a paperback volume written in popular style (Stamp 1965).

Medical geography was stimulated by the generally increasing interest in environmental and behavioral interactions as causes of disease. Concepts of multifactorial associations and ecosystems replaced single-factor hypotheses for disease etiology which, by definition, drew in biological and cultural environments and behaviors as at least the context for disease processes. These concepts were applied to health concerns in the different cultural and environmental contexts of developing countries, to degenerative disease, behavioral illness, and accident problems that were seen to have their roots in human environments and behaviors, to emerging problems of environmental pollution, and to problems of equitable distribution of health and medical services.

The application of the concepts that gave new purpose for medical geography was in large part made possible by the development of computers and information science. The ability to handle large volumes of data led in turn to social surveys on a new and vaster scale, and the undertaking of complex field research studies that were impractical in the past. Computers allowed quantification to proceed at a faster pace and the application of mathematical models to the behavioral, social, and medical sciences.

Communication of ideas through professional associations and journals identified with medical geography was important in giving momentum to advances in concept and method. From 1949 to 1976 the Commission on Medical Geography of the International Geographical Union functioned as a forum for exchanging ideas. The medical geographical section of the Hungarian Geographical Society published three annual volumes of papers in medical geography from 1966 to 1968 (Hungary 1966), and the Commission continued publication with two more volumes under the title of *Geographia Medica* (Commission on Medical Geography 1969 – 70), but the series did not survive. Soviet medical geography crystallized at a conference in 1962 (Shkurlatov 1963), and numerous publications appeared in geographical and biological science journals (Gelyakova *et al.* 1967). In the United States in 1979 a medical geography section emerged in the Association of American Geographers, and a section was proposed for the American Public Health Association. The International Society of Biometeorology, founded in 1956, and the Society for Environmental Geochemistry and Health (USA) in 1971, are two examples of several other organizations concerned with particular aspects of medical geography. The initiation of an English-language journal devoted to medical geography took place in 1978 when *Social Science and Medicine* created one section for this purpose.

Recent Advances

The objective of medical geography is to explain the significance of the geographical variable in questions of health and disease in ways that contribute to an understanding of those questions. In recent years the subject has achieved this objective in greater detail and with more precise measurement, using new concepts and methods, and applied to a wide variety of subject areas at the full range of geographical scales – from international through national, regional, urban, household/family, to individual persons.

Increased quantification of data measurement and analysis in the last twenty years has been a key element in crystallizing concepts and methods and allowing more vital application. May (1950) pointed the direction in a paper that provided a provisional correlation of disease related factors (pathogens) and environmental and behavioral factors (geogens). The correlation, regression, or factor analyses that were anticipated by this work were not applied until the mid-sixties in limited ways, for example, by Girt (1972) in the correlation of bronchitis and urban structure in the city of Leeds. Multivariate analyses were an obvious tool to apply to the problem of extracting a few significant variables from the maze that exists in any medico-geographical question. But the application has so far been of limited success either because data do not exist for precisely those variables that are relevant, or they are not on the levels of measurement needed for the analytic tools. Much has been done to refine the potential application of multivariate techniques and experience has led to guidance in procedures. For example, Pyle (1979) has outlined a modeling sequence using univariate, bivariate, and multivariate steps.

Measures of association have been more successful in applications that parallel epidemiological research, as in studies involving individual patients and control subjects, or specific populations. The statistical significance of the association of geographical variables and individual subjects is examined in the context of case and control 2×2 contingency tables. The relative risk is calculated as an odds ratio and statistical significance evaluated by chi-square. Confounding between variables is usually examined by log-linear correlation techniques. Associations between populations and geographical variables have been most often examined as mapped distributions and the statistical significance tested in terms of relative randomness. Case-control designs that have examined associations between geographical variables and a disease have not seen frequent application (Armstrong *et al.* 1978), although the method is clearly the most important for study of individual subjects. More widely applied has been the examination of spatial distributions of population, disease, and other geographical factors (McGlashan and Chick 1974; Rose and McGlashan 1975). A major contribution from this kind of work has been to draw attention to geographical variations and to indicate the potential research importance of the spatial aspect of epidemiology.

Geographers, generally, in recent years have been grappling with the problem of spatial analysis and particularly with trying to apply abstract mathematical models to real situations. In medical geography there has been some success in attempting to describe the diffusion of communicable diseases through space and time. Brownlea (1972) applied a random-walk model to the spread of an infectious hepatitis epidemic in an urban population in New South Wales, and Haggett (1972) planar graphs and network theory to the spread of measles in southern England. These and other studies attempt to fit a mathematical model to a spatial process already described in less quantitative terms, with the objective of obtaining a more accurate and precise model of the pattern which could then have general application. So far the achievement of general models has been elusive and a major advance in the offing is for someone to synthesize from the growing number of specific applications a general model with clear utility.

More success has been obtained from less quantitative applications. The diffusion concept was used by Hunter (1972) to support a hypothesis to explain the historical cycle of advance and retreat of populations from river valleys in Ghana due to the spread of onchocerciasis over time. Other descriptive studies of the spread of major epidemics of plague and cholera represent important contributions to the history of epidemics.

Difficulties in the synthesis of general models have also appeared in work attempting to apply ecological systems concepts. Theoretically there are many attractions to ecological concepts in medical geography. Human health may be viewed as successful adaptation to physical, biological, and cultural components of the environment. Disease and other kinds of obstacles to human health, that are not strictly genetic in origin, arise from the environment and behavior of individuals. Logically, we may examine disease and other such obstacles to health in the context of an ecological system of population, behavior, and environment. The universal geographical variable in this system is the special concern of medical geography. But there have been many barriers to the successful application of broad concepts to specific questions such as lack of precise theory, insufficient data, and often weak communication between scientists representing the various biological and social science disciplines.

Nevertheless, there has been a growing number of discrete studies that could lead to a distillation of general ideas and methods in the near future. Much of the Soviet work into the ecology of vector-borne diseases; the studies of possible relationships between African Burkitt's Lymphoma, climate, altitude, and a hypothesized vector for a virus; and work into possible geochemical associations with disease are in this vein. Important results have come from studies that attempt an ecological approach even though weak in theory and method. For example, Prothero (1965) demonstrated the significance of migrants in the transmission of malaria in northeastern Africa; Fonaroff (1968) the spatial and temporal interactions in malaria transmission in Trinidad; Meade (1976) the significance of a number of diseases in the social and economic success of new land development settlements in Malaysia; and Roundy (1978) relationships between disease patterns and transhumance in Ethiopia.

Maps are the hallmark tools of geographers and they have the capacity to show at once the geographic position, distribution, arrangement, and association of mapped phenomena. The application of mapping in medical geography continues to be hampered by problems with data. It is often non-existent for many parts of the world, it often varies in level and kind of measurement, and it often lacks geographical identification or coding as, for example, mortality data that do not give precise information on place of death. One major advance with considerable technical potential has been the application of computers to store and process data and to plot computer graphics, including maps. The Geographic Pathology Division of the Armed Forces Institute of Pathology (Hopps *et al.* 1968) undertook a pioneering effort to develop a computerized system for mapping disease, coupled with a comprehensive file of ecological factors. The project demonstrated that it was feasible to develop a system whereby disease and environmental data could be processed together to produce maps for particular places and time periods. It identified the major problems of data availability, comparability, and precision all of which can be expected to improve in time. The World Health Organization has continued to experiment with computerized mapping systems, and with the increasing availability of vital statistics and other health related data that have been coded geographically, there has been rapid development in computer mapping applications to such areas as health services planning.

Specialties

Activity in medical geography has become focused around a number of special areas of interest. The most prominent of these in recent years are the following:

Historical medical geography and the geography of health and disease in particular regions and places is the classical area of interest for geographers expressed as much in maps as in books and articles. The work of Howe (1972) in historical medical geography, and of Howe (1977) and Learmonth (1979) in the geography of diseases in the present is at the forefront of work of this kind. Several recent atlases of diseases have made important contributions to epidemiological research as, for example, in pointing up concentrations of incidence of cancers of the liver and bladder in local populations with certain industries (Mason *et al.* 1975). *Geographical epidemiology* has been advanced by both geographers and epidemiologists chiefly in terms of improved research design and data analysis. It has flourished in those research areas where the geographical aspects of the distribution and determinants of disease or other obstacles to health in populations can be more readily approached, as in vector-borne diseases, and in those diseases where incidence by geographic occurrence is carefully recorded (as by cancer registries). Computer mapping is being applied in epidemiology in more statistically rigorous form and there is increasing research into refinement of techniques (United States 1979). Least advance has taken place where epidemiology is also weak, as in psychiatric and psychological concerns and in deaths from violence.

Geographic pathology continues to be advanced principally by pathologists but with strong input from epidemiology and clinical medicine. It has made important contributions to the histological differentiation of certain cancers and revealed that each specific histological type may have a distinct epidemiology. International comparisons have found differences in the frequency of a number of disorders of the intestine such as ulcers, diverticulosis, and appendicitis. Newly discovered diseases have had their geographic pathology established: for example, in the case of primary amebic meningoencephalitis and Burkitt's Lymphoma a widespread geographical distribution, and in the case of Kuru a very limited distribution in New Guinea. Geographic pathology has also made effective use of maps in much of the recent work and in all respects is one of the strongest branches of medical geography.

Nutritional geography is an area of great potential but remains comparatively less developed in part because few people with sufficient knowledge of nutrition and geography have come to work in it. Jacques May and others (May and McLellan 1974) prepared a series of works for several world regions on the ecology of malnutrition. Although providing important insights into the inter-relationships between nutrition, health, and socioeconomic development these works did not have much impact on political policy or science because they were not focused at operational levels for administrators, and they were descriptive rather than analytical and soon out-of-date. Nutritional geography faces the same problems as nutritional science in general in attempting to measure the nutritional status of communities, and their actual diets and food supplies. Significant advances may have to await developments in field survey techniques.

Biometeorology is concerned with interrelationships between weather, climate, and season and biology, including human health and disease, and becomes a specialty for medical geography whenever associations with place become a focus. There has been a laboratory emphasis to much of the recent work as in the search for clarification of physiological responses to stresses of heat, cold, and altitude. The development of crude indices of 'comfort' for excessive heat and humidity, and for air pollution, have many geographical research implications but these have not been taken up. There is need to synthesize and apply purely biometeorologic work to geographical contexts. The effects of seasonal variation and other temporal variation on incidence and mortality patterns are beginning to receive attention in a number of countries, an interest stimulated chiefly by work in Japan (Sakamoto-Momiyama 1977).

Environmental geochemistry and its relationships with health has become an important interdisciplinary area for geologists, geochemists, geographers, and medical scientists. Evidence is accumulating that a number of trace elements, either in excess or deficiency, are associated with promoting or reducing risk for several diseases. For example, a rather consistent and significant geographic association has been demonstrated between deaths from heart disease and hardness of drinking water (Hopps 1979). Other work has demonstrated geographic associations between disease and natural and man-made radiation, and chemical pollution of foodchains. Considerable progress has been made in better understanding the pathways that link, say, trace elements in a Californian soil with the chemical composition of the diet of a disease patient in New Jersey. Mapping of the counties of the United States that produce speci-fied crops, studies of food origin and distribution, and surveys of dietary habits have all contributed to a sharper assessment of the relative im-portance of the geography of trace elements.

Health and medical services. As planning for more equitable health and medical services has become of growing concern to most nations, there has been need to understand spatial and temporal dimensions of patient behavior and of service location. The most advanced applications of medical geography in this specialty are to be found in those countries with national health services where population distribution and travel time were seen as basic considerations in planning for the distribution of services, as in the Soviet Union and in Sweden. In the United States, where national health planning legislation has preceded national health insurance legislation, the efforts to apply medical geography to locational issues have been so far less evident. Shannon and Dever (1974) provide an overview of the potential importance of geographic factors in health and medical services planning in the United States, and a review of the application of medical geography to this field. Since 1970 there has been a great deal of work in specific applications, such as the location of community clinics for mental health and family planning, emergency ambulance service location and time-distance analysis, hospital location, and patient-origin and physician preference for office location. There has been some work in association with medical anthropology in cross-cultural studies of medical services and traditions from a geographical perspective.

Conclusion

Medical geography is emerging as a more scientific and coherent field than it has been in the past. It continues to be dominated by several disciplines and to reflect the particular theories, methodologies, and preferred applications of those disciplines. The universal geographical variable has yet to be approached with universal theory and method but the trend is now clearly in that direction. The most important advances in recent years have been in the strengthening of concepts, methods, and precision of measurement to permit more effective application to vital geographical issues in the environmental and behavioral aspects of health and disease. The resurgence of diseases such as malaria and schistosomiasis, as a result of biological or cultural changes, are changing the map for these diseases in significant ways. Environmental pollution by chemicals and radiation have important spatial and temporal concerns. The recognition of environmental factors as being critical in the etiology of major causes of death such as cancer, heart disease, and accidents, presses for greater understanding of the geography of these factors. And the concern for equitable distribution of health and medical services calls for geographic inputs. These kinds of concerns assure the future significance of medical geography. As Shannon (1979: 2) recently put it: "The challenge is to develop an educated and viable medical geography community that will meet the challenge to provide input to analysis and solution of the problems."

REFERENCES CITED

Ackerknecht, Erwin H., 1965. *History and Geography of the Most Important Diseases*, New York: Hafner.

Armstrong, R. Warwick, 1965. Medical geography – an emerging specialty?, *International Pathology* **6**: 61–63.

Armstrong, R. Warwick, M. Kannan Kutty, and M. Jocelyn Armstrong, 1978. Self-specific environments associated with nasopharyngeal carcinoma in Selangor, Malaysia, *Social Science and Medicine* **12D**: 149–156.

Audy, J. Ralph, 1954. A biological approach to medical geography, *British Medical Journal* **1**: 960–962.

Audy, J. Ralph, 1958. The localization of disease with special reference to the zoonoses, *Transactions of the Royal Society of Tropical Medicine and Hygiene* **52**: 308–334.

Barkhuus, Arne, 1945a. Medical surveys from Hippocrates to the world travellers, *Ciba Symposia* **6**: 1986–1996.

Barkhuus, Arne, 1945b. Medical geographies, *Ciba Symposia* **6**: 1997–2016.

Brand, A.T., 1902. The etiology of cancer, *British Medical Journal* **11**: 238–242.

Brownlea, Arthur A., 1972. Modelling the geographic epidemiology of infectious hepatitis, in *Medical Geography: Techniques and Field Studies*, Neil D. McGlashan (ed.), pp. 279–300, London: Methuen.

Commission on Medical Geography, 1969–70. *Geographia Medica*, International Journal of Medical Geography, Vol. **1**, 1969–70; Vol. **2**, 1971. International Geographical Union and Hungarian Geographical Society. Budapest: Semmelweis Medical University Press.

Doll, Richard, (ed.), 1959. *Method of Geographical Pathology*, Springfield, Ill.: Charles C. Thomas.

Drake, Daniel, 1850. *A Systematic Treatise, Historical, Etiological, and Practical, on the Principal Diseases of the Interior Valley of North America*, Cincinnati: W.B. Smith

Fonaroff, L. Schyler, 1968. The decline of malaria in Trinidad, *West Indian Medical Journal* **17**: 14–21.

Gelyakova, T.M., A.G. Voronov, V.B. Nefedova, and G.S. Samoylova, 1967. The present state of medical geography in the U.S.S.R., *Soviet Geography* **8**: 228–234.

Girt, John L., 1972. Simple chronic bronchitis and urban ecological structure, in *Medical Geography: Techniques and Field Studies*, Neil D. McGlashan (ed.), pp. 211–231, London: Methuen.

Haggett, Peter, 1972. Contagious processes in a planar graph: An epidemiological application, in *Medical Geography: Techniques and Field Studies*, Neil D. McGlashan (ed.), pp.307–324, London: Methuen.

Haviland, Alfred, 1892. *Geographical Distribution of Disease in Great Britain*, London: Sonnenschein.

Hirsch, August, 1883–1886. *Handbook of Geographical and Historical Pathology*, 3 vols. Translated by C. Creighton. London: New Sydenham Society.

Hopps, Howard C., Roger J. Cuffey, Jerome Morenoff, Wayne L. Richmond, and Joseph D.H. Sidley, 1968. *The Mapping of Disease (MOD) Project*, Washington, D.C.: Joint Report of the Universities Associated for Research and Education in Pathology and the Armed Forces Institute of Pathology, Geographic Pathology Division.

Hopps, Howard C., 1977. Geographic pathology, in *Pathology*, William A.D. Anderson and J.M. Kissane (eds.), pp. 692–736, St. Louis: Mosby.

Hopps, Howard C., 1979. The geochemical environment in relationship to health and disease, *Interface (Society for Environmental Geochemistry and Health)* **8**: 24–29.

Howe, G. Melvyn, 1972. *Man, Environment and Disease in Britain*, Newton Abbot: David and Charles.

Howe, G. Melvyn (ed.), 1977. *A World Geography of Human Diseases*, London: Academic Press.

Hungary, 1966. *Geographia Medica Hungary*, Vol. 1, 1966; Vol. 2, 1967; Vol. 3, 1968. Budapest: Hungarian Geographical Society.

Hunter, John M., 1972. River blindness in Nangodi, Northern Ghana: A hypothesis of cyclical advance and retreat, in *Medical Geography: Techniques and Field Studies*, Neil D. McGlashan (ed.), pp. 261–278, London: Methuen.

Huntington, Ellsworth, 1924. *Civilization and Climate*, 3d. ed. New Haven: Yale University Press.

Learmonth, Andrew T.A., 1979. *Patterns of Disease and Hunger: A Study in Medical Geography*, Newton Abbot: David and Charles.

MacMahon, Brian, and Thomas F. Pugh, 1970. *Epidemiology Principles and Methods*, Boston: Little, Brown.

Markovin, A.P., 1962. Historical sketch of the development of Soviet medical geography, *Soviet Geography* **3**: 3–19.

Mason, Thomas J., Frank W. McKay, Robert Hoover, William J. Blot, and Joseph F. Fraumeni, Jr., 1975. *Atlas of Cancer Mortality for U.S. Counties: 1950–1969*, Washington, D.C.: Department of Health, Education, and Welfare Publication No. (NIH) 75–780.

May, Jacques M., 1950. Medical geography: Its methods and objectives, *Geographical Review* **40**: 9–41.

May, Jacques M., and Donna L. McLellan, 1974. *The Ecology of Malnutrition in Eastern South America*, New York: Hafner.

McGlashan, Neil D., and Neil K. Chick, 1974. Assessing spatial variations in mortality: Ischaemic heart disease in *Tasmania*. *Australian Geographical Studies* **12**: 190–206.

McKinley, Earl B., 1935. *A Geography of Disease*, Washington: George Washington University Press.

Meade, Melinda S., 1976. Land development and human health in West Malaysia, *Annals Association of American Geographers* **66**: 428–439.

Pavlovsky, Evgeny N., 1966. *Natural Nidality of Transmissible Diseases*, Norman D. Levine (ed.), Urbana, Ill.: University of Illinois Press.

Prothero, R. Mansell, 1965. *Migrants and Malaria*, London: Longmans.

Pyle, Gerald F., 1979. *Applied Medical Geography*, New York: John Wiley.

Rodenwalt, Ernst, and Helmut J. Jusatz (eds.), 1952–1961. *World Atlas of Epidemic Diseases*, 3 vols. Hamburg: Falk.

Rose, E.F., and Neil D. McGlashan, 1975. The spatial distribution of oesophageal carcinoma in the Transkei, South Africa, *British Journal of Cancer* **31**: 197–206.

Rosen, George, 1953. Leonhard Ludwig Finke and the first medical geography, in *Science, Medicine and History*, E.A. Underwood (ed.), Vol. 2. pp. 186–193, London: Oxford University Press.

Roundy, Robert W., 1978. A model for combining human behavior and disease ecology to assess disease hazard in a community: Rural Ethiopia as a model. *Social Science and Medicine* **12D**: 121–130.

Sakamoto-Momiyama, Masako, 1977. *Seasonality in Human Mortality: A Medico-Geographical Study*, Tokyo: University of Tokyo Press.

Shannon, Gary W., and G.E. Alan Dever, 1974. *Health Care Delivery: Spatial Perspectives*, New York: McGraw-Hill.

Shannon, Gary W., 1979. Editor's Corner, *Medical Geography Newsletter* (Department of Geography, University of Kentucky, Lexington) Vol. 2, June.

Shkurlatov, O.V., 1963. The first Soviet conference on problems in medical geography, *Soviet Geography* **4**: 55–57.

Simmons, James S., Tom F. Whayne, Gaylord W. Anderson, and Harold M. Horack, 1944. *Global Epidemiology, A Geography of Disease and Sanitation*, Philadelphia: Lippincott.

Sorre, Maximilien, 1947–52. L'organisme humain en lutte contre le milieu vivant, in *Les Fondements de la Géographie Humaine*, Livre III, pp. 291–419. Paris: A. Colin.

Stamp, L. Dudley, 1965. *The Geography of Life and Death*, Ithaca: Cornell University Press.

Stocks, Percy, 1935. The frequency of cancer deaths in the same house and in neighbouring houses, *Journal of Hygiene* **35**: 46–63.

United States, 1979. Department of Health Education and Welfare, National Center for Health Statistics. *Proceedings of the 1976 Workshop on Automated Cartography and Epidemiology*, DHEW Publication No. (PHS) 79–1254. Washington, D.C.: U.S. Government Printing Office.

6 Medical Anthropology:
A Critical Appraisal

David Landy

Introduction

The field of medical anthropology, despite the fact that it has under-gone explosive growth both in literature and in the number of individuals identifying themselves as medical anthropologists, has suffered a number of "personality" problems. Reviewing books and articles that attempt to pronounce upon the area (e.g., Colson and Selby 1974; Fabrega 1972; Comaroff 1979; Kaufert and Kaufert 1979; Firth 1979; Scotch 1963; Foster 1974, 1976; Foster and Anderson 1978; Kleinman 1978; Landy 1977a; Lieban 1973; and many others), one comes to imagine that a host of afflictions plague writers in the field: What is the field? Where are the boundaries? Who are we? Are we doing "real" anthropology? Are we really medical behavioral science? Should we concentrate on the practical implications of sociomedical phenomena and risk alienating our "pure" colleagues, or shall we maintain our objective distance from the data and risk alienating our "applied" colleagues? These pains of split personality, identity diffusion, and alienation cannot be addressed here, although they are worthy of study by philosophers and historians of science as well as by medical anthropologists. Nor shall we go beyond the attempts already made by others to define the field. To paraphrase Descartes, "Medical anthropology exists, therefore it is!"

What is impressive to this participant observer and native is that the human group that calls itself by the name of medical anthropology is a lively, heterogeneous community, busily engaged in myriad activities, studying, thinking, and writing about behaviors of human collectivities and individuals in understanding and coping with disease and injury. Medical anthropologists constitute a strange and scattered tribe that unites once annually in a corroboree marked by reports of victories and defeats, divination toward prophesying future events, ritual drinking and eating, soul-searching and occasional confessionals, induction of new members and leaders, and discreet explorations of new niches by members who feel the ecological resources of old sites have been threateningly degraded. What I attempt here is not a "total" ethnography of this lively society, but rather a report on some of those victories and defeats.

It may be true, as Scotch (1963), Wellin (1977) and others have said, that medical anthropology is no more poverty-stricken in theory and conceptualization than the other fields of anthropological study. It is certainly true that anthropology has had both a public and private image of being a discipline long on data and short on theory. These images have provoked more than a little defensiveness on the part of anthropologists vis-à-vis their colleagues in other behavioral sciences, and medical anthropologists have been perhaps more defensive than others, in part because of the relative youth of the field and its "taint" of being an applied science. Although within medical anthropology there is a good deal of righteous indignation about why more scholars should be even more "applied" in their work (and some advocacy of a "purer" approach), it is worth noting that the major journal, the *American Anthropologist*, still groups book reviews in the field almost invariably under "Applied Anthropology," regardless of content, orientation, or subject matter. Such retrograde narrowness and provincialism have been noted as well by medical anthropologists in England (Comaroff 1979; Kaufert and Kaufert 1979; Firth 1979), where even those within British medical anthropology – admittedly "a small band" – tend to disdain the study of practical aspects of health and illness.

I believe it will be evident, by the end of this piece, that if there have been no theoretical or conceptual revolutions as yet in medical anthropology, and if it may still be suffering from self-doubt more than *amour propre*, it is a thriving field. Much of its literature, it seems to me, is of high quality, often teeming with new (or new ways of looking at old) theories and concepts, and trying out explanatory models that sometimes provide theoretical opportunities not only for medical anthropology but many other subdisciplines of anthropology as well. When Alland (1966) pointed out some time ago that medical anthropology offered huge potentials for ecological research in anthropology, and, by its very nature, could serve as a vital nexus among *all* branches of the discipline, he was close to the mark, and many of the studies reviewed herein bear him out.

It is true that we do not have an overarching theoretical approach that unites the field and that everyone agrees upon. A kind of ecological-evolutionary perspective, as Alland (1966, 1970) proposed, has achieved, I believe, a broad tacit consensus, and informs many of the more significant and provocative studies. Some variations of that approach are less widely accepted, for example, Alland's (1970) notion that one could apply a game-theory model to human cultural adaptation:

Such a game involves a population as one player and the environment as the other. One aspect of the environment's strategy involves periodic changes in such relatively simple variables as rainfall, wind velocity, and temperature. These may in turn lead to rather complex fluctuations in floral and faunal composition, including disease agents and their carriers. Such fluctuations may include changes in both numbers and types of organisms. Variations of this type occur even in relatively stable environments, even those upon which man has asserted a considerable mastery (Ibid.: 3).

One may make an analogy between a population or group and a player, although a group "developing a strategy" is a very different process than when it is done by a single individual. But the environment as a player? Rain, wind, and temperature as "relatively simple variables?" I suggest that game theory applied at this level will not hold up very well. Nevertheless, one can forget this aspect of Alland's model and use the other parts, having to do with the population developing minimax strategies not simply to win a "game" but to provide the basis for adaptive decision-making in dealing with ecological and social-cultural problems of adaptation. Alland's little book is the first to attempt to provide the kind of encompassing theory that many feel is needed in medical anthropology, and for that, as well as for many other reasons, it represents a significant contribution to the field.

As medical anthropological research and thinking continue to increase in breadth and depth, as goals and methods become more clearly focused and theoretical and conceptual models begin to pay richer dividends, the growing pains of adolescence will become transformed into the assurances and solidities of maturity. The conflicts of childhood with the parent discipline will be resolved by the mutual respect that comes with the recognition of parent and offspring that each has a place in the sun and much to offer each other. The achievements of many scholars whose work is represented herein, and of many, many more whose equally fine accomplishments could not be included because of space limitations, attest to the successful growth and maturation of medical anthropological studies. In my assessment and critique of their work I have concentrated more on strengths than on weaknesses. Thoughtful analysis requires that criticism be constructive, though far from muted. The kind of idol-smashing criticism that attempts to annihilate a body of work simply to reflect upon the superior intellect and acumen of the critic usually results in a hot flow of invective, endless recriminations in print, huge symposia at meetings of anthropologists, and enormous expenditures of energy shedding glaring heat and little light.

It will soon be time for one or more scholars to begin to assemble a history of medical anthropology, so that we may begin to gain both a theoretical and sociocultural perspective upon our field. A history of medical anthropology is important in itself, so that reviews and assessments such as this one as well as research, can be placed in a temporal and culture-historical framework. But it is also important as part of the history of general anthropology, of which it is and will be a significant part. Such a history should deal, of course, with the men and women, great and small, who have toiled in these vineyards, but more importantly it should attempt to assess their research and their ideas against the backdrop of the social and cultural currents swirling about them in their own societies and in their world. For better or worse medical anthropology is very much a reflection of, and a response to, the social and political actions of its times. Such a history would make us not only aware of the contributions and limitations of our disciplinary ancestors but would help to prevent the sin of what I would call *temporacentrism*, of using one's own time as a baseline against which to judge everything past, present, and future, and of blindly pouring old wine into new bottles because our historical ignorance makes us oblivious of the vintage of many "new" ideas.

My aim here is to move away from the necessarily synoptic periodic inventories of earlier reporters (Scotch 1963; Fabrega 1972; Colson and Selby 1974), although each of these had useful and important summary statements of the broad areas surveyed. I have selected nine topic areas on which to report. In those areas I have chosen from among those papers and books appearing mainly during the decade 1969–1979, although in each area I have also referred to earlier studies when it seemed useful and appropriate to do so, and when they could lend a temporal or theoretical perspective. The literature that one could say directly falls into medical anthropology is itself vast, covering most anthropological journals and a large number of specialized journals (for example, *Medical Anthropology, Social Science and Medicine, Culture, Medicine, and Psychiatry*, and at least a dozen others). In addition, many journals in history and in the other behavioral sciences (including such specialized periodicals as the *Journal of Health and Social Behavior*), and literally hundreds in medicine and the health professions, all carry articles from time to time of direct or indirect relevance to medical anthropology. Similarly, journals in the natural sciences and particularly in biological and biochemical research, carry much of interest.

Clearly, I could not attempt to survey all or even some of these. What I have done is to sample some more or less representative (as I see them) research and theoretical statements more or less directly lying within medical anthropology that bear upon the topic areas I have marked out. No doubt many readers will be disappointed not to find a favorite article or book here. The selections have been made not only for representativeness, but also because I felt they had something important to say, although they may not have always said it as I or others would have preferred. In many, perhaps most, instances, the contributions were not only substantive in terms of empirical findings, but they also offer new concepts or theories or endeavor to sharpen and refine existing ones.

If one views the massive outpouring of medical anthropological publications, the overall effect is staggering. Certainly we have come a long way from Scotch's (1963) original survey, and even from the more recent ones by Fabrega (1972) and Colson and Selby (1974). In less than two scant decades we have been established, at least in the United States, as an organization of about 2,000 members in the Society for Medical Anthropology. Evidently there was an intellectual and action vacuum into which we moved with near superabundance. Nowadays one is hard put to keep up with this overflowing stream, not to mention the need to continue one's acquaintance with other anthropological writings. The prospect is pleasing and exciting, and at times a bit frightening as one fears one's ability to embrace and assimilate it all (for this means reading in adjacent fields as well).

The aim of this essay is to highlight some of the kinds of things going on during (and before) 1969–1979 so that we may begin to perceive the outlines, however dim and shadowy, of where we have been, where we are, and where we may be going – or should be going. For the purposes of this reassessment I have tried to avoid the quick run-through of an exhaustive or encyclopedic survey. Such summations are handy ways to catch up quickly with what kinds of things have been appearing in the literature, and especially in the case of such reviews as Caudill (1953), Fabrega

(1972), Lieban (1973), Scotch (1963), and Polgar (1962, 1963), brief evaluations as well. What I have done here is to examine some examples of work in the topic areas selected in order to assess the following: research objectives; major findings; significance of the study for some aspect of medical anthropological interest; methodology and problems therein; and finally, a critique of each and a pointing up of what else might be done. (This analytic approach is not followed, for reasons which will be obvious, in assessing the volumes in the section, The Coming of Age of Medical Anthropology.) This has required examining most of the studies discussed in some detail, and therefore including fewer than one would have liked. Since I recently completed an anthology which in part also attempts to assess and place a large portion of the literature into theoretical context (Landy 1977a), I have occasionally used a few brief passages from that work, much modified, and with a good deal of rethinking since that work appeared.

I have not offered here a separate section on applied medical anthropology. As in the literature as a whole, many of the studies examined deal directly or indirectly with practical aspects of health care delivery, diagnosis and treatment, or some other factors. Such separation would only perpetuate the myth that there is, in fact, a real barrier between "pure" and "applied" research. Even idle tinkering unrelated to any perceived human problem may eventually have a practical pay-off. But if the history of science tells us anything, it destroys the misplaced notion, however some may still cling to it, that a "pure" science can avoid its applications or practical consequences; or, the reverse myth, that applied research will contribute little to "real" science. If professional organizations and editors of professional journals remain bemused by this imaginary dichotomy, it is they who are out of step with the real world. It is somewhat dismaying to find a prominent British anthropologist, Rosemary Firth (1979), comparing medical anthropology in England and the United States, and stating that while it may be true that American anthropologists are deeply involved in applied research, most of their counterparts in the British Isles are not, and furthermore, it would be best if they did not. She finds it an advantage that the anthropologist is closely involved with his/her informants while the sociologist or the physician is not, although "On his return, in writing up his notes he tends to remain in contemplative comparison of his material. The prolonged contact of the field work survey also yields a different kind of information from that collected by the sociologist, even when the latter practices

first-hand observation, and abandons his questionnaire and computer."
Firth urges not only that British anthropologists have done well to
remain aloof from the practical consequences of their work, but they
should also avoid the temptations of interdisciplinary research:

> It is my belief that, at root, modern anthropology is nearer to a humanist philosophy than
> to a reforming social science today. Such a view may be no more than a personal predilection.
> But it may be worth considering, in the light of the history of frustration generated between
> medicine and anthropology described here, and the tentatives to collaboration some
> are now seeking. What is it which especially distinguishes an anthropologist? I think it may
> be that he will always try to keep his distance from other social scientists, and also from social
> engineers and social reformers. He may prefer to remain the outsider, looking in, looking on.
> As the translator of symbolic systems – which he is – he does not choose to evaluate or to
> try and change the social language of those systems in which he deals. While the physician
> is an interventionist by definition, and the sociologist by tradition, it may be his obsession
> with being the eternal outsider which makes the anthropologist what he is. If so, perhaps
> it is well for the rest of the world that we remain a small band, after all.

The last sentence is in response to a question probed by Firth: Why
has medical anthropology in America grown so rapidly while it has been
confined to a small group in Britain? Is it due to the willingness of Americans to engage in interdisciplinary research? To deal with applied problems? All of us who have engaged in interdisciplinary research in the
health and medical fields will understand the frustrations she refers to.
I know that I do (Landy 1958, 1961a, 1961b). For some the response
has been, as Firth suggests, to retreat into the walls of academe and
"remain the outsider, looking in, looking on." But it would be a fatal error
if medical anthropology as a whole followed Firth's counsel. Some of the
most vital problems that face us require interdisciplinary research,
especially with the health professions, and those problems are not likely
to be solved without this kind of collaboration. In these times of dwindling
research budgets and the rise of skepticism about such collaboration
on all sides (medical as well as social scientific), we must still pursue
joint goals jointly.

I should like to note here some areas of study that I consider of equal,
perhaps even greater, importance than those covered in this essay. The
present selection is in part due to the limited number of topics in which
I am myself deeply interested and with which I have a more than passing
acquaintance. Problems of space and time also dictated that more should
be excluded than included. And I wish to stress that in none of the areas
included do I make a pretense as to their being fully or exhaustively
covered, and, perhaps some would contend, even fairly represented.

Certainly any one of them is worthy of a full assessment in itself. In any case, I hope that in this series of volumes, or in other places, assessments of the following will soon appear:

– Social and cultural components of death and dying (see Landy 1978b).

– Social and cultural correlates of hallucinogens, trance states, possession, and/or dissociative states.

– Social-cultural and health factors in drug dependency.

– Interrelations between disease and nutrition in the context of culture, social organization, and demography. Also, the relationships between disease, nutrition, and starvation with social structure and economy. (These topics are partially touched upon herein under Health and Disease in Ancient and More Recent Preindustrial Populations.)

– Sanitation, environmental pollution, preventive medicine, and public and social health. Obviously this must be done for preindustrial as well as industrial societies. Brothwell (1972) has made a beginning for the former by addressing "The Question of Pollution in Earlier and Less Developed Societies."

– Surgical and anatomical knowledge and practices in preindustrial and industrial societies. So far this has been largely *terra incognita* for medical anthropologists.

– Cross-cultural perspectives on gynecology, embryology, and obstetrics. The statuses and roles of midwives and/or others involved have been occasionally studied by anthropologists (e.g., Cosminsky 1976, 1977; Paul 1975; Paul and Paul 1975; Spencer 1949–1950), but as an area of study surprisingly scant attention has been paid. Somewhat more study has been given to questions of population control and demography.

– Medical ethnography and ethnology. (These terms are defined and a few of such studies are briefly represented in this essay under The Coming of Age of Medical Anthropology.)

– The anthropology of medical and health institutions in industrial and industrializing societies in the West, in the East (on which there has been a beginning in the volumes edited by Kleinman, *et al.* [1975] and Leslie [1976]), and in the Third World.

– The medical and health systems of ethnic and social groupings in industrial societies, where so far surprisingly little anthropological work has been done.

– An assessment of ethnobotany and ethnopharmacology and their possible relationships to environment, ecology, technology, and medical and health systems.

– Statuses and roles of healers. (Healer roles in sociocultural change have been considered briefly herein under Changing Healing Roles and Differential Use of Traditional and Cosmopolitan Medicine. Statuses and roles of patients have been included in the present essay since they are in more immediate need of attention.)

– The anthropology of aging. In connection with aging, degenerative diseases must also be considered. And since they are increasingly important in Western societies, and will be in the developing countries, anthropologists will want to turn their attention to them.

The Coming of Age of Medical Anthropology

When there has been a sufficient accumulation of ideas, concepts, theories, bodies of data, and points of concern to generate basic books devoted to a subject, it may be said justifiably that a field of study has begun to come of age, or at least to have left its childhood and entered its adolescence. In recent years a small spate of books has appeared, textbooks and anthologies designed to serve as surveys, inventories, or guides to study of most or a portion of medical anthropology, and each in its own way attempting to characterize the field through a presentation of some of its salient concerns. While such books may require periodic revision, they should serve as prolegomena to assist in the codification and delimitation of the field, and pave the way for future research and study. They aid academic medical anthropologists in introducing the subject in their courses, and provide for general use different versions of the scope and important problems of the field as they appear to a range of scholars.

In addition, some medical ethnographies and medical ethnologies have been published; these terms are defined later in this section. I shall comment briefly on a sampling of these publications.

Culture, Disease, and Healing: Studies in Medical Anthropology, edited by the present writer (Landy 1977a), was the first anthology of this kind to appear. The editor's approach is "at once ecological, evolutionary, historical, and structural-functional; it is also epidemiological . . . ," and attempts to define the field. This book presents some theoretical and medical orientations to the study of medical anthropology, searches out the boundaries of the field, and provides selections dealing with paleopathology; ecology and epidemiology; medical systems and theories of disease; diagnosis; sorcery and witchcraft; public health and preventive medicine; anatomy, surgery, and medical knowledge; obstetrics and population control; pain, stress, and death; emotional states; and statuses and roles of patients and healers in mainly traditional societies and under the demands of sociocultural change and acculturation. In introductory statements in each section and to each of 57 selections, the editor attempts to place each chapter in its historical, ethnological, and theoretical context, and to link it to other relevant work. The focus is on preindustrial "little tradition" societies, with some selections dealing with the "great tradition" cultures of the East and West. There is an effort to provide a sense of historical continuity by including selections from anthropological past and recent classics, e.g., Fortune's *Sorcerers of Dobu* (1963), Geertz's *The Religion of Java* (1960), Lévi-Strauss' *Structural Anthropology* (1963), and from more recent work by anthropologists, historians, physicians, and other behavioral scientists.

Health and the Human Condition: Perspectives on Medical Anthropology, edited by Michael H. Logan and Edward E. Hunt, Jr. (1978), defines medical anthropology as "the comparative and holistic study of culture and its influence on disease and health care," and the task of the medical anthropologist as examining "the evolution and geographic distribution of disease, the means by which societies have learned to cope with illness, and ways to improve the delivery of modern medicine in traditional settings." As in the Landy volume, Logan and Hunt "expand on the purpose, history, methods, findings, and applications of medical anthropology," and its main, but not exclusive, concern is with "non-Western cultures" and "pluralistic societies." Its major sections cover definition and identification of the field and its methods and development; the interrelations between adaptability, culture, and disease stress; the scope and nature of nonWestern medical systems and healers; the interaction of culture and mental health; and the problems of health care delivery under the pressures of "modernization," culture change, and cultural pluralism.

Culture and Curing: Anthropological Perspectives on Traditional Medical Beliefs and Practices, edited by Peter Morley and Roy Wallis (1979), assumes that the medical beliefs and practices of preindustrial ("traditional") peoples are "inextricably intertwined with many others, not only situationally, but in the thought of those who inhabit technologically less developed societies." The editors assume such societies have a "complex *materia medica*" and "some measure of scientific status must be recognized in addition to the plethora of magicoreligious beliefs and practices . . . ." The linkages and meanings of such attitudes, values, and actions are intelligible and the papers in the anthology "are directed towards exploring some of these intelligible connections and their social meaning." Furthermore, since medical historians and anthropologists have conceptualized their analyses "specifically at supernaturalistic explanations of illness, particularly in terms of witchcraft, it is upon these that we shall focus." The supernatural vs. the empirical aspects of indigenous medical beliefs appears to vary in emphasis from one contribution to another. Medical systems described include those of Baja California (Mexico), rural Serbia, peasant Filipinos and city dwellers, the Admiralty Islands, the Fipa of Tanzania, the Yoruba of Nigeria, and rural Vermont, U.S.A. (according to the book *Folk Medicine* by D.C. Jarvis).

Culture, Curers, and Contagion: Readings in Medical Social Science, edited by Norman Klein (1979) oscillates in its 27 selections between preindustrial and Western societies, and while the majority of its readings are taken from the work of anthropologists, it draws heavily upon the writings of other social scientists and upon the popular press. The main thrust is based upon the assumption that "the perception of health differs from culture to culture as well as from individual to individual." In the editor's words, "All of the articles . . . reflect a basic relativist perspective." The major sections include some general considerations in relating cultural factors to health and illness; ecological determinants in disease; relationships between patients and health practitioners; health care in the pluralistic (ethnic minorities, women) society of the United States; and health belief systems. Theoretical and conceptual concerns are incidental, and selections were chosen as much for their style as their content; "clearly, effective style," says the editor, "assists readers in remembering important concepts when it is able to transform reports or discussions into *experiences*." In my opinion, these selections are not, taken as a whole, representative either of medical anthropology or medical social science, and in relying so heavily upon popular rather than scientific literature the editor underestimates students and undervalues the caliber and readability of the majority of scientific papers and books in the field.

Social Anthropology and Medicine, edited by Loudon (1976), demonstrates that medical anthropology is beginning to thrive in the United Kingdom (but see Firth 1979; Kaufert and Kaufert 1979). British anthropologists and some physicians have been interested in social and cultural factors in medicine since the 19th century. This book is very much in that tradition, with five of the 15 contributing authors being physicians. The convener, Meyer Fortes, of the conference of the Association of Social Anthropologists from which the papers were taken, urged a "refocussing ... on the human actor as such, rather than on abstract problems of, for example, role and status or the apparatus of custom at the disposal of the actor." Thus, patients and healers would be viewed as humans caught in the pain and vulnerability of illness, attempting to meliorate suffering not as robotic slaves of rule and tradition but as individuals pondering, weighing, and choosing among possibilities.

Most contributors to this collection responded to some degree successfully to the conference call. They were asked to orient their reports around indigenous concepts of health and of what constitutes departures therefrom (structures and functions of the body; physiological processes such as conception, birth, growth, maturation, senescence, and death; comparability of local notions with those of Western biology); ideas of etiology and pathology (disease as a consequence of contagion, pollution, sin, or environmental or human assault); and concepts of disease as distinguished from concepts of illness (presumably the former more biological, the latter more social and psychological). The conference objective, in its nature makes strict comparability unlikely, and while these studies are excellent, they do not obviate the need for additional research into the status and roles of patients and healers in order to achieve reliable transcultural comparisons (Landy 1977b).

Medical Anthropology, edited by Grollig and Haley (1976), also presents a collection of papers derived from a conference (the Ninth International Congress of Anthropological and Ethnological Sciences), but unlike the previous volume, contributors to this one were not guided by a focus or set of guiding categories, and the result is a rather haphazard pastiche of papers of variable length, quality, and importance. Many seemed to be based upon casual observation or programmatic notes and the whole hardly fulfills the editors' expectations of a ground-breaking book. Nearly one-third are from nonWestern countries, a commendable aim of the editors, but little editing has been done so that frequently the reader encounters anachronisms or generalizations of questionable accuracy or validity. Perhaps one-fifth of the contributions are noteworthy, although they do not relate to each other or to much else in the book, but they do stand out in bold relief to the generally unimaginative approaches and tired themes of the remainder (Landy 1978a).

Cultural Illness and Health, edited by Nader and Maretzki (1973), consisting of papers presented to a conference on Anthropology and Mental Health, seems to conceive of "mental health" in a broad and rather indeterminate fashion. This can be seen in the topics covered by the articles: mental retardation, crime, drug addiction, marriage and divorce, aging and the aged, sociolinguistics, altruistic and egoistic behavior, the individual in society, decision-making and uncertainty, mental health research and the nature of cultural systems, practical implications of cultural constructions of reality, and biological bases of behavior as indicated in primate studies. Obviously almost everything that happens in human society is related to health and mental health in some way, but the relevant connections of some of the topics covered here are not always made explicit. Nevertheless, most of the papers are interesting and valuable in themselves, frequently pointing to fruitful avenues of anthropological inquiry, a few of which will be totally unexpected. The direct usefulness of all contributions to medical anthropology is not uniformly clear, but the volume as a whole is worthwhile. The orientation is almost totally toward applications of anthropological concepts and methods, but many ideas here have important consequences for anthropological theory.

The Anthropology of Health, edited by Eleanor E. Bauwens (1978), is devoted primarily to the guidance and insights that anthropology can provide in applications of medical care and preventive medicine. It does not attempt to define the scope of medical anthropology, although it clearly lies within the field. The editor's objective is to "communicate to a broader audience the many facets of anthropology. Members of the health professions are beginning to extend their knowledge about health beliefs, practices, and the needs of individuals from different cultures." It is a unique anthology and most of its contributions will not be found in other volumes in medical anthropology. Its major sections deal with clinical anthropology ("the relation and application of anthropological principles to health care"); strategies for health care ("attempts to relate medicine to culture, society, and health care programs"); nutritional anthropology ("the sociocultural value attached to various foods by various groups and the concern with changing the food habits in different cultural settings"); and anthropological perspectives on aging and dying.

There were a number of earlier anthologies that were relevant and useful to medical anthropology which shall not be commented upon beyond noting a sample of such collections: *Health, Culture, and Community: Case Studies of Public Reactions to Health Programs* (Paul 1955); *Culture and Mental Health* (Opler 1959); *Magic, Faith, and Healing: Primitive Psychiatry Today* (Kiev 1964); *Magic, Witchcraft, and Curing* (Middleton 1967); *Medicine and Anthropology* (Galdston 1959); and *Man's Image in Medicine and Anthropology* (Galdston 1963). All of these and many others were tributaries that fed into the developing mainstream of data and conceptualization that became the emerging new-old body of interest and knowledge called medical anthropology.

Adaptation in Cultural Evolution: An Approach to Medical Anthropology by Alexander Alland, Jr. (1970) was the first book to present a specialized theoretical orientation to the field, and although small in size and scope it presents an introductory guide to the field and could be used, with other materials, in lieu of a textbook. Alland's theoretical framework is ecological and evolutionary and is built around a series of theoretical propositions that require cross-cultural testing. The introductory chapter includes useful definitions and is followed by chapters on evolutionary theory with special reference to medical anthropology; human disease ecology; adaptation to disease; indigenous customs concerned with health and sanitation; ethnomedical systems; and medical systems in acculturation and change. (The book was discussed more fully in the introductory section of this essay.)

Medical Anthropology by George M. Foster and Barbara Gallatin Anderson (1978), is, to my knowledge, the first textbook as such to appear on the subject. The authors provide "a general overview of the field of medical anthropology as we see it, concentrating on the topics that we know firsthand from research, consulting activities, and teaching, and that we have found to be of interest to our students." They assume that "health-related behavior ... tends to be 'adaptive'" and that "the comparative method of anthropology gives the greatest insight into the structure and dynamics of health behavior." The general orientation is "eclectic" and discusses the origins and scope of the field; medicine and medical systems in the non-Western and Western worlds; and the practice of medical anthropology in dealing with problems of sanitation and health care and behavior in preindustrial and industrial societies. There is strong emphasis on public health programs and the impact of culture change and industrialization on traditional societies.

Human Sickness and Health: A Biocultural View by Corinne Shear Wood (1979) is a textbook that takes an ecological and evolutionary approach to medical anthropology. The author assumes that "disease is one of the most critical components of environmental stress" and plays a crucial role in human and cultural evolution, and that "the presence or threat of disease has shaped, and continues to shape, all human cultures and societies." The eight chapters of the book discuss the paleopathological record; the diseases shared by humans with other primates; the role of nutrition in health and disease; the relationship of the social status of women to their health, especially to reproduction; an historical perspective on the role of disease in the conquest of the New World; the still lively debate on the origins of syphilis; the relationship between culture, environment, and malaria; and the statuses and roles of traditional healers. While the author assumes that health and medical practitioners need the knowledge of medical anthropology to practice their art successfully, only scant attention is paid to the applied aspects of the subjects and problems she examines in the book. But some areas here are dealt with uniquely, for example, women and reproduction.

Medical Anthropology in Ecological Perspective by Ann McElroy and Patricia K. Townsend (1979) is perhaps the most genuinely innovative of the recent textbooks. It begins with the assumption that most students taking a course in medical anthropology will not be anthropology majors or professional anthropologists, and attempts to incorporate fundamental principles and concepts of anthropology for such students. However, enough ground is covered and ideas evoked that more advanced students and professionals will find the book helpful and stimulating. The authors make no effort to be comprehensive but present a limited range of salient topics that they feel have been useful in capturing student interest: disease and health ecology; health problems requiring an interdisciplinary approach; human adaptation with special reference to health and disease; the life cycle from reproduction to death, with special reference to demographic phenomena; nutrition, malnutrition, and their consequences in health, disease, and the life cycle; stress, strain, and some effects in individual and group health; and the costs of modernization and culture change on the health status of populations. The unit of analysis is the population and the ecosystem rather than the society or individual, although these units inevitably receive consideration. The approach is ecological and evolutionary and is followed consistently with each major topic. In the process the authors manage to include a spectrum of concepts and data in order to document their point that "A primary concern of medical anthropology is the way health and disease are related to the adaptation of human groups over a wide geographic range and across a broad span of time, from prehistory to the future." Each chapter is tightly integrated around a series of "health profiles" or case studies to illustrate significant concepts and ideas and the book as a whole hangs together remarkably well.

It is useful to have data on the medical systems of societies in major geographic-cultural regions of the world as well as of ethnic groupings within these regions. The three collections reviewed below present just such reviews, and represent important additions to medical anthropology's corpus of knowledge.

Medicine in Chinese Cultures: Comparative Studies of Health Care in Chinese and Other Societies, edited by Arthur Kleinman, *et al.* (1975) is one of a number of recent collective works directed toward delineating and understanding the medical systems of geographic-ethnographic areas. This nearly encyclopedic survey includes papers on China, Taiwan, India, Hong Kong, Burma, Thailand, Malaysia, and other societies, as well as Chinese-Americans. According to the introductory statement, "It is intended that the reader will gain a general notion of where we stand today in our developing understanding of how medical systems relate to societies (particularly Chinese societies), and how medical systems can be studied cross-culturally." The orientation is comparativist and the many different approaches of the 33 contributors present "a spectrum of themes and problems that bridge both of these subjects [Chinese medicine and cross-cultural studies of health care], and that are centrally concerned with the relationship of medical systems (representing various combinations and groupings of traditional and modern elements) to their social and cultural contexts as well as to one another."

Asian Medical Systems: A Comparative Study, edited by Charles Leslie (1976), covers some of the same societies as the above collection, and includes certain others (e.g., the Soviet Union, the Arab world, Japan, Sri Lanka, Sumatra, and the United States). While the contributors represent many disciplines (including anthropology, sociology, history, philosophy, medicine, and pharmacology), the entire collection is of direct interest to medical anthropologists. The volume's papers are based upon the editor's assumption that "the health concepts and practices of most people of the world today continue traditions that evolved during antiquity," that folk medical traditions – little traditions in Redfield's classic phrasing – fed into cultural mainstreams (Redfield's great traditions) and these mainstreams fed into and influenced each other. The major great-tradition medicines "originated in the Chinese, South Asian, and Mediterranean civilizations, . . . maintained their individual characters although they were in contact with each other," but "nevertheless share general features of social organization and theory that allow us to describe a generic great-tradition medicine which can be contrasted with cosmopolitan medicine." Leslie coins the latter term in preference to "Western" or "scientific" or "modern" medicine, since each of these is misleading in various ways. Leslie's introductory chapter is enormously useful for the reader unversed in Asian medical systems and cultures, and places them into medical anthropological perspective. The major sections include chapters on the great-tradition medicines of Indian, Arabic, and Chinese cultures; the organization and character of cosmopolitan medicine; the significance of these medical traditions in the adaptation of their practitioners; plural medical systems; ecological factors in medical practice; Asian medical revivalism; and relationships between Asian medical systems and world views.

Ethnic Medicine in the Southwest, edited by Edward H. Spicer (1977), presents materials on the medical beliefs and practices of four of the many ethnic groups living in the American Southwest: Blacks, Mexican-Americans, Yaqui Indians, and Anglos (the latter described as lower-income, constituting less than a third of a town's inhabitants, and not otherwise ethnically identified). The ethnic medical beliefs and practices are little traditions in the sense in which they were used by Leslie in the volume cited above, but they do not so much feed into the cosmopolitan great tradition as exist in competition with it. The editor uses the term "popular" medicine. There is obvious confusion about all such terms and that confusion is not completely dissipated in this volume, though in context each contributor makes clear what is being described. The objective of the book is to increase knowledge of the cultural environments in the Southwest in which cosmopolitan medical practitioners operate and to which they must adapt. No special theoretical orientation informs the work as a whole or the contributions individually.

A number of volumes have appeared in recent years that I would term medical ethnography and medical ethnology. Pelto and Pelto (1979:414) define ethnography as "that aspect of cultural and social anthropology devoted to the first-hand description of particular cultures," and ethnology as "theoretical analysis and interpretation based on ethnographic data." *Medical ethnography* includes studies having as their primary objective description of a society's medical system, or some sector of the medical system, set within the context of the total ethnography. *Medical ethnology* has as its primary objective theoretical analysis and interpretation of medical ethnographic data, or of a health program or epidemiological data based on medical ethnography.

One example of medical ethnography is *Knowledge of Illness in a Sepik Society: A Study of the Gnau, New Guinea*, by Gilbert Lewis (1975). It is a unique monograph, not only because Lewis is a qualified physician who is also a professional anthropologist, but because the amount of rich, detailed data on the epidemiology, recognition, diagnosis, and theories of etiology and disease classification are unsurpassed in my experience. Never has the medical system of a preindustrial people been subjected to such intensive, detailed, and systematic investigation. There are also very detailed analyses of the social structure and of the role of environment in disease. The sheer quantity of material is unequalled in medical anthropological studies of this kind, and because of Lewis' special qualifications – he could do physical workups and estimates of health status of the people as easily as he could elicit a genealogy – it may be a long time before another study as this kind is accomplished. In the British medical anthropology tradition (see Introduction, this essay), Lewis does not explore the practical implications for programs of prevention or health care delivery. And admittedly, he barely touches upon treatment, upon the management of illness; and to have done so would probably have doubled an already long (365 pages) book. But the materials will constitute a bounteous resource for anthropologists and medical personnel interested in New Guinea cultures.

Another fine medical ethnography is *Body and Mind in Zulu Medicine: An Ethnography of Health and Disease in Nyuswa-Zulu Thought and Practice*, by Harriet Ngubane (1977). Like Lewis' volume, this study is also unique: it is a rare medical ethnography which in this instance encompasses the whole medical system from recognition of illness to treatment; and it is the work of a British-trained anthropologist who is herself a Zulu. It is also rare for British medical anthropologists in explicating methodology clearly (see Comaroff 1979; Kaufert and Kaufert 1979), and for surveying a large sample (about 10%) of a large population, as well as participant observation. Ngubane provided a good deal of material on the role of women in the society and in the medical system (only women qualify as diviners) and has one of the most original and incisive analyses of the role of female pollution in society and in healing yet to appear. She also has a fascinating account of the significance of color symbols in Zulu thought and in Zulu medicine, in the tradition of Victor Turner. The study has more scope than Lewis' but considerably less detail. But like Harwood (1970), she lays bare the many conjunctions between healing and social structure (Landy 1976).

One example of medical ethnology is *Medicine is the Law: Studies in Psychiatric Anthropology of Australian Tribal Societies*, by John Cawte (1974). Despite the subtitle, the material includes consideration of many diseases in addition to psychiatric ones. While the studies all hang together, more or less, although each chapter was originally published as a paper, the subject matter is far too various to summarize. But the quality of the book is generally high, since Cawte is trained in anthropology as well as being a practicing physician and psychiatrist. There is much valuable information on many tribal peoples among whom Cawte worked in dispensing health care, and at the same time carefully recording his observations. The book should be read in conjunction with an earlier one by Cawte (1972) also analyzing more systematically health and ethnological data on Aborigines.

In *The Doctor-Patient Relationship in an African Tribal Society* G. Jansen (1973) retrospectively applies some anthropological concepts to the analysis of a long-term health care program of which he was director. While there is much data in the book, one must interpret it with caution since Jansen is attempting to assess a clinical program for which he had charge, and such self-assessments are not easily made objective. More than this, Jansen has a muddled notion of what constitutes medical anthropology, or even anthropology, and his approach to his patients is patronizing and ethnocentric in the colonialist mode. As a white physician and missionary he seems scarcely conscious that a system of apartheid exists in South Africa and that the conditions it imposes may play a role in the resistance of his patients to his medicine (Landy 1977c).

Finally, a book which is partly ethnographic, partly ethnological, is *Kuru Sorcery: Disease and Danger in the New Guinea Highlands* by Shirley Lindenbaum (1979). The major focus of the study is on the interrelations between ecology, social structure, sorcery, culture change, sex roles, cannibalism, and the epidemiology and etiology of the degenerative disease, *kuru*. It is an excellent field study and analysis and is discussed in more detail subsequently under Ecology and Epidemiology of Disease in Human Populations.

Other medical ethnographies and ethnologies are discussed in subsequent sections of this essay (Fabrega and Silver 1973; Harwood 1970, 1977a; Janzen 1978).

Theory and Conceptualization

It is artificial, and perhaps unjustified, to treat theory and conceptualization in a separate section, since there are theoretically and conceptually important ideas in many of the studies considered under sundry headings throughout this essay, and here and there I attempt to tease out and discuss some of them. But the selections that follow have purportedly been written *primarily* as theoretical investigations and this is why they have been separated from the others. In fact, of course, some conceptualizations and model-building in connection with analysis of a body of data may be more significant than those discussed apart from specific applications to anthropological material (see final section of this essay). In any event, serious attempts at theory-building and sharpening of concepts are much-needed in medical anthropology, and while I interpose at times forceful critiques of the studies in this section, I also welcome their appearance and appreciate the purposes of the authors.

Foster (1976) suggests that "disease etiology is the key to cross-cultural comparison of non-Western medical systems," and that this can best be done by reducing types of such systems to two: personalistic and naturalistic. It follows that theories of causation, categorization of illness, functions of the healer/diagnostician, locus of responsibility, levels of causality, and measures of prevention are dichotomized along the dual division, and that magic and religion are intimately interrelated with one (personalistic) and "largely unrelated to illness" in the other (naturalistic).

A personalistic medical system is one in which disease is explained as due to the *active purposeful intervention* of an *agent*, who may be human (a witch or sorcerer), non-human (a ghost, an ancestor, an evil spirit), or supernatural (a deity or other very powerful being). The sick person literally is a victim, the object of aggression or punishment directed specifically against him, for reasons that concern him alone. Personalistic causality allows little room for accident or chance . . . .
    . . . Naturalistic systems explain illness in impersonal, systemic terms. Disease is thought to stem, not from the machinations of an angry being, but rather from *natural forces or conditions* as cold, heat, wind, dampness, and, above all, by an upset in the balance of the basic body elements. In naturalistic systems health conforms to an *equilibrium* model . . . .

Foster feels that the two etiological theories are not mutually exclusive but both exist in most societies. It is rather a question of which system of explanation is most often stressed in a given society. Personalistic etiologies are part of a more comprehensive theory of misfortune whereas naturalistic etiologies "are restricted to disease as such." Personalistic etiologies require specification of the agent and the instrument or technique. Naturalistic ones are based on a single level of causality (the person "causes" his own illness through doing what he is not supposed to do). The personalistic curer must specify not so much the "how" or "what" of the disease as the "who" and "why." Personalistic curers must divine the diagnosis, whereas the person himself makes the diagnosis in naturalistic systems. In personalistic systems responsibility lies outside the control of the patient, in the naturalistic system with the patient. Personalistic systems require individuals mainly to "do" certain things, naturalistic systems require mainly "don'ts."

I am in agreement with the need for cross-culturally valid etic categories for fruitful comparison of the medical systems of preindustrial peoples, but Foster's two-fold breakdown, as he admits, is "painting with a broad brush," and for a number of reasons is not, in my opinion, a presently useful comparative classification scheme. For one thing, it will not do to lump etiologies that fix the cause of illness in *human* agencies (witches, sorcerers) together with *nonhuman* agencies (ghosts, spirits, deities). Systems that emphasize the former will tend in general to generate distrust, suspicion, and conflict, since theoretically anyone could be a witch or sorcerer. Systems that emphasize the latter are placing the cause of disease beyond their fellows, beyond their society, and in this sense belief in spirits is unifying rather than divisive. It also seems confusing and unnecessary to distinguish between nonhuman and supernatural agents: are not ghosts, spirits, and ancestral shades supernatural? The notion of "supernatural" as opposed to "natural" is itself an ethnocentric way of dichotomizing nature, peculiar more to Western thought than to the thinking of the people whose thought systems are observed by Westerners, as Hallowell (1963:266–268) has insightfully pointed out. If one decides to use supernatural, however, what is the point in excluding spirits, ghosts, etc.?

It also seems to me confusing to characterize naturalistic etiologies as equilibrium models in contrast to personalistic ones, since in most explanatory systems of spiritual causation of disease and spiritual therapy the aim is not only to reduce the patient's suffering but to bring him/her back into a viable balance with the social system and the cosmos.

Indeed amelioration does not precede the re-establishment of social and cosmological equilibrium but follows it, or at least the patient is not likely to achieve one without the other.

Finally, it seems to me wrong to assign "purposive, active intervention" exclusively to personalistic systems. While it is true that the patient is a "victim" of such attacks, they usually come, as Foster himself states, from failing to "do" what is necessary for maintaining appropriate social and spiritual relationships. In other words, if an Ojibwa violates a socioreligious taboo, for example, not sharing the proceeds of a hunt with appropriate others, then he is likely to be punished by spiritual attack for what amounts to a "don't" – something Foster associates with naturalistic etiologies – and not simply failing to perform a "do." Personalistic systems may indeed be more complex and indeterminate, as Foster notes, than naturalistic ones, but it may be just as vague as to what degree of violation brings about a "naturalistic" disease as a "personalistic" one.

Foster's effort is commendable since we badly need classificatory schema that will facilitate cross-cultural comparisons of medical systems. But as Hart (1979) recently noted, "Some refinement of Foster's personalistic-naturalistic taxonomy is desirable." Hart analyzes with rich data the disease etiologies of Samaran Filipino peasants, using Foster's dichotomous model as his guide. While it did help to organize the data, it also presented certain problems both of exclusion and inclusion, some of which I've suggested here and others that I shall not take the space to list.

Another attempt at the classification of medical systems is offered in a stimulating essay by Young (1976a) on *internalizing* vs. *externalizing* types of systems. He suggests them as polar types, with the notion that at their extremes they are fictions since no actual medical system is wholly one or the other, but each is marked by which pole is emphasized in its orientation and model of sickness. Internalizing systems emphasize physiological explanations which "work by means of images and analogies which make it possible for people to order events within the sick person's body from the onset of symptoms to the conclusion of the sickness episode." Physiological explanations "link etiological events to the sequence of biophysical signs which mark the course of disease episodes." Externalizing systems stress etiological explanations which "have the form of narratives in which at least some medically important events take place outside the sick person's body. Such explanations (a) identify a point in time before which it is unnecessary to search for the causes of the onset of sickness episodes and (b) link agencies and events in time and through causes and effects in such a way that responsibility for the sick person's behavior can be allocated onto causes beyond his volition."

Young uses his own data on the medical system of the Ethiopian Amhara to illustrate his argument and decides that it lies "somewhere between these polar types." Both sets of explanations are utilized, but the Amhara are neither a tribal society nor an industrial-scientific society, each of which lies closer to the extremes in their culture, social system, and medical system.

Young's explanation of Amhara medical beliefs is most illuminating when placed against his typology and demonstrates why it is misleading to break down systems by natural-supernatural, empirical-abstracting, or generalizing-specializing. In each society there are elements of social organization, culture, and history that tend to introduce ambiguities and inconsistencies into the belief systems, in addition to the huge elements of uncertainty that are inherent in the vague shadings between "health" and "disease." In all systems these ambiguities and uncertainties are manipulated by medical practitioners who hedge in much of their knowledge with the armor of esoteric theory and terminology.

The internalizing-externalizing continuum helps us to order the data of medical systems cross-culturally (including *all* societies, not only nonWestern, preindustrial ones) in terms of "how people structure their explanations for the onset and course of sickness episodes, and how these explanations rationalize their therapeutic strategies."

Some additional important conceptual and methodological advances have been made by Young (1976b) in the analysis of medical beliefs and practices. He distinguishes between the *practical*, the *social*, and the *ontological* aspects of medical systems. He cautions about the misleading application of the Western medical paradigm to the analysis of non-Western systems and shows how both an emic and etic analysis (Glick 1967) are required for a full understanding of both the practical and social consequences of healing systems and of their meaning for societies and individuals. The *practical* aspects "answer questions about how medical beliefs and practices work, how they change a sick man's condition to some desirable state." The operative term is "work" and it has multiple meanings:

On the one hand, it can mean what people *hope* will happen, what *should* happen. On the other hand, "work" can also mean what people *expect* will happen, what *will* happen regardless of whether or not the sick person's situation has been improved by the healer's activities. ... A cure *sometimes* works in the sense of fulfilling the *hopes* or medical goals of the sick person and his kin; it sometimes restores the sick person to a condition of improved health. However, not even the most expert healer, someone known to possess an efficacious therapy for an ailment that he can correctly diagnose, is expected to be able to control all pathogenic and biophysical conditions that can possibly affect the sick person during the illness episode. Moreover, some therapies are known to be effective only in a minority of the episodes for which they are believed to be relevant. On the other hand, an established cure is *always able to work* in the sense that it meets the *expectations* of the sick person and his kin, that it produces certain results in a predictable way.

Those "certain results" are not necessarily cure or even amelioration, but effects that are expected to occur under given conditions when accepted medical practice is followed. To put this another way, the element of uncertainty which surrounds the phenomena of illness and disorder is also a component of medical procedures (Davis 1960) and therefore part of the expectable outcome in any healing process. Where the Western medical model explains that, given certain nonWestern practices, no "objective" change could result since the cures are medically "worthless" (and if the patient does improve it is because of "acute or self-limiting diseases, transient symptoms, or etiological mistakes"), members of nonWestern societies will tend to attribute symptomatic relief to the ministrations of the healer and appropriate thoughts and actions of patient and community. The healers' successes are further incremented by their ability to recognize and refuse to treat conditions with poor prognoses. Similarly, where the Western practitioner would attribute etiological "mistakes" to a confusion between pathogenic and nonpathogenic agencies, these may not be emically distinguishable or important. "What people get during sickness episodes, then, are medical proofs consistent with their expectations. Of course, this does not answer the question of how people can reconcile their assumptions about sickness and healing with instances where their therapies fail to cure or their prophylaxes fail to prevent."

Reconciliation of failure occurs because in preindustrial societies people tend to engage in "everyday" rather than in "systematizing" thinking. Such thinking is more concerned with conditions that directly affect the patient's life rather than by the need for consistency and for abiding by the principle in Western logic of the "law of non-contradiction." An unsuccessful healing ritual may still provide diagnostic information and referral to another healer. The mystical and recondite knowledge of the specialist is beyond the layperson's grasp, it may be dangerous to possess, and he does not hold the qualifications or certification of the healing role. Even the coexistence of alternative healing systems may not directly contradict or compete with the indigenous one, since they are assumed to deal with "new sicknesses," they may relieve only symptomatic complaints, and they may be relevant only to other categories of people. Furthermore classes of pathogenic agents and healers are differentiated according to their intrinsic power – some are more powerful than others – and the degree of power cannot be determined except contingently in the specific case.

Social explanations of illness include the obviously negative aspects of a serious, disabling episode. It disrupts the individual's daily routine, incapacitates him from carrying out his occupational and often his other role functions, causes alarm, anxiety, and potential economic and psychological sacrifice and conflict in the family (Parsons 1951; Parsons and Fox 1958; Sigerist 1951, 1960; Mechanic 1968). Sickness marks a sundering of the social fabric at the family, kin, clan, and community levels (Harwood 1970; Turner 1964, 1967, 1968). But, on the positive side, illness episodes and the activities of diagnosticians and healers, "may also contribute to the orderliness of social life, since they are a useful vehicle for communicating and legitimizing changes in how social relations are distributed in a community (Young 1976b: 12)." Etiologies comprise four categories of information: agencies (causal, precipitating, intermediating), events, actions, and processes. Diagnosticians vary in how they use these, and are chosen by patient and/or kin on the basis of their special competence. The diagnosis then defines the etiology to be used, the rules, procedures, personnel, cost, etc. The diagnostician's, and the healer's, actions serve not only to reduce suffering, but to legitimate the "extra-ordinary" (Young's term in preference to Parsons' "deviance" categorization of the sick role) behaviors of the sick person. This exculpates (also Young's term) "the sick person, and [reinforces] the fact that social accountability for his behavior can always be transferred onto some agency beyond the sick person's will." The agency may be human or nonhuman, material or spiritual, internal or external – a witch, a virus, a spirit, an intruded object, etc.

The *ontological* significance of serious sickness is that while it "is an event that challenges meaning in this world, medical beliefs and practices *organize the event into an episode* that gives it form and meaning." The practical meanings are translated through the social meanings into a dramaturgical event that provides a model to individual and group for reality-testing – to use the psychodynamic notion – and since sickness recurrently may affect all categories of persons in a society, they provide a model of reality that may be readily and continually tested and re-affirmed. As Young and many others (e.g., Turner, Lévi-Strauss, Geertz), have demonstrated, the management of illness is a process pregnant with significant symbols, and it provides the stimulus for praxis – for taking action to correct the diseased condition – and for returning individual and group to a viable equilibrium. Sickness episodes are especially useful and significant for testing and affirming reality since they "... are able to communicate complex models in a readily re-cognizable way." Despite the cloud of uncertainty that enshrouds illness and healing, they offer the opportunity to "do something" about an event and condition that otherwise are beyond individual control, and therefore to participate in matters affecting one's health and even life itself.

Analysis of medical systems at these varied and multiplex levels helps us to understand why they persist and why they overlap the Western medical paradigm at some points and diverge from it at others.

A half-century ago the first world-wide cross-cultural study was done of the distributions of theories of disease by Clements (1932), using a nonsystematic sampling of the then known cultures of the world and attributing classes of disease causation or etiology to object-intrusion, spirit-intrusion, sorcery, soul loss, and breach of taboo. In the old diffusionist tradition, the work sought to establish centers of origin and routes of diffusion of disease theories of preindustrial societies, and at the same time to map their geographical distributions. In an incisive critique, Wellin (1977) has pointed out that Clements failed to acknowledge that the same classificatory scheme had been published earlier by Rivers (1926, 1927) and that the unsystematic approach rendered the whole into "a conceptual morass," characterized by "conceptual and methodo-logical muddiness." Clements inferred a time sequence based upon his distributions with sorcery assigned the greatest antiquity, followed by object-intrusion, soul loss, spirit-intrusion, and breach of taboo, but Wellin cautions against accepting the chronology on Clements' evidence. Other defects in the culture-trait approach are too well-known to repeat here. Nevertheless, it was the first study of its kind and, for all its errors and ambiguities, a landmark in medical anthropology. Nothing ap-proached its scope until Whiting and Child, (1953), as part of their own important cross-cultural study of socialization, tested a series of hy-potheses regarding disease beliefs where the determining variables were factors in the socialization process.

Nearly five decades after Clements a careful scientific analysis was offered by Murdock, Wilson, and Frederick (1978) entitled 'World Distribution of Theories of Illness." The study is significant for a number of reasons. Using the World Ethnographic Atlas which Murdock and associates designed earlier (involving "the personal coding of a wide range of data for more than 1,300 distinct cultures" to compile 186 different ethnographic "provinces" world-wide), these investigators analyzed data from a stratified sample of one society from each of 139 of the 186 provinces. Lack of funds and/or of sufficient ethnographic data forced the elimination of 47 societies. Such samples are superior to the random selection required by probability sampling because they are "not only more accurate but more representative of the universe they sample." Theories of illness are judged as predominant in a society, important (but subordinate), minor or exceptional, or absent.

As in many classifications, they use the broad categories of "natural" and "supernatural" theories of causation, but in a novel fashion that calls for some explication. For notions of natural causation they superimpose an etic theory, that of Western scientific medicine, upon the emically structured theories of preindustrial societies. They reason that "primary reliance must be placed on categories recognized by medical science, and the anthropologist's role is confined to ordering them in a framework suitable for comparative analysis with the least possible distortion of their scientific accuracy." They define natural causation theory as "any theory, scientific or popular, which accounts for the impairment of health as a physiological consequence of some experience of the victim in a manner that would not seem unreasonable to modern medical science."

Five types of natural causation are posited: (1) *Infection* ("invasion of the victim's body by noxious micro-organisms, with particular but not exclusive reference to the 'germ theory of disease'"): Predominant in one society (Japan), minor in 31. (2) *Stress* ("physical or psychic strain"): Predominant in none, important in three, minor in nearly half the sample. (3) *Organic deterioration* ("decline in physical capacities attending the onset of old age, or the earlier failure of particular organs ..., or the appearance of serious hereditary defects ... "): Minor in 29, predominant or important in none. (4) *Accident* ("physical injury under circumstances which would appear to exclude both intention on the part of the victim and suspicion of supernatural intervention"): Minor in 38, predominant or important in none. (5) *Overt human aggression* ("willful infliction of bodily injuries on another human being, as in violent quarrels, assault or mayhem, brawls, crimes of violence, warfare, and even attempted suicide … "): The authors added this category *ex post facto*, stressing its universality and noting ruefully that they had specifically instructed coders to ignore it. But while it is true that overt human assaults "indisputably impair the health of the victims," it is not at all clear that cultures in the sample considered these conditions as illness, nor indeed that Western medical nosology so classified them. Somewhat confusingly they add,

> … it is aggression of this type, not "disease," that man everywhere has generalized or "projected" to the supernatural beings he has created, with the result that the motive of aggression is central to many of the supernatural theories of illness …. Along with the phenomenon of death, it lies at the root of all supernatural ideology.

The last statement is at least debatable. Expectably, theories of supernatural causation are more numerous and more complex. Murdock, Wilson, and Frederick recognize eight types divided into three groups: *mystical*, *animistic*, and *magical*. A mystical causation theory "accounts for the impairment of health as the automatic consequence of some act or experience of the victim mediated by some putative impersonal causal relationship rather than by the intervention of a human or supernatural being." These are (6) *Fate* ("ascription of illness to astrological influences, individual predestination, or personified ill luck"): Predominant only among the ancient Romans, minor in 28, important but subordinate in none. (7) *Ominous sensations* ("dreams, sights, sounds, or other sensations which are believed actually to cause and not merely to portend illness"): Predominant or important in none, minor importance in 37. (8) *Contagion* ("contact with some purportedly polluting object, substance, or person"): Important in one, minor in 48, predominant in none. (9) *Mystical retribution* ("violation of some taboo or moral injunction when conceived as causing illness directly rather than through the mediation of an offended or punitive supernatural being"): Predominant in five, important in 34, minor in 71.

An animistic causation theory "ascribes the impairment of health to the behavior of some personalized supernatural agent – a soul, ghost, or god." These are (10) *Soul loss* ("ascription of illness to the voluntary and more than temporary departure of the patient's soul from his body"): Predominant in none, important in one, minor in 37. (11) *Spirit aggression* ("direct hostile, arbitrary, or punitive action of some malevolent or affronted supernatural being"): Predominant in 78, important in 40, minor in 19.

A magical causation theory ascribes illness to the covert action of an envious, affronted, or malicious human being "who employs magical means to injure his victim." They are (12) *Sorcery* ("ascription of the impairment of health to the aggressive use of magical techniques by a human being, either independently or with the assistance of a specialized magician or shaman"): Predominant in 28, important in 44, minor in 50. (13) *Witchcraft* ("ascription of the impairment of health to the suspected voluntary or involuntary aggressive action of a member of a special class of human beings believed to be endowed with a special power and propensity for evil"): Predominant in nine, important in 18, minor in 27.

Earlier Murdock had divided the world into six geographical regions "with approximately equal areas and equal numbers of distinct peoples and cultures, so that the selection of roughly the same number of societies from each would produce a first approximation to a representative world sample for the statistical testing of cross-cultural hypotheses." Culture areas, of course, "are now recognized as strictly empirical constructs almost wholly lacking in theoretical support." In the intervening decade research experience indicated that geographical boundaries were more permeable than previously believed, "racial" boundaries yielded "too many contradictory facts," but linguistic boundaries (when added to cultural identity) "are not only relatively easy to establish but extraordinarily stable over time." So now the regions were revised to comprise "ideological regions" but there is a close approximation to linguistic regions and to a lesser extent geographical ones. Regional summaries yielded some interesting results but they are too numerous to recapitulate briefly. The regions are Sub-Saharan Africa, Circum-Mediterranean, East Asia, Insular Pacific, North America, and South America.

No doubt this system of classification of concepts of etiology will occasion some criticism. Certainly violence is done by forcing the thought categories of preindustrial societies into the culture-bound framework of Western medical diagnosis. For example, while all societies believe some disease is "natural" they do so, as Westerners do, because they are part of the routine of everyday life and expectedly part of every person's lot. They may, as we do, include some common ailments as colds, headaches, indigestion, etc., in this category. But they may also include some that would be considered not only pathological but serious in Western industrial societies (for example, pinta or yaws). They do so because such diseases have become endemic and therefore are likely to be visited upon anyone. Furthermore, how do we deal with a concept like "stress" which Murdock, *et al.* not only place into notions of natural causation, but include, in addition to "physical or psychic strain," "the emotional disturbances which constitute the province of modern psychiatry?" At the same time, such emotional states as possession (since "caused" by a spirit) are included in their scheme in theories of supernatural causation under soul loss. One could note other demurrers here and there. All such schemes inevitably will elicit less than universal agreement.

Murdock, Wilson, and Frederick express disappointment that "the natural causes of illness receive remarkably little attention in the ethnographic literature," and suggest that it may be due to "a special interest in the supernatural among anthropologists," rather than because pre-industrial societies are not interested in them. However, I suggest that precisely because they are considered natural, common, and pervasive, as I indicated above, they are seen to "come of themselves" (Sigerist 1951:125–126), require no special explanation, and assume scant significance in indigenous disease theory. These authors also take rather curious note "of a category of theories of illness which occupy a sort of twilight zone between those of natural and supernatural causation," including "such practices as acupuncture, chiropractic, osteopathy, and various versions of faith healing."

None is generally accepted by medical scientists, and none has substantial experimental support, yet there are seemingly valid grounds for assuming that they are not wholly lacking in therapeutic effectiveness. A common characteristic is the organization of their supporters in cult-like groups, often with charismatic leadership, as in India. They are no less frequent in simple than in complex societies, as witness the widespread prevalence of "medicine societies" among North American Indians.

If they are indeed found frequently in "simple" societies, are they to be excluded from cross-cultural analysis because they are not recognized by medical science? Would that not expunge many of the other categories included by the investigators as well? Murdock, *et al.* cite as additional reasons for exclusion from their data that they are "derivative rather than primary," "imprecisely defined," and while "not necessarily supernatural . . . they often have religious overtones." Some of the examples seem to me easily to fit into one of Murdock's natural causation types, and certainly "various versions of faith healing" (also cited) could apply to many of the categories of supernatural causation they have described.

Still, Murdock, Wilson, and Frederick, in my estimation, have performed a significant service to medical anthropology in this attempt to provide a systematic scientific basis for the careful cross-cultural comparison of theories of illness causation. They have done this by carefully and sharply defining their "ideological regions," by providing a schema with clear and careful operational definitions for each classification, by coding of the data by independent judges, and by offering the bases of their reasoning and judgments openly and frankly. The data base has been constructed for testing many hypotheses of interest to medical anthropology, especially in searching for the social, cultural, and ecological concomitants of various types of medical belief systems across cultures. The dilemma posed by the study is the same one that classically has confronted any attempt to investigate the parameters of social and cultural action across a sample of the world's societies. Without going into that dilemma in detail (for example, the perplexing paradoxes in dealing with "Galton's problem" and a series of other considerations [Pelto 1970: 276–319]), what faces the comparativist here is whether to accept the indigenous categories of belief and action, the emic theories of illness causation, whatever their differences and variations, or to impose upon the ethnographic material an etic theory, that of the predominant (but not sole) theory of illness in Western industrial society, in the interest of consistency, rigor, and the provision of a common basis for cross-cultural analysis. There may be no sure way out of this puzzle. We may throw up our hands in hopeless surrender and assume that true cross-cultural comparisons on a planetary basis are not possible in the nature of the case. Or we can move ahead, as Murdock and others have been doing, becoming sensitized to the myriad and treacherous problems inherent in such research, dealing with them as carefully and systematically as possible, and building the road to a true comparative science. With all its enigmas and questions, I subscribe to that aim.

One of the important contributions of anthropology to medicine is the frequent observation that healing in preindustrial societies is "effective" not only because some of the *materia medica* are in fact active in promoting beneficial physiological change, but, perhaps more significantly, even in the face of medications that may be placebos (and essentially inert in their biochemical effects), or perhaps chemically dangerous. The symbolic consequences of the healing process have been credited with major responsibility for therapeutic potency. The assumption usually has been that patient and healer share a set of common beliefs (which may, however, be cosmological but not necessarily medical beliefs [Fabrega 1970; Fabrega and Silver 1973; Willis 1972]). The common belief system – whatever, in fact, it may be – is mediated through whole clusters of symbols in the healing process. A paper by Moerman (1979) analyzes this point in light of a number of discoveries and assumptions in neurophysiology, endocrinology, and psychosomatic medicine, and purports to find that the mind-body duality is still present in much medical thinking and even some anthropological thinking. As a number of commentators on the article noted (it appeared in *Current Anthropology* together with invited comments), the propensity in Western thought for mind-body and other binary oppositions "hardly comes as news to contemporary behavioral sciences." And Moerman's argument is partially damaged by a superficial, and apparently in some respects inaccurate, gloss of neurological and endocrinological research findings. It also suffers from an oversimplified approach to current theories and practices among physicians and psychotherapists. Finally, he claims that he has

... tried to describe a unitary conceptualization of the human organism which will provide us with a context for understanding the "effectiveness" of symbolic healing, as well as metaphor itself, the power of meaning, and the significance of the symbol, without having to resort to "inner selves," "souls," or other mystical explanations, by showing there are no fundamental boundaries between the mental and the physical.

But as one commentator (Giovanni in Moerman 1979) has stated, the article is flawed by "a lack of a clearly formulated conceptual frame ... ." He implies that he has presented a model, but the model is neither explicitly described nor easily inferred. Nevertheless, the paper performs a service to medical anthropology in reinforcing the need to avoid the mind-body dichotomy, in calling attention to some critical relevant research in fields in which most of us are ignorant or poorly-read, and in indicating that progress in the search for mediating (possibly physiological or biochemical) links between symbol, self, and society – or between extraorganic and intraorganic events – will come about only in collaboration among anthropologists and members of other disciplines.

The Logic of Indigenous Medical Systems

An important task confronting medical anthropologists is to develop not only models for the comparative study of medical belief systems, but viable methods and techniques for analyzing such systems. A basic part of that objective is to create a data base of cross-cultural studies of the distribution of systems of beliefs about health and illness. Also, as Fabrega and Hunter (1979) put it, "there is a need to study the ways in which beliefs about disease are used during actual episodes of illness. An eventual benefit of a functional comparison of medical belief systems is better explanations of how different types of social groups handle disease and cope with its burdens." Fabrega and Hunter set about this task by developing a procedure "which would lend itself to quantification." Intuitively, they say, "regardless of what kind of ontology is assigned to disease . . . one observes that it is in behavioral disruptions that disease is realized." What they wish to do is to identify the domain "wherein much of the meaning of disease is calibrated." In the highland town of Tenejapa (Chiapas, Mexico) they applied the following eliciting procedures: One adult in every household was interviewed about four folk diseases: *pulmonia, riñones, colico,* and *espanto* (*susto*), each one qualified as *un poco* (mild), *mal* (serious), or *muy mal* (very serious). These 12 disease-severity combinations were studied in relation to 26 different behaviors or behavioral states (8 negative, 18 positive) that would be disrupted by the presence of one of the disease states. In all 42 respondents were asked 312 yes-no questions.

A meticulous statistical methodology included analysis of various disease-behavior clusters and yielded the following interesting results: *Espanto* did not prove to be homogeneous by comparison with the other 3 folk illnesses, a finding that puzzles the investigators, but bears out Uzzell's (1974) contention that this syndrome is subject to great variability according to individual selection of symptoms. The data indicated that respondents seemed to be classifying the four diseases and three degrees of severity as 12 different conditions of disease-severity, and each "may be seen as referring to a different disease." Behavioral tolerance limits and rank orders of behavioral frequencies seem to stay the same in each disease. "And for diseases at the same level of severity, we found in our data that the correlations among different diseases were approximately just as high as correlations within the same disease . . . . The folk diseases are consistently held to produce similar relative degrees of interference at each level of severity."

Fabrega and Hunter believe that their model "provides not only an explanation for the nature of individual differences in response to illness, but also an explanation for the causal nature of differences due to severity and illness type. . . . A continuum of effort and reaction serves to account for the way subjects of Tenejapa judge the way in which the effects of disease are realized in behavior." Nevertheless, each individual will "ascribe personal or idiosyncratic effects to disease." It remains to be seen whether this model and this technique is equally useful when applied in other cultures. As these investigators admit, their "respondents were not necessarily reporting on actual experiences during illness but on hypothetical conditions. Moreover, they were making projections based on the same behavioral models of disease which are current in the culture. . . . The subjects were relying on unorganized memories that have little immediate salience; those memories would have a very large random element." One legitimately may raise the question of whether it would not have yielded more meaningful results if the questionnaire had been designed to tap *actual experience* with illness. And there is the problem of how cross-cultural comparisons can be standardized, if in each culture subjects are asked to deal with "behavioral models of disease which are current in the culture." Of course, what can be effected, even so, is systematic knowledge of the *kinds* of behavioral interferences which are considered to be characteristic of the perception and handling of disease, and this is in itself a valuable objective.

Fabrega has long been interested in the emic structures and consequences of disease belief systems and has reported a number of such studies, especially in the Chiapas community of Zinacantan (Fabrega 1970, 1971; Fabrega and Silver 1973; Fabrega and Metzger 1968). These studies comprise a body of highly systematic data in a field in which such precision is rare. In one study (Fabrega 1970) the objective was (1) to determine "the extent to which subjects differentiate between various symptoms, signs, and the clustering of these syndromes," and (2) "the extent to which conceptions of illness are specific or special to folk medical practitioners." He found that there were almost no statistically significant differences in the way healers and nonhealers associate "discrete symptoms and signs with discrete illnesses." He also found that healers and nonhealers "tend to link a relatively large proportion of the disturbances with most of the illnesses," so that all in all he could reach the conclusion "that knowledge involving features of illness in Zinacantan is widely shared among the male members of the culture." This finding in turn leads Fabrega to suggest that in this culture the power and efficacy of healers come not from differences in knowledge about the nature of illness but rather in the powers ascribed to the healer's role by the society and culture plus individual personality attributes. One must also wonder how women, the other half of this society, perceive and specify folk maladies.

It seems probable, on the basis of a statistical analysis of categories of disease in American-English and Mexican-Spanish (D'Andrade, Quinn, Nerlove, and Romney 1972), that the "domain of disease exhibits a relatively small degree of isomorphism between the properties which determine the labelling and the properties which determine other behavior." The subjects were English-speaking Americans, Spanish-speaking Ladinos, and bilingual Tzeltal-Spanish speaking Indians. They were shown 30 disease terms and 30 belief frames with the objective of discovering "how individuals organize diseases with respect to a wide range of properties, rather than concentrating solely on properties which serve to define disease states." The investigators found that unlike the clear specificity of kinship terms, many different properties go into defining disease states: type and identity of the agent, anatomical site, symptom types, order of appearance, duration, degree of disability, etc. In fact, a good degree of uncertainty seems to surround the definition of disease terms. And this may help to account for some of the findings in regard to the low degree of specificity of folk illnesses by Fabrega, and Fabrega and Hunter.

The Zinacanteco practice of including many different illness syndromes within similar clusters of signs and symptoms is reminiscent of Selye's early observation as a medical student that many diseases seem to have similar symptoms in their early stages and the syndromes differentiate only as they progress to later, more severe stages. In any event, the general absence of specificity in associating specific disturbances with specific illnesses that seems to obtain in Zinacantan may be peculiar to that community or perhaps to the Mayan culture area. There is some evidence that it may not obtain across cultures. One example is from the work reported by Willis (1972) in a study of the Fipa of Tanzania. Willis here is not dealing with *hypothetical* choices of symptom and disease signs, but with *actual* cases of illness, some observed by him, and by their diagnosis and treatment by Fipa healers. He does not report the quantity of cases of illness and treatment but in this qualitative assessment he adduces two models of sickness etiology existing in complementarity: the "lay" or "folk" model, and the "doctor" or "professional" model. He avers that the latter conforms to the specifications of Kuhn's "scientific paradigm" in that it derives not from folk wisdom but the thinking of a series of small numbers of elite intellectuals, and provides a corpus of "organized thought and professional practice" even though it depends on nonWestern thought models. The lay theory "is a condensed and simplified version of the doctor's paradigm."

Both Fipa models are based on indigenous views of the person-body in the Fipa universe. The doctor theory places the self at the center of all social relationships, which may be injured by ancestral and territorial spirits and sorcerers and therefore cause illness, but the model also provides the cure. The folk model places blame for illness on the machinations of a small number of baleful antisocial members who work sorcery on food and drink to contaminate them. Since the Fipa conceive the self as the resultant of constructive social transactions (shades of G.H. Mead!), "the folk theory sees sickness as the manifestation of a kind of injurious communication among human beings," and therefore as the negation of the kind of social environment required by the Fipa world view. The doctor theory sees illness as a temporary failure of the self (located in the head) to dominate and control the forces of the body. But both theories

... are built on a set of shared assumptions about humanity and the universe which permeate the thought and emotions of laymen and doctors alike. In modern Western societies, however, it appears to be the case that scientific paradigms (for example, in physics) can exist in flat contradiction of corresponding social paradigms and there is an absence of shared cosmological assumptions which might serve to integrate these disparate areas of knowledge and experience.

These different characteristics can be correlated with different degrees of labour specialization in Fipa and Western society. *Asinaanja* [healers] form a distinctive social category, generally enjoying high prestige and frequently a substantially higher standard of living than their fellows in village society; nevertheless they remain only part-time specialists, being cultivators who practise their craft after labour in the fields and during the dry season of reduced agricultural activity. ... Their position is in marked contrast with that of most professional "intellectuals" in Western society.

Further qualification of the findings of Fabrega in Tenejapa and Zinacantan comes in a study by Young (1978) in the Mexican Tarascan community of Pichataro in which a sample of 10 (6 females, 4 males) were presented a set of 34 illness terms (including, but not confined to, folk terms), and were asked about 43 attributes (what does it feel like? what do you do? etc.) concerning occurrence of these illness states. Abstracting results from a highly complex analysis of the data, Young posits three general distinctions that presumably represent the salient trends:

First distinction: Internal vs. external cause. Internal causes are associated with body imbalances, external causes with environmental threats. The individual must therefore be constantly aware of these twin sources of menace.

On the one hand he must be able to recognize and defend himself against external threats to his health, while on the other, he must continually attend to his bodily intake and emotional state to guard against upsets. Ability to identify sources of illness (however they may be defined) is clearly important, and failure to do so has, in native theory, potentially severe consequences for the accomplishment of the tasks and goals of everyday life. This distinction has clear significance for personal behavior, aimed at preventing illness and is reflected in the illness classification . . . .

Second distinction: Degree of seriousness. This serves as a guide to action and determines whether the victim will seek home treatment, a folk healer, or physicians or medically-trained nuns. Non-serious illness is remedied primarily in terms of cost of treatment, but serious illness by what is deemed most effective regardless of cost, within the physical and financial limits of the victim.

Third distinction: Life stage of the victim. Though all illnesses may occur at all stages of the life cycle, some are seen as primarily children's illnesses. If these are classified as lasting for a known length of time, they are permitted to run their course with no medical intervention. Others are considered to be within the province of local healers, not physicians. For still others, young persons and children often will receive more costly treatments than adults since "Children are in general thought to be less resistant to illness than adults, a belief reinforced by a relatively high infant mortality rate."

Interestingly, the "hot-cold" distinction which most previous studies (e.g. Currier 1966; Harwood 1971; Foster 1953) have long assumed to be a basic explanatory attribute of disease etiology, receives rather lower salience than certain other attributes (e.g., weakness, appetite, chills). Young suggests that this may be because in addition to their concern with customary etiological labels, "most people are also evidently interested in the conditions and situations that lead up to these states of disequilibrium, so that they may be avoided, and in their consequences, in terms of discomfort, danger to life, and impaired abilities, so that appropriate steps may be taken to deal with them." He also suggests that if the respondents had been curers instead of laypersons, "the categories that resulted might very well be much more consistently related to specific etiologies." The "hot-cold" distinction is not ignored but it is less important in determining a course of remedial action than degree of seriousness and relative age of the sufferer. Finally Young proposes that "some [illness categorical] distinctions may vary in significance from one place to another" much more than the kind of implicit homogeneity assumed in studies of other Mesoamerican groups.

There is some reason to believe that the hot-cold syndrome is perhaps more closely associated with beliefs about health and disease in warmer than in cooler climates. In the semi-tropical climate of Yucatan McCullough (1973) has found that the concept is important in biocultural adaptation to a hot climate. He points out that peasants in this area are very careful not to overexert and thus to overheat themselves, since being in an extremely "hot" state is considered dangerous. The result is that they carefully pace their labor, rest frequently to "cool" their bodies, and drink water with salt in the belief that this, too will "cool" their bodies. They are, of course, replenishing their body salt, and possibly reducing susceptibility to heat disorders. McCullough suggests that the hot-cold belief has important evolutionary and epidemiological implications, since here it seems genuinely connected to health preservation and survival, but he does not fully spell out these possible implications.

An ecological-economic factor may loom large in the incidence of disease in a community and in fact it may be incorporated into the medical belief system. Suarez (1974) found that in the Venezuelan Andes the medical system consisted of a core of beliefs and disease etiologies shared with other Spanish-Indian belief systems throughout Spanish America. But an additional concept has been added in recent times – hunger! The people have the usual two broad categories of disease etiology: natural and preternatural. But now the subsistence economy is in sharp decline as a result of single cash cropping. Scant income means excessive carbohydrate intake and deficiency diseases are rife in the population, because while other sectors prosper with the huge sales of petroleum, agriculture is stagnating. Now hunger itself has been fixed in the etiological model. "Incorporated as an explanation of ultimate causation for the natural category, hunger diseases are the most prevalent, accounting for 46% of the cases in the sample." Since so many peoples studied by medical anthropologists, whether in preindustrial or industrial societies, live with the constant presence of hunger, they have perhaps overlooked its importance not only objectively in being implicated in disease and disease susceptibility, but emically in the medical perceptions of these populations.

Indeed Ohnuki-Tierney (1977), reporting on research on the Sakhalin Ainu of Japan, suggests that the category of "natural" diseases (as they are emically structured), has received relatively little attention on the part of anthropologists, perhaps because the subject peoples take it for granted and because they may not be deemed as intriguing as the magically or spiritually caused ailments. From a rich body of data on the Ainu Ohnuki-Tierney examines the categorization of headaches and boils which they consider as habitual conditions and are unconcerned about the cause, though not about the painful effects. At least 10 types of headaches were recorded and even more types of boils. The Ainu perceive these habitual illnesses through all their senses and liken the symptoms of the different types to the characteristics of animals in their environment ("octupus headache," "lamprey boil"). Furthermore there are permutations between symptoms and Ainu time-space classifications of their universe. For example, there are aquatic and land headaches and boils, and the stages of each represent time categories.

In his study of the therapeutic system of Lower Zaire, Janzen (1978) has contributed both to conceptual understanding and methodology. He set about to study the medical system of the Bakongo peoples of this region convinced that "Componential analysis promised great things, largely because the techniques of soliciting information appeared simple to administer and productive in the data one could gather." The disarming simplicity of the questions to be asked in the ethnoscience frames ran up against the puzzlement of the respondents. The underlying rationale of such question-answer techniques is to elicit perceptions of *a* culture as though cultures exist as integrated wholes. What Janzen found was that contemporary Kongo culture, caught up in the sweep of Euroamerican culture and technology, as most of the world's cultures, is pluralistic. It followed that the medical system was also pluralistic, but it consists not of an amalgam of traditional and new ways, not of a syncretism of native and Western elements, but of several systems working in parallel, transacting with each other as each case of illness seems to demand. Janzen had to forgo his "primary concern with 'what people think' for a concern with 'what they do,' and how it is rationalized." He had to approach his task etically in order to discover what was going on in the system, rather than simply what the practitioners perceived the system to be. He also found that the most useful technique on his voyage of discovery was the intensive case method, inspired directly by the work and advice of Victor Turner (1967, 1968, 1969). The quest of a sick BaKongo for treatment often takes him/her tens, scores, even hundreds of miles in seeking a satisfying resolution of the "dis-ease." Logistics thus limited Janzen from following to closure more than a small number of cases.

The nature of medical pluralism here arose out of the peculiar history of colonialism in the Congo, and of its agents: military, missionary, and medical. Here as in so many other places, improving the health of the natives became a prime objective of the imperial occupiers, so as to maximize their efficiency as a work force. The task was to transform Kongo society into a local replica of Belgian society. The goal was not achieved, but in the process much of traditional culture was suppressed. But the general level of health improved as indigenous and introduced diseases were eradicated or brought under control.

The BaKongo gained an appreciation for Western culture, technology, and medicine, but they never really relinquished their need for or devotion to traditional culture, including medical concepts, theories, practices, and personnel. Western medicine became firmly established, or at least its local variants, and in the contemporary situation, it co-exists along with several traditional medical systems. The pluralistic medical system, then, consists of several: the art of the *nganga* (generic name for a whole range of healers and diviners); kinship therapy, centering around the family and clan; ceremonies of initiation and purification, handled mainly by prophets or other religious figures; and Western medicine (as practiced rather differently by its dwindling European practitioners and its BaKongo adherents, medical and paramedical). For the most part, the European physicians are aware of the other systems, but continue to practice in isolation. Each of the others, including the Western-trained BaKongo, participate in a network of mutual referral. Healing takes place at any number of levels, from self-treatment, to a dyadic group (patient-healer, kinsmen-healer, patient-kinsmen), to a triadic group (patient-kin-healer, patient-kin factions), to larger groups (patient-kin factions-healer), to the complex formation of therapy managing groups (consisting of all of the preceding plus non-kin and non-kin factions). The key concept here is the *therapy managing group*, which is formed at all of the levels noted, and requires consensus at all levels, "combined with correct diagnostic judgment" and is "an absolute prerequisite for effective delivery of medical care." In my opinion, this concept is generalizable to *all* medical systems transculturally, and represents an important conceptual contribution. The group coordinates, controls, and monitors the healing process, and even when it refers to, and allocates responsibility to, hospital staff, it maintains these functions. It is a warrant to the patient of kin and non-kin concern, help, responsibility, and the sure knowledge that termination, often marked by a ceremony, is obtained so that the patient will know not only what has been done but that the process is at last completed. The group not only manages therapy of the patient, but of the kin and non-kin clan relationships as well.

The practical and theoretical implications of this notion are myriad and cannot fully be explored here. But the concept was derived through a "shift in focus from an exclusive analysis of practitioners' techniques and concepts to an analysis of these *and* popular expectations and images of practitioners, [and this approach] has afforded a much greater insight into the phenomenon of illness and therapy management in Lower Zaire." And it required not only painstaking and sustained follow-through on selected cases, but research into historical documents as well. One effect of this approach and the discovery of the therapy managing group as the critical focus of healing was that the concept of the sick role had to be seen in a much more complex network than simply patient-doctor, or even patient-family-doctor. Janzen's work nicely illustrates a number of points made elsewhere in this essay under *The Status and Role of the Patient*, especially in connection with the Parsonian concept of the sick role.

Janzen was also able to broaden and sharpen the concept of the "lay referral system" as proposed by Freidson (1970). Like the lay referral system the therapy management group of the BaKongo sets the boundaries of the sick role and may itself seek the services of a professional.

Similarly, the Kongo therapy managing group exercises diffuse sanctions upon the sufferer, organizes and channels information, and pressures the sufferer to consult a professional. But unlike the lay referral system in Europe and North America, which is described as discharging its duties after a professional takes over, the Kongo therapy managing group continues to exercise its authority and frequently even increases it while the sufferer is in the hands of a specialist. Other contrasts may be noted. The strongest lay referral system, according to some writers, is present in folk societies with an indigenous therapy tradition and in lower classes of society where knowledge of available professional medical services is not widespread. BaKongo have their own indigenous therapeutic tradition, to be sure, but at the same time they are quite cognizant, as well as supportive, of Western cosmopolitan medicine. Thus, other factors influence the strong institution of lay therapy management in Zaire. To explain this we may look at the pluralistic character of traditional and contemporary medicine in which loosely affiliated cults, services, clinics, and specialists must be mediated. The mediatory function served by the therapy managing group is situated within a broader structure of rights and organization of decisions shared by therapy, litigation, and ceremony (Janzen 1978: 134–135).

Janzen documents these points through an analysis of the interlocking structures and functions of Kongo decision-making, litigation, traditional and modern courts, religious, political, and medical institutions. This type of analysis is rare, if not unprecedented, in medical anthropology. It certainly needs to be done for most African societies and probably for many other strongly political cultures as well.

Like Janzen, Durrenberger (1979) was "heavily influenced by the proponents of the 'new ethnography' when I began fieldwork with the Lisu, [but] I soon concluded that formal eliciting techniques would not be sufficient to develop a description of Lisu categorical systems relevant to curing, much less how these categorical systems inform analysis of particular situations which in turn inform remedial action." And like Janzen Durrenberger found that he had to depend first of all upon observations of what people did about curing in order to develop some hypotheses for further testing through the use first of informal, then of formal, systematic interviewing. But unlike Janzen, Durrenberger did not use the completed case method. Working in one village of Lisu, a Tibeto-Burman people living in Thailand, Burma, and China, he collected chronologically cumulative data on "why are sick people treated as they are?" (his major research question) by visiting each household every week for a year and obtaining a range of data on not only what people did about sickness but the amount of energy and income expended.

The Lisu, as most societies, have two broad categories of illness etiology: natural and supernaturally caused diseases. Durrenberger found that "Although the Lisu theory of disease allows that most symptoms may be natural in origin, it is more likely that they will be interpreted as supernaturally caused, since effective therapies for these diseases are more available." Availability of various therapies were largely a function of distance and household wealth, and "it seems reasonable to suggest that availability of therapies is an important aspect in the conception and treatment of disease." In other words, availability influences diagnosis, treatment, and outcome.

Many household remedies were available and usually would be tried first after a self-diagnosis, but if an ameliorative response did not occur quickly, the diagnosis would be changed to a supernatural cause. Supernatural remedies were also readily at hand from herbalists or shamans. Remedies may also be sought from iterant "injection doctors." At a distance of three hours walk to a Thai town the services of a government health station, hospital, and missionary hospital were available. These were a last resort, not only because of distance and expense, but because the Lisu were distrustful of Thai doctors and other personnel. Should a hospital be used, the missionary one would be preferred since "one was better off to trust an unknown foreigner than a known Thai."

Borrowing from the work of Kuhn (1970) on scientific revolutions, Durrenberger argues that "because the most available technology for curing is a supernatural one, most of the observations are in terms of a supernatural paradigm of disease." Kuhn also suggests that "when there is no shared paradigm in terms of which to construct theories about a certain subject matter, each individual proposes his own more or less unique paradigm," and this is the case regarding Lisu ideas of causation for natural diseases. So, "There is no general paradigm to account for natural diseases, or in terms of which a theory could be constructed. There is, in contrast, a well developed paradigm for understanding supernatural disease." And this also helps to explain why Lisu so readily change a diagnosis from natural to supernatural. Finally, as Kuhn asserts that events "outside a particular field may contribute to the acceptance or articulation of a new paradigm in science," Lisu who can afford it will provide a feast as part of a therapeutic ritual in order to enhance their prestige without being charged with ostentation (since therapy is a socially approved activity). This reinforces the resort to supernatural diagnosis and treatment, redistributes wealth, and integrates the theory of disease with other parts of Lisu culture and social structure. Durrenberger's contribution consists not only in his successful application of Kuhn's theory to the problem of explanation of Lisu disease theory and medical action, but in suggesting a paradigm for the hierarchy of curative resort (Romanucci-Ross 1977) based on the nature of Lisu disease theory and the facts of availability of different forms of treatment and of ability to pay.

Changing Healing Roles and Differential Use of Traditional and Cosmopolitan Medicine

Through internal evolutionary processes and as a result of the forcible or peaceful influences of other cultures, each society and its culture – and its medical system – undergo continual change. When the term "traditional" is used to describe an indigenous society, it should not necessarily imply that its culture is a replica of, or even in direct continuity with, its ancient medical heritage. In most systems there are clearly some lines, however tenuous, of continuity with the past, but a "traditional" system and its roles do not necessarily reach very far back into the historic or prehistoric record. Like most terms in anthropology, "traditional" must be used in a relativistic rather than absolutistic sense. Having said this, there is no question but what traditional cultures, whatever their vintage, are being strongly impacted in the contemporary world not only by the direct effects of colonial domination, but by ever-mounting efforts from within to industrialize, urbanize, and modernize. Whatever the ensuing stresses and social and personal damage, the forces of industrialization, urbanization, demographic expansion and movement, and formal education, all play a part in the transformation of traditional societies.

Medical systems and roles are also impacted by these processes. The result is that they are also changing in many different ways, not all of which could have been predicted even from a profound understanding of the traditional culture. How are these systems and statuses changing? To what extent may systems and healers cling to the traditional ways and to what extent do they reach out to touch, to select from, or to embrace the dazzling and frightening new possibilities? To what extent do lay persons make use of the many new opportunities for treatment? Huge bureaucratic central governments decree some healing roles, for example, the Chinese barefoot doctors (New and New 1977), while some small traditional societies formulate a "hierarchy of resort in curative practices" (Romanucci-Ross 1977) as the natives of Manus, Admiralty Islands, have done to enable them to rationalize their choices of which illnesses and which types of curing will be allocated to the indigenous and to the "modern" systems.

To examine the role of the curer responding to the stresses of rapid culture change under the influence and challenge of Western medicine, technology, and culture, Landy (1974) reviewed changing curer roles in 32 traditional cultures in major ethnographic regions, "partially representative of the world range of acculturation situations." He found that "The indigenous curing role may exist in complementarity to the scientific medical system in a variety of ways, from almost complete isolation to almost complete interaction." A typology was derived of curing role adaptation to include at least the following three broad classes of response to the demands of the powerful industrial system: (1) *Adaptive curing roles* eventuate where the indigenous healer is able to objectively assess the conditions in which he/she must operate, and incorporates elements of the impinging medical role while maintaining strong ties to his/her home culture. The traditional curing role is not only maintained but often enhanced by selectively adding some new elements and dropping out ones that no longer seem functional in the changed situation. (2) *Attenuated curing roles* occur in acculturation or culture change situations when the impact of Western medicine and culture are so overwhelming that (a) the people prefer it to traditional medicine, (b) the traditional curer is unable to relinquish even partially his allegiance to traditional medicine, and/or (c) he/she is willing to accept diminished status and power and a decrement in clientele as the price of resistance to change. Such roles seem headed for oblivion, although under the force of cultural revitalization, new interest in the past may lend attenuated curing roles a new lease on life. (3) *Emergent curing roles* come either in response to the conditions of change and/or urbanization (e.g., the many healing and health sects in Western and Eastern cities), or at the instigation of the dominant culture as a means of delivering medical care to a dominated society. Such emergent roles either substitute for traditional roles that have become attenuated or extinct, or may serve to mediate between them and scientific medicine.

There may be more than the three broad types of role responses noted above. Furthermore, there will be considerable variation within the three classes in each locality in accordance with the nature of the traditional structures undergoing change, the dominating society, and the conditions under which change is taking place. What is clear is that the cultural transformation of traditional societies into parts of the world capitalist industrial system need not necessarily mean the end of traditional healing roles, or even of traditional healing systems. To explain this possibility, Landy introduces the concept of *role adaptation*: " . . . the process of attaining an operational sociopsychological steady-state by the occupant of a status or status set through sequences of 'role bargains' or transactions among alternative role behaviors." He states further:

In situations of rapid culture change, alternative behavior possibilities, expectations, rewards, and obligations will originate both within and without the indigenous social system. All individuals in any sociocultural system are confronted with "overdemanding" total role obligations but must manage to equilibrate role relationships and role sets through continual bargaining and consensuses with other actors in the system, and consequently reduce role strain. Therefore, the instance of the traditional curer's role under potential stress from the demands and temptations of the competing medical system represents an extension of Goode's theory of role strain.

Landy points out that role adaptation of the curer can be seen as an analog of the notion of cultural broker, a key individual who mediates between his own traditional culture and the impinging industrial system, selecting out those new elements that enhance his own role, or that he sees of potential benefit to his society. At the same time, he serves as a cultural conservative, not only in conserving the basic lineaments of the traditional curing role, but in holding the lid on too-rapid raising of aspirations and expectations whetted by the acquisition of new appetites. The analogies to the "successful" modernizing men in Graves and Graves' (1979) study in the Cook Islands seem apparent (see the Health of Preindustrial Peoples in this essay). Both represent instances of role adaptation (the concept is of course generalizable), though it may be that the Polynesian "leaders" functioned less than folk healers to conserve traditional culture even though maintaining traditional group orientation. One could hypothesize that there would be some biological and psychological health correlates of the several curing role types as there seemed to be of the types of modernizing and non-modernizing men in Aitutaki. I would predict that there would be fewer psychic and physical costs attached to the adaptive and emergent curing roles and more attached to the attenuated roles. However, this must be qualified by such considerations as the fact that most emergent curing roles seem to be created from outside traditional cultures by Western medical personnel, and therefore may be beholden to the latter, or suffer the strains of marginality between two cultures, since neither society may accept them into full membership. A study by Swantz (1979) indicates that in times of cultural and demographic shifts a people's patterns of medical belief and selection of treatment will shift accordingly. The cultural group known as the Zaramo, dwelling in and around Dar-es-Salaam, Tanzania, traditionally maintained a medical system based on communal participation in healing rituals. Life and health were conceived as a state of wholeness, with oneself, one's kin, neighbors, community, and the universe. Illness was seen as symbolic of discord in one's social as well as biological body, and healing sought to relieve conflicts at both levels. As the Zaramo become acculturated to the city (urbanized, "modernized"), "there is ... an observable decrease in communal aspects of healing and an increasing tendency toward more individualized forms of treatment." Somewhat unexpectedly, visits to hospitals *and* to traditional healers are accelerating.

Both modern and traditional practitioners are commonly consulted by the same people. The traditional practitioner can be consulted either before or after hospital treatment, or even simultaneously, as is evidenced by the many cases in which traditional medicines are smuggled to hospital patients.

Rural Zaramo tend still to attribute illness to spirits and accordingly to disturbed social networks, whereas urban Zaramo tend to find etiological agents in their fellow humans, in sorcery. This is the case even though urban Zaramo still cling to many traditional ritual forms, including circumcision, and often seek relief in communal rituals conducted by rural practitioners. More often, however, sorcery predominates as an explanation of urban illness. This differs from findings of other anthropologists that in African cities illness is allocated to spiritual domains, the result, says, Swantz, of "both the legal practice and Christian religious belief [that] prevent people from taking a revenging action against a fellow-being when tensions occur in a social group. The Zaramo of Dar-es-Salaam are 98 percent Muslim and do not have the same inhibitions against an avenging action."

Resort to sorcery as etiological explanation in the city results from the greater fragmentation and individualism, with consequent mistrust, and in turn reinforces that mistrust. Like the physician, the traditional healer in the city has a heavy patient load, sees his patients very briefly, but increasingly individualizes treatment by divorcing it from the communal and religious context. Spiritual causes cannot be invoked easily since the communal rituals require a community context and community support, elements lacking in the urban environment. As Swantz puts it:

> Thus the diviner must keep her/his finger on the pulse of the society, and be ready to change with the changing society, while providing also the element of continuity. The urban diviner-*mganga*, medicine-man, sees the physical and financial difficulty for the clients if there are to be extensive rituals and may on that account avoid them both in his/her diagnosis and in his/her method of treatment. He/she lives in an urban situation which is in itself divisive. He/she succumbs to the divisive tendencies of his environment and through his interpretation of disease and healing practice secures for himself a lucrative business. In the action of rural *mganga* there seems to be almost conscious effort to perpetuate certain communal forms of life as long as possible.

While still using some of the symbolic elements of traditional practice, the urban healer is characterized by great role resiliency and leads rather than follows his people in change. He becomes increasingly secularized because of the pressures of urban culture and "his methods would most likely not be acceptable to the more orthodox Muslim devotees," in the rural areas. Swantz suggests that despite these changing patterns of illness and care, both physicians and traditional healers should play some part in the "creation of new viable communities by referring to a person's social group in their method of healing." On the other hand, she acknowledges that a market economy and individual profits will militate against that goal.

In any event, it is now clear that traditional healers will not necessarily disappear, even where cosmopolitan medicine is available to portions of a population. In India Bhatia, *et al*. (1975) report that there are 400,000 traditional healers in India and "These traditional healers or IMPs [Indigenous Medicine Practitioners] are very popular among the ruralities and their ranks are being augmented every day." Because there is one IMP for every 1,300 people compared with one Medical Doctor for every 4,700, these health service personnel propose a "Rural Health Scheme" that would involve 250,000 IMPs to work in "the present skeletal rural health services." However, when they surveyed 93 IMPS, only one in six expressed interest in such a plan, although 90% reported increasing utilization of "Western" allopathic medicines (especially for patients desiring a "quick cure.") Less than 10% used "modern" medicines exclusively, about three-fifths used traditional and modern medicaments about equally, and fewer than 10% used traditional medicine exclusively. Majorities used injections, performed minor surgery, and referred difficult cases to hospitals, health centers, and private physicians. Most of those using allopathic medicines claimed they did so in response to demands of their patients, while themselves preferring traditional medicines. A revival of interest in Ayurvedic healing is dismissed by these writers as mainly tied to sentimental values rather than a renewed belief in pluralistic medical systems, such as Ayurveda, Yunani, and homeopathy, that other writers report for modern India (see Leslie 1976).

Chen (1975) also reports a strong persistence of traditional medical systems in Malaysia. The main systems are indigenous: Malay, Orang Asli, Iban, and Kadazan; and Chinese, which is imported. As Chen puts it:

> Modern medicine has become well-established in all the major towns in Malaysia and is also available to the rural population. . . . In spite of this, a diversity of traditional medical systems thrive with vigor both in towns as well as in rural areas, and play an important part in satisfying health care needs in Malaysia.

Chen suggests that the traditional and modern systems are borrowing elements from each other and one could infer that a kind of mutual symbiosis seems to be emerging. But he does not explain why Malaysians cling so devotedly to traditional medicines, except to suggest, as so many others have, that cosmopolitan medicine is more impersonal, less supportive, less cognizant of, or sympathetic to, folk illnesses.

This poses a critical problem that Lieban (1976) examines. When traditional medicines purport to have cures for diseases for which cosmopolitan medicine has not developed sure therapies, loyalty to the former is understandable. Even if traditional curers are equivocal in regard to some practices, "objective evidence of medical efficacy can be neutralized as a cognitive factor in the choice of practitioners if modern medicine is also ineffective." But where both attempt to treat similar diseases and cosmopolitan practice is demonstrably more effective, traditional medicine should come off "second best." But in fact this is not always the case. Why this should be so is not at all apparent. Lieban asserts the persistent strength of traditional medical beliefs in Cebu City, Philippines, "despite the significant therapeutic advantages of modern medicine in numerous cases where the traditional beliefs are relevant." This is especially puzzling since cultural disease etiology is secular and not integrated with religious beliefs. And costs of selecting a traditional healer may be high, involving even "a matter of life or death." Lieban pursues his research objective by focusing on a folk illness called *piang*, which in children is attributed to be the result of a softening of bones in the rib cage (and consequent impairment of the lungs), due to a fall. Physicians diagnose the illness as being pneumonia or bronchitis, the first and fourth leading causes of death in Cebu City, and other respiratory diseases. Paradoxically, *piang* in adults is held to be due to "natural" causes and may be taken to a physician, but the same symptoms in children are held to be due to a fall and hence require the services of a traditional masseur or masseuse who is highly skilled in alleviating many diseases, but not serious respiratory ailments. Lieban found some cases had been referred to a physician after failure by a masseur, but by then they were terminal. But despite the high recovery rate of cases treated by physicians with chemotherapy, most children stricken with *piang* are still referred to the traditional healer.

Lieban reasons that in part this is because the remedy is not almost 100% effective, as in the case of yaws, and that the minority of cases that die or show little immediate improvement create a confused cognition of modern medicine's superior efficacy. But there are other misleading cues as well. The indigenous concept of *piang* "covers in a single taxon what, from a modern medical standpoint, are such diverse respiratory infections as the common cold, bronchitis, pneumonia, pulmonary tuberculosis, etc." Since in mild forms some of these may be self-limiting, native curers will be credited with cures where physicians will not be. Another source of miscues is those cases treated by both traditional healer and physician. While the physician is using chemotherapy the child has a fall, may coincidentally begin again to display *piang* symptoms, and be returned to the traditionalist. The child continues to recover, due to chemotherapy, and the curer is credited with the success. Another source of confused cognition, of course, is the failure of confidence in the physician who receives the case after the child was seen by the curer but is by this time beyond repair.

Lieban feels that availability is not a reason not to use physicians since they are concentrated in the city; and he rejects economic factors since" ... the effect of medical costs on the choice of one practitioner over another is not determined by economic considerations alone. It is related to the perceived therapeutic advantage or necessity of such a choice." He also rejects the frequently-cited psychological functions of religious or magical elements in traditional healing of *piang*, since the treatment is essentially manual and secular. The presumed complementarity often invoked by medical anthropologists between traditional and cosmopolitan medicine does not apply, since the very kinds of illness that are taken to physicians (critical incapacitating dysfunctions) are in the instance of *piang* taken to curers. Furthermore, the masseur is an empiricist who is not involved in healing the interpersonal conflicts of the social system, so often described as an important function of traditional healing.

More important factors in determining patient choice of treatment, Lieban asserts, are: (1) degree of formal education; and (2) higher social status (associated with higher education and with modern medicine). For the socially disadvantaged segments of the population Lieban feels some hope lies in early health education in the schools. But such efforts should not attempt to dismiss *piang* as a nonexistent disease. Rather, " . . . a more practical approach might be to emphasize that when young children have a respiratory illness, it may not be *piang*, it may be dangerous, and it may be best to seek a physician's help."

From the patient's point of view, a medical system is set into motion when he perceives himself to be ill and he and/or those around him begin to do something to relieve him. Freidson (1970) has referred to the process of seeking help in widening circles, beginning with the patient's self-diagnosis, as the "lay referral system," and help-seeking along lines of specialization as the "professional referral system." Polgar (1963) wrote of illness referral behavior as occurring in three phases: (1) self-addressed phase (self-perception, self-diagnosis, self-action); (2) the lay health action phase (usually by kin and acquaintances of the patient); (3) the professional phase (one or more lay actors bring in a health specialist).

In a study of Spanish Americans in the United States Southwest, Weaver (1970) combines features of Freidson and Polgar's schemes to create an original model of what he terms the "illness referral system," which he defines as "a subsystem of the medical system which includes all health actors and their expected and actual behavior in illness situations." The initiating "self-addressed" phase is followed in order by the kinship phase, community phase, folk specialist phase, and urban professional phase. The professional phase may include all possible versions of professional medical and paramedical personnel and facilities together with "the accompanying roles, social relationships, groups, norms and behavior." These are within a two-hour drive of any rural village. Folk curers may be found in urban as well as rural settings. Both urban and rural dwellers move from the self-addressed to the kinship phase, since in Spanish American culture a wide network of affinal and consanguineal relatives and friends rally to the aid of the sick person. In the folk specialist phase the most significant actor is the midwife-curer, but she is more central to traditional rural people than to urban dwellers, although some of the latter may also use her. And both categories of Spanish Americans consider such alternative healers as chiropractors and osteopaths as professionals, as they do any who are not filling a traditional healing role. In general, in operating within the illness referral system, "The chief difference . . . between rural and urban Spanish Americans is that the latter have a rather truncated referral group, normally consisting of a nuclear family and friends from a small neighborhood or work group, a limited number of folk health specialists, and a more readily available team of modern medical specialists." Because of the costs of professional medical care, unfamiliar people and procedures, lack of privacy, impersonality, cultural misunderstandings and misperceptions of both parties to a professional medical transaction, loss of work time, need for emotional support, etc., Spanish Americans still depend heavily on folk health specialists.

Thus, although cosmopolitan health services may be available, there is no assurance that peoples in traditional societies will utilize them, nor, if they do so, that it will be done on the basis of full and unequivocal acceptance, coupled with rejection of traditional healing and healers. Davis and Kunitz (1978) attempted to test the hypothesis of use as associated with accessibility of cosmopolitan health services for the Navajo Indian reservation which is spread over an area of 25,000 square miles in three states. All costs of medical care save transportation expenses are borne by the Indian Health Service of the United States Public Health Service. They found that morbidity patterns tended to resemble those of a developing nation, "a poverty-stricken population still undergoing an epidemiologic transition from acute infectious to chronic diseases." The single most important precipitator of hospitalization was accidents and mortality rates from this cause are increasing, although we are not offered an explanation for this.

Navajo patients spend about as long in the hospital as the general population. Davis and Kunitz conclude that " . . . in regard to hospitalization utilization Navajos behave much as other populations under other systems: the more accessible the facility, the greater the utilization," despite cultural differences. They found that elective surgery increased in those health centers where it is readily available, so that " . . . the probability is that availability of services rather than need is a better explanation. ... " Still, they also offer their "impression" that the Navajo "general morbidity experience requires more preventive and curative services than are presently available." Although Navajos maintain a strong traditional orientation, Davis and Kunitz suggest that their relatively frequent use of cosmopolitan medicine is based on the "pragmatic" element in their culture.

Folk Healing Alternatives in the Urban Milieu

In pluralistic societies in which various social and ethnic groupings press for a place in the sun and encourage revitalization of their traditional cultures, new attention is being paid to traditional healing systems by medical practitioners and behavioral scientists. Such systems offer members of these groups a set of therapeutic options for dealing with illness alternative to that provided by whatever portions of Western scientific medicine are accessible to them. One such system which has been studied in recent years is spiritism as this is practiced by Puerto Ricans and other ethnic groups of Hispanic origin. Harwood (1977) has contributed significantly to these studies with his report on investigations of spiritism among lower-class Puerto Ricans living in New York City. He focused on several *centros* (spiritist centers) and upon their mediums, cult leaders, and clients with a two-pronged objective:

The practical purpose ... was to examine Puerto Rican spiritism as a mental health resource. The theoretical concern was to consider, on the basis of the spiritist data, the nature of psychotherapeutic healing in general (Harwood 1977: 178).

His findings are carefully detailed and made lively thorough presentations of much case material on individuals, mediums, and the *centros*. He discovered that they indeed offer a significant community mental health resource in this ultra-urban environment and perform a number of the same quasi-familial, quasi-kinship functions for the individual as voluntary organizations everywhere (including, presumably, those of earlier immigrant groups), as a job-referral agency, as a resource in time of crisis, as a means of social control through the gossip network, as a socializing medium for adapting to the demands of life in New York (e.g., how to deal with landlords, where to buy *materia medica* used in curing, as a source of ritual gratification and even of recreation through sponsorship of social events). Such services have a preventive function, according to Harwood, since they "contribute importantly to mental health." They also provide a set of standards for ordering social relations, for dealing with the uncertainties and ambiguities, the distrust and antagonisms, of their class and ethnic life-situation. Through their manipulation of important symbols they act as a kind of religion by providing, in common with many other types of cults, "therapeutic status transformation," as they move through the cult from an ill-adjusted member of an ethnic minority to mediumship, especially for the doubly-deprived women members. Spiritism is roughly analogous to the concept of "soul" among blacks and therefore lays the groundwork for a stronger social identity.

As psychotherapy spiritism can be utilized for short-term or long-term intervention. They usually consist of a combination of individual and group sessions. Most consultations are short-term, involve interpersonal relations, crises, loss, or psychic or physical malaise. Diagnosis is commonly of *envidia* (envy,) *brujeria* (sorcery), and *mala influencia* (bad influence); and includes a "sociospiritual" diagnosis for improving relations with spiritual protectors. Diagnoses of *facultades* (symptoms such as seizures, dreams, fugue states, deep depression, etc., that indicate spirit possession and potential for mediumship) and *castigos* (regression in mediums to earlier uncontrolled possession states, punishment of nonmediums for failing to keep a promise to a saint) require long-term therapy. Therapy consists of persistent group encounters in which the individual learns gradually to assume, or reassume, control over the spirits, resulting in a therapeutic personality transformation in the successful case and resumption of a lifelong commitment for the medium.

Harwood develops a number of points of convergence and divergence between spiritist and "mainstream" psychotherapy. Spiritism and psychiatry share the goals of "face validity," subjective comfort, capacity for rewarding relationships in and outside the family, gratification for successful occupational performance, social skills; but differ in regard to the goals of "construct validity" ("goals specific to certain techniques and theories of therapy," for example, "the psychoanalytically oriented therapies would be evaluated on the basis of the patient's awareness of his inner needs, conflicts, etc."). The construct validity of spiritist psychotherapy includes a cultural assumption of a spiritual world which is part of the therapeutic paradigm and, for some clients, a permanent relationship with a *centro*. Both of these assumptions are critical to the spiritist psychotherapeutic model, but could be seen as a sign of disease in the "scientific" models. There are also important similarities and differences in technique; for example, the spiritist encouragement of trance induction, the differing uses of patient anxiety and hostility, physical contact between client and therapist, etc.

Harwood presents a number of practical implications of his findings and those of other investigators for community mental health programs. In spiritism client and healer share a cultural and symbolic system and criteria for evaluating a healer's efficacy. This plus the ready availability of spiritist healers make it the treatment of choice for lower-class Puerto Ricans. Furthermore, belief in spirits is acceptable instead of a stigmatized condition requiring institutionalization. The therapist knows Puerto Rican culture as a member and uses this knowledge to positive effect. A community mental health worker should favor group or family therapy for the strongly family-centered and community-centered Puerto Rican client, whereas the therapist is much more likely to be an active participant in spiritist therapy. If a client is receiving both forms of therapy, which is not uncommon, consultations between spiritist and psychiatric personnel are called for, and under ideal circumstances there could be formal relationships established between spiritists and community mental health programs, as Lambo has done with indigenous healers in Nigeria. Finally, Harwood sees the spiritist healing process as a rite of passage ("clients in therapy ... being in a liminal state that I have called status remission") that "equips clients either for admission to a new status or statuses or for returning to the acceptable performance of roles associated with remitted statuses"), and recommends that mainstream therapists consider incorporating this model into their own therapeutic planning and procedures.

Koss, whose work is frequently referred to by Harwood, has published a number of papers on spiritist healing in Philadelphia and Puerto Rico, and in a recent paper published concurrently with Harwood's book (Koss 1977) suggests that, at least as regards mediums, "not all cults are equally effective in promoting and maintaining lasting personal transformations in healers who can maintain their own health and well-being at some optimum level." While Koss does not negate the generally optimistic view of spiritist healing, her study does serve to point out some potential negative and even antitherapeutic aspects of spiritism (a potential that exists, of course, in mainstream therapies as well), and provides a

useful caution and corrective. Thus, while Harwood points up the therapeutic features of spiritist ideology and organization and how they are
positively reinforcing in the transformation of client personality and social
status, Koss shows that for some groups, at least, there is another side of the
coin. Her longitudinal studies have led her to hypothesize that often
spiritist groups may be unstable in character, engendering factionalism
and conflict and challenges to the cult leader's authority. This poses a
keen dilemma for the healer, since to maintain authority he must maintain
control over spirit protectors and most of all self-control. But the more
he increases the impressiveness of his performance, the more his own
vulnerability is laid open. Even for the nonmedium adept there are many
traps along the route to personal salvation. As Koss states:

> If we metaphorically consider the cult as a special rewarding system, at least minimal
> reinforcement must persist throughout the initiand's ritual career. . . . The likelihood of
> this persistence depends, in part, upon the extent that crucial substitute personal-social
> relationships, a new personal network, can be formed and can persist. This will vary with
> the individual and with the cult group; many cult adherents easily cycle through their cult
> careers to attain the status of adept or even cult leader. But even at this stage the rewards
> and punishments may lose their attributes as reinforcement because the interpersonal
> relationships crucial to maintaining the new behavior and self-concepts take on negative
> attributes. When the medium leaves the cult group or when the group fragments and dis-
> solves, reinforcement derived from solitary ritual practice may persist, but improvements
> in behavior are either reversed or stablized at a maladaptive level and await positively
> rewarding cult participation to be renewed. Yet even when affiliation with another cult
> group is achieved and cult process again becomes relevant to desired behavioral change,
> a miscarriage of process is likely to occur again (Koss 1977: 467).

In another study of spiritism published simultaneously with those of
Harwood and Koss, Garrison (1977) was interested in determining
multiple use of mental health resources in a New Puerto Rican neighborhood. Some intriguing differences and similarities with other studies
are reported. Garrison states:

> There is a general impression among health professionals and in some of the anthropologi-
> cal literature that spiritist clients are primarily women, particularly older women, and that
> they are drawn from the lowest socioeconomic stratum, the least educated, and the most
> backward, rural, unacculturated migrants. The results of this study do not support these
> impressions. . . . The results indicated that spiritists were serving all sex, age, educational
> and socioeconomic groups proportionally to their representation in the population. . . . A
> much greater proportion of women in the spiritist client samples than in the neighborhood
> were employed. Similarly, a larger proportion of the males in the spiritist client sample than
> in the general neighborhood were married (Garrison 1977: 106–107).

These findings also held up when compared with 1970 census data for New York City Puerto Ricans as a whole. The heads of 9 of 14 *centros* studied were male and all of 9 *centros* observed by Koss were male (quoted in Garrison). Harwood (1977) found that women outnumbered men by 3 or 4 to one in *centro* meeting attendance. He also found that more mediums were female and suggested this was an attractive route to status transformation for the socially subjugated Puerto Rican female. He also noticed that females outnumbered males in the younger age categories, "but with increasing age, the proportion of male and female spiritists tends to reach parity," which he attributes in part to a smaller number of cases in the older age categories.

Garrison found that 86% of the spiritist clients in her samples had seen a physician within the past two years and 56% had done so within the past month, for psychiatric and somatic complaints, a greater proportion than in the nonspiritist sample. She estimates that less than one percent used the Neighborhood Service Center's mental health facilities, and these were usually brought involuntarily in a crisis. She also discovered that spiritists here were mainly of urban origin, more acculturated than nonspiritists, and, "The clinic is *not* serving only those with greatest English facility and the spiritists [mediums] are *not* serving only those with the least English." All of this runs counter not only to many other studies of Puerto Rican migrants but, one could add, of Third World and developing nations migrants generally. Using the Cornell Medical Index of perceived health status Garrison uncovered few significant differences between spiritists and nonspiritists. There were a number of possible methodological reasons for the finding, including certain problems inherent in the CMI as a measure of organic health status, but face validity at least leads to the tentative inference that "spiritist clients are no more physically or emotionally disturbed than the general population" of Puerto Ricans. The foregoing generally could not have been predicted from previous studies or "conventional wisdom."

Generally spiritists bring organic complaints to physicians or are referred to them by mediums who classify them as "material" because they are so diagnosed by physicians, but "they do purport to 'cure' some somatic complaints 'when the doctor has said there was nothing wrong' or 'when the doctor could not cure.' " The mediums also feel competent to heal almost all psychiatric disorders regardless of how severe they seemed to Garrison's psychiatric consultant. However, some clients report having chronic disorders that were not "cured" by spiritual procedures. Spiritists "In general . . . view the same things as disorder that could be considered psychiatric disorder in the clinic and they attempt to bring about change in these." Etiologically, of course, they are considered of spiritual origin. While the study generally agrees with the earlier one by Rogler and Hollingshead (1965) "that spiritism serves people with a variety of psychiatric disorders," it finds "that the role of *Espiritismo* in the Puerto Rican community is greater in the treatment of the problems of living, personality and neurotic disorders, and in primary and secondary intervention, than in the maintenance of the chronic schizophrenic." Rogler and Hollingshead were dealing with Puerto Ricans still living on the island, however.

As Harwood and others, Garrison found that "Spiritism is a ubiquitous feature in the Puerto Rican community . . . familiar to all, and utilized episodically by a large proportion of the population at some time in their lives, . . . but regularly by a relative few . . . . " It serves people in time of personal crisis, most especially those "who for a variety of reasons have not been fully satisfied or 'cured' by professional medical treatment." And psychiatrists are sought " . . . as the last resort only for the hopelessly mentally ill and as the source of the pills for nerves and not as a source of help for the problems of living." Mediums are not substitutes for physicians but are used for complaints emically defined as spiritual and as lying outside the physician's domain of competence; but they are substitutes for other kinds of professional mental health care.

The foregoing, plus the large number of earlier studies of spiritism, provide the building blocks for a fuller understanding of the more competently researched alternative healing systems, a body of work that will continue and that will be plumbed from a variety of angles in the future. We need to have similar quantities and quality of data for other optional healing systems. The studies, particularly those by Garrison and Harwood, are done with considerable methodological skill, with attention to problems of sampling and reliability, and with concern for care and caution in interpreting findings in light of sampling limitations, deductive logic, and the possibility of alternative explanations.

Belief in the role of spirits in human health and behavior is not confined, of course, to ethnic minorities in the contemporary United States. Many sects oriented around spiritism, or spiritualism (to use its more common English version), have existed for more than a century in American society. A study by Fishman (1979) of a small spiritualist church in an urban community of Western New York indicates that spiritualist healing possesses therapeutic efficacy for the lower-middle-class blue-collar workers that constitute its membership. Fishman finds three types of healing: (1) *prayer healing* during the service when the collective healing energy that is assumed to be present can be transferred into ailing bodies or even serve to prevent illnesses to which some are susceptible; (2) *faith healing*, due to spiritual potential for self-healing being implanted in an adherent through belief and church attendance, and based on the assumption that the mind can cause illness but only firm belief in the healing power of spirits can counteract its effects; and (3) *magnetic healing*, usually occurring in a private encounter after the general group session, when there is a laying on of hands through touching, massaging, and manipulating the ailing area, but with other healers and congregants present as a kind of support group. The sect is based upon the premises that life of the spirit continues forever, that Christian teachings are healing as well as life principles, that a believer may learn to share divine power, and that the individual through obedience to natural and spiritual law can control his own health and happiness. Thus a believer who enjoys good health assumes this is because he is a true believer, but if he does not, it is due to his own moral weakness, not a failed spiritualism.

Fishman concludes that this variety of spiritualism serves a practical purpose by meliorating the anxiety and emotional upheaval of serious organic or emotional disturbance, that the healers refer biologically-based problems to cosmopolitan physicians while they work on the psychological and social correlates, and that belief in spiritual healing power ensures its own success. While there are some similarities with Puerto Rican spiritism, there are also some important differences, not the least being that Puerto Ricans are far more likely to find corroboration and support for their beliefs in their ethnic communities than the former Catholics and Protestants in this sect will find in theirs. Very much needed in such studies are some clear epidemiological data as well as case studies, and some attempt to relate membership in the sect to medical, social, cultural, and psychological factors in the patient's life. Fishman does state that half the members were "widows and housewives over sixty years old," that most male members "were retired widowers," and that a relatively few younger members, including healer initiates, attended. These tantalizing sociological data are not further explicated or linked to factors that might help to explain sect membership and belief in spiritual healing, but these are precisely what we need to know anthropologically.

It would be useful to have many more such field studies dealing with such healing alternatives to mainstream cosmopolitan medicine (or its handmaidens in social work and psychology). But they should be done with the thoroughness of the studies on Puerto Rican spiritism cited previously.

In a series of papers Press (1969, 1971, 1973, 1978) has elucidated with provocative insight the phenomena of folk illness, folk medicine, and folk healers in the urban environments of Bogota, Colombia and Seville, Spain. In Bogota Press (1971) found an unexpectedly large number of folk healers operating. He presents evidence that conventional studies of Latin American folk healers (and by implication, healers in other regions) tend to typecast them into rather rigid, almost caricatured role patterns, and that in fact, there is likely to be considerable heterogeneity among them even in rural cultures and most assuredly in urban ones. Press then presents data on five "urban curanderos" to show how these folk healers in the city refute the conventional stereotype in at least the following variables: broad range of personalities; varied spectrum of illnessess managed; huge numbers of clients treated by each (often several hundred in the course of a week); brevity of treatment (often only a few minutes); wide series of diagnostic categories; highly pecuniary nature of prescriptions and fees, and wide range of fees (cash, non-cash, "honoraria," "donations," etc.); range of diagnostic techniques (almost anything from oil stains and coffee grounds to "pseudo-scientific and scientific instruments"); degree of privacy or nonprivacy of consultation; sources of their calling and of their curative and diagnostic powers; degree of empiricism, magic, or spiritual involvement; range of personnel involved in the curing process; "socio-cultural identification of the curer ('local,' 'foreign,' medical, non-medical, lower or middle-class, *ladino, indio*, etc.);" and degree of specialization.

In addition to these "professional" healers, there are alternatives other than resort to cosmopolitan or scientific medicine, including religious or quasi-religious leaders who cure individuals or sufferers en masse; healing through the sale of saints' images or holy water in established churches, for handling a broader spectrum of illnesses than may be available in rural churches; venders of patent medicines and herbal remedies; and a wide variety of books and pamphlets on all aspects of illness and other misfortunes.

Press (1973) also challenges another preconception when traditional medical systems compete with cosmopolitan medicine:

By and large, the resiliency and dominance of folk medical practice is stressed. Data thus far suggest that the mere presence of medical practitioners and facilities, whether it be in tribal, peasant or urban milieux, may not be sufficient to seriously threaten a strong folk medical complex. . . . In each case, medical "competence" of the facility is subordinate to social-cultural differences between the competing complexes. Even in cities, where modern medical facilities are numerous and "official," folk medical practitioners and treatments may continue with vigor (Press 1973: 232).

While this may be the case in many instances, it is by no means universal, as Press demonstrates in the case of Seville. Due to the totalistic bureaucratic organization of life in contemporary Spain, the pervasive availability of a wide array of medical and social services at no, or very little, cost has all but wiped out competing folk medical complexes. Every salaried worker must participate both in the socialized medical system and in the varied social services. Since absence from work because of sickness maintains a person on half-salary, certification into the role must be done by a physician. In addition, private practitioners (often themselves employees of the socialized system), government clinics, private health plans, Red Cross facilities, etc., are also at hand. A small cohort of folk and other nonofficial healers struggle to survive, but both city-dwellers and their rural neighbors most frequently patronize the bureaucratic services. Some people go to folk healers only as a desperate last resort, for example, the chronically or terminally ill, and then after having tried the official medical services. Even so, primary loyalty remains with the bureaucratic rather than the folk system. Thus, *under these conditions* of urban life, folk illness and folk therapy become of weak or scant functional significance. Other conditions that serve to attenuate folk medicine in Seville are: instead of urban anonymity and alienation, a sense of community in urban barrios; social mobility and envy of social-economic success are not frowned upon; because of governmental social and medical services, there are less interdependence and a weakening of the "image of limited good," and thus a weakening of support for belief in sorcery and witchcraft and a strengthening of superordinate social controls; rural migrants to the city find Sevillanos with similar speech and values, and cultural identity maintenance is not problematic; and subsidized housing makes for geographical stability and easy orientation to the city rather than the country. In Press' words, "Folk illness is thus not needed to maintain an 'us versus them' orientation in the face of urban threat to 'traditional' cultural values."

However, more recently, Press (1978) suggests that where the totalistic bureaucratic organization of life is less integrated and pervasive than in Seville, folk medicine and/or folk illness will tend to persist, since they serve critical adaptive functions for recent migrants or for less-adapted ethnic minorities. In the rural setting, Press believes that the major functions of folk illness appear to be "relief of stress and excuse for failure to meet role expectations;" "social or economic leveling;" "punishment for antisocial behavior, failure to reciprocate, etc.;" and "attribution of cause to human sources [to] allow for the expression and amelioration of interpersonal hostility within acceptable and limited bounds." In the city, in fact, such peoples find the environment "downright unhealthy," and frequently resort, and remain loyal to folk illness and/or folk medicine. It is convenient, accessible, and affordable. It is less threatening in an already traumatic situation than the cold impersonality of cosmopolitan medicine. In procedure and style it is more congenial to the cultural values of migrants and minorities. Curanderos "offer a guarantee that the patient's peculiar anxieties and sick role preferences will be validated;" by incorporating some "modern" elements they permit patients to "feel more 'modern' while still relying upon familiar causal concepts, remedies, and healing personnel" Folk medicine reduces "individual (not group) stress resulting from breakdown of interpersonal relationships and failure to achieve" Paradoxically, since community pressures in the city are weak compared with the country, "urban individuals and their families may make strategic responses to illness for filling a greater variety of idiosyncratic needs, with less reliance upon a limited community repertoire of diagnoses and sick roles" Folk medicine may aid in reinforcing group identity in the bewildering heterogeneity of the city. Under competition from pervasive bureaucratic medicine folk medicine "may shift toward adjunct functions of healing such as (a) prognosis and (b) treatment of chronic or medically irremedial conditions," and new healer functions may evolve "such as prediction and manipulation of fortune or future events" (though it should be added that in tribal and peasant cultures such functions are not uncommon).

The corollary of all this, as Press recognizes, of course, is that with upward mobility, fewer of these ego supports are needed while status consistency will demand adherence to "modern" medicine. But as Press points out, urban and middle class persons increasingly are using the nonmedical functions (advice, prognosis of fortune) of "an equally growing body of largely urban psychics, spiritualists, spiritists, mediators, palmists, aura-readers, and faith healers."

The range of health and medical alternatives in the urban environment is vast and the foregoing is meant only to indicate some types of research and problems. We are beginning to realize that far from ending folk healing options for ethnic and formerly peasant and tribal peoples in the city, not only are many traditional healing roles transferred to the urban context, but fertile ground exists for the growth of new varieties of "non-official" healers and techniques. Furthermore, populations long urbanized and exposed to cosmopolitan medicine have also begun to turn to "non-official" alternatives. There is much work here for medical anthropologists in terms of identifying the characteristics of such healers and their clientele.

Health and Disease in Ancient and More Recent Preindustrial Populations

Research into the health and disease patterns of ancient peoples and of more recent preindustrial societies yields data useful for a number of reasons. It tells us something of the history of particular diseases, of the ills to which the flesh of historic and prehistoric peoples was heir, of the relation between disease, subsistence systems, settlement patterns, and social and ecological adaptation, and of the effects of disease on human evolution, especially natural selection. Since some early fossils carried traces of diseases that affected the human bony structure, interest in the reconstruction of ancient epidemiology has been evident from the beginning of a scientific study of the remains of early humans. Until recent decades the occasional and random fossil find was one of the only sources of such data. In Ackerknecht's 1953 survey of paleopathology he stated that "Only a small percentage of diseases leave their mark on the bones," and suggested that mainly through the study of mummies was it possible to study diseases of the soft tissues. But in recent decades anthropologists, physicians, and others have begun to capitalize on the significant advances in methods of data collection and analysis in archeology, medicine, and other sciences, and have begun to uncover great storehouses of new knowledge regarding infectious and degenerative diseases in prehistoric and historic peoples (Brothwell and Sandison 1967; Jarcho 1966; Wells 1964).

One example is a report by Mensforth, et al. (1978) of an analysis of the skeletal remains of a Late Woodland site (A.D. 800–1100) in Ohio. Of 1327 articulated skeletons 452 were classified as infants and children. Thorough ecological research was done on all flora and fauna.

This report dealt mainly with porotic hyperostosis ("a descriptive term referring to cranial lesions which affect the anterior portion of the supraorbital plate, and the pericranial surfaces of the frontal, parietal, and occipital bones") and periosteal reactions ("another type of nonspecific skeletal lesion which occurs in association with a wide variety of pathological conditions"). The authors use the results of recent medical research that demonstrate that a much larger number of soft-tissue diseases leave their record in human bone than was known at the time of Ackerknecht's survey. They find that while in general the population of this site could be regarded as healthy, there was an age-stage of high morbidity in infants (6–24 months), and in this period diseases related to iron deficiency resulted in high rates of infant morbidity and mortality. Age-related synergistic processes in this age group, implicating an iron-deficient nutritional intake with a variety of infectious diseases, leads to the conclusion that

... Age-specific distribution of periosteal reactions strongly coincides with, and appears to be a response to, infectious disease as it occurs in infants and children. More importantly, survivorship and growth data indicate that porotic hyperostosis and periosteal reactions are strongly associated with patterns of infant and child morbidity and mortality, and therefore appear to play an important role in selection and fitness at Libben.

Classifying their population not in the broad classes usually used in paleodemographic studies but by more specific age intervals thus results in much more definitive findings and inferences. This prompts them to conclude that at the population level the nutritional status of infants and children may be revealed by the incidence of porotic hyperostosis, since this bone condition "is a response to nutritional stress," and "periosteal reactions are a fundamental response to, and therefore a valuable indicator of, infectious disease in infants and children."

Ackerknecht's survey did note the frequent finding of arthritis in many of its variations in ancient humans and nonhuman animals extending very far back in the evolutionary record, at least to the age of the dinosaurs. In a more recent study of another degenerative disease Jurmain (1977) compared four populations (protohistoric Alaskan Eskimos, 12th century American Indians from Pecos, New Mexico, and early to mid-twentieth century black and white Americans – the latter not further identified) with regard to the incidence of degenerative knee disease. These groups were further broken down by age and sex. The results indicate that Eskimos suffered the highest incidence of degenerative knee disease, the Pecos Indians the lowest incidence, and blacks somewhat more than whites among 20th century Americans. Eskimo females show more than all other ethnic females, Eskimo males the greatest frequency of all, male or female. In general, as might be expected, impairment of the knee joint in both sexes accelerates with age in all ethnic categories. Jurmain attributes the variation in rates of degenerative knee disease to differences in life-style, most especially in the conditions of work and subsistence activities. The Arctic hunters were subjected to continual, jarring stresses on the skeletal frame the year round (including probable frequent falls on ice, snow, etc., although Jurmain does not mention this). The Pecos Indians were agriculturalists who worked for only part of the year and in a much more benign environment. The recent American blacks are more frequently employed in onerous and strenuous occupations than their white contemporaries. As a whole the study lends strong support for the stress hypothesis of knee joint disease first promulgated in 1920, according to Jurmain, that is, to the close link between culture, behavior, and degenerative disease.

An even more extensive study of prehistoric skeletal material was that of Armelagos (1969) of four successive populations in the Wadi Halfa area of Lower Nubia (Mesolithic, Meroitic, X-group, and Christian) spanning a time period of about 8,000 years (A.D. 500–7,000 B.C.). These latter three peoples were irrigation agriculturalists, with, according to archeological interpretations, Nubian culture reaching its peak during the Meroitic, subsequently declining during the X-group span of 200 years, and then regaining solidarity as a Christian culture. In addition to many diseases commonly found in early skeletons, some were discovered that only rarely appear in prehistoric material (e.g., carcinoma, Legg-Calvé-Perthes disease, hydrocephaly), plus head lice and frequent evidence of traumatic injuries, the highest frequency of the last occurring, interestingly, during the Christian era. Arthritis was also most frequent in the latter period, perhaps due to increasing longevity. In general, epidemiology varies with cultural period, here nicely illustrated by a population-based study rather than by the kind of haphazard sampling of earlier work.

As one might anticipate, dental caries and loss increase with degree of "civilization," but the pathological picture of the X-group is *not* what might be surmised from previous archeological accounts, inducing Armelagos to suggest that these people "may not have experienced the cultural decline expected from the archeological record." Osteoporosis is shown to increase with age and these "prehistoric populations were losing as much bone by age 51 as modern populations lose by age 60." This study, and others from the same project, represent models of their kind.

Drawing together evidence from a great array of sources in archeology, primatology, ethnology, art, epidemiology, paleopathology, medicine and public health, Cockburn (1971) constructs a series of hypotheses to indicate the "probable development and routes of transmission of a number of infectious diseases in prehominid and hominid populations" (Landy 1977a: 83). He aims toward a paradigm of the evolution of infectious diseases that will exemplify his (and others') contention that the development of many diseases, perhaps most, has been influenced by the course of human evolution, but that this relationship is transactional, since human evolution in turn is influenced by the fate and history of infectious disease. This is perhaps not surprising, since "Infectious diseases result from the interplay of three main factors: the host, the parasite, and the environment" (Cockburn 1971), but these assumptions remain to be fully documented as additional work in the above-noted disciplines is carried out. Cockburn attempts to demonstrate that infectious diseases are mainly shared among humans and their closest evolutionary primate relatives and both received them from the same prehuman ancestors. Changes in environment and culture are reflected in the patterns of infectious disease in human populations. Resistance to pathogens increases in a population through natural selection, but is extremely low in a population which has not previously been exposed to the disease. It is now obvious that diseases that afflicted early humans affected their biological and cultural evolution, and much more study must take place, using as many lines of evidence as possible.

While there has been a tendency to idealize and romanticize "primitive" life and to assume that such peoples lived in idyllic Edens free not only of the cares, but of the diseases of modern life, there *is* a line of evidence that points to a relatively high health status among many preindustrial peoples prior to, or at the time of, contact with Europeans. On the basis of the testimony of early explorers, missionaries, colonists, traders, and military personnel, Dubos (1968) has suggested that the health status of preindustrial peoples prior to European invasion was generally good, and often superior to that of the "civilized" conquerors and colonists. While noting that the skeletal evidence of fossils leads him to conclude that "ancient man rarely lived much beyond the age of fifty," Dubos nevertheless states:

> Most of the skeletal remains found in Paleolithic and Neolithic sites are of vigorous adults essentially free of organic diseases at the time of death. Human remains of more recent origin provide further evidence of primitive man's ability to resist harsh natural conditions, at least until he is exposed to the influences of Western civilization [in Polynesia]. . . . Recent medical surveys of contemporary African, American Indian, and Australian tribes give us even more convincing evidence that health and vigour can be achieved under primitive conditions in extremely harsh climates. . . . Several investigators have recently called attention to the scarcity of cancers, vascular disorders, and other degenerative diseases among the most carefully studied primitive populations. Unfortunately, so few old people existed in most of these populations that the significance of such findings is unclear. . . . Life under primitive conditions helps human beings become stronger and tougher, but it is obvious that those who are seen and counted are the favoured ones who have survived precisely because they had the innate attributes to become strong and tough.

From this Dubos infers that "Man has in his nature the potentiality to reach a high level of physical and mental well-being even without nutritional abundance or physical comfort." Recent studies have tended to confirm this hypothesis. At least some hunter-gatherer groups, for example, the !Kung people of the South African Kalahari desert, have had a diet of at least 50% vegetable foods (Kolata 1974), and Lee (1979) estimates that, while the !Kung prize meat, it varies as a proportion of their diet from a low of 20% to a high of up to 90% when hunting is especially successful. Perhaps more importantly, their environment provides an abundance of edible plants. Lee considers them "superb botanists and naturalists, with an intimate knowledge of the natural environment" and he lists over 200 food plants the !Kung commonly recognize, though there is a decided gradient of desirability in terms of their tastes. A fair proportion of these peoples live to be 60 or more years of age, and Lee and his associates concluded that, despite the fact that medical intervention by the research team saved some lives, as a population they were remarkably free of infectious and degenerative diseases, and their diet appears to be nutritionally sufficient (see also Lee and DeVore 1976).

Dunn (1968) notes that disease is but one variable in population size and ecological stability, others including recruitment through reproduction, immigration, emigration, other mortality factors (accidents, predation, and other uncontrollable losses), and controllable losses such as abortion, infanticide, war, cannibalism, homicide, suicide, etc.

His survey of health and disease among hunter-gatherers results in eight propositions: (1) "Patent (and perhaps even borderline) malnutrition is rare." (2) "Starvation occurs infrequently." (3) "Chronic diseases, especially those associated with old age, are relatively infrequent." (4) "Accidental and traumatic death rates vary greatly. . . . " (5) "Predation, excluding snakebite, is a minor cause of death in modern hunter-gatherers; predation may have been relatively more important in the past." (6) "Mental disorders of hunting and gathering peoples have been so little investigated that no generalizations about incidence can be justified." (7) "'Social mortality' has been and is important in the population equation for any hunting and gathering society." (8) "Parasitic and infectious disease rates of prevalence and incidence are related to ecosystem diversity and complexity. Although many of these diseases contribute substantially to mortality, no simple, single generalization is possible for all hunter-gatherers."

Despite Dunn's final point, Black (1975) compared nine Amazonian Indian tribes with each other, revealing past infections of a large number of diseases measured serologically by identifying specific antibody titers, and concluded that

Diseases that affect only man fall into two distinct categories. Those which can persist in an individual for a prolonged period are highly endemic, but those which are infectious only in the acute phase die out quickly after introduction. The suggestion is made that the latter diseases could not perpetuate themselves before the advent of advanced cultures and did not exert selective pressures on the human genetic constitution until relatively recently.

This study lends confirmation to Dubos' generalization and to the findings in regard to the !Kung, since it now seems likely that many of the deadly infectious diseases that afflict modern and recent populations probably did not exist in earlier times. Furthermore, they require concentrated, sedentary host populations for their continued prevalence. In small nomadic populations, even if contacted through exposure to Europeans, if that confrontation is not prolonged and continuous, the diseased members will die off and the survivors thus selected out will retain a degree of immunity, even though the initial effects could have been explosive and epidemic. Clearly, among other factors, the *conditions* of culture contact will play a decisive role. Recent studies have tended to confirm much of the preceding, but also show that under some conditions the health of a preindustrial people may be seriously – and perhaps permanently – damaged. For example, a team of physicians and anthropologists (Larrick, *et al.* 1979) did careful medical workups on 60% of a population of 612 Waorani Indians in Eastern Ecuador, most of whom have managed to stave off White contacts until little more than a quarter-century ago. They found that

> The Waorani appear to be very healthy. . . . What accounts for the unusual good state of health of these Amerindians, and what will happen to their health as the Waorani increase their contacts with the outside? (Ibid.: 176)

The answer may be found in part from the extreme isolation of these people until very recently which "has prevented the introduction of many infectious diseases which commonly affect more cosmopolitan tropical populations." But since that contact, the Waorani have been increasingly plagued by scabies, helminth parasites, and upper respiratory infections, and a significant number died during a polio epidemic. Apparently their highly protein and vegetable diet insures that "in general these people are well nourished and have no evidence of specific vitamin deficiencies." They seem remarkably free of the allergies that affect city dwellers and "have less atopic disease than populations in temperate climates . . . " but they do suffer "very poor dentition," and are subject to a high incidence of trauma and snakebites. The forces of commerce and colonization move ever closer, encroaching on their territory, and the investigators hope that "Perhaps, with the proper concern of the government of Ecuador and the continuing medical assistance of the Summer Institute of Linguistics, these unique people will not be humiliated, dehumanized, and eventually decimated, as have so many other indigenous populations of South America."

In the case of an indigenous people in North America, the Cree-Ojibwa of northern Ontario, who have been in contact with Europeans for hundreds of years, a physician serving them found, through study of historical documents, that while their health status prior to contact was probably good, it deteriorated rapidly very soon after the foreigners entered their territory, bringing with them new diseases, many of which, like measles, smallpox, and influenza, took a dreadful toll, and exploitation through the fur trade, which often resulted in death through exposure in the harsh climate (Young 1979). Epidemic disease decimated their ranks many times in the 17th, 18th, and 19th centuries, and observers throughout this period were in agreement that their health status was poor. While in the 20th century many infectious diseases have been brought under control, and their dependence upon store-bought foods and the largess of the Canadian government for social, educational, economic, and medical assistance has somewhat improved their health, their nutritional status is low.

High rates of injuries and accidents have replaced infectious diseases as the major health hazards. In addition, the wholesale transformation of dietary intakes (including the increase in consumption of alcohol) produces the paradox of an economically marginal population suffering from "diseases of affluence," including obesity, with attendant health problems.

Thus we find again that availability of health and medical services is not in itself an assurance either of adequate medical care or of the maintenance of good health. And we glimpse the process whereby the diseases of industrial civilization begin to afflict a dependent and economically and politically disadvantaged native population. But under somewhat more favorable conditions, health effects of Westernization may not be so devastating.

The search for information about health and disease of preindustrial societies in the historic past involves methods being developed in the emergent field of ethnohistory. Krech (1978a) investigated the diet used to feed children of the Fort McPherson Kutchin, a Canadian Northern Athapaskan people, at a mission school. As ethnohistorical epidemiology the study is important for several reasons: (1) It shows how discrepancies between the recall of living informants can be checked against the surviving records (mainly from the Hudsons Bay Company and the school) and how the differences can be reconciled. (2) It demonstrates that these Indians, as many other groups, were in fact eager to send their children to mission schools for education and to equip them to deal with the white-dominated world. (3) It also indicates that when evidence of malnutrition leading to several deaths occurred, the Indians quickly withdrew their children. (4) It presented a very careful reconstruction of the diet of these Indian students, comparing them with dietary standards of the United Nations Food and Agricultural Organization, the U.S. Department of Agriculture, and the National Research Council's Food and Nutrition Board (which differ at points among themselves) to show that while the diet (mainly whitefish and white potatoes) provided food high in protein and in several critical vitamins, calorie, iron, and calcium intake were extremely deficient. There is thus strong evidence of under-nutrition and some evidence of deficiency diseases (the boys often fought with the dogs for food), and this "surely affected all aspects of the adaptation of children to the Hay River mission residential school." (Other important work by Krech on the Kutchin is examined in this essay under Epidemiology and Ecology of Disease in Human Populations.)

While it has long been assumed that Westernization of tradition-oriented societies is usually accompanied by physical and psychological stresses and that these may lead to physical and psychological stress-related diseases, many studies have shown that stress is not an inevitable concomitant of rapid cultural change and that when it does occur the populations undergoing change vary considerably in their response to stresses in cultural transformation. Using the island of Aitutaki in the Cook Islands, a New Zealand protectorate now self-governing but affiliated, Graves and Graves (1979) studied the effects and concomitants of Westernization upon a traditionally generous, cooperative Polynesian society. They began with three hypotheses: "(1) those Aitutakians with the greatest exposure to Western influences would also display a more individualistic, competitive orientation toward life; (2) . . . they would experience more conflicts with their family and friends, and (3) . . . they would report more physical and psychological health problems than traditional segments of the community." Using observation, interviewing, and a battery of tests, they confirmed the first hypothesis strongly but found that data concerning (2) and (3) were "far more complex than we had anticipated, and to understand them has required that we extend our analysis to include . . . a wide range of changes taking place in the traditional reward structures. . . . "

For men emerging as community leaders they found that while social skills and group orientation were still important, they were less so than for traditional leaders. "Instead the new leadership appears to be selected more on the basis of Western education, New Zealand experience, occupation, and economic position." But they also found among these that "Those modernizing Aitutakians who retain their traditional group orientation should experience relatively few social conflicts as a result of the modernization process and should remain in good health in contrast to other segments of the community." They discovered as well that "traditional islanders, regardless of their group orientation, are reporting just as many social conflicts and health problems as the modernizing individualists. It is *only* those who are both modernizing *and* retaining their group orientation who are reaping the benefits of improved health."

As Graves and Graves point out, their results coincide with a growing body of research and theory on "'the stress-buffering role of social support' in promoting better mental and physical health among persons in stressful life situations." In other words, in a situation of rapid Westernization – becoming part of the money economy of the industrial world – the most healthful response is not to sever all kin and community ties on the route to cultural transformation, but to maintain them in the transformation process. Either clinging blindly to traditional culture or rushing blindly along new paths will lead to a high incidence of stress-related physical and psychic symptoms of disturbed health. While these results must be received with some caution since measures of health and illness were taken as reported by respondents rather than measured objectively by medically-trained professionals, they are highly suggestive. They are also reminiscent of a number of studies dealing with changes in medical systems and healing roles under the stress of acculturation and rapid change (see section on Changing Healing Roles and Differential Use of Traditional and Cosmopolitan Medicine).

The Epidemiology and Ecology of Disease in Human Populations

The quickening interest of anthropologists in making human populations their unit of analysis, and in ecological approaches to the study of social-cultural processes during the past two decades, have been the results of many factors. The story is too complex to consider here although Montgomery (1973) and Wellin (1977) have useful comments on it. In any case, there seemed to be an increase in attention to biological factors in behavior (and correspondingly a decrease in "racial" studies) and to environmental factors as they impinge on social-cultural processes. Whether or not anthropologists were aware of it, I suggest that this movement represented in part a renewed appreciation for that portion of the anthropological heritage that was in fact, if not in name, ecological and environmental. I further suggest that the growth of medical anthropology, with its epidemiological concerns, probably also played a part. In any event, epidemiological and ecological approaches to the study of problems of concern to medical anthropology have begun to yield some useful and even significant returns, a tincture of which we now examine.

One of the advantages of ethnohistorical research into pathological events of the past is that new documents and archival resources may be discovered from time to time and new methods of analysis applied, so that previous work can be built upon, modified, or in some cases, corrected. An apposite example is the re-examinations – there have been several over a period of three decades – of the precise epidemiology and ecology of the disease described variously as "fever and ague" or "intermittent fever" in early accounts, which in the 1830's very nearly exterminated Native American Indian populations in the American Northwest, especially the Chinookan and Kalapuyan peoples in Western Oregon. The first study, done by a physician in 1947, concluded that the disease was actually typhus, with malaria, influenza, and dysentery also present. Ten years later a restudy of the evidence resulted in a finding that the prevalent epidemic disease was not typhus but malaria. The first anthropological study of the evidence in 1955 concurred with the finding of malaria. But these findings were thrown into doubt by a study published in *Ethnohistory* in 1962 (Taylor and Hoaglin), which concluded that the "fever and ague" was viral influenza. In my (Landy 1977a) anthology I accepted that conclusion. But a subsequent article in the same journal (Boyd 1975) reassesses the evidence plus a wealth of new sources and seems, in a most convincing manner, to agree strongly with the earlier studies that found the epidemic disease (or pandemic in the sense that whole populations were nearly wiped out) to be malaria. Since that journal was about two years behind in publication dates, and since the manuscript of my volume went to press in 1975, Boyd's paper was not then available. Not only do I find his presentation of the historical data persuasive, but his use of ethnohistory and cultural practices as etiological agents also seems significant.

Boyd's reconstruction of the cultural and epidemiological factors is as follows: A hot and rainy summer left much standing water in which to breed anopheles mosquitos and the muck of these and of lakes and ponds was incremented by runoff from plowed fields of white farmers at Fort Vancouver. The Indians sought the edible plant *wapato*, or arrowleaf, by pulling up the roots with their toes, stirring more muck, and adding to the breeding potential for mosquitos. In addition, they camped near these bodies of water, making themselves easy targets for the insects. Since traditionally they took sweat baths followed by plunges into cold water, when sweating and feverish from malaria they attempted to cool their condition similarly, but now with fatal results, namely, frequent attacks of pneumonia and influenza. Malaria does not normally produce a high death rate, but pneumonia and epidemic flu do. The diseases were new to the region and the Indians were genetically and culturally defenseless to combat them. Whites in the area survived by meliorating the effects of malaria with quinine, but for the most part the limited supply was not shared with the Indians. Frightened survivors fled from the *wapato* area, settling into villages as yet uninfected. But the next year when anopheles again bred, the survivors with the parasite now present in their blood, became agents of transmission for spreading malaria in the unaffected areas. This cycle was repeated annually until few Native Americans were left to be infected and the Chinookan and Kalapuyan peoples were depopulated. Thus, according to Boyd's hypothesis, malaria complicated by pneumonia and influenza, became "the major factor in the depopulation of the Western Oregon Indian." And, as he further concludes, these Northwest cultures "were not only totally unprepared for new diseases, but possessed traits that proved dysfunctional in their presence, actually increasing the aboriginal mortality rate and assuring the Indian's ultimate extinction."

Another ethnohistorical study of epidemic malaria (Friedlander 1969) found that the disease accounted for the depopulation of the Indian peoples of the Mexican lowlands and their replacement by blacks and whites. Whites, possessing high resistance from their European experience, and black slaves with genetically acquired immunity in Africa, brought malaria into the region. Deforestation of the lowlands to make way for sugar plantations prepared these areas for breeding the anopheles. The Indians, not only genetically and culturally vulnerable, but with their resistance further lowered through overwork by their Spanish exploiters and malnutrition, succumbed in overwhelming numbers to the disease, while those living in the highlands survived. Those who endured in the malarial regions, of course, were debilitated by the effects of malaria.

Wood (1975) argues also for a late introduction of malaria into the New World, and her recent textbook (Wood 1979) features a major section on this devastating disease which is estimated still to be present in the environments of nearly half of the world's people (nearly 2 billion), 343 million of whom "still live in malarious areas that [in 1978] were not yet protected by specific antimalarial measures." Annually 150 million persons are stricken with it and "In Africa alone each year a million children die of it and one-quarter of the adult population suffers recurring bouts." While people in malarial areas frequently accept it as part of their fate and come to terms with it, it takes a deadly toll not only in lives lost but in wreaking further disease and misery upon the survivors. As Wood shows, there is an "intimate relationship" between malaria, society, and culture. Both for scientific and humanitarian purposes medical anthropologists can find many ways, in conjunction with physicians, public health personnel, and others, to do research that will be rewarding to them as anthropologists and potentially useful to the human populations they study. As Wood points out so well, such efforts could actually lead to the complete eradication of the disease, although they may require a degree of international cooperation difficult – perhaps impossible – to obtain.

The work of Krech (1978a, b, c) on the ecology, social organization, and participation in the fur trade of the Kutchin Indians of the North American subarctic, has involved ethnohistorical research into the health and disease patterns of these Indian hunting bands. All these factors have been shown to have produced, through their synergistic effects, critical alterations in the demographic and ecological balance of the Kutchin in their extremely harsh environment. Krech's careful and painstaking ethnohistorical epidemiology (part of which I have discussed under Health and Disease in Ancient and More Recent Pre-industrial Populations) enables him to challenge some existing theories regarding kinship and demographic size and change. For example, bilocality and bilaterality, which traditionally have been thought to have been associated with the strong ecological demands of a harsh environment on a hunter-gatherer people, may in fact have been the effects of such postcontact factors as disease, starvation, and the fur trade and ensuing competition and warfare with other Indian groups. Krech is able to offer some support for the notion, advanced by others as well, that matriorganization, "subsuming matrilocality and/or matrilineality" may in fact have been characteristic of the precontact Kutchin and some of their neighbors.

More relevant to our present concerns, Krech cogently argues that earlier population estimates are too low because they did not sufficiently consider the effects of disease and starvation that, by the mid-19th century had reduced the population by 80% or more. The precarious equilibrium between the Kutchin and a fluctuating animal and plant population on which they were profoundly dependent was frequently disrupted by devastating outbreaks of disease and ingroup aggression (sorcery) and outgroup aggression, caused in part by trade competition, game and plant scarcity, and perhaps most of all, by epidemic disease. Krech insists that, contrary to the notion that the effects of undernutrition on disease susceptibility flows mainly in one direction, sweeping epidemics may themselves be wholly or partially causal of starvation (by reducing strength, numbers, motivation). In any case, "The major cause of mortality was epidemic disease: disease was a proximate cause of death, and disease predisposed mortality from warfare (inexplicable death being due to sorcery, hence the need for revenge) and starvation (with adult male and female mortality in virgin soil epidemics, cooperative resource exploitation became difficult)" (Krech 1978b:718).

Krech also suggests that the response of the Kutchin to incessant disease and frequent mortality was maladaptive. Not only did they continue to practice female infanticide, but their methods of disease treatment – sweating, bleeding, and continuing to gather into groups and to contact other groups with contagious disease – and their responses to death – food and property destruction, sorcery accusations, self-multilation, suicide – could have exacerbated the effects of specific diseases (e.g., increasing the chances of bronchial pneumonia), and probably added to the fearful mortality rate. Epidemic diseases that struck the Kutchin included measles, diptheria, smallpox, cholera, tuberculosis, influenza, scrofula, and whooping cough. Starvation was common, and a constant threat. The resulting depopulation may have made bilocality/bilaterality a necessary social adaptation.

An Australian psychiatrist (Cawte 1972, 1974, 1978) has contributed greatly to ethnopsychiatry and to social psychiatry generally by his studies of Australian Aborigines based in large part upon his treatment of their medical and emotional disorders. In the provocative anthology, *Extinction and Survival in Human Populations* (Laughlin and Brady 1978), Cawte suggests two concepts as useful for the study of disease and disturbance in human populations under stress: "macropsychiatry," and "gross stress." While neither notion is original with him, Cawte demonstrates powerfully how they are especially advantageous for anthropologists interested in the role of ecology in the epidemiology of disease, particularly in the case of human populations who stand poised between survival and extinction. "Gross stress" or "gross stress reaction" came into use in World War II to conceptualize a causative syndrome occurring in cases of massive catastrophe, proceeding in four phases: anticipatory, impact, recoil, and post-traumatic.

Macropsychiatry is concerned with the *pathology* of adaptive processes employed by human groups. By focusing on group pathology, macropsychiatry reflects the customary medical orientation toward sickness rather than toward health. It studies the maladaptive responses which may be employed by groups under stress, including the stress produced by prolonged or extensive resource deprivation. ... Macropsychiatrists study corporate groups which, when confronted by environmental stresses or cyclical privations, behave in ways that make matters worse – for example, by reducing rather than maximizing the production of resources (Cawte 1978: 96).

He suggests that while psychiatrists have erred in placing overemphasis on the intrapsychic, anthropologists and other behavioral scientists have also erred in focusing almost exclusively on the effects of group pressures on individual behavior; and neither has been much concerned with the effects of individual behavior on the adaptation of groups. The latter, of course, is best seen in the instance of small populations and is perhaps not as perceptible in large populations. Cawte's studies of aboriginal populations led him to suggest the following hypotheses:

(1) People are less disturbed when they perceive they have access to sufficient resources; (2) ... if they have some social protection from the retroflexive effect of individuals with mental disorders of sociopathic or paranoid kinds; (3) ... if physiological stresses related to shelter, sanitation, and nutrition are reduced; and (4) people react to frustration in one aspect of role fulfillment by overactivity in another (Cawte 1978: 120–121).

The hypotheses derive from his findings of studies of the Kaiadilt, a small band living in an extremely isolated island environment; the Lardil, a rather larger band living in a less isolated and less ecologically and socially deprived environment; and a sample of mainland aborigines. Under the conditions of extreme limits on natural resources, almost no outside assistance, a harsh environment (including effects of weather, sun, rain, etc.), a series of prolonged droughts, and scant hope of change, the Kaiadilt resorted to behavior self-destructive of social solidarity and personality integration, with profound negative consequences nutritionally and psychologically. The rates of mental disorder were very high by comparison with both the Lardil and mainland group, most especially of paranoia, aggressive behavior, and depression. Adult males compensated for the destruction of their traditional role as good providers by attacking other males (to the point of homicide), stealing and marrying their wives, and even most desperately at times, eating their children. When their numbers had been reduced from 123 in 1942 to "47 very sick survivors" in 1948, and the whole island was inundated by monsoonal flooding, they were removed by a mission to the island occupied by the Lardil. There "they were literally nursed, fed, and calmed into survival," but nevertheless psychologically continued to suffer disorders of apathy and aggression turned inward as even such survival – in Kaiadilt eyes – behaviors as wife-stealing were prohibited. And yet the Kaiadilt men perceive their situation antithetical to the perception of the "objective" outsider. "They relate the high stress to persistent fighting *over women*, and to its complications. They dispute that hunger and sickness were important to them. They wanted women." Which leads Cawte to the interesting observation which is really another hypothesis: "People on the inside and undergoing stress define the stress differently from the way outsiders define it."

This Hobbesian, Malthusian situation (both analogies made by Cawte) not only demonstrates that one sociopathic, aggressive individual can set a pattern (homicide and wife-stealing) that infects the group as a whole but leads Cawte to an absorbing conclusion for the function of ecology under great, sustained stress:

> The basic role of ecological privation in mental disorder has been neglected by the modern psychiatric sects, especially those drawing their data chiefly from the middle and upper socioeconomic strata of Western society. The Kaiadilt data highlight the role of ecology. They suggest that ecological privations, for which a group can find no escape or relief, set in motion severe interindividual conflicts and hostilities, sometimes to the point of madness. Ecological privation comes first, frustrating man's need to hold his place in the ecology; interpersonal disturbances follow, with man against man; then intrapsychic disturbances complete the pathological sequence as fears and suspicions reverberate around the society and down into the new generation. The concept of powerlessness, or perceived inability to cope, is thus a suitable place as a starting point in this macropsychiatric process (Cawte 1978: 116).

Implicit in the preceding statement is a model for the effects of gross stress on a small society, one that, combined with the hypotheses previously noted, sketches a dynamic framework for much needed studies of this kind.

For the first time in 1978 anthropology shared in a Nobel prize which was awarded to Dr. D. Carleton Gajdusek, a medical virologist and anthropologist, for his (and his co-workers') discovery that the mysterious disease *kuru* was caused by a slow acting virus. The probable route of transmission and infection, furthermore, was proposed earlier by two anthropologists, Shirley Lindenbaum and Robert Glasse, as a result of their fieldwork among the Fore peoples of the New Guinea highlands, where *kuru* seemed to have reached epidemic proportions. The whole exciting story of this discovery is reported against the epidemiological background of the disease in the context of Fore culture, social structure, and environment in one of the finest monographs ever produced in medical anthropology (Lindenbaum 1979).

The symptomatology pointed to the central nervous system: tremors, loss of balance, lack of coordination, ataxia, dysarthria – moving toward greater and greater incapacity, exaggeration of the symptoms, and rigidity, and leading finally to complete incapacitation and death. Early cases were reported to be accompanied by inappropriate fits of giggling and Australian papers termed it the "laughing death." Fore men, perceiving the women (the most frequent victims) as temporarily deranged, at first took sexual advantage of them. Later the seriousness of the affliction caused the men to attribute the sickness to sorcery. Western observers also linked it with fear of sorcery and labelled it a psychosomatic disorder (one example: "acute hysteria in an otherwise healthy woman"). Gajdusek in the United States and Zigas in Papua New Guinea began to work on the disease in 1957. They soon declared that *kuru* "cannot by any stretch of the imagination be identified with hysteria, psychoses, or any known psychologically-induced illnesses" and pointed to the high incidence in certain families and settlements, among the Fore and their neighbors, and mainly among women and children.

This epidemiological picture suggested a genetic basis of *kuru* "determined by a single autosomal gene that was dominant in females but recessive in males." Fore men, by now engaged in migrant labor, were discouraged from leaving their home region for fear they would transmit the disease to other groups. However, doubt was soon cast on the genetic hypothesis because the malady did not seem to occur strictly along lines of kinship, since logically the sure death of its victims would soon kill off the host if it were restricted to family lines.

The anthropological research of Glasse and Lindenbaum demonstrated that the disease had been introduced among the Fore relatively recently in the 1920s and 1930s. Most importantly, the two anthropologists showed that it was highly probable that the disease was related to patterns of cannibalism, which although suppressed by the Australian authorities continued surreptitiously among the Fore. *Kuru* also seemed more prevalent in the South Fore, where cannibalism flourished longer than in the North. The following critical cultural and social factors could be implicated in *kuru* etiology and epidemiology: Neighboring groups practiced exocannibalism (eating dead enemies), the Fore practiced endocannibalism (eating kin members of one's own hamlet). The Fore adopted cannibalism a decade after the turn of the century. Before that they had been hunters as well as horticulturalists, but conversion to the

sweet potato as the subsistence mainstay resulted in progressive denuda-
tion of the forests and disappearance of game. The Fore then intensified
the raising of pigs but the men, strongly dominant in the society, laid
first claim to the supply of pork, forcing women and children to derive
their animal protein from rodents, reptiles, and human flesh. When
kuru victims died before emaciation their flesh was especially prized
since it more closely resembled fatty pork. Women and children of both
sexes maintained cannibalism and were its chief victims.

Fore eating practices made infection by the virus inevitable, since
every part of a dead human except the gall bladder was eaten. The brain,
later to be implicated as the site of the pathogenic agent, and very highly
desired along with marrow, was alloted, according to kinship rules to the
victim's mother, sisters, daughters, and brother's wives. Small bits of the
brain might also be handed to children. By the middle 1960s *kuru* incidence
seemed highest in adolescents and young adults of both sexes and older
women, but the total rate was decreasing. As Lindenbaum (1979: 25),
says, "A purely genetic explanation of kuru no longer seemed plausible."
Meanwhile research in England and the United States indicated a close
resemblance between *kuru* and scrapie, a CNS degenerative disease in
sheep, and brain material of *kuru* victims injected in chimpanzees resulted
in the clinical syndrome appearing after incubations of as long as 50
months. Such experimental evidence has been added to a number of
epidemiological and etiological findings to suggest very strongly that
kuru has been caused by a slow-acting virus transmitted by absorption
through Fore cannibalistic practices. Thus it is known that young adult
victims had engaged in such practices four to eight years prior to the
appearance of symptoms; outlawing of such practices has led to a
progressive decrease in *kuru* incidence among women and children;
but incidence continues relatively high among the Gimi, a neighboring
people who resorted to cannibalism even later than the Fore and surreptitiously continued the now illegal behavior.

While the disease has been produced experimentally in several primate
species, the actual virus has not yet been isolated. However, the *kuru*
epidemiologic and etiologic model is now being used to study other
baffling diseases of the central nervous system, including the Creutzfeldt-
Jakob disease among some Jews of North African and Middle-Eastern
origin, subacute sclerosing panencephalitis, progressive multifocal leuko-
encephalopathy, amyotrophic lateral sclerosis, Alzheimer's disease, and
other senile or presenile dementias. Slow acting viruses may also be
responsible for degenerative diseases of other organs besides the brain.

Belief in sorcery is still strong among the Fore, exacerbated by the stresses of social and cultural change, and they continue to hold sorcerers as the malefactors in the rare cases that still appear. The Fore have long held a reputation as powerful sorcerers, and the epidemiology of *kuru* has enhanced that image. While Fore men may have basked in this limelight of admiration-fear, they were genuinely worried about the critical depletion of women in their ranks. They realized that if the trend of female *kuru* deaths continued they would face extinction. They visited other tribes seeking the wisdom of diviners and healers, but the crisis continued and so they rallied their own numbers to large meetings (*kibungs*), anyone was permitted to speak, and many attacked the work of the sorcerers in their midst. Men were beseeched to avenge a death by killing a substitute – pig, dog, garden produce – rather than a human enemy. Male sorcerers, most people felt, had gone out of control and threatened the very existence of the group. Some sorcerers came forward to confess their guilt, thus reinforcing the belief system. First in the South, then in the North, internal sorcery was forbidden (though not external sorcery against tribal enemies). The ban gained strength from increasing fears of punishment by Australian territorial police. But after a few months, new cases of *kuru* appeared and the *kibungs* ceased. An eclipse of the sun, predicted as inconsequential by the Australians, was perceived by the Fore as another cosmic threat to their survival. Disillusionment was further buttressed by failure of the cargo cults or other new ways of life to enrich them materially as the whites had been. Internal hostilities and an intensification of religious activity occurred and finally the seeming threat to their way of life by the Australians led to shifting alliances within, and outside with other groups.

Illness, witchcraft, sorcery, and fear of ritual pollution are all involved in the struggle within Fore society for power and status in a nonstratified social system. Not only external enemies in other tribes and in the Australian authority menaced Fore men; they are also threatened, they believe, by the very women upon whom they depend, toward whom they harbor strong ambivalence, and whose envy and resentment they fear. Lindenbaum ends her fine study with a metaphor of powerful significance for further research in medical anthropology:

In a masterly illusion projected by an egalitarian ethic, the dispossessed are characterized as a threat, a casuistic line of argument we share with the Fore. People in marginal positions are portrayed as a danger to the establishment. If *kuru* becomes the prototype for studies of slow virus infections, Fore beliefs about mystical danger may contribute to our understanding of the emergence of social inequality.

Neither biological nor social communities offer truly equal shares to all. A society stratified as little as the Fore shows individual men and women living in relationships of mutual aid and as parasite and host. Just as infectious disease results from inconclusive negotiations for symbiosis between humans and a few species of bacteria, sorcery is portrayed as an overstepping of the line by one side or the other. In the absence of alternative methods of settling disputes, sorcery may serve to regulate relations between individuals who must cooperate and also compete. As has been postulated for immune reactions, sorcery seems designed not to interrupt but to modulate the process. Disease symptoms, like sorcery accusations, signal a corrective response, an attempted reassertion of dominance by the protesting host. It is a paradox the Fore repeatedly face: how to dispose of the enemy on whom you also depend.

Thus, an illness which at first seemed to be a kind of "ethnic psychosis" or "culture-bound reactive syndrome" (q.v.), a psychosomatic disturbance associated with fear of sorcery, proved to be due to a viral infection of the central nervous system with an extensive incubation cycle. Careful and patient medical anthropological research demonstrated both its organic etiology, its epidemiology, and its social and cultural ecology. From a Western viewpoint sorcery does not cause *kuru*, although the Fore continue that belief. But from an anthropological viewpoint, learning *why* the Fore cling to that belief provides understanding not only of the indigenous medical system but of a social system that excludes women from an ethic of equality, forces their inequality, and holds them responsible for the real or imagined ills that seem to undermine the position of the male holders of power.

Statuses and Roles of the Patient

I have suggested previously (Landy 1977a: 385–388) that compared with the attention paid to the admittedly dramatic roles of healers, we know relatively little about the roles of patients: the who, what, where, when, and under what conditions persons choose or avoid the many guises provided by illness, that is, by being socially and culturally defined as being ill. This is perhaps truer of our knowledge of nonWestern than Western societies, although some studies are now beginning to shed light on the sick role in preindustrial societies as well as in industrial ones. In a number of the studies reviewed here there are relevant findings in this regard, especially in the section dealing with 'ethnic disorders." The few examples of research in the present section are mainly from our own society, and many are concerned with the applicability of the sick role and patient role as formulated by Parsons (1951, 1953, 1958).

In order to "re-examine" the sick role concept, Arluke, Kennedy, and Kessler (1979) secured questionnaires on 1,000 recently discharged hospital patients in New York City, of which they termed 490 "usable." The sample "overrepresents older, retired, low income patients," and since each "chose" the sick role the results may not be generalizable to a "normal" population. They found

> ... Four interrelated normative expectations: (1) the right of the occupant of the sick role to be exempt from responsibility for the incapacity; (2) the right to be exempt from normal social role responsibilities; (3) the duty to recognize that illness is inherently undesirable and to try to get well; and (4) the duty to seek technically competent help and to cooperate in the process of trying to get well.

Thus, in general the Parsonian model of the sick role seems to find consensual confirmation in this sample of hospitalized patients, although the strength of each of the four expectations varied somewhat by age, sex, income, and family size. These investigators conclude that "The Parsons model applies to most people when the expectations are treated as discrete and unrelated dimensions rather than as a configuration of expectations." What we still do not learn here, and very much need to know, is: under what conditions (social psychological, cultural, environmental, nature and severity of illness, etc.) is this or that expectation of patient status and role stronger or weaker? The practical as well as theoretical significance of this question seems obvious.

Insofar as the perception of the sick role is in large part culturally defined, it becomes part of the culture of health and medicine and should be transmitted to new generations in the socialization process. Campbell (1978) studied 264 pediatric patients and their mothers and found that children's perceptions and interpretations of the sick role become sharpened with age and become strongest in adolescence. In general, the higher the social status of parents, the more Spartan-like becomes the sick role behavior of children; that is, the more it approaches agreement with the Parsons paradigm. Campbell's study has determined, then, that sick role characteristics begin to exert their influence on children's thinking "fairly early in the child's life." An important insight here is that " ... the sick role may represent an extension of normal age and sex roles to a special set of aperiodic circumstances." Expectably then, the sick role must be seen in the larger context of the complex of other social statuses and roles (in Merton's concepts: status sets and role sets) which are being filled by the individual, since we should assume some degree of linkage among roles (though this is not to deny the probability of role dissonance, as well).

A study by Stein (1979) suggests a dialectical model, "one which combines the conceptual opposition and dissonance inherent in Hegelian logic (thesis and antithesis) and the psychodynamic conflict central to Freudian metapsychology," in order to examine the concepts of "chronic illness," "disability," and "rehabilitation" within the context of American culture. In the aging society of the United States chronic illness is becoming an increasing concern, with medical and social institutions ill-prepared to deal effectively with it. The Parsonian definition of the sick role is relevant here since it presumably "legitimates deviance" and illness as deviance becomes even more significant for chronic than for acute sickness. In a youth-oriented society age itself is seen as a form of deviance and meets with the stigma, repugnance, anger, annoyance, and other hostile reactions of the "healthy" toward the "ill," of the "normal" toward the "abnormal." When physical or mental infirmity accompanies old age, these reactions are compounded. Furthermore, according to Stein, similar reactions greet chronic illness regardless of age, especially in such cases where the illness is defined as terminal or incurable and when the victim becomes apathetic, hopeless, and loses the will to live or to fight against his condition.

The deep ambivalence with which rehabilitators view their chronically-ill charges, who are in a sense unrehabilitatable, is a function at a psychodynamic level of the way that physicians, nurses, social workers, and other rehabilitators view themselves and see in the patient's disability and depression a reflection of their own self-repugnance and self-doubt. On the sociocultural level chronic illness is seen as "unAmerican," since it runs counter to the traditional values of American culture that stress independence, achievement, confidence in the future, optimism, youth, beauty, mobility, (and currently narcissism and "doing your own thing"), etc.

Rehabilitators not only meet the chronically ill with this emotion-laden negativism and ambivalence but seek to avoid them, shunt them away to other specialists, and rationalize their own gloom, avoidance, and probable failure through resort to stigmatization, humiliation, and denigration of the patient (a form of "blaming the victim"). Patients deal with the problem either through resignation or an unconscious splitting of the self between "me" and "not me," the latter, of course, being the diseased and/or aged self. Patient and therapists see clinical failure as moral failure in a "culturally shared projective system." Stein suggests that the health care-giver cannot really cope with the patient until "both in clinical training and practice, therapists . . . focus on their own expectations, attitudes and needs and talk less about the choreography of 'patient management,' because the former will influence the latter."

The same model may be applied to preindustrial societies (insofar as chronic illness is treated at all rather than considered as a "natural" and inevitable phenomenon), but eliciting the kinds of data Stein was able to collect in a medical school and hospital setting from patients, practitioners, students and others would, I believe, be extremely difficult. It would certainly require long-time immersion in the culture and language, probably more than most anthropologists can afford.

Elsewhere I have attempted a constructive critique of Parsons' landmark contribution of the sick role concept (Landy 1977a: 384–388). I should like briefly to summarize the major points of that assessment: (1) The sick role (and its complement, the doctor role) is formulated according to two different models which are superimposed upon each other: the sociological model of the middle-class family in the United States, in normative terms, and a psychodynamic – largely psychoanalytic – model of the patient-physician relationship. But the inherent paradox lies in the fact that while this relationship is structured somewhat as a child-parent relationship, it had to be characterized by behavior that was "universalistic," "functionally-specific," and "affectively neutral," in order to avoid the emotional entanglements that typify the family (Parson and Fox 1958). The problems involved in placing a socialized adult into a child-like status are not clearly worked out beyond assuming that the patient will accept the requirements of the role in order to recover, since the dimensions of the role have been "socially recognized" and "accepted" by society. (2) Being sick is seen by Parsons as a temporary form of deviance, and the sick role and physician role are seen as means of social control. But unlike other deviants, the role forbids the patient to "form a 'sub-culture' of the sick," defines the role as undesirable, and precludes the possibility "for everybody to get sick," since this would clearly disable the social system. Parsons does not deal sufficiently with departures from his model, assuming such persons or groups are "peripheral" or "marginal," and presumably not significant. (3) The model may apply more clearly to psychic than to physical illness, since, as I note, "the occurrence of physical illness brings with it a whole train of factors and consequences not involved in psychological disturbance, or at least very differently involved." (4) Parsons indicates here and there that he is aware that the model is culture-bound, and that "kin-based" societies probably deal with the role differently. But he does not spell out clearly what such differences might be. Similarly, it is class-bound, a point of which Parsons seems less aware. Insofar as different social classes possess different subcultures, we should accordingly expect some differences by social class in the way the role is conceptualized.

It is even possible to conceive of situations in which the sick role is eliminated as a viable option for persons who are otherwise undergoing genuine suffering. This happens when the cultural definition of being ill works to neutralize or cancel the legitimacy of the sick role. Lebra (1972) observes in Tenshō, a Japanese religious sect, which has healing as one of its major functions, that illness becomes symptomatic of spiritual power, but a spiritual attack of illness may indicate malign, benign, or neutral spiritual intent and such illness may be interpreted in various ways. Sickness may also be taken as a sign of testing by the Supreme spirit, Kami. Traditionally in Japan heavy demands for conformity stimulate frequent use of the sick role as a sanctioned release from stress and as a masochistic attempt to induce stress (guilt) in others. Tenshō changes all this since in it illness inspires shame and guilt in the victim, who is deemed to bring about his suffering through his own culpability. Sickness becomes supernatural punishment for religious or social wrong conduct. The Tenshō convert experiences deep, painful guilt when ill, thus in effect denying the legitimacy of the sick role. "The only way he can expiate his guilt is to save [his suffering, deceased mother's] spirit, which is signified by his own recovery."

Sickness represents a denial of the difficult Tenshō norms and of obligations of the member to sectarian comrades. Rewards of sect affiliation are economic, interactional, affectional, and tactile for persons who join because of strong needs in these areas. Recovery is proof of the sect's reward system which is activated by the convert's prayers. When one is sick one's sectarian colleagues avoid all contact for fear of contamination and sympathy for the patient is minimized. "... Change in desirability and change in legitimacy reinforce each other until the point is reached where the sick role is eliminated."

But in a culture in which the sick role is legitimate but particular disease states are not, assumption of the sick role is itself a symbol of suffering from a stigmatized condition. In diseases that are dreaded, but where a few recover, as in cancer, diabetes, etc., the result may be enhanced status through admiration for struggling successfully against a frequently mortal attack. But some diseases, in addition to actual or supposed impairment of the victim, carry with them an onerous burden of stigma that transforms the patient into a social outcast, for example, venereal disease or leprosy. The latter has been long surrounded by a complex mythology difficult for its victims to shake off. Not all victims of such culturally branded maladies accept their fate passively. A unique study by Gussow and Tracy (1968) shows how some of them struggle against the corrosive effects of stigma by assuming not simply the sick role, but a *career patient status*. Characteristics of the disease complicate the career patient status but do not deflect it.

To counter the opprobrious consequences of the conventional and medical theories of leprosy and its corresponding stigma, patients in a leprosarium create, as it were, a new subculture for themselves (and consequently new images of "impression management") by constructing their own theory of the disease and its stigma in order to destigmatize their disability, and of course themselves. As Gussow and Tracy point out, "such statuses and ideologies are not limited to this illness alone." For example, mental illness carries a strong stigma and "The entire mental health movement is in a sense directed toward attenuating the stigma of mental illness." Similarly with alcoholism and other diseases in which self-image and community definition are heavily stigmatized.

Such studies do not, in my opinion, invalidate the sick role concept. But they do help to correct and modify it, and extend its explanatory usefulness. I believe that in spite of the limitations to Parsons' conceptualizations, some of which I have dealt with above, his ideas are among the most important in social science and medicine. It is the task of medical anthropology further to refine the sick role model as it is adapted to nonWestern, preindustrial societies, and to various social, ethnic, and other collectivities within the structure of mass industrial society as well.

Witchcraft, Sorcery, Evil Eye: Human Causes of Human Sickness and Other Miseries

Witchcraft, sorcery, and the evil eye are held to be implicated in sickness and other misfortunes in all those societies (most of the world) where people believe their health and their lives may be harmed by the intentional or unintentional evil that others send their way through magical means. The assumption of baneful humans who can cause one to sicken, suffer, and/or die is a *sine qua non* of medical systems that include witchcraft and sorcery among their principal diagnostic classes. But since they occur in a wide variety of human groups in every kind of environment and ecological setting, the important question for medical anthropology is: under what kinds of conditions, or combination of conditions, can we expect they will occur? Beyond that, we shall need to know some of the consequences for individuals and societies of such medical beliefs.

For a number of reasons which I suggest elsewhere (Landy 1977a: 231) the terms witchcraft and sorcery are frequently confounded in the literature, and often there seems to be as much ambiguity regarding them in anthropological monographs as in the cultures where purportedly they are found. As I shall point out subsequently, this may be inherent in the way the concepts are formulated and operationalized in the societies that use them. They are certainly associated with anxiety about anticipated or experienced loss: of health, physical appearance, wealth, social position, power, reputation, and even life itself. But they also seem to be associated with the perception of threat to the welfare of the community or society as a whole and with the need to concretize that threat in persons or classes of persons. Public flogging or execution of witches no longer occur in industrial societies, but witch-hunting as a solution to real or supposed disease in the social body did not cease with the Salem trials.

Some years after Foster proposed his concept of "the image of limited good" in peasant society (Foster 1966), he published another essay on "the anatomy of envy" (Foster 1972) in which he suggested that (1) feelings of envy were universal in human society, (2) they operate with especially telling effect in peasant societies or others with scarce resources and the image of limited good (finite limits on resources impose a more or less egalitarian distribution and various levelling mechanisms in such societies work to effect equal allocation); (3) fear of envy is one such mechanism; and (4) one way in which fear of envy is expressed is in accusations of evil eye-caused disease. In other words, having too much wealth, beauty, etc. is punishable through terrible misfortune afflicting the envied status, and persons possessing the evil eye are to be avoided. To make his point Foster admittedly overdraws his argument so that almost anything or anyone may become the object of envy. He believes that in Western societies "man has rather successfully repressed his true feelings about envy, which he is taught is the most shameful of emotions. But even while denying it, man in all cultures has found devices, most but not all of which are symbolic, to cope with his fear of the consequences of envy." These consequences include "hostility and aggression capable of destroying individuals and even societies." Needless to say, this essay drew a good deal of both positive and negative criticism. It does seem to me, however, that used judiciously both concepts may help to explain *some* social behaviors, especially in societies with sparse supplies of the good things in life. They seem especially germane to notions of witchcraft and evil eye, the latter of which one may see as a variant or subclass of the former (Landy 1977a:196, 218).

In an analysis of the evil eye belief among a group of relatively wealthy landowning Amharic peasants in Ethiopia, Reminick (1974) utilizes Foster's notions of envy in "deprivation societies" (those holding the image of limited good) as well as those of Douglas (1970) in virtually equating evil eye with witchcraft beliefs, assuming their universality, and casting the concept of the witch as external or internal enemy or deviant. Reminick also alludes approvingly to Kennedy's (1969) insistence that, contrary to the concept of witchcraft and sorcery as having the more positive functions of revealing and healing dangerous tensions in the social system through diagnosis and treatment (as expressed in the work of such anthropologists as Gluckman, Turner, Harwood, inter alia), "witchcraft systems are forms of institutionalized patterns of psychopathology which tend to be pathogenic and which create built-in self-perpetuating stress systems . . . [and] tend to regularly generate the hate and aggression which they allegedly function to relieve." My own view is that Kennedy's dissent from the pervasive conceptions of witchcraft as a positive force in socio-political systems, often presented as part of elaborate structural and/or symbolic analyses, is a needed corrective to these at times almost simplistic functionalist approaches. At the same time, as so often seems to characterize such theoretical controversies, the conventional wisdom is not thus rendered obsolescent. As with many institutions in social and cultural life, witchcraft and sorcery (and the evil eye) may have *both* positive and negative effects on the social and medical system of which they are elements. Thus, one can easily think of positive *and* negative effects of Western scientific medicine, and of its many variants and alternatives, on both the individual and group levels. One function does not necessarily negate the other, but in terms of its overall effects, an assessment must be made of the net costs measured against the net gains.

In Reminick's study, the evil eye belief is part of a caste system in which

Amhara land-owning peasants conceive of themselves as a nobility who are both dependent upon, and threatened by, a class (caste) of skilled craftspeople, the *tayb*, who turn out the fine and very necessary implements required economically by the peasants, but which they do not deign to make for themselves since they despise manual labor. By definition these crafts identify their practitioners as possessors of the evil eye, since the *rega* (peasant nobility) assume that the *tayb* covet their wealth, land, and even their presumably handsome bodies and clothing. The terms *tayb* and *buda* (evil eye, evil spirit) are used interchangeably. The craftspeople are the *buda* people, and to neutralize their potential attack to cause serious illness while a *rega* is in a vulnerable state, the latter always attempt to portray themselves as composed and unworried, but also silent and guarded, dressing modestly and living simply, since the appearance of beauty and wealth will magnetize the evil eye. In Foster's terms, the evil eye represents envy and its belief represents the fear of envy in a "deprivation society." In Douglas' conception, while the *buda* seem to be insiders, since they are, after all, a segment of the same society, they are perceived by the Amhara as outsiders even though they live in the same area, participate to some extent in the same social network, and are part of a symbiotic socioeconomic system. Hate and tension are indeed generated, in Kennedy's idiom, but at the same time Reminick sees positive functions being served (for example, "The landless *buda*, who is dependent upon others for his livelihood, is the symbolic reflection of the threat of becoming landless and without authority, *ergo*, without identity, because of the ambitions of a more powerful relative or the father's curse of disinheritance.")

Projecting their fear and anger onto the outcaste *buda* people preserves asserts Reminick, "the internal solidarity (what there is of it) of the Amhara people." Perhaps. But since the outside observer may see the two groups as essential parts of a transacting social system, one may ask (1) whether the evil eye belief does anything for the *buda* people, and (2) whether the function of preserving the status quo of a caste system may be assumed to be an unalloyed good. Clearly one of the hazards of unthinking or uncritical functionalism is to find "integrative" positive purpose to institutions that operate essentially to preserve systems of grievous inequality. One must always ask of any social institution or cultural practice, "functional for whom, for what, and under what conditions and value-orientations?"

Messing (1959, 1975) also studied an Amhara people, and also examines the evil eye belief in terms of Foster's concepts. He infers that its strong persistence among a mainly rural people serves as a deterrent to positive change. He concludes: (Messing 1975)

(1) Ethnic outcasting of craftsmen discourages young people from entering skilled trades . . . .

(2) Encapsulation of ethnic craftsmen has not had the effect of reducing envy . . . . On the contrary, the syndrome cultivates attitudes of fear, witch-hunting, and scapegoating. It reinforces nonscientific beliefs in the causation of disease . . . .

(3) Health care programs in peasant societies require massive input of public health education. This should also have the effect of separating attitudes of disease causation from any lingering objections to craftsmen. Stigma attached to the latter can then be removed by general education.

While Messing's statements are interesting, and suggest support for Kennedy's view of witchcraft as a mainly destructive social institution, he does not present the data necessary to reach the three inferences made above and the reader is left with no evidence either to substantiate or refute Messing's statements.

As happens so frequently in theoretical generalizations in the social sciences, the conditions under which a theory is presumed to work are not clearly stated. Since no theory holds under any and all circumstances, the preconditions for the application of a theory must be specified as precisely as possible. This happens only sometimes in the social sciences, in part because of the complexity and ambiguity of human behavior and in part because many social scientists either ignore or are unaware of this fundamental principle. For example, the notion of the witch as deviant insider or outsider does not hold under all conditions. In a study of witchcraft in a "disease-ridden" Chontal-speaking community (Oaxaca, Mexico), Turner (1970) documents the case of a man in his fifties being executed for witchcraft by an assassin hired by another man who felt he and his family were victims. Far from being a deviant, or even embodying personal and social characteristics disvalued by the community, the accused witch "advanced through every office in the village until he was elected president and later became a member of the socially respected elders. He was not a social misfit in any sense . . . ". His turkey was killed by a neighbor's daughter and his mother-in-law predicted dire misfortune for the girl. Subsequently a burro belonging to the girl's father died, then the girl herself became ill and died. The mother-in-law declared this was because of her misdeed and the girl's father then accused his neighbor of killing the girl through witchcraft. Despite the father's request, village authorities refused to intervene, since they feared the power and retaliation of the accused. Later the girl's mother also died. The accused witch and his wife were arrested and fined, but since the man forced the wife to pay the fine, she spread the word that he was indeed a witch and his murder followed.

Thus, high social status and respect do not inevitably protect against witchcraft accusations. The conditions for this event were the witchcraft statements made by the man's mother-in-law and wife, frequent resort to coercive threats by the "witch" that could be interpreted as witchcraft intimidation, and the deaths in rapid succession of the burro, the girl, and her mother. It took the actual occurrence of the latter events to persuade the girl's father that he and his family had suffered from the machinations of the accused witch, and to carry out his vengeance. Why, then, risk the witchcraft accusation? Turner responds:

> ... The risk involved is not as great as it might appear because the statements are always ambiguous and can be interpreted in different ways. There must probably always be an element of ambiguity in witchcraft for it to be operative in any culture. If witches could be easily identified among the Chontal, they would be eliminated before they could cause any anxiety. But no Chontal openly admits being a witch, and any of them, when angry, can make a statement which may have witchcraft implications ... .
>
> Witchcraft among these people involves one person coercing others, and this is only possible when the one practicing witchcraft is known. The motivation of R as well as of the other accused witches ... seems to be a desire to exercise power over others. In the process they must expose themselves, at least in part. They have what Aberle has called negative charisma in the sense that they are disvalued but have unusual influence over others.

There is now a sufficient body of ethnographic data on witchcraft and sorcery that the whole needs to be reconsidered and recodified. The aim of this task would be to refine present theory so as to spell out clearly (1) the various social situations under which these phenomena seem to be implicated in disease etiology in human society; (2) the conditions that are essential for providing both a necessary and sufficient sociopsychological explanation of how they cause disease, i.e., their etiological functions; and (3) sociocultural, psychological, economic, environmental, medical, and other factors that may play a role in causing individual and group conflict and illness, and yet which do *not* implicate witchcraft, sorcery, or their variants. All societies experience stress and strain and many hold the image of limited good, yet neither envy nor anger nor balefulness necessarily always conduce toward the accusations of witchcraft or sorcery, nor tempt people into acts that will be perceived as involving these evil actions. Not every deviant or overreaching powerful individual will fall under the axe of the witchcraft indictment. Even in societies like that of the Chontal people in Turner's study where there is a high incidence of infectious disease morbidity and mortality (and to which the girl and her mother probably succumbed), one cannot assume that unexpected deaths will always provoke the cry of "witch!" What we badly need to know is why – and why not?

Except for Foster's essay on envy and its consequences for such beliefs as witchcraft and evil eye, insofar as I can determine during the past decade, only one other anthropologist has incremented significantly the theories and models previously utilized in this area. I shall discuss first very briefly the earlier theories and then consider the work of that anthropologist.

In the introduction to his outstanding anthology, *Witchcraft and Sorcery*, Marwick (1970) states: "The theories of witchcraft that have been implicitly or explicitly put forward fall into three main categories, historical or ethnological, psychological, and sociological; and the last of these may be subdivided into those theories that emphasize normative aspects of social organization and those centering on tension and social change." Marwick terms the first category "theories which, on the basis of history or conjectural history, account for the present distribution of witch-beliefs and for the developments within a particular society that have given rise to its characteristic pattern of beliefs." I should reserve this definition for mainly historical theories, as in the work of Caro Baroja (1965) as he traces the development of witchcraft beliefs in Western Europe from classic Greece and Rome to modern times, using an historical approach with some digressions to the work and theories of anthropology. I suggest that "ethnological" should be used for anthropological theories that are essentially cultural-functional, that explain witchcraft as it serves integrative or disintegrative functions in a culture.

I agree with Marwick's generalization that psychological theories "stem from Freud's doctrine of the displacement of affect and derivative neo-Freudian hypotheses about the projection of urges and conflicts into culturally standardized fantasies." Kluckhohn's (1944) study of Navaho witchcraft is an illustration, although he uses sociological notions of deviance as well.

The two variants of sociological theories are also worth noting: (1) Those that are built on the notion that witches embody the contrary poles of the norms that characterize a society, that they are, *par excellence*, the epitome of social deviants, but more than the embodiment of negative social values, witches may (a) perform actual harm, and (b) serve as negative role models. Marwick suggests that by indirection "they may also play positive moral roles in being the points of retrospective projection for feelings of guilt resulting from acts of foolishness and meanness that a believed victim may have committed." In the latter instance, Marwick has, perhaps unwittingly, introduced a psychological explanation into a sociological theory. (2) Those theories that are built around the notion of witchcraft accusations as indicators of social tensions and conflict, possibly symptomatic of social change. As Marwick phrases it:

> The relative frequency of accusations in various social relationships provides us with a set of social strain-gauges for detecting where the tensions and role-conflicts in a particular society lie. In keeping with the abandonment by anthropologists of a static functional model in favour of a more dynamic view of social trends and processes, this theory is undergoing modification, greater attention now being paid to the part accusations play in manipulating social situations and in involving the community as a whole in issues hitherto confined to those persons directly enmeshed in the quarrel from which the accusation stems.

As with all types, the preceding two are not mutually exclusive. One may think of studies that exemplify both types of explanation, for example, Epstein's (1967) account of a multicaste Mysore peasant village in India. Here, as a result of social change, some peasants have acquired great wealth, part of which they allocate to their wives, who, to put their money to "work," lend it to needy poor peasants at exorbitant interest rates. These usurious women are strongly hated by the poorer peasants, and when the interest payments become especially painful, a moneylender may be accused of witchcraft, especially if an additional misfortune, such as disease, strikes the borrower or a member of his family. These women symbolize evil values (usury, greed), and their actions and the perceptions of their actions also indicate sources of internal conflict and change. And the community is drawn in at a village council trial of the accused witch. Villagers prefer to settle their charges at the village level, since if the woman is denounced to the town police, this will richochet onto the accusers, as witchcraft accusations are officially outlawed by the central government.

Selby (1974) proposes a variation on these classes of witchcraft theory, basing his proposal on the work of Basso (1969). Three of the theory types he terms "functionalist," and a fourth is "based on social structure:" (1) The *social psychological* explanation, based on the notion that traditional societies stress harmony, order, and nonviolence, but witchcraft accusations serve as an outlet for repressed antisocial feelings and the witch serves as scapegoat to "deflect antisocial aggressiveness from the inner group, where it can do irreparable harm to social relations." (2) The *behavioral control* explanation, in which the witch serves as a negative role model, especially in socialization as a way of inculcating the social norms. Either the witch will harm the child, or if the child does not toe the cultural line, he may be isolated and punished as people treat witches. (3) The *tension and conflict indicators* model explains the points and sources of social tensions or disruption in times of sociocultural change. (4) The *social-structural psychological* model is based on the assumption that social structures and social relations may themselves stimulate the kinds of conflicts and tensions that call forth accusations of witchcraft or sorcery, for example, between ego and his mother's brother in a matrilineal society over matters of inheritance.

Selby does not refer to Marwick's classification, yet the two typologies clearly overlap. But these explanations are not mutually exclusive. As Selby points out, ". . . they are closely related and . . . social scientists, by and large, have tended to rationalize the local ideas about witchcraft in terms of the scientists' own prevailing folk model." In Selby's (1974) fine study, *Zapotec Deviance*, where witchcraft beliefs are one major focus, he shows how the anthropological folk model and the Zapotec folk model converge at most points. Selby's contribution lies not only in the cogency of his analysis of Zapotec witchcraft, in which his approach is itself a combination of the social structural and psychological, though mainly and essentially the former, but in his application of "labeling" theory, borrowed from sociology and social psychology, to witchcraft and other forms of deviance in Zapotec society. He asserts that psychological explanations of witchcraft, or other deviance, would be incomprehensible to the Zapotecs since they not only take their social structure for granted, but they tend to think in sociological terms, and to explain deviance in such terms. His analysis leads him to conclude that labeling theory provides a powerful explanation for witchcraft beliefs. It does not obviate the earlier explanatory models but goes beyond, and supplements, them. Without in any way denigrating labeling theory (indeed I agree with its powerful potential), I suggest that it is a kind of extreme relativistic model. For, as stated by Selby:

Finally, and ultimately, there is no deviance in the world, except as we create it by labeling offenders. Finally, and ultimately, there is no absolute character to the categories of deviance; they are creations of the social order and the ideas that we have about that order.

I submit, further, that all of the theory types used so far to explain witchcraft and sorcery are varieties of equilibrium theory. In one way or another each one, or any combination of them, assumes that a social structure – and an individual – is in equilibrium, in some degree of dynamic balance or steady state. Accusations of witchcraft or sorcery or evil eye are signs to the observer that things are not well, that the equilibrium has been invaded or disrupted, that the network of social relations or the physical organism of the individual is hurt, diseased, agonized. The task of the diviner or diagnostician is to detect these signs, both in the suffering person and the injured social system, to find the witch or sorcerer that has so foully assaulted the social-moral organism, and by trying and punishing the witch, pave the way for the repair of the insults that have harmed the person and his family, lineage, clan, or community. Harwood (1977) suggests "that this procedure of conflict resolution is necessary because of the vagueness of the norms specifying one's obligations to one's lineal kin." Similarly, Selby found not only the same kinds of vagueness among the Zapotec, but also vagueness about who, specifically, in the community was a witch. When he questioned eight trusted informants as to the identity of witches, they named collectively a total of 28 persons, but not a single one of the 28 was named by all informants and only a handful was identified by a majority of informants. In fact, the one person receiving the highest degree of agreement among informants was himself unaware that he was so considered. A wealthy farmer in another community reputed to be a powerful witch did not himself believe in witchcraft, but cynically exploited his baleful reputation as a way of obtaining workers for his huge farm (by making men afraid to refuse his request).

While Selby's Zapotec community conforms to Wolf's (1957) model of the "closed corporate community," where one would think "institutionalized envy" and the notion of "limited good" would help explain the operation of witchcraft, Selby finds that one need not assume that this notion is held uniformly in such a community, or that envy operates only as evil thoughts against someone having more of the limited good. Selby says, "envy is a relative thing," and, for example, if one farmer has had only an 'average' return during a year but another has had a bad year, the former may assume the latter may wish him ill as a way of restoring the balance. (It might be noted that the notion of limited good is itself an equilibrium type of theory, presumably a folk model of the availability of resources and social relations which has been abstracted by an anthropologist.) Envy in Selby's Zapotec village is loosely conceived, as is deviance, witchcraft, and disease itself. The general vagueness of specificity of disease categories may be inherent in their very nature in all human societies, as I discuss elsewhere in this essay (The Logic of Indigenous Medical Systems). Selby notes compellingly:

> The villager has a theory, or an explanation for witchcraft, just as the social scientist does. And they are not dissimilar. Where the social scientist looks for tension, the villager looks for envy. Where the social scientist examines interpersonal relations, the villager introspects about his relationships with other people. Where the social scientist looks for predisposing circumstances that will activate the process of a witch hunt, the villager looks at sickness and through diagnostics rationalizes the process of locating witches in the community. The social scientist admits the social definition of witches and accords them a reality that derives from cultural definition; the villager elaborates an ideology about the nature of the soul and its relationships with the animal and the spirit world. Both make the assumption that everyone agrees to the major propositions about the identification of witches (and in this village through *tonos* [a second soul, of an animal familiar, in addition to the Christian soul]) and the identity of witches. It is not important that people do or do not agree on the criteria that define witches, or on who the witches are. The importance of witchcraft lies in the general process that generates witch identification and in the sociological consequences of the activity of labeling.

Because there is widespread and continuing serious illness and frequent unexpected deaths, the process of witch-naming and hunting goes on constantly, first in the inner family circle, and through gossip and rumor to the whole community. The labeling of witches, in Selby's view, is more than a marking of deviants. It is a continual process of defining and redefining the insiders and the outsiders. By definition one cannot expect a person will be a witch who seems fully to express the key values of humility, trust, and respect – and who does not engage in actions expressing envy, aggressiveness, mistrust, lack of respect, and lack of generosity and reciprocity. As Selby puts it, "symbolic exchange is the major activity that creates community," and good and evil are summarized in the positive and negative values just enumerated. People are constantly concerned with maintaining the social order, which is also a moral order, and in creating ideologies and myths to explain the actions of themselves and others. Selby invokes psychology enough to suggest that people maintain such myths as witchcraft because they need to express and respond to their anxieties and conflicts. In the language of labeling theory, deviance is created as a way of defining and maintaining the norms.

Selby is aware of the tautology implicit in his analysis. Perhaps there is no way to break out of the kind of implicit circular reasoning of the mainly equilibrium-type theories of witchcraft. At least one escape hatch may present itself in Kennedy's (1969) insistence that witchcraft serves dysfunctional as well as functional ends, in the sense that, if it reduces the tensions of the accusers and the conflicts in the social system, it punishes the accused, often (perhaps usually) unjustly, and perpetuates an inequitable system of justice. If it reduces anxieties when stirred into motion, it also generates anxieties, and since ultimately no one can be certain that the finger will not point in his direction, such societies exist in a constant state of suspicion, distrust, and paranoia. It would serve a useful purpose, and perhaps could lead to a less tautological theory, if studies of witchcraft concentrated as much on the lives of the witches as of their accusers, and told us more about the consequences to them and their circle of kin as much as of their supposed victims. For the process is a kind of spiral of victimization, with the perceived victims in turn victimizing their putative oppressors. As I have remarked in commenting on the classic study of sorcery in Dobu by Fortune (1963), "In this highly competitive, profoundly suspicious culture, where in effect a kind of Hobbesian amalgam of fear, hostility, jealousy, and distrust rule the passions, where the greatly valued behaviors and achievements are also the most dangerous, sorcery and its concomitant, disease, exist side by side in a hazardous game of life" (Landy 1977a: 198).

I should like to note one final problem. Selby's analysis of Zapotec witchcraft indicates a general gradient of probability of witchcraft accusation that increased with the distance from the accuser's kin and neighborhood circles. But other studies have suggested that the accusation seems more likely to strike within the kinship or neighborhood orbit. Mayer (1970), for example, states the latter principle as follows:

Two general rules seem to emerge from the literature. The first is that witches and their accusers are nearly always people close together, belonging to one neighbourhood community or even to one household. This principle is expressed in the witchcraft myth by the notion that witches cannot harm you from far away but only from close by. The second rule is that a witchcraft accusation nearly always grows out of some personal antipathy or hostile emotion ... In the typical case, then, the alleged witch is a neighbour and perhaps a kinsman of the accuser who has not been getting on well with him or her. .... For example, among many African peoples it is specially common for a woman to accuse her husband's other wife of being a witch. ... We must conclude that witches and their accusers are individuals who ought to like each other but in fact do not.

Mayer admits some exceptions to his rule but feels they are the exceptions that prove the rule. My own reading of the literature suggests that these "exceptions" are not as "few" as Mayer insists, but clearly this is a point requiring further study. As one must ask for any kind of anthropological or sociological "rule," "under what conditions should we expect this rule to apply, and under what conditions should we expect a different rule to apply?"

Ethnic Disorders or Culture-Bound Reactive Syndromes

Anthropologists and some psychiatrists have long been interested in certain acute behavioral disturbances that seem to be peculiar to specific cultures, and which they have labelled variously as "ethnic neuroses," "ethnic psychoses," "cultural psychoses," etc. None of these labels is completely satisfactory since they are based upon nosological notions stemming from Western clinical psychiatric classification systems, and seem at once to place an ethnocentric judgment upon the data. Some of them may not occur with high frequency even within their own cultural milieux and thus even within a specific culture perhaps should be regarded as "atypical." LeVine (1973:29–37) labels such phenomena *rare-zero differentials*: "Some traits thought of as characteristic of a given population are actually rare within it but are totally absent in populations with which it is being compared. ... Insofar as they are truly absent in other populations they represent genuine rare-zero differentials."

There are some problems with even this qualification, since certain entities that the Western observer might view as culture-specific but sporadic in fact seem to occur with some frequency. Furthermore, there is some question not only as to whether these phenomena are considered locally to be atypical but even as to whether they are seen as severe disturbance. Among the kinds of phenomena that have come to be placed into these categories have been *latah, amok, susto, pibloktoq, koro, windigo* (*wittiko*), saka, "falling-out," and various states of dissociation, possession, trance, and "malignant" anxiety.

A psychiatrist, P.M. Yap (1969) made an important contribution to thinking about these phenomena by freeing them from premature ethnocentric classification and at the same time making it possible to compare them meaningfully with Western medical diagnostic categories by suggesting the concept of "culture-bound reactive syndromes." Yap states:

These terms are culture-bound in that certain systems of implicit values, social structure, and obviously shared beliefs produce unusual forms of psychopathology that are confined to special areas. Social and cultural factors bring about special forms of illness, although these are only atypical variations of generally distributed psychogenic disorders.

Undoubtedly some will debate Yap's reasoning in placing these "culture-bound reactive syndromes" into the symptom clusters of Western psychiatric nosology. But his effort, as he explains, helps to raise some important questions and research agendas for transcultural psychiatry and for medical anthropology. We shall consider some of these subsequently, but first we turn our attention to three symptom patterns that have been studied with some frequency by anthropologists and psychiatrists: (1) the disturbance called *susto* (or *espanto*) in Hispanic American cultures which Yap classifies as a "fear-induced depressive state;" (2) the behavioral deviation termed variously *windigo*, *wittiko*, etc., found among certain Northeastern Canadian Native Americans, which Yap designates as a psychotic possession syndrome involving dissociation; and (3) the spasmodic, hysteriform outburst found among some Eskimo groups that they call *pibloktoq*, frequently grouped with "ethnic psychoses" by anthropologists, but excluded from "culture-bound reactive syndromes" by Yap.

A classic early essay on *susto* by Gillin (1948) referred to it as "magical fright," and noted symptoms that paralyzed the victim into a state of extreme fear and apathy, triggered by a sudden shock or trauma believed to cause the soul to flee the body. Rubel (1964) labelled *susto* a "folk illness," which he defines as "syndromes from which members of a particular group claim to suffer and for which their culture provides an etiology, diagnosis, preventive measures, and regimens of healing." Rubel insists that this folk illness may be studied epidemiologically:

Despite localized embellishments on a general theme of soul-loss illness, there recurs in many societies a hard core of constant elements which lead one to conclude that this phenomenon is indeed subject to orderly description and analysis. Moreover, inferences of causality drawn from the ethnographic data offer great potential for understanding the nature of folk illness and some facets of the relationships which obtain between health and social behavior.

Rubel (1964) proposed four hypotheses: (1) *Susto* is chosen as a sick role in some, but not all, cases of self-perceived stress (evil eye, for example, might be invoked for other stresses), and such persons "elect the kinds of symptoms by which to make manifest to others an absence of well-being." (2) "The social stresses which are reflected in the *susto* syndrome are intra-cultural and intra-societal . . . ." Effects of alienation or blocked mobility due to stress between cultures or social classes "will not be reflected by *susto*." (3) *Susto* will come about because of inability to meet requirements of a social role for which the person has been socialized. Since male and female roles differ markedly, the sexes will be differentially affected by role stress, and *susto* rates will differ. (4) Personality and societal variables will operate to determine which individuals choose *susto* where two or more are otherwise matched for age and sex. Just as some cultures choose *susto* to express self-perceived social inadequacies, so some, but not all, persons will select this route to demonstrate their soul-sickness and their hope of social reintegration.

O'Nell and Selby (1968) sought to test the first three hypotheses by comparing data for two Zapotec (Oaxaca, Mexico) villages. Their general hypothesis was, "The sex which experiences the greater intra-cultural stress in the process of meeting sex role expectations will evidence the greater susceptibility to *susto*." Ethnographically they found females subject to greater sex role stress in both communities, as in most Meso-american studies. They also found corresponding statistically significant differences in the (reported) incidence rate of *susto* in both villages (Village A: 40% men [N = 15], 67% women [N = 15]; Village B: 20% men [N = 20], 55% women [N = 20]). These data, and additional findings which cannot be detailed here, appear to confirm Rubel's Hypotheses 1–3. They did not test Hypothesis 4 dealing with the critical question of why some individuals and not others, even within the sexes, prefer *susto* as a sick role. Apparently they did not have the requisite personality and other variables on each subject. And they matched them only for sex, not age.

Like Rubel, and O'Nell and Selby, Uzzell (1974) presupposes that assumption of the role of *asustado* (having *susto*) is a mode of behavioral deviance. His study is methodologically less satisfactory than the earlier ones. He tells us, for example, that he had 47 respondents reporting 23 cases of *susto* in their families – responding to a list of presented illnesses – but fails to supply the sex or age of the respondents. Uzzell says that the 23 cases comprised 12 women, four men, and seven children. The universe, and indeed the sample, is impossible to identify here. While the male–female differential is in the expected direction, Uzzell insists on some possible qualifications to the idea of *susto* as a "strategic role." The passivity characteristic of *susto* is more acceptable in the culture because it is closer to normal role expectations of women than of men. However, since the rate is "high" among children (how high, we are not told), certain assumptions of the earlier reports require reconsideration. For example, children should not be assumed to "elect" their symptoms, as Rubel proposed, since "it is adults, not the victims, who make the diagnosis." He also suggests that while Rubel's posited central core of common elements of *susto* is probably correct, the great flexibility of implementing the role and thus providing wide latitude for "peripheral" symptoms, considerably complicates a full understanding of its dynamics. But this very flexibility makes it a highly preferred form of deviance or "strategic role," one that may be less punishing than other forms of folk illness in the same cultures (evil eye, *muina*, *pasmo*, etc.). Uzzell argues that *susto* is a form of "misinvolvement" (following Goffman) in social interactions, but whereas misinvolvement usually elicits negative reactions from other participants in social interaction, *susto* permits the victim in a sense to "write his own ticket" in expressing his unhappiness, and this "enables him to impose his own definition on the situation, a definition that gives his otherwise deviant acts legitimacy." He points to the paradox that *susto* both signals withdrawl from interaction and "becomes a mechanism for maintaining interaction."

O'Nell (1975) more recently states that *susto* not only refers to an emotional syndrome widely distributed across Hispanic America as Rubel (1964) described, but that it "is a label applied by both native populations and ethnographers to several closely associated psychophysical conditions . . . ," in other words, to an illness cluster rather than a sharply delineated set of symptoms. It consists of a spectrum of conditions, symptoms, etiologies, and categories of victims, even though some general trends in all these may be detected. Thus, like many folk illnesses, including *pibloktoq*, and possibly *windigo*, *susto* lacks clear specificity. In this respect it is really not very different from any number of illnesses commonly referred to in the singular in Western medicine but actually representing a disease group, for example, schizophrenia, cancer, and diabetes.

O'Nell found in a sample of 24 substantiated cases in a Zapotec (Oaxaca, Mexico) community (14 female, 10 male), an age range from 15 to 65 years (actually some were younger but not included in the sample). *Susto* means "fright" in Spanish (also scare, shock), and is used by Zapotecs to describe both the initial traumatically-perceived event and the onset of *susto* symptoms. In these 24 cases the time lapse between the initial fright and the appearance of *susto* symptoms ranged from "immediate" to as much as seven years. Furthermore, there was no correlation between severity of fright and severity of symptoms. Dividing the cases between "rapid" (− 2 weeks) and "delayed" (+ 2 weeks) symptom development, and between human and nonhuman figures involved in the fright episode, O'Nell found a positive association between delayed onset of symptoms and nonhuman fright figures.

How does O'Nell explain these intriguing results? First, he rejects the notion that the indigenous etiological explanation is merely "a system of convenience, a post hoc rationalization for events with which a group of human beings must contend." The syndrome is deeply embedded in the culture and must have both individual and cultural adaptive significance, since it is nearly universally accepted. But how can the native and the social science explanations be reconciled? O'Nell finds that "Not only is there a convergence between folk and scientific explanations of folk illnesses, but a study of the convergence will provide the investigator with an added dimension of understanding within his own theoretical framework." (See also Selby 1974.) That framework for this analysis of *susto* is the theoretical model of role stress. The frequent long delay between initial fright and appearance of symptomatology "is consistent with a role stress theory of the etiology of the conditions that assumes that perceived deficiencies in meeting common role expectations tend to result from cumulative and protracted social psychological experiences of negative character." In other words, when the frustrating events and disappointed feelings that mark the cognition of a failed social role aggregate to a point where they can no longer be repressed, they are rationalized into a socially accepted act of deviance, or illness, symbolized in the signs and expressions associated with *susto*. Many of the themes in fright events, human and nonhuman, seem to symbolize directly and indirectly, feelings of anger. When the sensations of rage burst out in a culture that highly values nonviolence, such a person is said to be sick with another folk illness, *bilis*, and it is interesting to note that often an attack of *bilis* may be followed by an attack of *susto*. The apathy and listlessness typical of *susto* are favored cultural symptoms.

A logical question in regard to *susto* as well as similar folk disorders, and which has been investigated in the case of *pibloktoq*, as will be seen subsequently, is the role played by physiological or biochemical factors either in predisposing some individuals to greater susceptibility, or in some way being implicated in the onset, duration, severity, treatment, and outcome of these disorders. Klein (1978) has suggested this with regard to *susto* and calls this syndrome and similar disturbances resulting from trauma or fright "diseases of adaptation" after Hans Selye's notion that "many common diseases are largely due to errors in the body's adaptive response to stress, rather than to direct damage by germs, poisons, and other external agents . . . ." Such a concept would include role stress and other social, cultural, and psychological stressors as well as organic ones. It is one thing to insist, as Klein does, that there is an important physiological dimension to *susto*; it is quite another to demonstrate it specifically, and this she does not do. Rubel and O'Nell, with the collaboration of medical and psychological personnel, have performed epidemiological studies of *susto*, following Rubel's (1964) original proposal (see postscript at end of this section).

In the culture-bound reactive syndrome known variously as *windigo* or *wittiko*, the victim imagines himself possessed by a demon spirit, an ice-monster horrible of aspect, that craves human flesh and impels the victim to kill and eat people. Sometimes the victim imagines he is being transformed into the monster, becoming a *windigo*. The most frequent explanation by early anthropologists and other observers is that this apparently disordered behavior was a reaction to the cold and privation so frequently faced by the Algonkian Indians of North-eastern Canada in which *windigo* was both a manifestation of cultural belief and at times a fact. Starvation was both a frequent threat and a pervasive theme in the often-expressed anxieties of these people.

Rohrl (1970) suggests that an explanation may be found in nutritional deficiencies of the Cree and Chippewa (Ojibwa), especially of proteins and B vitamins (particularly thiamine), and possibly also Vitamin C. She derives this idea from one of her informants who noted that the cure was most often the administration of large quantities of bear fat or other fat (which contains the needed nutrients), the folk belief being that when the fat melted it melted the heart of the ice giant within. Rohrl also alludes to the data of a definitive study by Teicher (1960) in which bear fat appeared to be the remedy of choice, and she suggests that it "may reflect the result of long-term, not necessarily conscious, empirical observation . . . ." She insists that this does not do away with other factors cited as part of the etiology of *windigo*, and refers to Wallace's (1972) caution that "dietary deficiencies have different behavioral mani-festations in different cultures, depending on the total culture pattern."

However, Brown (1971) contradicts Rohrl's nutritional hypothesis, pointing out that the bear fat cure is noted in only two of 70 cases included in the Teicher study and cannibalism as directly caused by extreme hunger only in 25 cases. Additionally, the cure consisted of using bear fat to induce the victim to vomit his "heart of ice." Furthermore, the usual reaction of others was to kill the victim, either to forestall cannibalistic acts, or prevent further such acts after they had once occurred. Brown also reports that only 10 of Teicher's 70 cases are said to have recovered.

Teicher's (1960) study indicated that frequency of *reported* cases of *windigo* was highest in the 19th century, which might seem like a reaction to extreme acculturation pressures except that it was reported as early as the 17th century by Europeans. His total number is very low. While this is in part probably due to underreporting and the unlikelihood that Europeans would observe or easily be told of such occurrences, he feels that the phenomenon is rare, although today, in a population of at least 50,000, the *belief* remains widespread and persistent. Unlike common impressions that victims were usually male, Teicher's data are almost equally divided among both sexes and all stages of adulthood. He points out that this is unquestionably an example of spirit possession, which is noteworthy in that spirit possession is rarely reported for native North America, and that "the entire spectrum of psychiatric illness" was found among the cases. Teicher suggests that the belief is so powerful that it defines the character and content of the illness. Whether the victim resorted to expressed cannibalistic behavior voluntarily (through strong delusional fantasies) or involuntarily (through the pangs of starvation), once the symptoms appeared both victim and community inexorably followed the path of the culture pattern. Cannibalism was feared and tabooed, to openly express it was insane, and the culture designed the course for victim and community to pursue.

The problem with this explanation is that starvation is a fear among many other groups besides the Algonkian-speakers. Although the belief in *windigo* psychosis is universal among Algonkians, only a relatively small number succumb to the overt display of cannibalistic cravings. Some victims of *windigo* do not in fact eat human flesh, and when it does occur, it "is unritualized, socially uncontrolled cannibalism among people of a society in which cannibalism is strongly tabooed and regarded with horror" (Hay 1971:1).

Parker (1960), using a psychoanalytic model, suggests that roots of the illness can be found in the socialization of Ojibwa children in which emphasis "on self-reliance and individualism leads to unsatisfied dependency cravings and repressed hostility." Ojibwa modal personality and culture further frustrate these impulses, since the masculine role in this egalitarian social system is narrowly confined and prevented from special achievement. Only success in the hunt is permitted, so there is great anxiety around fear of hunting failure and loss of self-esteem. This leads in some men to rage, paranoia, and depression, and when defense mechanisms fail, they may be overtly expressed, accompanied by nausea, anorexia, and feelings of worthlessness and vulnerability. Repressed feelings can be converted to action through the culturally-constituted symbol of the *windigo* monster. While Parker suggests that "the *prototype* of the *wittiko* monster is the mother figure," in the adult Ojibwa "it is more fruitful, heuristically, to think of the *wittiko* monster as a phantasy figure symbolizing the wider circle of significant others who continue to frustrate the dependency cravings of the adult and constitute threats to his vulnerable self-esteem." The victim is transformed into the thing he fears most, in order to overcome it. Fearing his own impulses, he eats another lest he be eaten, and "the depressive conflict between the rebellious rage and the submissive fear is resolved." Thus, Parker's explanation rests on the impact of socialization, modal personality structure, and culture. But since he admits that "actual or even threatened starvation is not invariably part of the situation of the *wittiko* sufferer," one is left to conclude that socialization, modal personality, and culture have differing manifestations in different individuals.

Hay (1971) hypothesizes that "cannibalistic impulses may result in psychotic cannibalism, in psychosis without cannibalism, or in ritualized cannibalism without apparent psychosis, depending on the cultural and social conditions which surround the person whose cannibalistic tendencies have been intensified by some stress." He points out that in all societies many forms of psychosis may include a desire to eat human flesh (rarely implemented, of course). First, since only northern Algonkians seem in this region to surrender to cannibalistic impulses which may be widely experienced, this can be explained in part by certain cultural features, "first, their pronounced emphasis on individual acceptance of the promptings of the individual's unconscious as expressed in dreams, and second, the absence of alternative patterns for expressing these impulses in social controlled cannibalism or in symbolic fashion." In other words, there is a relative paucity of group ritual in the culture. Having *windigo* also depends upon

... the relative degree of control over their own cannibalistic impulses by those who are physically and emotionally close to the incipient *windigo*. If those around him have such good control that they are not frightened by his symptoms of loss of control, they treat him in ways which both strengthen his control and reduce the intensity of his cannibalistic impulses. If the self-control of those around the incipient *windigo* is less secure, so that they are frightened by his symptoms, then their behavior tends to exacerbate his symptoms and they usually kill the *windigo* before he and they give in to the desire to eat human flesh. If those around an incipient *windigo* are close to losing control of their impulses themselves, they may unconsciously encourage the incipient *windigo* to become a cannibal and, when he does, they may join him in eating human flesh (Hay 1971).

Finally we turn to the emotional disorder among some Eskimo groups known as *pibloktoq*, which Yap (1969) somewhat surprisingly excludes, along with certain others, from his classification schema, on the grounds that "they are only vague generic terms for mental illness or denote only ordinary, unspecialized hysterical reactions." Perhaps somewhat carried away with his point he adds, "Such terms should not be allowed to creep into the psychiatric literature." De Vos and Hippler (1969) nevertheless include *pibloktoq* in their category of "culture-specific forms of aberrant or unusual mental states," and Gussow (1960) hypothesizes that the etiology of the syndrome(s) can be derived almost completely from Eskimo culture and personality. Observers of Eskimo behavior in the 18th, 19th, and early 20th centuries remarked on the phenomenon, associating it with some of the conditions of Eskimo environment and culture: the sustained cold, the long nights, extended periods of close confinement in the small space of igloos.

A follower of Freud in the United States, A.A. Brill, characterized the syndrome as hysteria major, finding its genesis in frustration of emotional needs, especially love, on the part of women among whom it was most frequently observed. Gussow, building on Brill's notion of hysteria, saw the disorder as an attempt by women to gain attention through the symptomatology: sudden wild excited behavior with seemingly irrational, antisocial acts, including the tearing off of clothes, then fleeing into the Arctic cold, and requiring others to come to the rescue, which is usually successful. He found causes for this "seductive" behavior in Eskimo personality structure, culture patterns, and fear of environmental dangers and starvation during the long winters. Parker (1962) also finds etiological factors in Eskimo modal personality and culture, especially in certain social, economic, and religious aspects, and the socialization process. While utilizing a psychodynamic model like Gussow, he selects rather different elements to link to *pibloktoq*.

Psychogenic, sociogenic, and ecological explanations of "arctic hysteria" remained generally accepted until Wallace (1972) suggested an alternative hypothesis, namely that *pibloktoq* was at least in part a response to calcium deficiency, and that the symptom portrait was typical of the convulsive, spasmodic actions of persons suffering from hypocalcemic tetany. Wallace noted that others before him had also posited the calcium deficiency hypothesis, as well as the possibility that inbreeding in northern Greenland peoples might make many persons subject to epilepsy, and that "The hypocalcemia and epilepsy theories are not mutually exclusive ... since hypocalcemia would tend to precipitate a latent seizure in persons prone to epilepsy." He pointed to certain physiological characteristics of Eskimos noted by medical observers that might be associated with low concentrations of ionized calcium in the blood, and suggested that "the high arctic environment does not provide rich sources of nutritionally available calcium during all seasons of the year to technologically primitive populations." But Wallace also remarked on "the reported extreme rarity of rickets in Eskimo infants and of osteomalacia in Eskimo adults (for example, in pregnant and lactating women)," and admits that this could throw his hypocalcemia hypothesis into doubt, since he has also suggested that Eskimo diet is low "in sun-formed vitamin D_3." To account for this apparent negation of his hypothesis, he adds a corollary hypothesis that the Polar Eskimo through natural selection "chose" tetany rather than rickets "as the lesser of two evils," and that they tend to be "mildly hypoparathyroid," thus "yielding a type of hormonal balance which retains calcium in the bones even if calcium levels in serum fall occasionally."

Additionally, having found factors in Eskimo environment and technology for calcium dietary deficiency, he suggests somewhat paradoxically, it seems to me, that environment and technology still yield sufficient calcium and vitamin D_3 to prevent rickets in infants and lactating women, though restricting them at times through food taboos. Nevertheless, due to the needs of male hunters for "a strong and undistorted skeletal structure," the environment will "select the nervous and muscular system rather than the skeleton as the target tissue of any calcium and/or vitamin D_3 deficiency." And finally he states that Eskimo personality and culture may influence the form and content of *pibloktoq* symptomatology. Wallace even suggests that what has been psychiatrically termed "grand" hysteria, wherever it occurred, may have had such a biologic component as calcium and/or D_3 deficiency, even in Freud's Europe. He asks, "Why has hysteria virtually disappeared in Europe and the United States?" and he answers, "It has dissolved in bottles of milk and cod-liver oil . . . ."

Wallace admitted that his, as well as the purely psychogenic or psycho-cultural hypotheses, are "armchair theories" and urged a multidisciplinary approach to the study of such "exotic" disorders as *pibloktoq* (Wallace 1960, 1972). One of his graduate students, already trained in medicine, set out to do just that. Foulkes (1972) could not do fieldwork in Greenland, but did study the Innuit Eskimos of north Alaska in an attempt to implement the approach and methodology urged by Wallace. He employs the term Arctic Hysterias, and calls them "a group of mental disorders which have occurred with some frequency among circumpolar peoples from pre-contact periods to the present time." Foulkes concentrates on factors he feels are involved in these disorders: historical-cultural traditions, social organization, arctic environment, dietary patterns, general health factors such as parturition, prenatal morbidity, infant morbidity, central nervous system aberrations, and psychological factors. The overall aim was "not only to elucidate the particular causes of the Arctic Hysterias, but more importantly to demonstrate the inter-actions and summations of these factors as interdependent systems." One small village was the target community where six cases of *pibloktoq* were identified, to which were added four more from nearby communities to comprise a sample of 10. For each case data were collected on reported symptoms, associated circumstances, comparisons with known clinical entities, selection and ranking of alternative hypotheses, subsequent differential diagnosis by more intensive observation and interview, pursuit of the etiology "implicated by the confirmed diagnosis," and as much relevant ecological, psychological, neurological, biochemical, and socio-cultural data to be collected as could be done during the field period. While the medical model is used, a multisystems model is superimposed.

Foulkes notes that the Arctic Hysterias and other "related mental disorders" are found widespread in the Arctic regions. In the contemporary world Eskimo admissions to psychiatric hospitals in the Northwest Territory are about twice as high as Indian admissions and about three times as high as for whites *in absolute numbers*; the *rate* must be extremely high. However, while suicide rates of ethnic groups including Eskimos in the area are about the same, one observer has remarked that most Eskimo psychiatric hospital patients had suicidal tendencies. The data on psychiatric epidemiology are rich but too detailed to describe further here.

Despite the assumption by outsiders that the Arctic environment is so barren, bleak, and monotonous that it makes for sensory deprivation, Foulkes asserts that "through an Eskimo's eyes" the terrain, flora, and fauna provide a never-ending source of fascination and potential resources to sustain life. However, the absence of annual daily alternations of light and dark "affects the circadian cycling of calcium metabolism," and since calcium is required in the transmission of neural impulses, "abnormalities in the physiological functioning of calcium are capable of producing disorders including hysteria-like behavior." Although Foulkes' subjects had normal levels of calcium in the blood (contrary to Wallace's hypothesis), there is nevertheless an environmental effect on its functioning. Long periods of darkness plus the heavy clothing of the Eskimo reduce penetration of ultra-violet rays, decrease vitamin D, and thus affect calcium metabolism. Relatively small amounts of calcium are afforded the North Alaskan natives (though not in the South), resulting "in serum levels which fell on the low end of the physiological spectrum." All these factors "potentiated dysfunction of the Eskimo central nervous system." Furthermore, living now in houses rather than igloos, interior heat is no longer humidified, drying the nasal and respiratory passages and "rendering these surfaces vulnerable to infective agents." Respiratory diseases are common, leading to high fevers, middle ear disease, and meningitis, all of which affect the central nervous system and may result in serious behavior dysfunction and deficits.

Foulkes suggests many constraints inherent in the delicate balance between Eskimo culture and environment. Hunting large mammals required cooperation and the repression of competitiveness and anger. Emphasis was on mutual accommodation and achievement was confined to a very few roles, mainly hunting and shamanism. Tradition remained relatively unchanged for several thousand years since innovation and deviation threatened the gossamer human-environment equilibrium and was frowned upon and ridiculed. Fear of gossip and humiliation and constant monitoring kept people in line. Foulkes suggests that the outbursts of the shaman, the epileptic, and the victim of *pibloktoq* could provide some emotional catharsis, and while such persons are not interchangeable, "each behavior . . . obviously contains many causal elements shared with the others." What these are, however, is not spelled out. Foulkes also suggests that the demographic patterns of Eskimo bands living on the tundra (small, close-knit groupings, behaviors closely controlled, few emotional outlets) may also play a role in shamanistic or hysterical dissociative actions, and contrasts with the prevalence of the mental disorders of depression and alcoholism characteristic of Eskimos living in urban areas. The frequent visiting and interaction among Eskimo village bands provides the opportunity for rapid spread of infectious diseases. All 10 of his subjects were characterized by lifelong otitis media, with frequent suffering and impairment of the nervous system. An additional factor frequently found to affect calcium homeostasis and possibly contribute to the onset of Arctic Hysteria is hyperventilation which increases "the pH of the blood and binding the free calcium which reduces availability for neuronal functioning." Foulkes stresses that "There were many differences among our ten subjects in terms of which etiological agent acted as the major determinant of the Arctic Hysteria attack," though all were implicated.

The foregoing demonstrates that much effort and thought have gone into the attempt to understand and persuasively explain such seemingly exotic behaviors. We have indeed moved some distance beyond the hesitant, or overly-confident, explanations offered by earlier observers. But this presentation also makes it evident that the explanatory models we are offered, often intriguing and highly suggestive in themselves, remain to be more fully demonstrated as not only reasonable and plausible, but as better explaining these human events than alternative explanations. Each of the models – the psychodynamic or psychogenic, the sociogenic, the multicausal synthetic – have been utilized at the cost of ignoring or not cogently explaining many of the facts, and data at times seem to be pushed, pulled, and trimmed to fit each theory. This is said not so much as direct criticism as to point out what yet must be done. These scholars must be commended, for they have willingly undertaken an extremely difficult task, and each effort has added, whatever its flaws, an increment of knowledge, understanding, and insight, and often new dimensions of data, that are part of every scientific process toward reaching closer and closer approximations of "truth."

In considering the studies of *susto*, Uzzell proposes a series of interesting hypotheses for differentiating the "choice" of *susto* over other sick or deviant roles. He feels that we still know very little about how or why people choose this or that sick role while rejecting others. We must assume, of course, that each culture offers more than a single option in the process of expressing "dis-ease", and certainly for the cultures that utilize *susto* this appears to be the case. Assuredly, the question of sick role choice is a fundamental one for medical anthropologists. As I have noted (Landy 1977a:402),

> ... Though Uzzell does not say so, one could say that the assumption of the sick role under these conditions brings not only the usual "secondary gains" of illness (relief from normal role requirements) ... but that these rewards of the role may be seen as "primary." In converting the role for a given individual from the consensual fictions surrounding it to the reality of actual selection for action, the role performer achieves an altered identity.

The same questions of choice or avoidance of sick role may be raised for *windigo*, *pibloktoq*, and ultimately any sick role which is not the *direct* outcome of organic deficit or infection. Even in organic disease-states each culture provides some degree of behavioral choice, however slight it may seem to the observer or the patient. Role analysis of the selection of sick role variant aids us in understanding the often long delay found by O'Nell among Zapotec *susto* cases between originating fright episodes and the expression of *susto* signs. He states:

> Rationalized frights serve the function of alerting *susto* sufferers to cognitive elements in the stress conditions producing their illnesses. They also serve to validate the problems experienced in culturally meaningful terms, which facilitates the rehabilitation of the individuals in social context.
> Precipitating fright seems to be connected to problems of impulse control in interpersonal situations. Given an understanding of social and psychological factors relating to social control in the culture, the problems of the control of one's hostile impulses in situations not clearly governed by social cues or in situations provoking intense hostility, can be seen to relate clearly to role stress, in this case associated with the most general role a person can occupy [namely, being a Zapotec].

Some Zapotec victims of *susto* even seem to be dimly aware of this paradigm, although O'Nell feels that few cognize the dynamics fully. But the esoteric surface (to nonZapotec eyes) of this folk illness, this "culture-bound reactive syndrome," crumbles when the folk model is placed beneath the scientific model, and we can begin to appreciate the adaptive significance of this no-longer strange phenomenon. The symptoms of *susto* communicate to the community that the victim is now aware of his role deficiency and is suffering for it. This permits him/her to expiate the feelings of shame, and the treatment acts both to relieve the sufferer's pain and restore him/her to the status of a full-fledged citizen of the community.

As for the studies of *windigo*, except for Rohrl and Brown, none of them really contradict each other so much as they complement one another. None is completely satisfactory, in part because the data on this syndrome – like so many others that have come within the purview of anthropologists – are sparse, often unclear, inconsistent, and even self-contradictory, and in part because the studies themselves demonstrate that no single set of factors, ecological, social, cultural, or psychodynamic, can alone completely account for this seemingly strange malady. While they do explain more than the simple ecological or cultural explanations of the past, it is clear that much remains to be done. I suggest that a series of well-documented cases of known instances of cannibalism in several societies, including the United States and others in the West, carefully identifying as many factors as possible, would be enormously helpful. For if *windigo* is a culture-bound reactive syndrome, cannibalism and the cannibalistic impulse are not. As many writers have noted, it appears with some frequency in the hidden wishes and fantasies of several types of behavior disorders in Western societies.

Foulkes' interdisciplinary attack on the Arctic Hysterias, or *pibloktoq*, is highly laudatory, and rare if not wholly unique. It is only through such studies that medical anthropologists may be certain that biological, environmental, sociocultural, and psychological data will all be brought to bear in a systematic approach toward the clarification and understanding of ethnic disturbances. However, the study contains what appear to me to be some vulnerabilities. For example, in light of Wallace's and others' hypothesis that *pibloktoq* etiology could implicate hypocalcemia, he states,

Our analysis of several serological surveys of the North Alaska Eskimo do not support the notion that this population is unable to maintain normal calcium levels. Serum total calcium determination of ten Innuit who manifested Arctic Hysteria-like behaviors revealed normocalcemic levels during all seasons of the year. However, several subjects [among or outside of the "ten"?] demonstrated calcium levels which were decidedly on the low side of normal. Levels of the ultrafilterable fraction of serum calcium was also determined. These levels were again within normal limits and did not differ significantly from a group of matched controls. The subjects also maintained serum inorganic phosphate levels within the normal range.

... The ability of the Eskimo to generally maintain normal levels of calcium in spite of dietary deficiencies needs explanation, however. It has recently been demonstrated that there is an increased calcium absorption with increase in protein intake, presumably because of the formation of a soluble complex with amino acids. Thus the high protein diet of the Eskimo may allow more efficient utilization of the low amounts of calcium normally ingested. In addition, serum magnesium was measured in our subjects, since the action of this cation so closely resembles that of calcium in the central nervous system. The mean levels for this group of subjects was normal and did not differ significantly for a group of co-villagers who were free from hysterical symptoms (Foulkes 1972).

We are left with the puzzle, never fully explained by Foulkes, as to how low dietary intake of calcium can eventuate nevertheless in "normocalcemic levels" in these Eskimo. For if, as Wallace suggested, we should find dietary calcium deficiencies associated with hysteria everywhere, are we to assume that somehow Eskimo metabolize small amounts of calcium into normocalcemic blood serum levels, while the same did not occur in Europe? But Foulkes suggests, as I noted previously, that disrupted circadian rhythms from long arctic days and nights affected calcium metabolism, interrupted neuronal functioning, and resulted – possibly – in hysterical outbursts among the Innuit. Of course, Europeans did not undergo arctic circadian cycling patterns. Wallace (1972) speaks of the relationship between tetany and hysteria, of "a veritable endemic of tetany among the working class of Vienna, Paris, and other European cities . . . a plague of tetany," which "came at precisely the same time that hysteria reached its peak as a psychiatric problem." He further suggests that in the late 19th and early 20th centuries many cases which would be diagnosed as tetany today were earlier diagnosed "as mixtures of tetany and hysteria," that Freud and other physicians were unaware of the behavioral consequences of rickets and hypocalcemia and were prone to find hysteria frequently. Since psychoanalytic theory "was founded on the analysis of hysterics . . . it may be well to evaluate further the culture-historical dimensions of this issue," especially since Freud and others "were aware that hysterics might display unusual physiological profiles as well as disordered behavior."

While both Wallace's and Foulkes' studies have been valuable, even ingenious and courageous in their effort to break new ground, I doubt that they have thrown psychodynamic or psychoanalytic theories into oblivion. It scarcely needs repeating that orthodox psychoanalytic models used rigidly and unimaginatively have led many an incautious anthropologist into theoretical pitfalls and dead-ends. But the explanations offered by Gussow, Parker, and others (including the psychological factors noted by Wallace and Foulkes), combined with sociocultural and environmental factors, seem to me at least as persuasive as the calcium hypothesis for the etiology of Arctic Hysteria(s). I would still not dismiss a possible role for calcium, vitamin D, and other biochemical, biological, and physical factors. But we need both better data and theory than we have acquired so far.

One needs to raise, as Yap, LeVine, and others have already done, the question of rarity or atypicality of culture-bound reactive syndromes (or rare-zero differentials). Yap in fact suggests that many of the "exotic" syndromes may not be rare. This appears to be the case with *susto*. And, while Teicher and others have suggested that *windigo* is rare, and others have said the same for *pibloktoq*, the fact that Foulkes found 6 cases in a village of 350 does not seem rare, though he says he chose this village site precisely because research indicated higher frequency there than in other villages. I know of no statistics for *windigo* although it seems to affect Cree and Chippewa but not other groups in the same region.

Epidemiological studies, therefore, of such syndromes, are sorely needed, but may be difficult to carry out. We certainly need a better picture than we now have, of demographic and sociocultural variables so as more precisely to determine incidence patterns, life-history materials carefully collected to elucidate sociocultural as well as psychodynamic factors in the etiologic chain, anthropological identification of role and value conflicts that contribute to these disorders, and answers to such questions as why certain ego-defenses are employed and not others, how cultures organize emotional response patterns, etc. We also need to know which behaviors are considered as pathological by each society as opposed to deviance (which may or may not be more painful for the individual), which mark the individual as gifted or exceptional irrespective of how similar behaviors may be viewed elsewhere.

And, finally, we will wish to raise questions not only about the older designations of behavior disorders as "ethnic" neuroses or psychoses, but even more recent, presumably less evaluative notions such as "culture-bound reactive syndromes." For in a very real sense, if there is anything to the belief that culture provides not only the means and conditions for human adaptation but also for maladaptation, all behavioral deviancies may be seen as both culture-bound and reactive to situations or events within the physical and social universe of individual and group. *Susto*, *windigo*, and *pibloktoq* may seem exotic and bizarre to Western eyes, but syndromes in which the person imagines he/she is penetrated or attacked by rader or radio waves or the images on a television screen, or that his/her insides are rotting away, or that he/she is Jesus Christ, Joan of Arc, or the President of the United States, will certainly be seen as equally strange and alien to members of nonWestern societies. Perhaps the place for the anthropologist to begin to understand culture-bound reactive syndromes is at home.

Postscript: Additional materials on the results of epidemiological research on *susto* by Rubel and associates (O'Nell 1972; O'Nell and

Rubel 1976, 1980; O'Nell, Rubel, and Collado Ardon 1978; Rubel and O'Nell 1978; Rubel, O'Nell, and Collado Ardon 1978) and on *windigo* (Preston n.d.) reached my attention too late to be incorporated into this analysis. Similarily, a series of studies on the syndrome termed "falling-out," or *indisposition* (Charles 1979; Lefley 1979a, b; Phillipe and Romain 1979; Rubin and Jones 1979; Weidman 1979) came to my notice just before sending this to the editor. These will be included in a more complete treatment of ethnic disorders on which I am presently at work.

Some Methodological and Theoretical Requirements in Future Research

In each of the preceding sections of this paper I have attempted to point out, in light of critical assessments of the studies appraised, certain conceptual, methodological, and theoretical questions that need to be addressed, or reconsidered, by medical anthropologists investigating problems in these areas. I shall not burden the reader here with a re-counting of those points. I do wish to point up, however, a few of the more salient theoretical and methodological requirements of medical anthropological research, as they appear to me at the conclusion of this recension. Some studies are so well done, they need few of the adjurations that follow; most, I believe, are in need of some.

As a general principle, medical anthropological studies should report on methodology and techniques routinely. Such reports should not include a simple passing obeisance to this "ritual" requirement, but should make the exposition of method include certain basic essentials: identification of the sample and universe; problems of sampling; the rationale for using whatever approach and techniques have been selected; problems encountered in application of such techniques. While these have been supplied by an increasing number of publications, a surprising proportion still tend to slight or completely ignore these essentials of any competent reporting of research. Some attention must be paid, too, to shortcomings of the data presented and where the methods of eliciting data failed fully to achieve their purposes. It would be helpful to identify the unit of analysis as completely as possible. Indeed the problem of what unit of analysis to use, which has been a concern of other branches of anthropology, is scarcely considered so far in the writings of medical anthropologists.

In stating hypotheses, or in making generalizations based on inferences from data, it is necessary to state the *conditions* under which the hypothesis or generalization should be expected to hold. Since no principle, correlation, or general statement of relationship is expected to apply under any and all conditions, we are more likely to be able to establish a body of viable principles when we can qualify them in this fashion. This applies in any of the sciences, but is triply important in the social sciences in making statements about relationships among behaviors, and between behaviors and social, cultural, ecological, biological, and other espects of the human condition.

In historical and ethnohistorical studies, medical anthropologists must exercise utmost care in the use and interpretation of documentary materials. The principles of good historiography apply here but are sometimes overlooked. In this regard, as in all other kinds of research it is important not to select out only those data that seem to confirm one's hypotheses or preconceptions. Contrary evidence must never be eliminated, but fully considered and reported.

In the same way, it is incumbent upon the medical anthropologist to consider and present *alternative explanations* to the ones that he/she may feel offer the best understanding. It will then be left to the reader to decide whether the evidence and reasoning mustered in defense of an author's explanatory model is persuasive.

A good many papers and books in the field suffer from a holdover of the old functionalist fallacy: the assumption that cultures and societies are perfectly integrated, that all parts fit together in a smoothly running behavior-sentiment machine. If some part is found to be inconsistent, to fit less well, it is perceived as an anomaly, and dysfunctional. Surely by now anthropologists know that societies are not organisms and cultures are not physiologies. Apparent inconsistencies or lack of easy fit does not mean necessarily either that the behavior or institution is malfunctioning or that the society as a whole is in a state of *anomie* or falling apart. It may be symptomatic of necessary and adaptive changes which are occurring, and without which the group might indeed begin to lose its dynamic equilibrium. As Geertz (1973) states it so well,

... coherence cannot be the major test of validity for a cultural description. Cultural systems must have a minimal degree of coherence, else we would not call them systems; and, by observation, they normally have a great deal more. But there is nothing so coherent as a paranoid's delusion or a swindler's story. The force of our interpretations cannot rest, as they are now so often made to do, on the tightness with which they hold together, or the assurance with which they are argued. Nothing has been done more, I think, to discredit cultural analysis than the construction of impeccable depictions of formal order in whose actual existence nobody can quite believe.

We know, really, that culture, even in the so-called "tight" structures is rather loosely articulated. We also know that culture changes constantly (indeed we drum this into the refrains of introductory courses). We are aware of the inconsistencies and jagged edges and square-pegs-in-round-holes elements of the cultures we observe and the ones we live and participate in. But many of us remain bemused by the antique fictions so insistently and forcefully repeated by Malinowski, Radcliffe-Brown, and their legions of followers.

Medical anthropologists are rightly concerned with problems of theory and conceptualization, and I have addressed some of those problems. As I have indicated, we must also be concerned with methodology, and with the collecting of data that can be subjected to statistical analysis. However, some of the critics, and, I fear, some of their targets in their reactions, are erroneous in dismissing "descriptive" studies as though they are necessarily untheoretical or even atheoretical. In fact, I would suggest our field needs *more* description, rather than less. Many aspects of human behaviors concern processes and events that are not easily boiled down to variables discrete enough to quantify and manipulate statistically. Anthropology, especially ethnology, remains primarily a kind of natural history, and the approach and methods of natural history should apply. As Brown (1963) has shown in a book that should be required reading for all medical anthropologists, *Explanation in Social Science*, sociocultural description is more than reporting. It is a full presentation of the facts observed, of the relationships among those facts, and includes a systematic explanation of the relationships among the facts. Thus, good description is – or should be – as much informed by theory as any other form of data presentation and analysis. Ethnographic description and ethnological analysis are part of our anthropological heritage. Rather than discarding that heritage into the dustbin of history, we should be using it to the fullest, and sharpening our methods and theories thereby. Good description does not preclude other forms of data collection and analysis. The latter complement it. But for adequate anthropological explanations of out investigations, good description is indispensable.

For example, for our understanding of the process of becoming a healer, of the human and sociocultural events that play a role in that decision, we need careful descriptive biographies and autobiographies of healers and others concerned with health and illness. They can also help us answer a host of other questions, e.g., is the shaman a psychotic or self-cured neurotic? I think here especially of the work of Handelman (1967, 1972) on a Washo Indian shaman, and Harvey (1979) on the biographies of six Korean women shamans. Similarly, we could use more descriptions of various healing processes, such as divination (as diagnosis), treatment, etc.

What I am saying about description here is what Geertz (1973) has depicted with characteristic elegance as "thick description," which is, he says, the aim and business of ethnography. What is contained in a good ethnography is not a mere surface reportage of random or even systematic observations, or chronologically ordered events, or presumed processes, but a second- or third- or fourth-order set of inferences (interpretations), logically structured, of what we have observed and experienced. As Geertz puts it:

> What the ethnographer is in fact faced with – except when (as, of course, he must do) he is pursuing the more automatized routines of data collection – is a multiplicity of complex conceptual structures, many of them superimposed upon or knotted into one another, which are at once, strange, irregular, and inexplicit, and which he must contrive somehow first to grasp and then to render. And this is true at the most down-to-earth, jungle field work levels of his activity: interviewing informants, observing rituals, eliciting kin terms, tracing property lines, censusing households ... writing his journal. Doing ethnography is like trying to read (in the sense of "construct a reading of") a manuscript – foreign, faded, full of ellipses, incoherencies, suspicious emendations, and tendentious commentaries, but written not in conventionalized graphs of sound but in transient examples of shaped behavior.

Cultural description is a semiotic science, in Geertz' terms, in which we search ever more deeply for meaning, even though meaning, like culture, is public (at least once it has been made known or is experienced by the observer). "In the study of culture," says Geertz, "analysis penetrates into the very body of the object – that is, *we begin with our own interpretations of what our informants are up to, or think they are up to, and then systematize those* ..." [italics in original]. Necessarily, theory and conceptualization are embedded into our cultural descriptions, and it is for this reason that anthropology has by tradition insisted that theories separated from data and hanging suspended in the space of intricate speculation are not very useful, although theoreticians may play games with them to impress us – and each other. Again, Geertz phrases it cogently:

The major theoretical contributions not only lie in specific studies – that is true in almost any field – but they are very difficult to abstract from such studies and integrate into anything one might call "culture theory" as such. Theoretical formulations hover so low over the interpretations they govern that they don't make much sense or hold much interest apart from them. This is so, not because they are not general (if they are not general, they are not theoretical), but because, stated independently of their applications, they seem either commonplace or vacant. One can, and this in fact is how the field progresses conceptually, take a line of theoretical attack developed in connection with one exercise in ethnographic interpretation and employ it in another, pushing it forward to greater precision and broader relevance; but one cannot write a "General Theory of Cultural Interpretation." Or, rather, one can, but there appears to be little profit in it, because the essential task of theory building here is not to codify abstract regularities but to make thick description possible, not to generalize across cases but to generalize within them.

What Geertz means by the last sentence is of immediate relevance and importance to medical anthropology:

To generalize within cases is usually called, at least in medicine and depth psychology, clinical inference. Rather than beginning with a set of observations and attempting to subsume them under a governing law, such inference begins with a set of (presumptive) signifiers and attempts to place them within an intelligible frame. Measures are matched to the theoretical predictions, but symptoms (even when they are measured) are scanned for theoretical peculiarities – that is, they are diagnosed. In the study of culture the signifiers are not symptoms or clusters of symptoms, but symbolic acts or clusters of symbolic acts, and the aim is not therapy but the analysis of social discourse. But the way in which theory is used – to ferret out the unapparent import of things – is the same.

Thus we are led to the second condition of cultural theory: it is not, at least in the strict meaning of the term, predictive. The diagnostician doesn't predict measles; he decides that someone has them, or at the very most *anticipates* that someone is rather likely shortly to get them. But this limitation, which is real enough, has commonly been both misunderstood and exaggerated, because it has been taken to mean that cultural interpretation is merely post facto: that, like the peasant in the old story, we first shoot the holes in the fence and then paint the bull's-eyes around them. It is hardly to be denied that there is a good deal of that sort of thing around, some of it in prominent places. It is to be denied, however, that it is the inevitable outcome of a clinical approach to the use of theory.

There is much more to Geertz' argument, but enough of it has been included here that it should be apparent that the almost shuffling self-consciousness and hat-in-hand apology with which many anthropologists use descriptive ethnography is, despite the frequent assaults from outside and within the gates, unwarranted, if not demeaning. The best proof of Geertz' compelling propositions is found in his brilliant descriptions of Javanese religion, or social and economic change at the village and national levels of Javanese life.

A final note. I perceive a contradiction in medical anthropological writing in regard to our treatment of American society. Medical anthropologists rightly insist that we must study our own society with the same diligence and objectivity we apply to the study of nonWestern and preindustrial peoples. I concur, and in the review above of ethnic disorders I urged in fact that this be done, not only because we need to study ours as another of the many cultural variations in the world, but because it would help to clarify some of the vexing problems about such turbulent behaviors as those I raised in that discussion. Our society, our culture is one among many. But very frequently in the pages of medical anthropological writings we find that the medical system of that society, or of a broader conception that we imprecisely label as "Western" or "Euroamerican" society, is accepted as an established baseline against which to measure the disease concepts, classifications, and systemic processes (diagnosis, prognosis, treatment, cure, etc.) of other peoples. Becuase it is "scientific," we accept that it is a kind of universal standard to gauge the "fit," "validity," "rationality," or something else of the data of nonWestern and preindustrial medicine. This is especially ironic when one learns that the Western medical model is itself coming under increasingly sharp criticism and rethinking by Western physicians themselves, for example, in a compelling recent essay by Engel (1977), "The Need for a New Medical Model: A Challenge for Biomedicine." I am convinced that this has been heavily implicated in such bothersome and tangled questions as those I suggested in connection with ethnic disorders, or with folk illnesses generally, and even with the still unsettled disputes about whether shamans are deranged misfits or the repositories of tribal wisdom.

What will be needed here, and in all other attempts to compare health and illness across cultural systems, is a set of categories that are as culture-free as we can devise. We should not be put off by the assumption that we are prisoners of our own culture and language, for if we cannot design such truly objective classifications, we are unlikely to achieve a nonsubjective comparative science. Some commendable beginnings have been made, as in some of the work reviewed above in The Logic of Medical Systems and in Theory and Conceptualization. Much more remains to be done.

REFERENCES CITED

Ackerknecht, Erwin A., 1953. Paleopathology, in *Anthropology Today*, A.L. Kroeber (ed.), Chicago: University of Chicago Press.
Alland, Alexander Jr., 1966. Medical anthropology and the study of biological and cultural adaptation. *American Anthropologist* **68**: 40–51.

Alland, Alexander Jr., 1970. *Adaptation in Cultural Evolution: An Approach to Medical Anthropology*, New York: Columbia University Press.

Arluke, Arnold, Louanne Kennedy, and Ronald C. Kessler, 1979. Re-examining the sick role concept: An empirical assessment, *Journal of Health and Social Behavior* **20**: 30–36.

Armelagos, George J., 1969. Disease in ancient Nubia. *Science* **163**: 255–259.

Basso, Keith H., 1969. *Western Apache Witchcraft*, Anthropological Papers of the University of Arizona, No. 15, Tucson: University of Arizona Press.

Bauwens, Eleanor E. (ed.), 1978. *The Anthropology of Health*, St. Louis: Mosby.

Bhatia, J.C., Dharam Vir, A. Timmapaya, and C.S. Chutani, 1975. Traditional healers and modern medicine, *Social Science and Medicine* **9**: 15–21.

Black, Francis L., 1975. Infectious diseases in primitive societies, *Science* **187**: 515–518.

Boyd, Robert T., 1975. Another look at the "fever and ague" of Western Oregon, *Ethnohistory* **22**: 135–154.

Brothwell, Don, 1972. The question of pollution in earlier and less developed societies, in *Health and the Human Condition*, Michael H. Logan and Edward E. Hunt, Jr. (eds.), North Scituate, Mass.: Duxbury Press, pp. 129–136.

Brothwell, Don R., and A.T. Sandison (eds.), 1967. *Diseases in Antiquity: A Survey of Diseases, Injuries, and Surgery in Ancient Populations*, Springfield, Ill.: Charles C. Thomas, Publisher.

Brown, Jennifer, 1971. The cure and feeding of *Windigos*: A critique, *American Anthropologist* **73**: 20–22.

Brown, Robert, 1963. *Explanation in Social Science*, Chicago: Aldine Publishing Co.

Campbell, John D., 1978. The child in the sick role: Contributions of age, sex, parental status, and parental values, *Journal of Health and Social Behavior* **19**: 35–50.

Caro Baroja, Julio, 1965. *The World of the Witches*, tr. by O.N.V. Glendinning, Chicago: University of Chicago Press.

Caudill, William, 1953. Applied anthropology in medicine, in *Anthropology Today*, A.L. Kroeber (ed.), Chicago: University of Chicago Press.

Cawte, John, 1972. *Cruel, Poor and Brutal Nations: The Assessment of Mental Health in an Australian Aboriginal Community by Short-Stay Psychiatric Field-Term Methods*, Honolulu: University Press of Hawaii.

Cawte, John, 1974. *Medicine is the Law*, Honolulu: University Press of Hawaii.

Cawte, John, 1978. Gross stress in small islands: A study in macropsychiatry, in *Extinction and Survival in Human Populations*, Charles D. Laughlin and Ivan A. Brady (eds.), New York: Columbia University Press, pp. 95–121.

Charles, Claude, 1979. Brief comments on the occurrence, etiology and treatment of indisposition, *Social Science and Medicine* **13B**: 135–136.

Chen, Paul C.Y., 1975. Medical systems in Malaysia: Cultural bases and differential use, *Social Science and Medicine* **9**: 171–180.

Clements, Forrest E., 1932. Primitive concepts of disease, *University of California Publications of American Archeology and Ethnology* **32**: 185–252.

Cockburn, T. Aidan, 1971. Infectious diseases in ancient populations, *Current Anthropology* **12**: 45–62.

Colson, Anthony C. and Karen E. Selby, 1974. Medical anthropology, in *Reviews in Anthropology*, Bernard J. Siegel, et al. (eds.), Palo Alto, Calif.: Annual Reviews, Inc. **3**: 245–262.

Comaroff, J., 1979. Medicine and culture: Some anthropological perspectives, *Social Science and Medicine* **12B**: 247–254.

Cosminsky, Sheila, 1976, Cross-cultural perspectives on midwifery, in *Medical Anthropology*, Francis X. Grollig and Harold B. Haley (eds.), The Hague: Mouton Publishers, pp. 229–284.

Cosminsky, Sheila, 1977. Childbirth and midwifery on a Guatemalan finca, *Medical Anthropology* 1(3): 69–104.

Currier, Richard L., 1966. The hot-cold syndrome and symbolic balance in Mexican and Spanish-American folk medicine, *Ethnology* 5: 251–263.

D'Andrade, Roy G., Naomi Quinn, Sara Beth Nerlove, and A. Kimball Romney, 1972. Categories of disease in American-English and Mexican-Spanish, in *Multidimensional Scaling: Theory and Applications in the Behavioral Sciences*, A.K. Romney, N. Shepard, and S.B. Nerlove (eds.), 2 vols. New York and London: Seminar Press. Vol. 2: 9–54.

Davis, Fred, 1968. Uncertainty in medical prognosis: Clinical and functional, *American Journal of Sociology* 66: 41–47.

Davis, Scott and Stephen J. Kunitz, 1978. Hospital utilization and elective surgery on the Navajo Indian reservation, *Social Science and Medicine* 12B: 263–272.

DeVos, George A., and Arthur A. Hippler, 1969. Cultural psychology: Comparative studies of human behavior, in *The Handbook of Social Psychology*, Gardner Lindzey and Elliot Aronson (eds.), Vol. IV: 323–417. Reading, Mass.: Addison-Wesley.

Douglas, Mary, 1970. Thirty years after witchcraft, oracles, and magic among the Azande, in *Witchcraft Confessions and Accusations*, Mary Douglas (ed.), A.S.A. Monograph No. 9. London: Tavistock Publications.

Dubos, René, 1968. *Man, Medicine, and Environment*, New York: Mentor Books, New American Library.

Dunn, Frederick L., 1968. Epidemiological factors: Health and disease in hunter-gatherers, in *Man the Hunter*, Richard L. Lee and Irvin DeVore (eds.), Chicago: Aldine.

Durrenberger, E. Paul, 1979. Misfortune and therapy among the Lisu of northern Thailand, *Anthropological Quarterly* 52: 204–210.

Engel, George, L., 1977. The need for a new medical model: A challenge for biomedicine, *Science* 196: 129–136.

Epstein, Scarlett, 1967. A sociological analysis of witch beliefs in a Mysore village, in *Magic, Witchcraft, and Curing*, John Middleton (ed.), Garden City: Natural History Press, pp. 135–154.

Fabrega, Horacio, Jr., 1970. On the specificity of folk illnesses, *Southwestern Journal of Anthropology* 26: 304–314.

Fabrega, Horacio, Jr., 1971. Some features of Zinacantan medical knowledge, *Ethnology* 10: 1–24.

Fabrega, Horacio, Jr., 1972. Medical anthropology, in *Biennial Review of Anthropology*, Bernard J. Seigel (ed.), Stanford, Calif.: Stanford University Press, pp. 167–229.

Fabrega, Horacio, Jr., and John E. Hunter, 1979. Beliefs about the behavioral effects of disease: A mathematical analysis, *Ethnology* 18: 271–290.

Fabrega, Horacio, Jr., and Duane Metzger, 1968. Psychiatric illness in a small ladino community, *Psychiatry* 31: 339–351.

Fabrega, Horacio, Jr., and Daniel Silver, 1973. *Illness and Shamanistic Curing in Zinacantan: An Ethnomedical Analysis*, Stanford, CA: Stanford University Press.

Firth, Rosemary, 1979. Social anthropology and medicine – A personal perspective, *Social Science and Medicine* 12B: 237–245.

Fishman, Robert Gary, 1979. Spiritualism in western New York: A study in ritual healing, *Medical Anthropology* 3: 1–22.

Fortune, Reo F., 1963. *Sorcerers of Dobu: The Social Anthropology of the Dobu Islanders of the Western Pacific*, New York: E.P. Dutton & Co. (Orig. 1932; new copyright 1959, London: Routledge and Kegan Paul.)

Foster, George M., 1953. Relationships between Spanish and Spanish-American folk medicine, *Journal of American Folklore* 66: 201–217.

Foster, George M., 1966. Peasant society and the image of limited good, *American Anthropologist* 67: 293–315.

Foster, George M., 1972. The anatomy of envy: A study in symbolic behavior, *Current Anthropology* **13**: 165–202.

Foster, George M., 1974. Medical anthropology: Some contrasts with medical sociology, *Medical Anthropology Newsletter* **6**: 1–6.

Foster, George M., 1976. Disease etiologies in non-western medical systems, *American Anthropologist* **78**: 773–6.

Foster, George M., 1977. Medical anthropology and international health planning, *Social Science and Medicine* **11**: 527–534.

Foster, George M., and Barbara Gallatin Anderson, 1978. *Medical Anthropology*, New York: Wiley.

Foulkes, Edward F., 1972. *The Arctic Hysterias of the North Alaskan Eskimos*, Anthropological Studies No. 10. Washington, D.C.: American Anthropological Association.

Freidson, Eliot, 1970. *The Profession of Medicine: A Study of the Sociology of Applied Knowledge*, New York: Dodd, Mead & Co.

Friedlander, Judith, 1969. Malaria and demography in the lowlands of Mexico: An ethnohistorical approach. *Proceedings of the American Ethnological Society*, Seattle: University of Washington Press. pp. 217–233.

Galdston, Iago (ed.), 1959. *Medicine and Anthropology*, New York: International Universities Press.

Galdston, Iago (ed.), 1963. *Man's Image in Medicine and Anthropology*, New York: International Universities Press.

Garrison, Vivian, 1977. Doctor, espiritista, or psychiatrist?: Health-seeking behavior in a Puerto Rican neighborhood of New York city, *Medical Anthropology* **1**: 2, Pt. Three: 65–191.

Geertz, Clifford, 1960. *The Religion of Java*, New York: The Free Press.

Geertz, Clifford, 1966. Religion as a cultural system, in *Anthropological Approaches to the Study of Religion*, M. Banton (ed.), London: Tavistock.

Geertz, Clifford, 1973. Thick description: Toward an interpretive theory of culture, in *The Interpretation of Cultures by Clifford Geertz*, New York: Basic Books.

Gillin, John, 1948. Magical fright, *Psychiatry* **2**: 387–400.

Glick, Leonard B., 1967. Medicine as an ethnographic category: The Gimi of the New Guinea highlands, *Ethnology* **6**: 31–56.

Graves, Theodore D., and Nancy D. Graves, 1979. Stress and health: Modernization in a traditional Polynesian community, *Medical Anthropology* **3**: 23–59.

Grollig, Francis X., and Harold B. Haley (eds.), 1976. *Medical Anthropology*, The Hague: Mouton Publishers; Chicago: Aldine.

Gussow, Zachary, 1960. *Pibloktoq* (hysteria) among the polar Eskimo: An ethnopsychiatric study, *Psychoanalytic Study of Personality* **1**: 218–236. New York: International Universities Press.

Gussow, Zachary, and George W. Tracy, 1968. Status, ideology, and adaptation to stigmatized illness: A study of leprosy, *Human Organization* **27**: 316–325.

Hallowell, A. Irving, 1963. Ojibwa world view and disease, in *Man's Image in Medicine and Anthropology*, Iago Galdston (ed.), New York: International Universities Press.

Handelman, Don, 1967. The development of a Washo shaman, *Ethnology* **6**: 444–464.

Handelman, Don, 1972. Aspects of the moral compact of a Washo shaman, *Anthropological Quarterly* **45**: 84–101.

Hart, Donn V., 1979. Disease etiologies of Samaran Filipino peasants, in *Culture and Curing: Anthropological Perspectives on Traditional Medical Beliefs and Practices*, Peter Morley and Roy Wallis (eds.), Pittsburgh: University of Pittsburgh Press.

Harvey, Youngsook Kim, 1979. Six Korean women: The socialization of shamans, *American Ethnological Society Monograph* **65**: St. Paul, West Publishing Company.

Harwood, Alan, 1970. *Witchcraft, Sorcery, and Social Categories Among the Safwa*, London: Oxford University Press.

Harwood, Alan, 1971. The hot-cold theory of disease: Implications for treatment of Puerto Rican patients, *Journal of the American Medical Association* **216**: 1153–1158.

Harwood, Alan, 1977a. Rx: *Spiritist as Needed: A Study of a Puerto Rican Community Mental Health Resource*, New York: John Wiley & Sons.

Harwood, Alan, 1977b. Some social structural consequences of divination as diagnosis among the Safwa, in *Culture, Disease, and Healing: Studies in Medical Anthropology*, David Landy (ed.), New York: Macmillan Publishing Co., pp. 169–175.

Hay, Thomas H., 1971. The windigo psychosis: Psychodynamic, cultural, and social factors in aberrant behavior, *American Anthropologist* **73**: 1–19.

Jansen, G., 1973. *The Doctor–Patient Relationship in an African Tribal Society*, The Netherlands: Van Gorcum.

Janzen, John M., 1978. *The Quest for Therapy in Lower Zaire*, Berkeley: University of California Press (with collaboration of William Arkinstall).

Jarcho, Saul (ed.), 1966. *Human Paleopathology*, New Haven: Yale University Press.

Jurmain, Robert D., 1977. Paleoepidemiology of degenerative knee disease, *Medical Anthropology* **1**: Pt. 1, 1–23.

Kaufert, P. Leyland, and J.M. Kaufert, 1979. Alternate courses of development: Medical anthropolgy in Britain and North America, *Social Science and Medicine* **12B**: 255–261.

Kehoe, Alice B., 1973. The metonymic pole and social roles, *Journal of Anthropological Research* **27**: 266–274.

Kennedy, John G., 1969. Psychosocial dynamics of witchcraft systems, *International Journal of Social Psychiatry* **15**: 165–178.

Kiev, Ari (ed.), 1964. *Magic, faith, and healing: Primitive psychiatry today*, New York: Free Press.

Klein, Janice, 1978. Susto: The anthropological study of diseases of adaptation, *Social Science and Medicine* **12**: 23–28.

Klein, Norman (ed.), 1979. *Culture, Curers and Contagion: Readings for Medical Social Science*, Novato, Calif.: Chandler and Sharp.

Kleinman, Arthur, 1978. International health care planning from an ethnomedical perspective: Critique and recommendations for change, *Medical Anthropology* **2**: 71–96.

Kleinman, Arthur, Peter Kunstadter, E. Russell Alexander, and James L. Gale (eds.), 1975. *Medicine in Chinese Cultures: Comparative Studies of Health Care in Chinese and Other Societies*, Washington, D.C.: U.S. Dept. Health, Eduction, and Welfare.

Kluckhohn, Clyde, 1944. Navaho witchcraft. *Peabody Museum Papers*. Vol. **22**. Cambridge, Mass.: Peabody Museum of Archaeology and Ethnology.

Kolata, Gina B., 1974. !Kung hunter-gatherers: Feminism, diet, and birth control, *Science* **185**: 932–934.

Koss, Joan D., 1977. Social process, healing, and self-defeat among Puerto Rican spiritists, *American Ethnologist* **4**: 453–469.

Krech, Shepard III, 1978a. Nutritional evaluation of a mission residential school diet: The accuracy of informant recall, *Human Organization* **37**: 186–190.

Krech, Shepard III, 1978b. Disease, starvation, and northern Athapaskan social organization, *American Ethnologist* **5**: 710–732.

Krech, Shepard III, 1978c. On the aboriginal population of the Kutchin, *Arctic Anthropology* **XV–1**: 89–104.

Kuhn, Thomas S., 1970. *The Structure of Scientific Revolutions*, 2nd ed., Chicago: University of Chicago Press.

Landy, David, 1958. The anthropologist and the mental hospital, *Human Organization* **17**: 30–35.

Landy, David, 1961a. Some problems of research in psychiatric rehabilitation, *Diseases of the Nervous System, Monograph Supplement* **22**–4: 1–5.

Landy, David, 1961b. An anthropological approach to research in the mental hospital community, *Psychiatric Quarterly* **35**: 741–757.

Landy, David, 1974. Role adaptation: Traditional curers under the impact of western medicine, *American Ethnologist* **1**: 103–127.

Landy, David, 1976. Review: Body and mind in Zulu medicine: An ethnography of health and disease in Nyuswa-Zulu thought and practice, by Harriet Ngubane, *Medical Anthropology Newsletter* **10**: 16–17.

Landy, David, 1977a. *Culture, Disease, and Healing: Studies in Medical Anthropology*, New York: Macmillan.

Landy, David, 1977b. Review: Social anthropology and medicine, edited by L.B. Loudon, *Science* **197**: 1174–1175.

Landy, David, 1977c. Review: The doctor–patient relationship in an African tribal society, by G. Jansen, *Medical Anthropology Newsletter* **9**: 26–27.

Landy, David, 1978a. Review: Medical anthropology, edited by Francis X. Grolling and Harold B. Haley, *Man: Journal of The Royal Anthropological Institute* **13**–1: 149–150.

Landy, David, 1978b. Death: Anthropological perspective, in *Encyclopedia of Bioethics*, Warren T. Reich, Editor-in-Chief, New York: The Free Press-Collier Macmillan, Publishers. **1**: 221–229.

Larrick, James W., James A. Yost, Jon Kaplan, Garland King, and John Mayhall, 1979. Patterns of health and disease among the Waorani Indians of Eastern Ecuador, *Medical Anthropology* **3**: 147–189.

Laughlin, Charles D., Jr., and Ivan A. Brady (eds.), 1978. *Extinction and Survival in Human Populations*, New York: Columbia University Press.

Lebra, Takie Sugiyama, 1972. Religious conversion and elimination of the sick role: A Japanese sect in Hawaii, in *Transcultural Research in Mental Health, Vol. II of Mental Health Research in Asia and the Pacific*, William Lebra (ed.), Honolulu: University of Hawaii Press.

Lee, Richard Borshay, 1979. *The !Kung San: Men, Women, and Work in a Foraging Society*, Cambridge: University Press.

Lee Richard B., and Irven DeVore (eds.), 1976. *Kalahari Hunter-Gatherers: Studies of the !Kung San and Their Neighbors*, Cambridge, Mass.: Harvard University Press.

Lefley, Harriet P., 1979a. Prevalence of potential falling-out cases among the black, Latin, and non-Latin white populations of the city of Miami, *Social Science and Medicine* **13B**: 113–114.

Lefley, Harriet P., 1979b. Female cases of falling-out: A psychological evaluation of a small sample, *Social Science and Medicine* **13B**: 115–116.

Leslie, Charles (ed.), 1976. *Asian Medical Systems: A Comparative Study*, Berkeley: University of California Press.

LeVine, Robert A., 1973, *Culture, Behavior, and Personality*, Chicago: Aldine.

Lévi-Strauss, Claude, 1963a. *Structural Anthropology*, New York: Basic Books.

Lévi-Strauss, Claude, 1963b. The effectiveness of symbols, in *Structural Anthropology*, New York: Basic Books.

Levis, Gilbert, 1975. *Knowledge of Illness in a Sepik society: A Study of the Gnau, New Guinea*, London: The Athlone Press; New Jersey: Humanities Press, Inc.

Lieban, Richard W., 1973. Medical anthropology, in *Handbook of Social and Cultural Anthropology*, John J. Honigmann (ed.), pp. 1031–1072. Chicago: Rand McNally.

Lieban, Richard W., 1976. Traditional medical beliefs and the choice of practitioners in a Philippine city, *Social Science and Medicine* **10**: 289–296.

Lindenbaum, Shirley, 1979. *Kuru Sorcery: Disease and Danger in the New Guinea Highlands*, Palo Alto, Calif.: Mayfield Publishing Co.

Logan, Michael H., and Edward E. Hunt, Jr. (eds.), 1978. *Health and the Human Condition: Perspectives on Medical Anthropology*, North Scituate, Mass.: Duxbury Press.

Loudon, J.B. (ed.), 1976. Social anthropology and medicine, *A.S.A. Monograph* **13**, New York: Academic Press.

Marwick, Max (ed.), 1970. *Witchcraft and Sorcery: Selected Readings*, Harmondsworth, Middlesex, England: Penguin Books.

Mayer, Philip, 1970. Witches, in *Witchcraft and Sorcery*, Max Marwick (ed.), Harmondsworth, Middlesex, England: Penguin Books, pp. 45–64.

McCullough, John M., 1973. Human ecology, heat adaptation, and belief systems: The hot-cold syndrome of Yucatan, *Journal of Anthropological Research* **29**: 32–36.

McElroy, Ann, and Patricia K. Townsend, 1979. *Medical Anthropology in Ecological Perspective*, North Scituate, Mass.: Duxbury Press.

Mechanic, David, 1968. *Medical Sociology*, New York: Free Press.

Mensforth, Robert P., C. Owen Lovejoy, John W. Lallo, George J. Armelagos, 1978. The role of constitutional factors, diet, and infectious disease in the etiology of porotic hyperostosis and periosteal reactions in prehistoric infants and children, *Medical Anthropology* **2**: Part 2, 1–59.

Messing, Simon D., 1959. Group therapy and social status in the zar cult of Ethiopia, in *Culture and Mental Health*, Marvin K. Opler (ed.), New York: Macmillan.

Messing, Simon D., 1975. Health care, ethnic outcasting, and the problem of overcoming the syndrome of encapsulation in a peasant society, *Human Organization* **34**: 395–397.

Middleton, John (ed.), 1967. *Magic, Witchcraft, and Curing*, Garden City, N.Y.: Natural History Press.

Moerman, Daniel E., 1979. Anthropology of symbolic healing, *Current Anthropology* (With 15 commentaries) **20**: 59–80.

Montgomery, Edward, 1973. Ecological aspects of health and disease in local populations. *Annual Review of Anthropology*, B.J. Siegel, A.R. Beals, and S.A. Tyler, eds. Palo Alto, Calif.: Annual Reviews, Inc.

Morley, Peter, and Roy Wallis (eds.), 1979. *Culture and Curing: Anthropological Perspectives on Traditional Medical Beliefs and Practices*, Pittsburgh: University of Pittsburgh Press.

Murdock, George P., Suzanne F. Wilson, and Violetta Frederick, 1978. World distribution of theories of illness, *Ethnology* **17**: 449–470.

Nader, Laura, and Thomas W. Maretzki (eds.), 1973. Cultural illness and health, *Anthropological Studies No. 9*, Washington, D.C.: American Anthropological Association.

New, Peter Kong-Ming, and Mary Louie New, 1977. The barefoot doctors of China: Healers for all seasons, in *Culture, Disease, and Healing: Studies in Medical Anthropology*, David Landy (ed.), New York: Macmillan Publishing Co., pp. 503–510.

Ngubane, Harriet, 1977. *Body and Mind in Zulu Medicine: An Ethnography of Health and Disease in Nyuswa-Zulu Thought and Practice*, New York: Academic Press.

Ohnuki-Tierney, Emiko, 1977. An octopus headache? A lamprey boil? Multisensory perception of "habitual illness" and world view of the Ainu, *Journal of Anthropological Research* **33**: 245–257.

O'Nell, Carl W., 1972. Severity of fright and severity of symptoms in the susto syndrome, *International Mental Health Research Newsletter* **XIV-2**: 2–5.

O'Nell, Carl W., 1975. An investigation of reported "fright" as a factor in the etiology of susto, "magical fright," *Ethos* **3**: 41–63.

O'Nell, Carl W., and Arthur J. Rubel, 1976. The meaning of Susto (magical fright). *Actas del XLI Congreso Internacional de Americanistas* (1974) **III**: 343–349.

O'Nell, Carl W., and Arthur J. Rubel, 1980. The development and use of a gauge to measure social stress in three Mesoamerican communities, *Ethnology* **19**: 111–127.

O'Nell, Carl W., Arthur J. Rubel, and Roland Collado Ardon, 1978. An assessment of relationships between social and organic measures of a folk illness: One direction in research in medical anthropology. Paper read at Annual Meeting, Central States Anthropological Society.

O'Nell, Carl W., and Henry A. Selby, 1968. Sex differences in the incidence of susto in two Zapotec Pueblos: An analysis of the relationships between sex role expectations and a folk illness, *Ethnology* 7: 95–105.

Opler, Marvin K. (ed.), 1959. *Culture and Mental Health*, New York: Macmillan.

Parker, Seymour, 1960. The Wittiko psychosis in the context of Ojibwa personality, *American Anthropologist* 62: 607–623.

Parker, Seymour, 1962. Eskimo psychopathology in the context of Eskimo personality and culture, *American Anthropologist* 64: 76–96.

Parsons, Talcott, 1951. *The Social System*, Glencoe: Free Press.

Parsons, Talcott, 1953. Illness and the role of the physician, in *Personality in Nature, Society, and Culture*, C. Kluchkhohn, H.A. Murray, and D.M. Schneider (eds.), 2nd ed. New York: Alfred A Knopf.

Parsons, Talcott, 1958. Definitions of health and illness in the light of American values and social structure, in *Patients, Physicians, and Illness*, E.G. Jaco, (ed.), New York: The Free Press.

Parsons, Talcott, and Renee Fox, 1958. Illness, therapy, and the American family, in *Patients, Physicians, and Illness*, E.G. Jaco (ed.), New York: Free Press.

Paul, Benjamin D. (ed.), 1955. *Health, Culture, and Community: Case Studies of Public Reactions to Health Programs*, New York: Russell Sage Foundation.

Paul, Lois, 1975. Recruitment to a ritual role: The midwife in a Maya community, *Ethos* 3: 449–467.

Paul, Lois and Benjamin D. Paul, 1975 The Maya midwife as a sacred specialist: A Guatemalan case, *American Ethnologist* 2: 707–726.

Pelto, Pertti J., 1970. *Anthropological Research: The Structure of Inquiry*, New York: Harper and Row.

Pelto, Gretel H., and Pertti J. Pelto, 1979. *The Cultural Dimension of the Human Adventure*, New York: Macmillan Publishing Co.

Philippe, Jeanne, and Jean Baptiste Romain, 1979. Indisposition in Haiti, *Social Science and Medicine* 13B: 129–133.

Polgar, Steven, 1962. Health and human behavior: Areas of common interest to the social and medical sciences, *Current Anthropology* 3: 159–205.

Polgar, Steven, 1963. Health action in cross-cultural perspective, in *Handbook of Medical Sociology*, H.E. Freeman, Sol Levine, and L.G. Reeder (eds.), Englewood Cliffs, N.J.: Prentice-Hall, Inc.

Press, Irwin, 1969. Urban illness: Physicians, curers and dual use in Bogota, *Journal of Health and Social Behavior* 10: 209–218.

Press, Irwin, 1971. The urban curandero, *American Anthropologist* 73: 741–756.

Press, Irwin, 1973. Bureaucracy versus folk medicine: Implications from Seville, Spain, *Urban Anthropology* 2: 232–247.

Press, Irwin, 1978. Urban folk medicine: A functional overview, *American Anthropologist* 80: 71–84.

Preston, Richard J., n.d. The Witiko: Algonkian knowledge and Whiteman knowledge in hominid monsters: *Proceedings of the Conference on the Anthropology of the Unknown: Sasquatch and Similar Phenomena*, Marjorie Halpin and Michael Ames, eds. Vancouver: University of British Columbia Press (in press).

Reminick, Ronald A., 1974. The evil eye belief among the Amhara of Ethiopia, *Ethnology* 13: 279–291.

Rivers, W.H.R., 1926. *Psychology and Ethnology*, London: Routledge and Kegan Paul.

Rivers, W.H.R., 1927. *Magic, Medicine, and Religion*, London: Routledge and Kegan Paul.

Rogler, Lloyd H., and August B. Hollingshead, 1965. *Trapped: Families and Schizophrenia*, New York: John Wiley and Son.

Rohrl, Vivian J., 1970. A nutritional factor in Windigo psychosis, *American Anthropologist* **72**: 97–101.

Romanucci-Ross, Lola, 1977. The hierarchy of resort in curative practices: The admiralty islands, in *Culture, Disease, and Healing: Studies in Medical Anthropology*, David Landy (ed.), pp. 481–487, New York: Macmillan.

Rubel, Arthur J., 1964. The epidemiology of a folk illness: Susto in hispanic America, *Ethnology* **3**: 268–283.

Rubel Arthur J., and Carl W. O'Nell, 1978, Difficulties of presenting complaints to physicians: Susto illness as an example, in *Modern Medicine and Medical Anthropology in the United States-Mexico Border Population*, Dr. Boris Velimirovic (ed.), Scientific Publication 359, Washington, D.C.: PanAmerican Health Organization, pp. 147–154.

Rubel, Arthur J., Carl W. O'Nell, and Rolando Collado Ardon, 1978. Changing a psychiatric test to conform with cultural reality. Paper presented at Annual Meeting, Southern Anthropological Society.

Rubin, Jeffrey C., and Judy Jones, 1979. Falling-out: A clinical study, *Social Science and Medicine* **13B**:117–127.

Scotch, Norman A., 1963. Medical anthropology, in *Biennial Review of Anthropology*, Bernard J. Siegel (ed.), Stanford, Calif.: Stanford University Press. pp. 30–68.

Selby, Henry A., 1974. *Zapotec Deviance: The Convergence of Folk and Modern Sociology*, Austin: University of Texas Press.

Sigerist, Henry E., 1951. *A History of Medicine: Primitive and Archaic Medicine, Vol. 1.* New York: Oxford University Press.

Sigerist, Henry E., 1960. The special position of the sick, in *Henry E. Sigerist on the Sociology of Medicine*, Milton I. Roemer (ed.), New York: MD Publications.

Spencer, Robert F., 1949–1950. Primitive obstetrics (Introduction to primitive obstetrics, pregnancy among primitive peoples, childbirth among primitive peoples, primitive obstetrics and surgery), *Ciba Symposia* **11**: 1158–1188.

Spicer, Edward H. (ed.), 1977. *Ethnic Medicine in the Southwest*, Tucson, Ariz.: University of Arizona Press.

Stein, Howard F., 1979. Rehabilitation and chronic illness in American culture: The cultural psychodynamics of a medical and social problem, *Journal of Psychological Anthropology* **2**: 153–176.

Suarez, Maria Matilde, 1974. Etiology, hunger, and folk disease in the Venezuelan Andes, *Journal of Anthropological Research* **30**: 41–54.

Swantz, Maria Lisa, 1979. Community and healing among the Zaramo in Tanzania, *Social Science and Medicine* **13B**: 169–173.

Taylor, Herbert, and Lester Hoaglin, 1962. The intermittent fever epidemic of the 1830's on the lower Columbia river, *Ethnohistory* **9**: 160–178.

Teicher, Morton I., 1969. Windigo psychosis: A study of a relationship between belief and behavior among the Indians of Northeastern Canada. *Proceedings of the 1960 Annual Spring Meeting of the American Ethnological Society*, Seattle: University of Washington.

Turner, Paul R., 1970. Witchcraft as negative charisma, *Ethnology* **9**: 366–372.

Turner, Victor W., 1964. An Ndembu doctor in practice, in *Magic, Faith, and Healing: Primitive Psychiatry Today*, Ari Kiev (ed.), New York: Free Press.

Turner, Victor W., 1967. *The Forest of Symbols*, Ithaca, N.Y.: Cornell University Press.

Turner, Victor W., 1968. *The Drums of Affliction*, London: Oxford University Press.

Turner, Victor W., 1969. *The Ritual Process*, Chicago: Aldine Publishing Co.

Uzzell, Douglas, 1974. Susto revisited: Illness as strategic role, *American Ethnologist* **1**: 369–378.

Wallace, Anthony F.C., 1960. An interdisciplinary approach to mental disorder among the Polar Eskimo of northwest Greenland, *Anthropologica*, *N.S.* **11**: 1–12.

Wallace, Anthony F.C., 1972. Mental illness, biology, and culture, in *Psychological Anthro-*

pology, F.L.K. Hsu, ed. Cambridge, Mass.: Schenkman Publishing Co. (Reprinted from orig. ed. 1961, Homewood, Ill.: Dorsey Press.)

Weaver, Thomas, 1970. Use of hypothetical situations in a study of Spanish American illness referral systems, *Human Organization* **29**: 140–154.

Weidman, Hazel Hitson, 1979. Falling-out: A diagnostic and treatment problem viewed from a trans-cultural perspective, *Social Science and Medicine* **13B**: 95–112.

Wellin, Edward, 1977. Theoretical orientations in medical anthropology: Continuity and change over the past half-century, in *Culture, Disease, and Healing: Studies in Medical Anthropology*, David Landy (ed.), New York: Macmillan.

Wells, Calvin, 1964. *Bones, Bodies, and Disease: Evidence of Disease and Abnormality in Early Man*, London: Thames and Hudson.

Whiting, John W.M., and Irvin L. Child, 1953. *Child Training and Personality*, New Haven: Yale University Press.

Willis, R.G., 1972. Pollution and paradigms, *Man* **7**: 369–378.

Wolf, Eric R., 1957. Closed corporate peasant communities in Mesoamerica and Central Java, *Southwestern Journal of Anthropology* **13**: 1–18.

Wood, Corinne Shear, 1975. New evidence for a late introduction of malaria into the New World, *Current Anthropology* **16**: 93–104.

Wood, Corinne Shear, 1979. *Human Sickness and Health: A Biocultural View*, Palo Alto, Calif.: Mayfield.

Yap, Pow Meng, 1969. The culture-bound reactive syndromes, in *Mental Health Research in Asia and the Pacific*, William Caudill and Tsung-Yi Lin (eds.), Honolulu: East-West Center Press and University of Hawaii Press.

Young, Allan, 1976a. Internalizing and externalizing medical belief systems: An Ethiopian example, *Social Science and Medicine* **10**: 147–156.

Young, Allan, 1976b. Some implications of medical beliefs and practices for social anthropology, *American Anthropologist* **78**: 5–24.

Young, James E., 1978. Illness categories and action strategies in a Tarascan town, *American Ethnologist* **5**: 81–97.

Young, T. Kue, 1979. Changing patterns of health and sickness among the Cree-Ojibwa of North-western Ontario, *Medical Anthropology* **3**: 191–223.

7 Uses of Medical History

Stanley Joel Reiser

THE QUESTION is frequently asked: "What has medical history to offer those seeking to understand modern health problems?" The answer is difficult, and dependent on concepts of what history is, and what sorts of problems require clarification.

Without making an excursion into various positions in historiography, let me state briefly what history is not. It is not simply collecting facts. Facts are important to history, clearly. Without facts that are accurate history becomes philosophy, or fiction. Veracity to the historian is as important as veracity to a judge: without it neither is credible. A task of history is to view the past without self-consciously imposing a personal bias on events. But the person whose sole purpose is to collect data about people or events and painstakingly verify their accuracy is a chronicler, an antiquarian. The historian collects and verifies facts too, but submits them to searching selection and interpretation, with an eye to seeing things as they were. Facts to the historian are disordered building blocks, necessary to locate in a structure that explains them. It is the centrality to historians of deciding which facts are significant, and explaining why, that distinguishes them from antiquarians.

If history is a discipline that explains as well as describes in acting on the past, in what ways is this activity useful to the present – in this case to those interested in medicine? One way is to look to history as a source of natural experiments, of efforts undertaken to meet past issues, and to abstract the meaning and understanding from them in dealing with present ones. For example, a troubling question of modern practice is how to handle those patients whose illness seems beyond the help of current therapeutic measures. In seeking to fathom our own attitudes towards this issue, and alternatives to it, a view of historical development is useful.

This question was debated in the body of literature mainly compiled between the fifth and fourth centuries B.C. and known as the *Corpus Hippocraticum*. Although written by different people, these essays are influenced by a medical genius, Hippocrates. He and his disciples gave much thought to the relation between the forces of nature that produced and healed disease, and the power of the medical art. What role, they asked, should medical therapeutics play in the process of healing? The position taken was determined by a view that the power of nature was significantly greater than the power of medicine. This meant, principally, that the physician made great efforts to closely follow the course of illness in the patient so that his limited powers could be used at strategically significant points in the illness – and so exert their most telling effects. The doctor viewed his role as *assisting*, not overwhelming nature. Yet in cases judged irremediable, what was the Greek physician to do? One Hippocratic writing, *The Art*, offered advice: "I will define what I conceive medicine to be. In general terms, it is to do away with the sufferings of the sick, to lessen the violence of their diseases, and to refuse to treat those who are overmastered by their diseases, realizing that in such cases medicine is powerless." The writer of this essay went on to justify his directive: "For if a man demand from an art a power over what does not belong to the art, or from nature a power over what does not belong to nature, his ignorance is more allied to madness than to lack of knowledge. For in cases where we may have the mastery through the means afforded by a natural constitution or by an art, there we may be craftsmen, but nowhere else. Whenever therefore a man suffers from an ill which is too strong for the means at the disposal of medicine, he surely must not even expect that it can be overcome by medicine" (Jones 1959: 193, 203).

This passage asserts that each physician must critically determine what his therapeutics can do and, from that evaluation, decide their use. For doctors to employ measures that would likely fail was, for the Greek physician, damaging in three ways: To the patient – who would be needlessly subjected to the rigors of the remedy. To the physician – whose reputation would suffer for failing to evaluate the ailment adequately or understand the limits of his remedies. To medicine as an art – which, to those witnessing the failure, would seem to rest on a foundation of sand.

The view of the Hippocratics that nature should be dominated by being lived with, was gradually succeeded around the seventeenth century when the scientific revolution began by the view that nature should be dominated by being overwhelmed. A belief grew that investigation of nature by an emerging technology could uncover the secrets of its structure and functioning. As powerful instruments of fact-finding have been focussed on nature, discovery piled on discovery has strengthened this conviction. The modern medical armory is filled with weapons to turn upon a disordered nature. But when they succeed, as many do, in producing temporary arrest rather than cure, questions of when use is appropriate are raised. Today the usual answer – continue to treat as long as there is some response – seems inadequate. The purposes and goals of therapy are being questioned, and are tested by cases such as that of Karen Ann Quinlan. Her life was sustained by mechanical means while in coma for more than a year. She now continues to live without her machines, taken from her by court order, still in coma five years after the accident that produced it.

As we seek ways of meeting the dilemma of applying medical therapy it is instructive to understand the ideology of an age of medicine which treated nature differently than do we, and to recognize the origins of the therapeutic attitudes we hold. This means a view not only of the physical events that have taken us from helpers of nature to interventionists, but of the ideas and values that directed this shift. Such a quest has contributed to a significant modern movement – concern with the ethics of medicine.

For some medical ethics is basically the application to medical situations of forms of analysis developed in philosophy and ethics. This belief fails to comprehend a crucial dimension of the subject – an understanding of the actual behavior of physicians and patients trying to form a set of moral standards to accompany medical care. Without recognizing the context in which ethical principles were and are applied, and the reasons for selecting some as more important than others, one cannot judiciously apply ethics in medical situations. Medical ethics, thus, is grounded not only in the ideology of ethics and philosophy, but in the cumulative experiences and traditions that are part of the evolution of medicine.

But what of the modern interest in the ethics of medicine? How to account for it, and comprehend its place in the present, even the future? The catalyzing events began in the America of the 1960's. Before this time, much of what was called medical ethics dealt with concepts that guided the conduct of physicians towards each other. The first code of ethics of the American Medical Association, for example, written in 1847, devotes a majority of space to statements about professional duties, such as the requirement that doctors support the good character of the profession: "Every individual, on entering the profession, as he becomes thereby entitled to all its privileges and immunities, incurs an obligation to exert his best abilities to maintain its dignity and honor, to exalt its standing, and to extend the bounds of its usefulness." It suggests too that doctors treat colleagues exceptionally: "All practitioners of medicine, their wives, and their childern are entitled to the gratuitous services of any one or more of the faculty residing near them, whose assistance may be desired" (AMA 1977: 31). Aspects of moral problems connected with the therapeutic relationship of doctor to patient are also discussed in this document, but without penetrating insight about their content.

What had changed more than a century later in the 1960's to focus the attention of doctors on these neglected problems? This was a time when, stimulated by the growing civil rights movement of the previous decade, physicians, like others, grew more attentive to the moral elements of their interventions. An early, important expression of this was the attention given to exposing a case in which the right of patients to knowingly consent to participate in an experiment was abridged. It involved 22 elderly and senile patients at the Jewish Chronic Disease Hospital in Brooklyn who, in 1961, were inducted into an experiment that involved the injection of live cancer cells into their skin. The ensuing controversy raised questions about the conditions of oversight needed to assure moral behavior in experimental settings. It rekindled a process of soul-searching that had begun when the Nuremberg War Trials in 1947 revealed atrocities in the name of human experimentation – only to lapse in the 1950's. The debate over conditions under which humans should elect to become research subjects drew attention to the question of the nature of consent. It also made clearer the vexing dilemma of assuring, on the one hand, that the benefits of medical knowledge-seeking should not be needlessly endangered and, on the other hand, that individuals be adequately protected against experimentally-caused harms they did not understand or expect.

Other events were occurring at the same time that drew attention to the painful decisions bedside clinicians were required to make bearing on the choice of therapy. In the 1960's a new armory of therapeutic weapons was introduced that gave the physician powerful tools to sustain life under what used to be impossible circumstances – the artificial kidney machine, the heart-lung machine, to name a few. With this capability came the recognition that knowing when to use and when to withdraw such machines posed new ethical dilemmas. They were illustrated by the comment of a physician in 1966: "I have seen patients with brain-stem failure, with dilated, fixed pupils, decerebrate rigidity and cessation of spontaneous respiration, who have had a tracheostomy and were assisted with a mechanical respirator. With fluids, and good nursing care, the essentially isolated heart in such a patient can sometimes be kept beating for a week. I have never seen such a patient begin to breath spontaneously and survive, and autopsy always shows advanced liquifaction necrosis of the brain, for it died several days before the heart did" (Williamson 1966:793).

Doctors now began to reexamine some of the basic ethical ideas with which they lived. For example, what was death? In 1968 a report emerged, written by a committee of Harvard faculty members that included physicians and scientists, as well as a lawyer and an ethicist. It sought to establish a new definition of death, which took account of the fact that physiological activity could be sustained in a human being whose brain was not functioning. This committee redefined death around brain activity.

Events and problems such as these led growing numbers of physicians to suspect that perhaps discoveries in science and technology were not enough to maintain medical progress. Recognition slowly dawned on the medical profession, as well as on society, that serious investigation and learning about the moral values that underlay clinical decision-making were essential: that perhaps technological progress was only possible if accompanied by ethical progress.

The modern medical ethics movement illustrates the interplay between evolving ideas and traditions within medicine and the society in which it is embedded. A study of this relation had become of growing interest to historians of medicine in recent decades. A newly published volume of essays honoring a leading exponent of exploring the interaction of medicine and society, George Rosen, demonstrates the variety of ways in which this concern is expressed. Examining Rosen's contributions, the volume's editor, Charles Rosenberg writes: "All medicine was social to him. There was no aspect of the healing art from the definition of disease categories to the development of specialism that did not reflect social and economic, demographic and attitudinal factors. The labelling of witches, the nineteenth century's broadening conceptions of insanity were as much a product of intersecting social forces as the diseases which afflicted sixteenth-century miners or the rickets which crippled children in Europe's new industrial cities" (Rosenberg 1979:1).

Thus, just as the application of ethics to medicine requires knowing the context of the medical ideas and institutions in which it is used, so does comprehension of medicine itself involve recognizing the social and cultural context within which its techniques are applied.

Understanding the historical development of medicine can help most people concerned with medicine. It can make clear ideas and beliefs which act as invisible hands or bonds in stimulating or constraining what we think and what we do. How can we hope to effectively change the behavior of institutions or people, through private actions or public policies, without appreciating the circumstances of the past that have made them what they are? Knowing where we have been can help direct us to where we want to go.

But knowledge of the past is no infallible guide to the future. It can indicate the directions that previous events and ideas have propelled us towards. It cannot predict the course in which present events will lead us. Nor can the past give us sure guidance about which direction to go. It can provide useful evidence, which broadens our comprehension of the alternatives before us. It can give us analogies, suggesting what sorts of outcomes occurred given certain sorts of actions. It can help us recognize whether we are part of a traditional way of solving problems, or breaking new ground. Learning ways of handling certain problems that contrast with our own approaches also can stimulate a clearer view of our actions: looking into the mirror of history is sometimes the best way to see ourselves.

REFERENCES CITED

American Medical Association, 1977. First code of medical ethics, in *Ethics in Medicine: Historical Perspectives and Contemporary Concerns*, Stanley Joel Reiser, Arthur J. Dyck, William J. Curran (eds.), pp. 26–34, Cambridge, Mass.: MIT Press.

Jones, W.H.S. (Ed.), 1959. The art, in *Hippocrates*, Volume 2, W.H.S. Jones (ed.), Cambridge, Mass.: Harvard University Press.

Rosenberg, Charles E., 1979. George Rosen and the social history of medicine, in *Healing and History: Essays for George Rosen*, Charles E. Rosenberg (ed.), pp. 1–5, New York: Science History publications.

Williamson, William P., 1966. Life or death – Whose decision? *Journal of the American Medical Association* **197**: 793–795.

8 Beyond the Germ Theory: Reflections on Relations between Medicine and the Behavioral Sciences

Charles C. Hughes and Donald A. Kennedy

A GENERATION ago Iago Galdston, a psychiatrist with wide-ranging interests in the social context of medicine, edited a book which bears the title *Beyond the Germ Theory* (1954). With thanks to Galdston, we adopt that title for use with this chapter, for our purposes, similar to his, are to "go beyond the germ theory" in responding to the charge given for this paper, which is to present an overview and commentary on interrelations between medicine/health care and the behavioral or social sciences. Indeed, as we shall see, we *must* broaden the restrictive conceptual boundaries implied by that particular model if we are to take adequate account of the numerous contributions to human thought and practice that come from conjoining these two complex bodies of knowledge labelled "medicine" and the "behavioral sciences."

The overview will look at the topic not only abstractly, that is, at the level of the theory of nature and broad conceptual schemes implied in this problem area (e.g., what is disease? where is "it" located? what are "its" causes? what is the most effective point of intervention?) but also at the level of empirical research, training, and collaborative activity. Finally, some assessment will be made of successes and contributions, persistent problem areas, and prospects. Through such an overview, we hope to convey, if not the complete "state of the art," then at least a *sketch* of the evolving picture to both students and faculty colleagues unfamiliar with this area of interest. Because it is an overview, we will cite only a few of the most directly relevant bibliographic references. More detailed treatment of some of the content of this chapter, together with pertinent bibliography, will be found in the literature cited, other chapters of this collection, as well as in two recent publications oriented to some of these issues (Eisenberg and Kleinman 1980; Brenner *et al.* 1980).

The "Behavioral Sciences"

In the past few years there has appeared in print an apparent distinction between the "social sciences" and the "behavioral sciences" (frequently seen, for example, in the title of academic units which deal with these disciplines, e.g., College of Social and Behavioral Sciences). In this chapter we will use only the term "behavioral sciences" in referring to the several disciplines implied, and it is useful to discuss the reasons for this preference. There are several: parsimony of phrasing, historical precedent, and conceptual clarity.

The term "behavioral sciences" was coined in the late 1940's as one way of designating those disciplines whose root phenomena are *behavioral events* (Berelson 1968). One reason for the neologism in preference to the then current general designation, "social sciences," was the anti-communist national political climate of the times in the United States, when "social" appeared to many people uncomfortably too close in sound – and therefore possibly in meaning – to "socialism." But it was coined also in order to encourage *interdisciplinary* research that would place the study of human behavior even more firmly on an empirical and scientifically-informed basis. As we shall see, the interdisciplinary intent has, in fact, been realized to a gratifying extent, especially in many areas of research and the training of student physicians and others in health care.

Over the past three decades the phrase "behavioral sciences" has become widely employed in referring to the basic disciplines of anthropology (except for the sub-fields of archeology and physical anthropology), psychology, sociology, some aspects of economics, geography, political science, and history, as well as other disciplines in which the patterning of and antecedent factors involved in shaping behavior are the object of study. Psychiatry, at least in some of its aspects, clearly fits in the latter category. Perhaps the first most notable institution-alized use of the phrase was in the founding of the *Center for Advanced Study in the Behavioral Sciences* in 1952 at Stanford, California. A more recent application of the term was in the formation of the "Behavioral Sciences test committee" as part of the National Board of Medical Examiners in 1971. In between these two events there has been considerable use of the term in other contexts, such as for university departments or in journal titles (e.g., *Behavioral Sciences*).

One of the most significant aspects of the term is that it is more theoretically inclusive than the term "social," which, as a concept, implies *inter*-organism interactions and therefore conceptually sets off a *group* level of analysis from the study of *individual* behavior and thought. Yet it is the *behavior* of individual organisms that lies at the observable bottom of the conceptualization chain for those more comprehensive abstractions that deal with such ideas as groups, institutions, social structures, value systems and the like. An excellent notable example of the conceptually interlocking systems point of view applied to the behavioral sciences is Yinger 1965 (see also Hughes 1976). Hence, to reinforce a hierarchical, mutually interacting *systems* view of behavioral events and their conceptual consequences – and to avoid reinforcing the "super-organic" fallacy with its fruitless imputations of concreteness to what is essentially a conceptual construct – many researchers and authors dealing with the study of human behavior have preferred a single inclusive term to a cumbersome and possibly misleading joint designation.

But whatever the utility, historical precedent, and conceptual rationale, there remains confusion with a contending term deriving from earlier days of psychology as a discipline: "behaviorism." Thus we now have "behavior modification," "behaviorism," "behavioral medicine," and the like, which by and large take an avowedly individual-centered focus and rely upon particular types of psychological theory regarding determinants of behavior. And recently there has once again emerged an attempt at drawing a distinction between the "social" and the "behavioral" sciences, even though the objective of both remains the same (Simon 1980). What we are contending here, however – and it will no doubt be somewhat controversial even if clearly defined – is that the above terms and conceptual approaches to the study of behavior are *part of*, not coterminous with, what we will refer to as "the behavioral sciences" in relation to the study of medicine, disease, and health care.

Perspectives

At first glance, if looked at in terms of the many disciplines implicated, the topic "the behavioral sciences and medicine" does not appear to represent anything like a homogeneous subject matter, even though the common denominator is a given *problem domain*, namely the conceptualization, diagnosis, treatment, and prevention of disease. Indeed, the phrase refers to a complex of highly diverse literature, activities, purposes, and perspectives.

It is important in this regard, however, to remember that a "subject matter," being found free and unconfined in the natural flow of events, is not the same thing as "a discipline," itself the bounded creation, often evanescent, of intellectual, social, and situational influences. The effects of different *disciplinary* perspectives upon a common problem domain are obvious to all – occasionally, for example, leading to mutual enrichment of the fields brought into close working relationship with each other; but more commonly, perhaps, leading to further entrenchment of compartmentalized viewpoints and a self-righteous illiteracy in fields seen as "poachers" on one's own academic turf.

There are other perspectives, however, which can also fractionate a problem domain and lead, as can those from a disciplinary perspective, to contentiousness and academic pettifoggery. Especially in the problem domain of medical behavioral science it is important to recognize the implicit assumptions involved and the major differentiating conceptual points of view from which the topic is approached by various participants in research and applied activities.

One way of appreciating the first of such latter perspectives is to recall Straus's pithy and contrasting phrases of a generation ago (1957), when (using a particular discipline as an example) he spoke of the difference between "the sociology *of* medicine" and "sociology *in* medicine." In the first instance, medicine is viewed as a social institution and set of activities which is as appropriate a focus for behavioral science analysis as any other psychosocial content area, e.g., religion. In short, medicine is viewed from the "outside"; it is the "figure" in perceptual terms which is highlighted against the background of a particular conceptual context, in this case, the behavioral sciences. With the second phrase, "sociology *in* medicine," *medicine* is taken as the ground, the behavioral sciences figuring into the implementing of *its* assumptions, goals, tasks, and ways of operating. This is the perspective whose focus is from *within* the practice and research fields of medicine.

To draw such a conceptual distinction is not to be trivial or merely pedantic. These different perspectives have consequences in the real world, and failure to appreciate the assumptions upon which these perspectives are based, many of them covert, can well create problems of adaptation for the academician or practitioner or miscommunication among like-disciplined colleagues, as well as of misunderstandings and premature judgments of the "irrelevance" or "insignificance" of someone else's professional activity and interests. The different perspectives may well imply different reference or peer groups deemed appropriate to judge competence and adequacy, as well as different bodies of relevant literature and publishing outlets. The sociologist, for example, whose well-received seminar presentation to sociology department colleagues dealing with needed refinements in macrostructural social theory relating to the health care system, will be unenthusiastically if not shabbily received in a grand rounds presentation by most third year medical students.

Perhaps the key conceptual element distinguishing these two perspectives is the familiar contrast between what is often called "basic" as contrasted to "applied" values and ends of action. This distinction – often conceived as a dichotomy but more accurately thought of as a continuum – may be taken as the first of two fundamental, intersecting conceptual dimensions that fractionate the general subject matter of this article, two dimensions that can be singled out to help organize one's thinking about the broad topic (see Figure 1). (The second dimension, the continuum in *levels of analysis* that the behavioral sciences bring to bear upon medical issues, will be commented upon in a moment.)

The typical medical school curriculum and relations among medical school faculty members is a good example of the tensions that exist between these first two contrasting modes of organizing thought and behavior, i.e., the basic versus the applied. Although some of the newer medical schools in the United States and Canada have formulated their curricula in such a way that students begin early on to learn *clinical* problem-solving in parallel with their acquisition of knowledge in the fields of anatomy, biochemistry, microbiology, genetics, pathology, pharmacology, physiology, etc., most medical schools still operate in a framework of the Flexnerian division between the preclinical first two years of the "basic" sciences followed by two years of applied or clinical activity on hospital wards. While the "basic scientists" often complain of students' lack of fundamental interest in their subject matters, most students rather impatiently "put in their time" in the basic sciences until they can qualify to be on wards in contact with patients. All the while, the clinician faculty members may keep encouraging basic science faculty members to make their offerings more relevant to the clinical tasks of diagnosis and treatment, and the basic scientists mutter under their breaths about the lack of *scientific* and theoretical curiousity on the part of their clinical colleagues.

Yet both groups insist that they are involved in "medical science."

And indeed they are. The differentiation lies in the *context* of the activity, in the question of "science for what *purpose*?" Science for the purpose of generating new knowledge in and of itself, or science to be put to use in problems of *patient care*, which reflects a different basic orientation? While, of course, the dichotomy is not in all instances drawn in so absolute a fashion, it is widespread enough to be recognized as a salient theme in medical education. And this dialectic, this tension, is as applicable to the biological sciences as the behavioral sciences, for many first year students tend to complain almost as much about the perceived "irrelevance" of biochemistry as about sociology or the other behavioral sciences.

Despite clear evidences of territoriality in a university setting and the strong imprinting of students to use the techniques and special language of the disciplines into which they are being inducted, it is clear that the several behavioral science "disciplines" are by no means independent entities, each with exclusive, internally-consistent, and well-bounded concepts and techniques (Sherif and Sherif 1969). This is one reason one can comfortably and with further conceptual justification refer to them by the collective term, "behavioral sciences." There is considerable overlap in analytic concepts employed, level of conceptualization chosen, problem-interest, and even research techniques. Campbell (1969), for example, argues this point persuasively and presents a "fish-scale" image of the overlapping content areas of the behavioral sciences. He notes further:

> There are no doubt many natural divisions within the domain of the social or behavioral sciences – but they are not employed in the allocation of content to disciplines. A hierarchy of levels of analysis exists in which the focus of differential description at one level becomes the assumed undifferentiated atoms of the next; this is the atom-molecule-cell-organ-organism-social group- etc. model. On this hierarchy, sociology, political science, geography, and anthropology are all mixed across the individual and group levels, and so is experimental social psychology. The experimental laboratory work of Sherif, Lewin, Lippitt, and Bavelas in many instances represents psychologists doing experimental sociology, experimenting with social structure, developing laws about social norms in which persons are treated as undifferentiated atoms, and in which the resulting laws relate social structural and group-product variables. (1969: 332)

Although there is in-house arguing among its various disciplinarians, perhaps the greatest single contribution of the behavioral sciences *taken as a whole* to medicine lies in exemplifying a comprehensive, ecologically-informed conceptual framework, a "systems" framework if you will, that operates with the data of human psychosocial life at several levels of abstraction and goes "beyond the germ theory" in grounding processes of disease and the practice of medicine in a multifaceted natural context. A particularly succinct statement of the essence of this framework was made a generation ago by Murray and Kluckhohn in their pioneering book in the field of culture and personality. Attempting to give the student a sense of the theoretical and conceptual mapping which study of such a field entails, they noted that:

Every man is in certain respects

a) like all other men,

b) like some other men,

c) like no other man. (Kluckhohn, Murray, Schneider 1953:53)

Interestingly enough, such a "levels" approach, such a contrast between "nomothetic" and "idiographic" perspectives for understanding much of the division of labor among the behavioral sciences, can also be found in medical education and medical practice although not with as wide a range of empirical content as the behavioral sciences. It is often useful to point this out to medical students. For example, the thrust of much of the first year in "basic science" biological subjects is to present the abstract universals, the accepted generalizations about human physiology, anatomy, ect.; while, in the clinical years, those universals become modified somewhat to meet the patient's situation as a member of a *class* of persons with that particular disease. Further, however, the *particular* idiosyncracies and individual characteristics of the patient are always a factor to be reckoned with in patient care (as, for example, in the immunologic response in organ transplants or in side-effects of drugs). Indeed, Williams, on the basis of extensive biochemical, physiological, and anatomical studies reported in his book *Biochemical Individuality* (1963), demonstrates how each person, at the ultimate level of individuality, is a "deviate," and that while "standards" and "universals" are of course useful first approximations on the way to delineating the *specific* patterns that comprise a given organic whole, they are constructs and should not be reified.

From the area of medicine itself, this tiered approach to sorting out the relevance of the basic sciences to the study of disease, as well as to designating significant points of entry for the behavioral sciences, has been well expressed by Temkin in his paper, "The Scientific Approach to Disease: Specific Entity and Individual Sickness." He notes:

When a man is ill, that is when he feels dis-ease, he has experiences which are partly his own, partly open to others. This is his individual sickness which in exactly this particular form with all its details will never repeat itself in others or even in himself . . . Speaking of "sickness", or "illness", or "disease", we have introduced a conceptual denominator uniting many such individual events. The individual may not think of himself as being ill or diseased. By thus labelling him, his friends, physician, or society, have classified his experience. From here on it becomes possible to approach the matter scientifically ... Each patient's sickness is truly individual in the role it plays in his life; it has a meaning for him. But here where disease melts into the patient's whole life, science finds its limits. In bringing a patient back to health the physician will take as his frame of reference what is commonly considered as health ... The case history is the form in which the physician links the science, which does not deal with the unique directly, and the patient, who requires attention as an individual. Replete with scientific data and possibly utilized to serve the advance of medical science, the case history documents the physician's art. (1963: 629, 630, 644)

One may thus broadly conceive of the empirical domain of the behavioral sciences as a hierarchical continuum, one end anchored in the visible single human organism (and, indeed, perhaps even in events conceptualized at systems levels less inclusive than that of the total organism with all its attributes, such as psychophysiologic phenomena); and the other, in assemblages of behavioral events in populations conceptualized at the level of broad social structures. It can also be pointed out in this connection that the scope of the behavioral sciences so conceptualized – ranging from the study of individual behavior to group phenomena – parallels the distinction in the health field between "numerator medicine" and "denominator medicine," i.e., between the individual person as the focus of clinical activity and the group or collectivity as the focus of epidemiological investigation or preventive intervention.

A continuum of this nature illustrates the second of the two intersecting conceptual dimensions that fractionate the "field" of the behavioral sciences and medicine as defined in this context. A pervasive issue in the philosophy of science is the question of the relationship – often posed antithetically – between what some call a "holistic perspective" toward understanding phenomena and a "reductionistic" perspective. The issue has both epistemological and methodological implications of considerable importance in the present discussion. Other terms are often used in referring to the basic ideas involved; for example, *synthesis* (putting back together what has been broken out for closer examination) and *analysis* (breaking down a phenomenon into manageable and more easily understood pieces, whether tangible or conceptual). Or, in less grandiose but perhaps pithier terms, one hears of the "lumpers" and the "splitters."

Especially in the view of some types of researchers, the word "holism" is suspect, charged with being obfuscatory, mystical, certainly "soft" and therefore not "scientific." Perhaps the clearest justification for *thinking* holism, however – even if not using that particular term – is that a strategy of radical reductionism (often followed in the biomedical sciences), while necessary for the study of some problems at a given stage of investigation and clearly of great significance in the development of some aspects of medical science, nonetheless has the disadvantage of *losing information* about the dynamic properties of the constituents which have been abstracted out of their naturally-occurring contexts; and that missing information can be critical in a proper interpretation, and certainly any extrapolation, of the findings. This is the old problem of the whole being something qualitatively different from the mere sum of its parts.

As one example of many that could be used Weiss (1977:25) illustrates this with his studies of chick embryos. He shows, quite graphically, what happens to the "chick" when it is first crushed into a homogeneous suspension in order to conduct chemical analyses of its properties, and then further fractionized by centrifugation to separate out the physical properties of the solution thus produced. His implicit question, "What happened to the 'chick' in this process?", underscores the parochial nature of the understanding thus obtained by adherence to only a single level of analysis.

Dubos (1966) also concretizes this epistemological problem on the basis of his own laboratory work and emphasizes the need for flexibility in applying hierarchical frames of reference appropriate to the level of phenomena being investigated. Indeed, that is the crucial point: these contrastive approaches for acquisition of knowledge about the world are not mutually contradictory, but rather, complementary. They are not inherent polarities fixed in nature, each of which denies the validity of the other; rather, as Turbayne (1970:29–53) points out, each is a human construct, a conceptual model for understanding events at a particular level of organization and, as such, cannot totally mimic the entirety of events themselves. The problem comes, of course, when either idealized approach becomes rigidified or mis-applied and then is taken as the exclusive, all-purpose mode of understanding.

Perhaps a better term to express the basic concept of "holism" is "field," a word expressing the notion that conceptualizations should approximate as closely as possible the context in which an object of study is found in the empirical world. Even in the field of physics it has been found more useful theoretically to move from the study of conceptually isolated particles to that of particles situated in a *field* of electromagnetic forces (Brandt 1973, Einstein and Infeld 1961 ed.), and analogously this basic theoretical stance has also been very influential in the behavioral sciences (e.g., Lewin 1951).

Such a hierarchy-of-systems approach or continuum provides us with the second of the two constituent fractionating dimensions in the world of the behavioral sciences and medicine referred to earlier. These dimensions (the *basic* vs. *applied* and the *holistic* vs. *reductionistic*) may be graphically suggested in the following fashion:

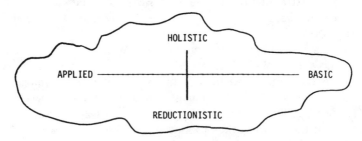

FIGURE 8.1   The "field" of the behavioral sciences and medicine.

While this is not the place exhaustively to locate aspects of the various disciplines or subject matters of the behavioral sciences *vis-à-vis* medicine on this grid, some examples of problem areas which may help fix familiar subject matters can be cited. Thus, for instance, a study of the social organization of a hospital or medical school that has no clear-cut recommendations for action or intervention would fit somewhere in the upper right-hand quadrant; research dealing with behavioral effects of a particular drug would be placed in the lower right-hand quadrant; behavioral change programs oriented to weight loss could well be located in the lower left quadrant; and a community development effort directed at improving environmental facilitators of health promotion would be found in the upper left quadrant.

The Concept of Disease

We have been speaking of the background and largely implicit assumptions which figure into the diverse activities undertaken in the domain of the behavioral sciences and medicine. These assumptions imply another, usually covert, conceptual feature that often confounds easy understanding and agreement among the diverse actors in this scenario. That feature is the vexatious question of the conventional "medical model" *vis-a-vis* the behavioral sciences. This is the type of consideration in which Kuhn's "paradigms" (1962) or Engel's "biopsychosocial model" (1977) come to mind. The extent to which thinkers at various times have theoretically conceived the relationship between sociocultural factors and medicine has depended principally upon the implied empirical scope of the "medical model" with which they were working, upon their response to that basic question: "What are the factors conceived to be related in some way to the genesis, prevention, or course of a disease?" And without directly addressing this question of the implicit model involved, we will be able to do less than what is otherwise possible to strengthen the study of interrelations between medicine and the behavioral sciences.

It seems we are always tempted to go back to the Greeks. Perhaps with good reason. For example, in speaking of the context of various diseases (and anticipating the current *conceptual* emphasis upon a "holistic," comprehensive perspective that considers environmental factors in health, ecologic awareness, epidemiologic forecasting, and "life-style" issues), Hippocrates prophetically remarked in his essay, "On Airs, Waters, and Places":

Whoever wishes to investigate medicine properly, should proceed thus: in the first place to consider the seasons of the year, and what effects each of them produces (for they are not at all alike, but differ much from themselves in regard to their changes). Then the winds, the hot and the cold, especially such as are common to all countries, and then such as are peculiar to each locality. We must also consider the qualities of the waters, for as they differ from one another in taste and weight, so also do they differ much in their qualities. In the same manner, when one comes into a city to which he is a stranger, he ought to consider its situation, how it lies as to the winds and the rising of the sun; for its influence is not the same whether it lies to the north or the south, to the rising or to the setting sun. These things one ought to consider most attentively, and concerning the waters which the inhabitants use, whether they be marshy and soft, or hard, and running from elevated and rocky situations, and then if saltish and unfit for cooking; and the ground, whether it be naked and deficient in a hollow, confined situation, or is elevated and cold; and the mode in which the inhabitants live, and what are their pursuits, whether they are fond of drinking and eating to excess, and given to indolence, or are fond of exercise and labor, and not given to excess in eating.

From these things he must proceed to investigate everything else. For if one knows all these things well, or at least the greater part of them, he cannot miss knowing, when he comes into a strange city, either the diseases peculiar to the place, or the particular nature of common diseases, so that he will not be in doubt as to the treatment of the diseases, or commit mistakes, as is likely to be the case provided one had not previously considered these matters.   (1964: 19–20)

Obviously the key term linking the investigative domains of the behavioral sciences and medicine is "disease" and, provoked by the comments from Hippocrates, one is led to wonder what type of concept, what type of process or thing is so pervasively embedded in nature and can act in so many diverse ways? Were the word interpreted uniformly and unequivocally there would perhaps be no problem tracing out areas of relationship between these two sets of disciplines. But, as is so often the case, a given term is subject to different meanings, not only across disciplines but within the historical evolution of any given discipline.

An important distinction can be drawn between two widely different orientations in thinking about disease which have been (and remain) elements in a conceptual dialectic. Interestingly, both can be found in the historical and cross-cultural records of both medicine and the behavioral sciences. The first of these orientations has been called the *ontological* view of disease; the second, the *physiological* view (Dubos 1966; Temkin 1963; Engelhardt 1974a).

In its extreme form the ontological view considers a "disease" an *entity*, a self-contained "thing" having discrete boundaries and an existence in and of itself. Its ontological status is assumed to be in nature and not in man's analytic conceptualizations *of* nature. Thus a disease "attacks" a person; "it" can be prevented and "cured." Perhaps the phenomenon that comes closest to fitting this conception is an infectious disease, in which there is a micro-organism that putatively "causes" the illness in a person and that illness, that disease, is often so labelled (e.g., "tuberculosis" from the tubercle bacillus). Closely implicated in such a view is another conceptual feature which has been called the "doctrine of specificity," by which is meant that each disease has a *specific* cause that can be identified, an approach which became crystallized in Koch's famous "Postulates":

(1) the organism should be found in each case of the disease; (2) it should not be found in other disease; (3) it should be isolated; (4) it should be cultured; (5) it should, when inoculated, produce the same disease; and (6) it should be recovered from the inoculated animal (Ackerknecht 1968: 179).

This disease-as-an-entity, specific-focus type of concept emerged in a fully intellectualized form during the 19th century in European medical thought and was greatly strengthened, of course, by the development of the germ theory and medical successes in identifying specific pathogenic organisms. No doubt its considerable utility as a concept for certain stages of investigation is a significant factor in the persistence in modern medicine generally of much outright "entity-thinking," if not at least overtones of such thinking (as illustrated, for example, in the phrases "diagnostic entities" or "disease entity").

It is of interest to note that such "entity-thinking" has its parallel in ethnomedicine. In Clements's classic cross-cultural study of beliefs about disease and causation (1932), he noted that widespread throughout the world's societies are several mechanisms which, upon reflection, bear structural similarity to the doctrine of specificity and "disease-as-a-thing" thinking: intrusion of a harmful object, intrusion of a spirit, malevolent activities on the part of other people, breaking of a taboo, and loss of one's soul or essential spirit.

There has, however, also been another and quite different conceptual approach taken to understanding disease, an approach which has been called the *physiological* or what here we might more ecumenically term a *processual* orientation. "Disease" is seen not as an entity, but rather as a conceptual construct inferred from interactive processes or interrelations within a naturally-occurring system (be that a body or a social system); as a concatenated series of normal physical and mental dynamics that have exceeded the boundaries of balance or homeostatis that defines "normality." This second view of disease is thus an expression of the "field of forces" type of concept discussed earlier and has sometimes been referred to as an "epidemiologic" model, in which the

organismic condition of the individual is bound up in the complex of relationships which exist between the genetically given individual, on one hand, and the physical and social environment, on the other. Disease, or more accurately, pathogenesis, is generally recognized as arising from the interaction of some combination of external exposure to infectious agents, toxic substances, or stressful circumstances, and the internal integrity of the human psycho-physiology at the time (e.g., the immune system).   (Kelman 1980: 135)

Again the Greeks, with the humoral theory of pathology, provide a familiar illustration. Given that there are a number of basic elements or "humors" that comprise the functioning of the body, health consists in the proper balance among these several elements. Disease is *disharmony*, an imbalance among elements which, in proper adjustment, are constitutive of the "normal" state of affairs. In this conception, then, disease is seen as the organism's failure in *adaptation* to either disturbances in the internal *milieu* or the external environment (in the manner first formulated a century and a half ago by Claude Bernard in his classic,

Introduction to the Study of Experimental Medicine, and more recently discussed by Dubos in his series of scientific as well as popular books on disease and medicine in the natural world – e.g., 1959, 1968). It thus involves not only specification of the nature of the threat to the viability of the organism, but also of such factors as resistance threshold, strength of immunologic response, physical and emotional and social resources (see Ader 1980).

Such a mode of conceptualizing disease has been very widespread in human history and has come down to us in the present day. It is a fundamental characteristic of the belief systems of many people of Latin-American descent, for example, as expressed in the "hot-cold" theory of disease and appropriate treatment. And notions of balance as health and imbalance as disease are still found in China, India, and numerous other non-Western systems of medical thought, such as many native American groups.

With reference to this *processual* type of conceptualizing disease, one of us has written elsewhere:

In speaking of "health and well-being" we are, essentially, confronting one aspect of the ancient and persistent conceptual problem of adaptation, adjustment, and equilibrium. Dislike it as we may because of the methodological and operational snares involved in use of these terms, we cannot avoid them; for health and well-being are but indicators or phases of the more comprehensive phenomenon, life itself; and life is rooted in processes of adaptational efforts directed at specific environments ...

Life and adaptation (and therefore health) are, then, *contingent* phenomena, not to be discussed except with reference to the specific *conditions* of life. One must ask what is adjusting, is attempting to adapt, and to what? ...

Health and disease are thus concepts which inherently imply the necessity of considering context, both in terms of definition and of causation. For "health" is, first of all, rooted in transaction, in the continuous activity on the part of the organism to establish and maintain patterns of relative adaptive success in dealing with its environment, both its "external" environment and its "internal" milieu. In this light health is, then, an ecological phenomenon, always to be considered in terms of contextual relations ...

Life is therefore an expression of a stable, continuing constellation of adaptive processes, and disease represents an exaggerated or abnormal use of defense reactions or mechanisms on the part of the organism in its attempts at adaptation to threatening circumstances, either internal or external.   (Hughes 1966: 122–125.)

Although the "entity-thinking" approach to disease still predominates in institutionalized western medicine, there are numerous voices being raised to point out its shortcomings and defects for adequate understanding of disease causes, mechanisms, prevention, and treatment (e.g., Cassell 1979; Engel 1977, 1980; Engelhardt 1974 a&b; Temkin 1963;

Wolf 1961). Such questions arise in numerous areas, not only in regard to the study of infectious diseases (when not everyone exposed to the presumably "causative" microorganism becomes ill), in many varieties of mental disorders (e.g., "Is Grief a Disease?" Engel 1961), and perhaps also in the major mortal afflictions such as cardiovascular disease or cancer, in which behavioral patterns or *non-specific* stress (cf. Selye 1976) are postulated to play a significant role. Dubos, for example, has stated (as have others, of course) that it is not the tubercle bacillus itself that can be said to "cause" the clinical symptoms – except as associated with a wider context, a field of linked physical and/or emotional deprivations, such as a poor nutritional state and low standard of living (1966).

Actually, the background already exists in medical practice which could accommodate such a conceptualization. Often a distinction is made between an "organic" and a "functional" or behavioral etiology – between an etiology which is discernible at the level of tissue alteration or laboratory test, and one in which there is "dys-ease" reflective of disordered behavioral, psychological, or emotional processes that in themselves may or may not have tissue effects. Stress is a prime example of the latter type of conceptualization, and, within the medical disciplines, only psychiatry traditionally has made very much use of that type of disease etiology. In most medical practice, however, the functional – the processual – approach is usually considered a residual category. It receives secondary billing; only after all other factors have been "ruled out," as the phrase has it, is this level of analysis thought appropriate. Although discussed in medical textbooks, most students come away from exposure to such an alternative explanatory model of disease with an ingrained practice of giving it only afterthought consideration in their diagnostic and therapeutic approaches.

Dubos's assertion that tuberculosis is a disease of poverty raises another kind of issue in regard to locating the concept of disease in its natural context of linked events; namely, when speaking of "cause" and especially of *specific* cause, how far "upstream" must one go in order to be able to predict the occurrence of a given event, such as appearance of given symptoms? Does one seek only to observe the existence of a given pathogen and then predict that the disease will eventuate? Or is there a need to outline more specifically the contextual physical, emotional, social, economic, etc., conditions that predispose the organism to vulnerability and perhaps eventual exhaustion of immunologic resources to such an extent that the organism is clearly at risk? To follow through that chain of associated circumstances might seem, of course, to lead to infinite regress; and for the practicing clinician some mundane issues (such as the time required) usually supervene to prevent such philosophic meandering. But for those in the health care field who are concerned with wider issues of prevention as well as fuller understanding of the natural history of a disease, such conceptual follow-through becomes vital. It is especially important for those considering the place of the behavioral sciences in medicine and the kinds of mutually-productive interpenetrations that occur between the fields.

The issue becomes, then, one of choice between a proximal and a distal point of entry into the chain of implicated events and situations leading to disease; for there is no *inherent* dichotomy or illogic in looking at the practice of medicine on an individual-centered basis rather than a group basis (or vice-versa). Especially with a systems-within-systems framework, there is an overall conceptual coherence that more or less matches the coherence of events in nature, and (in the abstract) it comes down to the arbitrary choice of the individual practitioner or researcher as to where along that continuum one wishes to park and do business. However, seen within the context of *a particular environing sociopolitical structure* there may well be problems involved in trying to articulate these two points of view in daily practice, as we will see below. (For a discussion of these two contrasting medical orientations, an individualistic compared to a group orientation, see Sokolowska 1973.)

Of these two conceptions of disease – the *ontological* and the *physiological* – the behavioral sciences (and much of psychiatry as well) probably have a much greater chance of making significant contributions to medical thought under the explicit aegis of the *physiological*, the *processual* conception than under the *ontological* umbrella, given the prominence in these fields of the notions of adaptation, interaction, function, "field" or gestalt, and of the search for *patterns* of variables rather than simply the delineation of uniformly acting single elements. Certainly there is a vast literature of relevance in the behavioral sciences that speaks to this kind of concept with relation to breakdown of a given system – e.g., "social pathology," "social problems," "social disorganization," "anomie," "alienation," "personality disorder," and like terms. The largely fruitless search for highly specific traumatic events (in the manner of Koch's postulates) as the "cause" of neuroses or for the "ulcer personality" and other presumed univocal psychological predisposers to disease that characterized the early days of psychosomatic medicine a generation ago illustrates this as well. More recently the failure to find one-to-one specific relationships between types of stressful situations and the onset of disease is another expression of the difficulty of using a simple schema without placing such interactions in a context of buffering and ameliorating forces (cf. Antonovsky 1979).

Engelhardt has expressed very well the theoretical and philosophical problems consequent upon a radical ontological position, as well as points of entry for the behavioral sciences into the chains of linked circumstances which bring about a diseased condition in a person. With his observation we can bring to a close consideration of the central conceptual models which underlie much of the activity in the arena of the behavioral sciences and medicine:

Diseases are, in fact, not only multifactorial, but multidimensional, involving genetic, physiological, psychological, and sociological components. The presence of these various components does not merely entail a superimposition of modifying variables upon basic disease structures. Rather, it implies that diseases have a basically relational, not a subject (i.e., substance) predicate (accident) nature. That is, there is not necessarily a *bearer* for every disease, a substrate for each type of disease.

This view of disease emerges from consideration of the complex of etiological structures involved in modern "disease entities." Diseases such as asthma, cancer, coronary artery disease, etc., are as much psychological as pathophysiological in that the likelihood of such illness is closely bound to experienced stress and the availability of support for the person stressed. They are thus sociological as well. The result is a multidimensional concept of disease with each dimension – genetic, infectious, metabolic, psychological and social – containing a nexus of causes bound by their appropriate, usually different, nomological structures. The multiple factors in such well-established diseases as coronary artery disease suggest that the disease could be alternatively construed as a genetic, metabolic, anatomic, psychological, or sociological disease, depending on whether one was a geneticist, an internist, a surgeon, a psychiatrist, or a public health official. The construal would depend upon the particular scientist's appraisal of which etiological variables were most amenable to his manipulations. For example, the public health official may decide that the basic variables in coronary artery disease are elements of a lifestyle which includes little exercise, overeating and cigarette smoking. He may then address these social variables and consider such disease to be . . . ways of life.

This shift in nosology is back to a "Hippocratic" notion of disease in the sense of a "physio-logical" or contextual concept (1974a: 133).

What, then, is being done in the worlds of education and research in response to such an encouraging conceptual mandate?

The Workaday World of the Behavioral Sciences and Medicine

Despite the existence in general academia of fractionist tendencies representing specific disciplinary interests (expressed for example, in the existence of separate professional associations oriented to medical sociology, medical anthropology, and medical psychology), it may well be that medical behavioral science comprises an arena in which there is relatively more movement toward functional integration of many of the concepts and techniques of anthropology, psychology, and sociology than in any other substantive problem area. Such a development bears out some of the hopes of that group of scholars, foundation officers, and others influential in coining the concept and phrase "behavioral sciences" in the late 1940's. While, of course, such movement has not resulted yet in anything like a new "discipline," social organizational evidence of such mutual influence is found, to a limited extent, in the formation of inter-disciplinary professional societies or university administrative units, such as departments.

Another, and perhaps more significant, expression of the trend toward *de facto* synthesis is the frequent use ("borrowing," as we academics sometimes say) of concepts as well as research techniques from neighboring fields, both in the teaching of health care personnel and in the basic research that builds the body of knowledge used for teaching. A number of significant, shared analytic concepts, research areas and methodological approaches tend to be used by behavioral scientists of various disciplinary persuasions, though not always called by precisely the same terms. The extent of such diffusion is attested by perusal of the contents of relevant journals (e.g., *Journal of Health and Social Behavior; Medical Anthropology Newsletter; Culture, Psychiatry and Medicine; Social Science and Medicine; Journal of Behavioral Medicine; Journal of Psychological Medicine; Human Organization; Journal of Psychosomatic Research; Psychosomatic Medicine; Medical Care*), textbooks (e.g., Stone *et al.* 1979), and names of courses in the medical school curricula. Several of these common concepts, or at least conceptual areas, will be discussed below.

Medical education

We will first look at the arena of medical education to assess the extent of incorporation of various behavioral science concepts and techniques – in this case medicine being the "ground," the behavioral sciences, the "figure."

For one thing, in this instance the balkanization of the three primary disciplines into separate departments – so typical of the general university – is not found. Rather, there is most commonly a "behavioral" or "social" science section or division of a department or even a department itself. Departments of behavioral science are included in medical schools at the University of Kentucky, the Pennsylvania State University at Hershey, the University of Toronto, the University of Alabama, and the University of Minnesota at Duluth. A number of schools have divisions of behavioral science, often in departments of family medicine, or else the term "behavioral sciences" is included as part of the formal name of a psychiatry department. Included in such departments or divisions (as of 1978) were 68 anthropologists, 156 sociologists, and 1,694 psychologists (data from Webster 1979). Many of the psychologists, of course, are involved primarily in clinical work, but at least some of them also participate in research activities and in teaching programs for medical students and residents. From one point of view, such an organizational form, such a collapsing of disciplinary boundaries, may be viewed as an ecological necessity; for medical students, and probably many medical school faculty members as well, perceive these several disciplines at the *generic* level – as all dealing one way or another with human behavior – and not at the species level, i.e., in terms of the disciplinary distinctions often cherished by behavioral scientists in other contexts.

Another kind of recognition or legitimation for a common core of behavioral science concepts can be found in the list of descriptive categories in terms of which questions for the National Board of Medical Examiners behavioral sciences examination are written. This examination is taken each year by approximately 16,000 sophomore medical students in the United States and Canada. The categories have been developed by a committee of behavioral scientists out of their own front-line experience in teaching medical students. Members of the original committee which formulated the first statement of these categories in 1971 were Evan G. Pattishall, M.D., Ph.D. (chairman); Peter L. Carleton, Ph.D.; David R. Hawkins, M.D.; Donald A. Kennedy, Ph.D.; Edward J. Stainbrook, M.D., Ph.D.; and Robert Straus, Ph.D.

The categories can be taken as a synopsis of the social, cultural, and psychological domains considered relevant to medical education by one of the most powerful and influential organizations in North American medical education. Note that the categories tend to follow a systems or hierarchical analytic format:

1) Behavioral Biology, including:
   a) Biochemical correlates of behavior
   b) Comparative behavior
   c) Genetics of behavior
   d) Pharmacological correlates of behavior
   e) Physiological correlates of behavior
   f) Psychophysiology
   g) Statistics

2) Individual Behavior, including:
   a) Emotions
   b) Growth and development
   c) Learning and memory
   d) Life cycle
   e) Motivation
   f) Perception and cognition
   g) Personality
   h) Psychodynamics
   i) Psychological assessment
   j) Psychopathology

3) Interpersonal and Group Processes, including:
   a) Adaptation
   b) Attitudes and beliefs
   c) Change
   b) Child rearing practices
   e) Communication (both verbal and nonverbal)
   f) Interaction
   g) Leadership
   h) Physician–patient relationships
   i) Prejudice
   j) Roles

4) Culture and Society, including:
   a) Community
   b) Ethnomedicine
   c) Family
   d) Health care systems
   e) Human ecology
   f) Norms and values
   g) Organizations

   h) Social institutions
   i) Social problems
   j) Stratification

A major empirical study which looked at what concepts and knowledge from the three principal behavioral sciences were actually being taught in the curricula of medical schools was conducted in the early 1970's under a proposal developed by the American Sociological Association and funded by the National Center for Health Services Research. The principal investigator was Richard C. Fletcher, who worked with an interdisciplinary behavioral sciences committee that consisted of Robin F. Badgley and Samuel W. Bloom, representing Sociology; Charles C. Hughes and Donald A. Kennedy, representing Anthropology; Carl Eisdorfer and Murray Wexler, representing Psychology; and Evan G. Pattishall and Edward J. Stainbrook, representing the general field of medical education. John Kosa served as senior consultant to the project, and Jack Elinson was the liaison to the American Sociological Association.

The study consisted of several parts: nine case studies, a systematic review of catalogues of the then 112 U.S. and Canadian medical schools, and a series of specialized position papers which dealt with a variety of topics, e.g., the relationships of each behavioral science discipline to medical education.

The review of the catalogues (Fletcher 1972) was especially interesting. It showed, for one thing, that there was significant input of behavioral science knowledge and techniques into medical education, although such input might not always take place as the offering of one of the "behavioral science" departments or divisions. For example, pediatrics or a department of preventive medicine might well include an instructional unit incorporating some behavioral science perspectives and data.

There were almost 1300 behavioral science entries in the 112 medical schools, these "entries" being either courses in themselves or included as sections of topical courses which did not necessarily carry a behavioral science title. For purposes of determining relative importance, the entries were classified into 12 behavioral science subject categories and then ranked on the basis of (1) the number of medical schools with catalog entries in the category, (2) the mean number of catalog entries per school, and (3) the number of entries in required courses of the curriculum. By combining these three ranks, the topics were ordered in descending frequency of appearance in the curricula as follows:

Psychosocial determinants of illness
Human Development
Health Care Provision and Utilization
Physician Role
Psychological Concepts
Biological Basis of Behavior
Patient and His Social Context
"Behavioral Science"
Human Sexuality
"Sociology"
Organization of Social Interaction
Anthropological Concepts

What is clear from the 1971 review is that the most common form which behavioral science input into the curriculum took was that of a course which had an interdisciplinary cast to it and did not derive straightforwardly from any of the three major behavioral science disciplines. For example, at the bottom of the list are grouped those relatively few entries (3.2% of the total) which explicitly refer to "anthropological" content, use that term in the title, or strongly suggest that discipline – e.g., "comparative cultural studies." Similarly, "sociology" does not fare too well, either, when that term is used in course titles.

Thus, as indexed by the 1971 data, the tendency exists in curricula to present behavioral science material under a course label that tends to be interdisciplinary and have easily discernible "applied" implications. Further, as the results of this catalog review showed, there was apparently a significant amount of behavioral science material included in the teaching programs of the 112 medical schools – 40% of the topical courses being found in the required curriculum.

More recently another, and far less ambitious, effort was made to assess the status and activities of the behavioral sciences in medical education. In a brief questionnaire survey that was not comparable in scope, method, or analytic detail to the Fletcher study, Petersdorf and Feinstein (1980) polled chairpersons of departments of pediatrics, family medicine, and internal medicine and received replies from most of the departments in medical schools in the United States. They asked about "medical sociology," intentionally not offering a definition. To judge by the types of replies they received, that term is taken as a collective phrase for what has been referred to in this paper (and elsewhere) as the "behavioral sciences," or even the "social sciences"; and the discussion by the authors does not indicate that they, themselves, recognize the complex relations that occur between the behavioral science disciplines, on the one hand, and the topics and language employed in teaching situations, on the other. For them, it all resolves down to "medical sociology."

But by whatever term, though it is represented in the curricula of their schools, in the opinion of these chairpersons the field is not held in high esteem. Perhaps one relevant factor is in lack of appropriately trained faculty from the behavioral sciences – they note, for example, that "many faculty teachers of medical sociology were medical social workers" in departments of family medicine or pediatrics. There were no such personnel in medicine departments, the teaching there being done by internal medicine generalists who "were active in ambulatory care programs or in student health services." Of interest also is the relative acceptance of the *theoretical* importance of the subject matter among the three types of departments: highest in family medicine, lowest in internal medicine.

The specific content categories mentioned for behavioral science input in the preclinical years, ward rounds, and grand rounds are familiar: personal behavior (daily living, causes of illness, response to illness), interpersonal behavior, physician behavior, the community and the environment, and the organization of care.

In their interpretive comments the authors note that some of these topical areas have been taught for years in medical schools – but in departments of preventive medicine or public health, and not in the context of *clinical* departments such as those queried in this case. They further comment that this may explain some of the negative reaction on the part of the clinical department chairmen to the inclusion of such subject matter under the aegis of their departments. The scope of data relevant to the *clinical experience* has obviously not been widened sufficiently to include such factors as, for example, cost containment or some of the other issues from the macrostructural perspective – nor even examples from some of the other more immediate areas of personal behavior (which are often thought to be handled by physicians in their normal clinical activities). In terms of this study, then, the "clinical model" has not been very widely breeched by behavioral science, although the latter is relatively well represented in the preclinical years. Once again, the reality of the difference in orientation between the "basic" and the "applied" uses of scientific knowledge is apparent.

Thus, to judge by both the 1971 study and the more recent survey, while the array of behavioral science subject matters taught may be encouraging, it should not be taken as meaning that everything taught is necessarily *learned* or put into clinical practice following formal medical training. For there remain issues of the structural constraints on the practicing medical profession, of the division of labor, payment mechanisms, etc., which are influential in shaping actual patterns of formal role performance of the physician with respect to incorporating and *using* behavioral science concepts and data – a topic discussed below.

The overlap between the medical world and the behavioral sciences has been expressed not only in curricula but also in the formation of professional societies devoted to teaching and research in this area. For example, at about the same time as the Fletcher study of behavioral science content in medical school curricula was being conducted, there was formed a new professional society, the Association for the Behavioral Sciences and Medical Education (ABSAME), with the objective of bringing together behavioral scientists and professionals from medicine, nursing, and other health care fields around issues of enhancing the teaching of the behavioral sciences in medical (health) education. This organization has strongly reinforced both the trend toward relevant behavioral science topics in the curricula, as well as the *interdisciplinary* approach to be taken toward such teaching. At its semi-annual meetings, for example, almost invariably there are discussions and workshops on the issue of optimal behavioral science topics, curricula, and modes of teaching (such as, for example, use of experiential approaches or "clinical rounds" for presenting the relevance of the behavioral sciences; cf. Stein 1979; Medical Anthropology Newsletter 1980). Workshops are always offered dealing with one aspect or another from a common pool of topics that can usually be approached from any of the behavioral sciences, and it is often difficult to ascertain the original "discipline" of the instructor from the language and concepts used.

Another example of an organization devoted to such interdisciplinary concerns is the more recently formed "Academy of Behavioral Medicine" (Holden 1980). Its purpose is " ... the integration of biological and behavioral knowledge in a multidisciplinary approach ... The disciplines include anthropology, sociology, and epidemiology as well as psychiatry, medicine, and basic biological disciplines." Avowedly eschewing the Cartesian mind/body separation central in so much western scientific and even popular thought, this field " ... treats mind and body as two ends of the same continuum. The core of basic research ... is an attempt to locate the specific neurochemical mechanisms by which subjective states – specifically those associated with emotional stress – lead to disease. Ultimately, it is an approach to disease and health that spans everything from research through etiology, diagnosis, treatment, rehabilitation, and prevention."

As illustrated, then, by the inclusion of the behavioral sciences in the National Board of Medical Examiners testing schedule, the 1971 survey of behavioral science content in medical school curricula as well as the more recent data reported by Petersdorf and Feinstein, and the existence of professional societies oriented to education and research in the nexus between the behavioral sciences and medicine, it is clear that significant steps have been taken in the institutionalization of the linkage between the behavioral sciences and medicine. At the same time, however, given the weight of established tradition, the extent to which these activities may result in a fundamental change in the dominant reductionistic conceptual frame of reference is probably moot at this point.

Let us now turn to a very brief overview of that body of research-based knowledge that both serves as the source of content for much of the behavioral sciences' contribution to medical school curricula as well as demonstrates the extent to which concepts drawn from the field have begun to diffuse into the study of the distribution and determinants of disease, its very conceptualization and definition, diagnosis, treatment, and prevention.

Toward a knowledge base for a "medical behavioral science"

The research record illustrating the mutual relevance of the behavioral sciences and medicine is impressive, obviously imperfect, certainly uneven, and, at the same time, a precursor of what is to come. Perhaps it is always so at the beginning of a potential shift in the conceptual paradigm organizing a field of thought. In any case, it is our purpose in this section to present the briefest of samplers of concepts or conceptual areas drawn from the behavioral sciences in terms of which there has been considerable research evidence developed by both behavioral scientists themselves as well as researchers drawn from medical fields who share this wider orientation in regard to linkages between the disease process and its psychosocial parameters. Obviously in such a limited space we must be highly selective. Our sample is, however, representative of the conceptual *scope* of the behavioral sciences, dealing as it does with levels of analysis, uses of the concept of role, the structural and psychogenic aspects of stress, concepts of primary and secondary group, bureaucracy and other forms of social structure, and the great realm of values, belief, and ethics. Interspersed in the discussion of these domains are also other behavioral science concepts implied by the particular conceptual point of entry chosen. Aside from briefly illustrating the scope of the behavioral sciences with respect to the study of disease, we hope that the principal effect of this exercise will be to illustrate a *method* of looking at the two sets of fields that can be extended to other concepts of choice which it is not possible to cover in this discussion.

But how is one to organize presentation of such a sampler so that there will be both some kind of logic and yet minimal redundancy? One could, of course, adopt a simple "levels of analysis" approach, starting with sub-organismic phenomena (such as psychophysiologic processes) and move upward to the individual human personality system, thence to interpersonal processes and finally to the macrostructural patterns displayed by institutions and groups at the level of societies, in a manner paralleling the system of categories devised by the National Board of Medical Examiners' Committee. A disadvantage to that organizational scheme is that it runs the danger of hypostatizing disciplinary boundaries and denying, by the very form of scheme chosen, the interdisciplinary nature of much of the research. Another problem is that one is usually forced to present such a discussion in terms of a linear analytic mode without illustrating relationships of a concept, for example, to other constructs in the relevant field of inquiry; and much of the pervasive contribution of behavioral science concepts to the study of disease and its treatment is thereby lost. The "medium is *too much* the message" in such a format.

For these reasons we adopt a cross-cutting matrix format to provide a visual and conceptual point of entry into the body of research literature (Figure 2). The matrix was developed by one of us (CCH) and has been successfully used with a graduate level seminar consisting of both medical and non-medical students and post graduate medical residents and fellows to demonstrate the central purpose of this chapter itself – the wide applicability of some common behavioral science concepts to the study and treatment of disease.

The horizontal axis of the matrix is comprised of several simple, primary concepts and topical areas frequently found in the medical and

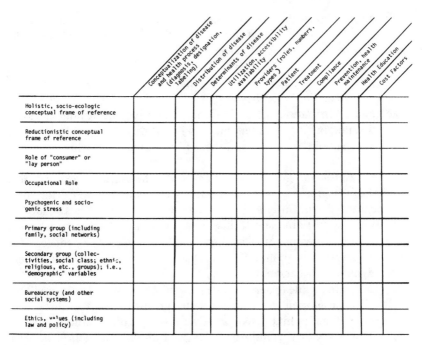

FIGURE 8.2 Matrix for interrelations between medical services system and behavioral sciences.

health services research framework, and the vertical axis is a sampling of familiar behavioral science concepts. Clearly neither axis is exhaustive of all possibilities. The behavioral scientist, for example, may well be appalled at how few concepts are represented from the many the field works with, and those from medical fields will likewise wish to make additions. Such further development of analytic categories from both axes is not to be regretted; indeed, it is precisely the chief stimulus one wishes from use of such a paradigm. For its intent is to establish a way of thinking about multiple interrelationships and to belie the feeling that there are so many potential areas of intersection that no analytic order is possible in viewing the subject.

We will discuss the relevant literature by using the vertical axis – concepts from the behavioral science perspective – as the starting point for illustrating the content of some of the cells intersected by concepts from the "medical" axis.

Obviously, given the concerns raised earlier in this paper there is no need for further discussion at this point of the first two dimensions in the matrix from the behavioral science perspective – the contrast between a "holistic" or "field" conceptual frame of reference and the more restrictive "reductionistic" conceptual model. Suffice it to say that there is an extensive literature beyond that cited earlier that considers the place and contributions of both a comprehensive and a limited model for understanding disease phenomena, a literature contributed to by both medical behavioral scientists and those from biomedical fields.

Role of "consumer" or "lay person"   With the third conceptual area from the behavioral science perspective we encounter one of the most significant and fruitful analytic concepts we all work with, the idea of *role*. While specifically defined in varying ways by different researchers, its bottom-line meaning underscores its nature as a *bridging* concept, for it is the basic structural unit of social systems as well as a key constituent in the dynamics of personality systems.

It is not worthwhile to attempt assigning ultimate disciplinary credit for the explicit development of this key concept in the behavioral sciences. One person might point to George Herbert Mead's discussions of "taking the role of the other"; another to Ralph Linton's distinction between "status" and "role" in his 1930's book, *The Study of Man*; still another would refer to Talcott Parsons's elaboration of the concept and its eventual status as the cornerstone of a "general theory of action." Be that as it may, the concept well illustrates the purpose of the matrix; for what the term "patient" means in medical care transactions becomes in a behavioral science perspective expected *role behavior* on the part of the consumer or lay person when he or she presents to the physician. Parsons's classic formulation of the "sick role" stimulated considerable research in this area of linkage between malfunctioning biology and social norms; and, although, subsequent research has refined and sharpened the scope of relevance of that first formulation – pointing, for example, to its lack of fit with conditions of *chronic* illness (Gallagher 1976, Twaddle 1972) – its pioneering status and continued utility remain significant.

Other research has examined how different from the "medical model" is the lay person's conception of illness (Apple 1960; Mabry 1964); how the lay person's behavior, emotions, and outlook are significantly affected when in the role of "patient" (e.g., Cassell 1976; Lederer 1952);

how the decision to utilize medical care facilities is multiply influenced by factors in that person's life situation, especially the influence of family and friends (e.g., Stoeckle, Zola, Davidson 1963; Zola 1973); how, when the lay person has presented for *treatment* of an ailment, the response sought from the health care provider includes powerful psychosocial expectations and is not limited to the merely technological or pharmacologically effective (Cassell 1976; Eisenberg 1977); how disease and estimates of one's vulnerability and hence the relative importance of either taking preventive action or seeking medical aid are influenced by the conceptual model the person has, illustrated for example in the "health belief model" or ideas such as "locus of control" (e.g., Becker, Haefner, *et al.*, 1977; Wallston and Wallston 1978).

One can also point to how strongly a patient's compliance with medical directions is influenced by such psychosocial factors as the quality of the interpersonal relationship with the physician, or the sensitivity of the physician to the life situation of the patient and his understanding of the structural and psychological constraints inhibiting conformance to certair types of regimen (e.g., Stimson 1974; Sackett and Haynes 1976). Research in the field of health eduction shows the powerful force of habit in daily life, the inadequacy of utilizing only cognitive messages in an attempt to change behavior, and the strong role of affect in perception and conduct (Richards 1975; Farquhar 1978; Jenkins 1979; Ubell 1972).

To judge not only from the proliferation of easily available and popularized paperback manuals, as well as from professional literature, concepts and techniques drawn from the behavioral sciences are beginning to have important results in the *treatment* of various disorders, especially of such problems as obesity, alcoholism, cigarette smoking, and other indulgence disorders. One line of attack, of course, draws its theoretical justification from the behaviorist tradition in psychology and has developed behavior modification or behavior "shaping" techniques of intervention, now often called "social learning theory." Not concerned with internal images or psychological conceptualizations of what occurs, this activity applies techniques well-systematized in experimental settings toward behavior change through familiar reinforcement or aversive techniques (Katz and Zlutnick 1975; Leventhal 1973; Pomerleau *et al.* 1975). Perhaps because of the apparently greater "scientific" (i.e., quantified) rigor of such methods, they have won acceptance in broad circles of the medical establisment, and as noted before the term "behavioral medicine" is, by some, being distinguished from the more general rubric of "behavioral sciences" and medicine. One major theoretical issue that remains troublesome in the broad application of many such findings, however, is that of the *voluntaristic* nature of participation by many who seek out or agree to participate in behavior change programs. This prompts the further question of how widely such techniques can be applied – within ethical and legal boundaries – in the society at large on populations not necessarily *motivated to participate?*

Aside from the attractiveness of the techniques and methodological straightforwardness of the behavior modification approach, there still remains a great deal of research and teaching interest in the more elusive phenomenological constructs of the human psychosocial enterprise. Postulated concepts of the "inner" life which can be indexed only tangentially but which are theoretically crucial in interpretation of human behavior generally and more specifically in episodes of illness and treatment are very common. Not only general concepts such as personality structure and personality change, but also more specific concepts such as self-image, self-concept, identity, locus of control, satisfaction, personal constructs, and others of like *genre*, remain useful analytic tools for many researchers, and in recent years we have seen an astounding proliferation of cognition-based therapies and conceptualizations (e.g., Pelletier 1977). Techniques such as "guided imagery" (Jaffe and Bresler 1980) or "cognitive restructuring" have attained respectable status along with the more behavioristic therapies for treatment of a wide variety of disorders, something known in the Orient for quite a while, apparently, which has recently become respectable in this society through such techniques as cognitive control of autonomic activity and biofeedback (e.g., Miller 1969, Benson 1975).

Various conceptualizations at the level of personality structure in relation to disease have been found in the literature for some time. Early on these were associated with such specific susceptibility as "the ulcer personality," and most recently with the now quite notorious "Type A Personality," especially studied in relation to heart disease (Friedman and Rosenman 1974; Haynes *et al.* 1978). The "Type A Personality" is, in fact, so commonly referred to that it has almost become folk wisdom. Rosenstock, in an excellent early overview of many aspects of the mutual relevance of the behavioral sciences and public health, takes us directly to the nub of many of the problems in this field and long before the appearance of the phrase anticipated its essential meaning. He asks, "How can we teach motives for rest or relaxation to people, including health workers, when the culture now rewards those who work night and day? How many of us can fail to admire our co-workers or supervisors who pridefully inform us that they complete even more office work at home than the phenomenal amount they accomplish in the office?" (1960: 301).

While not at the level of conceptualization represented by "personality," other research has underscored the close association between certain habits of daily living – some of which used to be called "hygiene," e.g., regular exercise, eight hours of sleep a night, daily breakfast – and prevention of disease or promotion of health (e.g., Belloc and Breslow 1972; Breslow 1978), and in much literature these days the almost ubiquitous term "life style" is common with reference to generalized role behavior of the lay person in relation to health and disease susceptibility (e.g., Haggerty 1977). Indeed, some writers place much emphasis for the current "crisis" in the nation's health picture and escalating costs of medical care upon the behavior – the "life style" – of the consumer as a major *determinant of disease*. Knowles, for example (1977b), speaks of the responsibility of the individual to establish healthful behavior patterns as the only feasible way to prevent and thereby manage the crisis in medical care.

It is important to comment briefly upon the phrase "life style" in connection with matters related to the determinants and prevention of disease, since the phrase may be at risk of becoming so seductive a concept that it puts a stop to critical analysis of its ontological status as well as its empirical referents. It is included, for example, as one of the four determinants of the health status of a population in the highly influential "Lalonde Report" on the health of Canadians (1974). It also figures persuasively in the report of the U.S. Surgeon General on the need for health promotion and disease prevention in this country (Surgeon General 1979); and the most recent edition of a major text in this country on preventive medicine devotes a major chapter to the concept (Somers 1980).

"Life style" (or, as sometimes put as a single word, as if to emphasize the union of ideas), "lifestyle" is a concept that carries obvious face validity in discussions of the intersection between the behavioral sciences and medicine/nursing/health care. What else is meant by the term than an amalgam or concatenation of habits, behavior patterns, perhaps certain aspects of personality, "culture" (especially the "way of life" kind of definition), "social behavior," norms, values, themes, etc.? The word "style" itself connotes an overall, persistent and coherent patterning of parts or elements at any given level of abstraction; a construct pertaining to *quality* or *configuration* rather than simple quantity or enumeration; a structural rather than statistical conceptualization. It is in these conceptualizations of "pattern," "style" (if you will) that the behavioral sciences make much of their contribution to understanding and explicating the uniformities and differences in normal human behavior, both in individual persons and in groups.

Thus one can assert that attention to "life style" is of the essence in the behavioral sciences. And the relationship between life style or "way of life" (or whatever other term one wishes to use in characterizing cultural and individual habit patterns) and health is certainly not new. Recall Hippocrates's injunction, cited earlier, to investigate ". . . the mode in which the inhabitants live, and what are their pursuits, whether they are fond of drinking and eating to excess, and given to indolence, or are fond of exercise and labor." Practically a programmatic statement for the foci of many current behavior modification programs directed at major health problems!

But what is "life style" as a researchable idea? It is not a neat and clean variable, does not have discrete boundaries that are easily imposed for research purposes (as does, e.g., age, gender, occupational position). It may be thought slippery to work with – but nonetheless vital as a first approximation of the overall patterning of a series of more specific variables that can be broken out for detailed research. Its ontological status is different from some of the other variables that have proven helpful in dissecting stable, predicitve relationships between health and social condition, and the chief danger is that the *aspects* chosen to operationalize it for useful research may or may not include the most significant and critical features. This concept, somewhat like the concept of *culture*, simply cannot be used as a homogeneous and easily replicable "variable." Rather, like the concept of culture, it is a "mother-lode" of variables, which, entwined together in a natural setting, provide challenge for the analyst to choose particular features deemed theoretically most important for the problem at hand. "Life style," then, like "culture," is therefore best viewed as a primary *orienting concept*, a first approximation, out of which a selection of variables is made for more specific research purposes. Its understanding requires a different, but equally legitimate, modality of thought; like "culture," it is perhaps best apprehended on the basis of a synthesizing clinical or configurative *verstehen*, a type of understanding that may confound the more positivistic-minded type of methodologist.

What is meant by an "orienting concept" can be exemplified in other cognitive domains. The concept of "north," for example, is useful in distinguishing one broad directional orientation from the other cardinal directions, such as south, east, and west. And knowing the difference empirically between north and south in particular situations can be absolutely vital – as when lost in the wilderness. But in some other, more sharply-defined problem situations, it may be important to know something more detailed about "north"; for example, whether it is north-east, north-north-east, north by east, or north-west. And, of course, these verbal designations can be translated into quantified ("operationalized") terms as well.

So, we suggest, must it also be with "life style" – first, the descriptive characterization of what the term means whether applied to a person or to a group, a characterization done with all the sensitive observational and analytic skills at the command of the investigator. The behavioral sciences are rich with literature that offers a first approximation understanding of the different life styles in a population, a literature more abundant in some of the behavioral sciences than others. But then, building upon that base of understanding, which must include a *strong* phenomenologic component – *how the world is perceived and understood by the people studied* – there can come about the sharper specification of the significant variables operating in that behavioral pattern or set of behavioral patterns, with all the tools of operationalization, quantification, and analysis that the behavioral sciences possess brought to bear upon problems of disease in relation to "life style."

Occupational role   Obviously the concept of role can be used not only in a generalized sense, as with reference to "citizen" or lay person. It can also be used to designate specific sets of rights, duties, and expected behavior for persons occupying more circumscribed positions in the social system. And it is in this second sense that we now turn to illustration of the considerable literature that bears upon the relationship of particular role positions to disease and its treatment, in this case *occupational roles*.

The influence of a person's occupational role (an expression of the division of labor) in structuring one's place in society is of course enormous. Not only relative prestige factors are involved as well as access to and control of rewards and resources, but an occupational position has important effects on one's self-esteem and that of family members, and in many situations upon one's standing among peers. But because so much time in one's life is also spent working in a particular physical-social-psychological niche, an occupational role can also have major effects upon health – something that insurance companies have known for a long time, not to mention ancient peoples such as the Romans, who put captured slaves, not their fellow citizens, into the mines to work! Looking at just one type of disease, for example cancer, one can cite Pott's observations of scrotal cancer among chimney sweeps in 18th century England, and bring those observations up to date by reference to the many studies discussed in Epstein's book, *The Politics of Cancer* (1979).

The literature shows very clearly that there are major differences in morbidity and mortality between the manual labor occupations and the "white collar" jobs (APHA 1975), something graphically pointed out three centuries ago by Ramazzini, the "father" of occupational medicine (1964), and the hazards of the workplace are not simply limited to accidents from machinery or the harshness of inclement working conditions. They are also evident in the psychological repercussions of the work itself, as in assembly-line industrial work that may induce a high level of boredom associated with the increasing levels of dissatisfaction and alienation, drug abuse, and absenteeism (Coburn 1978; House *et al.* 1979; *Work in America* 1973). Work as a possible *determinant of disease* has also been related to the development of coronary heart disease (e.g., House 1974), and perhaps the most widely publicized suggested mechanism in that relationship is the famous "Type A Personality Pattern," cited earlier. But other disease outcomes are also associated with particular occupational positions, such as the highly stressed position of air traffic controller (Cobb and Rose 1973), or that of the foreman – typically a position caught between two contending sets of pressures, that of loyalty to management and that of peer affiliation with workers (Useem and Useem 1958). And the occupational role of housewife is also shown to be comprised of stresses of sufficient pathogenicity as to lead to depression and other disorders (Gove and Tudor 1973; Brown and Harris 1978).

And yet, perhaps paradoxically, while a given job situation may well predispose toward disease, the stresses associated with *loss* of a job may likewise be a significant factor in illness (Kasl *et al.* 1968) – a topic more

fully developed below. And continuing to work, perhaps thereby fulfilling a variety of psychosocial needs, has been shown to be protective
against premature mortality in retirement (Palmore 1969).

For this particular discussion, the role of physician is of special
interest from several points of view, not only its pathogenic implications
for the person in whose role repertory it is usually central, but also with
regard to consequences for patient care of the performance of this
significant role. There is a considerable literature dealing with what the
behavioral sciences call the "socialization" of a student into the role
of physician (see Coombs 1978 for a recent study), and such studies
underscore the pervasive and insidious shaping and molding of behavior,
attitude, and value that is an associated feature of biotechnical training.
That such role imprinting is successful is attested both by longitudinal
studies that show changes in the person's attitudes over the course of
formal medical training, as well as by the trend toward stereotypy of
behavior subsequently displayed by physicians in practice. Other features,
and these of a health-related nature, are also, however, associated with
the role, such as the considerable stresses of residency training (an
excellent portrayal of which is given for the field of surgery by Bosk
1979), and the high incidence of suicide, drug abuse, divorce, and accidental death as aircraft pilots, in some instances higher than most other
occupational categories (Bowden and Burstein 1974; Vaillant *et al.*
1972).

Another feature of the behavior displayed by those performing the
role of physician is the effect of much of that behavior upon the patient,
and the study of the physician/patient relationship has been the focus of
considerable attention. While the variety of affective needs and factors
felt by a patient in an encounter with a physician may be wide, many
of the role-trained behaviors on the part of the physician have the singular
effect of creating negative fellings in the patient because of the impersonality displayed, the lack of apparent interest in the patient as a
person and not just as a convenient vehicle for the disease, and the
sense of impatience with what are often seen as trivial complaints.
It is often precisely in this area of the *psychosocial needs of the patient*
in the medical care transaction, no matter how technically competent
the care in other respects, that major problems with the system of health
care delivery are cited – epitomized in the title of a recent critique,
"Doing Better and Feeling Worse" (Knowles 1977a; see also Bernarde
and Mayerson 1978).

Studies of affect in human behavior are common in the behavioral sciences, of course, and the powerful role of emotions in energizing the restorative and "self-treatment" processes in the sick person is highly relevant to discussion of the physician/patient relationship. This can be succinctly illustrated with the concept of the "placebo" and the potential "placebo-effect" aspects of the role behavior of the physician. (Indeed, Balint, 1972, spoke metaphorically of the "doctor as drug," in this case one of the most powerful of drugs.)

It was W.I. Thomas who noted many years ago that "if men define situations as real, they are real in their consequences." Perhaps the extreme illustration of that comment are the cases of death by witchcraft, reported in Cannon's classic article of some years ago (1942) as well as in more recent publications (e.g., Greene *et al.* 1972). In these studies the message is clear – belief can kill. The power of belief, an idea whose dynamic is emotion, is not to be disregarded in fundamental matters of medical care, either; and in the realm of practice, it is the unwise physician who does not recognize and attempt to foster the patient's "will to live" by explicitly reinforcing psychological forces as allies in the curative process (Frank 1975). The widespread popularity of Norman Cousins's recent account of his experience with a life-threatening illness (1979) in which he depicted the strong support of his physician, his own determination to recover against huge statistical odds, and his success in doing so, is a good example of phenomena widespread in actual medical practice.

The placebo tends to be much maligned in medicine. Commonly defined as a "sugar pill," a chemically-inert substance that parades as a pharmacologically-effective drug, it is usually dismissed as somehow belonging in the camp of the "quacks," charlatans, "witchdoctors" – as well as smacking of the unethical. The phrase "merely a placebo" is often used disparagingly by the physician or other health care providers to dismiss the importance of a patient's perceptual world as an active partner in self-healing processes.

To dismiss the so-called "placebo effect," however, is to operate out of the narrow biomedical model discussed earlier which implies that disease is a specific biologically- or chemically-based entity *sui generis* not influenced by psychological or other "subjective" factors. Among other things, adoption of such a restricted idea of disease sharply circumscribes the scope of the healer's perceived role and demonstrable effectiveness, as has been so widely demonstrated, for example, in studies of attempts to introduce western medicine into parts of the world not sharing such a conception, groups where the patient's will to restoration of health is actively fostered by the ethnohealer's use of all the power and transformational possibilities of drama, suggestion, and command. In fact, perhaps the placebo effect is the best succinct example one could cite of the need for enlarging the conventional medical model to include patterns of intimate interdependence between *soma* and *psyche*.

Psychogenic and sociogenic stress Of the world of stress there seems no end. Indeed, stress, when defined as perceived threat to the organism, is at least episodically a constant companion in life (Selye 1973), and the psychological and sociocultural sources of stressful stimuli provide grist for a huge literature of relevance to studies of the disease process (e.g., Levine and Scotch 1970). Quite aside from its being an associated feature of any serious illness, stress figures explicitly into the analysis of distribution and determinants of disease in the obvious instance of mental disorders (Leighton 1959; Hughes *et al.* 1960; Leighton *et al.* 1963; Weissman and Klerman 1978), in hypertension and heart disease (Scotch 1963; Syme *et al.* 1975; Jenkins 1976), resistance to infectious disease (Friedman and Glasgow 1966; Solomon and Amkraut 1972), and arthritis (Cobb 1976). It is a key factor involved in the utilization of health care facilities, as when Yudkin speaks of the "second diagnosis," that stress-induced reason for seeking the counsel of a physician (Yudkin 1961; see also Andersen *et al.* 1977; Zola 1973; Roghmann and Haggerty 1972); in psychological preparation for recovery and rehabilitation following surgery (Egbert *et al.* 1964; Skipper and Leonard 1968); and in efforts directed at prevention, illustrated in the considerable professional as well as popular literature on "stress reduction" or stress "management."

One of the principal antecedents of stress is drastic change in the psychosocial world of the person, with consequent deprivations, frustrations, or unclear expectations, and the burgeoning literature on the malignant effects of change in a person's life or circumstances is impressive. Whether at the level of the "normal" human life course and developmental "crises," e.g., marriage, retirement, aging; or more broadly in the action of *situational* life changes and their effects upon health (death of spouse or relative, moving to a new job, failure in school, etc.), many changes require major psychosocial readjustment (Cassel 1974; Kagan and Levi 1974). Brenner (1973, 1980) has illustrated this with regard to situations of economic depression. Although it is an ancient insight that changes in life circumstances can affect health, it has not been until recently that instruments have been developed and successfully replicated in many different studies in an attempt to measure and predict health effects consequent to social readjustment (e.g., Holmes and Rahe 1967; Rahe 1974; see also Dohrenwend and Dohrenwend 1974; Rabkin and Struening 1976).

Primary group   One of the most seminal conceptual areas for the behavioral sciences is the phylogenetic basis and profound psychosocial influence of a network of close, intimate social ties. Harlow's studies of infrahuman higher primates have shown the critical importance of *bonding* and the impact on healthy growth of an infant that nurturant ties with an adult female have (Harlow 1971). Of course, Spitz years ago (1965) and Bowlby (1969) have demonstrated the same imperative in human infants; Barnett *et al.* (1970) have pointed to the reciprocal need in mothers themselves; and a vast realm of literature as well as common observation points to the pervasive and critical importance of the *family* unit in human psychological as well as sociocultural life (e.g., La Barre 1954). But the idea of primary group is not limited to those socially-defined, genetically-based units called families; it also includes non-kin types of relationships to which a given person is linked in close, usually face-to-face interaction (such as a work group, an association or network of friends).

The relevance of the quality of a person's primary group affiliation to health status is enormous. To look first at family experience, the family, of course, has been considered by some to be the crucible of mental health (or ill-health), and both individual-focused therapies and "family" therapies have grown in response to the recurrent production of casualties of that experience. But the family is also an epidemiological unit having major impact upon the distribution of disease. It is, for example, an "infecting unit" in cases of contagious disease, the use of which term in a study of health care among the Navajo Indians illustrated dramatically for health care personnel the relevance of knowing particulars of family structure and living (Adair and Deuschle 1970). Knowledge of family relationships was also demonstrated to be the key factor in unravelling the theretofore perplexing transmission patterns of the viral disease, *Kuru* (Gajdusek 1977). But the impact of the family has been noted with a wide range of other types of diseases also (Litman 1974 presents a good review); and stability of family context has been shown to be enormously significant in matters of patients' compliance with a medical regimen (Becker and Green 1975), with success in rehabilitation (Peck 1974), with decisions to utilize the medical care system through consulting "lay referral systems" not only in industrialized societies (Freidson 1959; McKinlay 1973; Hamburg and Killilea 1979), but also in nonliterate societies and ethnic minorities (Clark 1959). Within the family, risk of premature mortality has been shown to be highly associated with death of spouse (Parkes 1964; Walker *et al.* 1977) or other significant persons (Lynch 1977) and has been demonstrated as a consequence of disruption of the close, supportive ties represented in a marital relationship (Holmes and Rahe 1967; Parkes *et al.* 1969).

Beyond the realm of family ties *per se*, the health-promoting implications of primary group ties is indexed by an extensive literature, which is reviewed by Hamburg and Killilea (1979), and by Kaplan, Cassel and Gore (1977). Cobb (1976) reviews a number of studies in which diverse types of disease were ameliorated by social support; Caplan (1974) speaks to the qualities of social ties with respect to mental health; and Finlayson (1976) studied the importance of social ties in assisting a woman adapt to her husband's myocardial infarction. Berkanovic (1976) reviews the importance of social supports in programs of prevention and health maintenance, and one of the most extensive studies to document the importance of primary support systems is that of Berkman and Syme (1979), in which a nine year longitudinal study of almost 7,000 persons, controlling for baseline health status, socioeconomic status, health practices, physical activity, alcohol consumption, obesity, sleeping and eating patterns, indicated significantly higher mortality risk for persons with fewer primary group social ties.

Secondary group Beyond primary social ties, which are rooted in demonstrable social relationships and tend to cohere around a given person to create a network of social affiliation, there is another dimension often used to characterize that person's placement in a social matrix. That dimension is the "secondary group" concept, in terms of which populations of people sharing defined characteristics may be *analytically* singled out from other populations in the society. Such populations are usually not "groups" in the generic sense, for when each is considered as a whole it does not incorporate networks of actual social interactional ties, as do primary relationships. These types of populations are better termed "aggregates" than "groups" and are what one usually refers to as the "socio-demographic" dimensions of a heterogeneous population – age, sex, race, ethnic group, and socio-economic status or *social class*. Because of its tradition in the behavioral sciences literature, we will retain use of the term "secondary group" in referring to these characteristics.

Social class standing is a key factor in susceptibility to disease and its differential distribution (Syme and Berkman 1976). There is an enormous body of evidence that underscores the inverse relationship between social class position and mortality, morbidity, and disability, and this relationship holds for most physical diseases as well as mental illnesses (Kitagawa and Hauser 1973; Yeracaris and Kim 1978; Fuchs 1974; Antonovsky 1972; Weissman and Klerman 1978; Kosa and Zola 1975). At the same time, while in recent years with the development of such programs as Medicaid there has grown greater utilization of health care facilities by the poor – such that utilization now is almost on parity with people from higher in the social class hierarchy (Andersen 1978) – the fact remains that, relative to need, the poorer social strata are still underserved. In terms of the "use/disability ratio" (Aday 1975), they still lag behind those more fortunately situated in the social class system. And when they do appear for health care, the coping skills developed as a result of socialization and life in a particular psychosocial niche are not as well adapted to the demands for service from the medical care system as are those of the better educated, more affluent, more facile members of the middle and upper class groups. Strauss (1969), illustrating the import of a vast literature, points out that the lack of interpersonal skills in dealing with the intricacies of a bureaucratic system, such as lack of language facility and ease in use of abstract terms, submissiveness to authority, and discomfort with an impersonal basis for a relationship, all militate against a satisfactory interpersonal outcome from such contact.

Preventive medicine and health education are also detrimentally affected by the structured experiences of lower social class persons (Ireland 1971; Coburn and Pope 1974; Hurley 1972; Bullough 1972), insofar as the perplexities of daily living often preclude having the necessary resources to carry out a better health plan (e.g., "better" – which usually means more expensive – nutrition), or militate against taking a long-range time perspective in which it is difficult to visualize problematic outcomes from current behavior in an often unpredictable environment. Further, typical techniques of health education, often geared to middle class symbols, aspirations, and cognitive styles, usually fall short of the mark in having an impact upon changing behavior. And there is the further complication of different conceptualizations of disease and of the meaning of symptoms, many of which are structured on a social class basis (e.g., Koos 1967).

But beyond social class parameters representing the secondary group concept, there is another, enormously important analytic concept that serves not only to group certain types of people together in the same category, but often also to serve as a major reference group for them and in many local situations to be manifested in primary group ties. This concept is that of *ethnic group* membership. While it is obvious, for example, that not all people listed as "Black" or "Spanish-American" in vital statistics tables ever do interact in a face-to-face manner with their cultural congeners, this designation does serve to group together large numbers of people who share certain characteristics and who may, in a symbolic sense at least, think of themselves as members of at least a powerful reference group *for* each other (as seen for example, in use of such terms as the "Black Community" when the reference is to all Blacks in the United States).

Much of the relevance for health status of ethnic group affiliation has been implicated in the discussion of social class standing, for many members of such ethnic aggregates are also characterized by poverty, less education, and less prestigeful occupations. And if the health status of the poor is bad, the health status of the ethnic poor is much worse (see *Health Status of Minorities and Low-Income Groups* 1979). Moreover, many of the same difficulties that impede optimal utilization of health care facilities are accentuated when the patient is Black, Chicano, Native American, Puerto Rican, etc., or (newly arrived on the scene) a refugee from southeast Asia. Lack of language facility; unfamiliarity with behavioral customs relating to touch, modesty, gaze and eye contact; active folk ethnomedical traditions and differential conceptualization of disease, symptoms, or the relevance of preventive behavior – all may create major obstacles in the way of a smooth articulation between most members of most minority or ethnic groups and the dominant medical care system (e.g., Quesada and Heller 1977; Mechanic 1972; Snow 1974; Harwood 1971; Falk 1979).

Social system level   Group membership or collectivity variables and their influence upon the behavior of individual persons are not the only useful insights concerned with collective behavior that the behavioral sciences contribute in research on medically-oriented problems. Some researchers have taken an institutional level of analysis and looked at *social system* aspects of medical care organization and health services. Taking one particular social organizational form, for example, that of what is perhaps the central social organizational "image" in the field of medicine – the hospital – there have been numerous studies analyzing its internal structural contradictions, its institutional impact upon shaping behavior and perceptions of both providers and patients, its iatrogenic and nosocomial properties, its increasing consumption of resources (e.g., Fuchs 1974), its celebration as the crowning justification of the reductionistic conceptual model. Mauksch (1973) has spoken of the several competing differential "cultural" systems in the hospital setting – patients, providers, family – and Duff and Hollingshead (1968) have presented an extensive case study. Georgopolous and Matejko (1967) and Caudill (1958) have looked at the hospital as a social system; Caudill *et al.* (1952) and Parker (1958) analyzed the hospital ward as a small scale social system; and Wilson (1963) and Smith (1958) have discussed the structural compromises built into the hospital system – the "two lines of authority" between administrators and the technically qualified "outsiders," the physicians, who are *in* but not *of* the institution in the typical community hospital.

When the lay person serves in the role of patient in a hospital, as contrasted to an outpatient clinic or physician's office, there are particular, institutionally-based and frequently demeaning effects perceived by that person, Tao–Kim–Hai (1960) has placed such treatment in a cross-cultural perspective, and Taylor (1970) has referred to the bureaucratic processing of the person into a patient as "sociological sheep-shearing," whereby the complexities and individuality of the person are disregarded in the interests of uniformity, standardization, and amenability to institutional requirements of the hospital as a social system.

When the "patient" happens to be, in another role, a physician or other health care provider, interesting complexities arise which may be commented upon in passing. Lipowski and Stewart (1973) and Glass (1975) and others have spoken of the confusions in interpersonal treatment and difficulties of adapting to a different role definition (for *all* persons concerned) when the situation of action is radically changed. Others have spoken of the inappropriate projection of rationality and self-sufficiency onto, for example, a physician as a patient, projection which occurs perhaps out of a reluctance to imply lack of competence or inability to care for one's self (Bowden 1974).

Other investigators have looked at middle-range social organizations that have certain features of the "ideal type" formulations of a bureaucracy, as described by Weber (1952). For instance, Bloom (1971) has analyzed the structure of a medical school at the institutional level. Others, of course, have taken on more ambitious analyses of the numerous social organizational aspects of the "medical care system" seen in the context of the broader social structure – some from a Marxist perspective (e.g., McKinlay 1975; Waitzkin 1980; Navarro 1978), and others from a more neutral position (Fry and Farndale 1972; Field 1980). The series of essays edited by Knowles (1977) – carrying the provocative title "Doing Better and Feeling Worse" – contains a balanced spectrum of such critiques.

Earlier, in connection with the role of the lay person and especially the "lifestyle" features of the behavior of individual persons, we referred to the point of view which implies that the ultimate responsibility for changing unhealthful living patterns in order to maximize health and prevent disease lies with the person himself. Saying that the individual is the locus of effective intervention represents a particular theoretical position, that of an individual-centered locus of behavior. In some major respects, however, there exist strong counter-arguments, appropriate to express at this point, to placing the major "cause" for disease or its prevention upon the individual person who exhibits unwise living habits, and some behavioral scientists (as well as scholars from other persuasions) adopt a stance closer to the broad, macrostructural level when viewing determinants of human behavior. Crawford (1977), for example, discussing the "ideology of blaming the victim," speaks not only for a significant body of social and social-medical criticism but also for a particular level of analysis and a theoretical framework, which emphasizes an environmental or "structuralist" as contrasted to the "individualistic" analytic perspective. Others who share such a perspective, especially emphasizing economic interests in the social structure, are Navarro 1978, Renaud 1975, Waitzkin and Waterman 1974, Kelman 1980, and Eyer and Sterling 1977.

This is, if you will, the ancient philosophical issue of the dialectic between the "free will" – "I am the master of my fate" – "I gotta be me" value orientation contending with the school of socioenvironmental, historical materialist determinism. For the behavioral sciences, it puts into sharp focus such issues as a person's relative degree of influence by peers, by role modeling, by economic resources, by social and cultural factors which shape basic character structure and consequent behavior, not to mention physico-chemical and ecologic features of the environment. The central question in the anthropological and sociological "subfields" of culture and personality, it also appears in psychology in diverse theories of personality development, and is the essential continuum along which numerous investigations in the field of social psychology proceed.

Currently this polarity also finds considerable expression in medicine and health policy discussion, especially those having to do with prevention, cost containment, or the increasing inutility of high-level technology for solving some of the most persistent and widespread health/medical problems, as Knowles has illustrated (1977b). Often such discussions tend to take on the cast, by implication if not direct statement, of what some have termed the philosophy of "blaming the victim" (Ryan 1976) for his or her sickness, in contrast to the etiologic role of impersonal genetic, environmental, and/or social structural factors in predisposing the person to disease.

The question, then, is where, along the continuum of "causation," does one begin when the issue is not understanding mechanisms but rather finding propitious points for intervention into a disease process? Often cited in this connection is the example of excessive dental caries in America's children from eating sugar-frosted cereals. Those who advocate the "blame the victim" philosophy would say that the problem clearly lies with the person (or, perhaps, the child's parents), for "they could stop the practice, couldn't they? The children don't *need* to eat that kind of cereal." On the other hand, those pointing to environmental inducements for and influences in behavior point to the power of the omnipresent commercial advertising – and its highly sophisticated and targeted appeal to children – as the locus of the "cause" of the deleterious health habit.

An even more insidious illustration is the problem of black lung disease among coal miners. Who is to "blame" in this case? The miners who "choose" to breathe while at their workplace, the company which did not institute appropriate safety measures, a particular form of socio-economic system which stresses productivity at minimal cost, or – railing against the perversity of Nature – the particular features of the physical environment which produce such a biological effect, etc.? This type of query can, of course, be extended far more widely these days, with references to the heavily chemicalized and polluted environments in which many people live and from which they must breathe the air, drink the water, and eat the food – hardly activities providing of easily available alternative options!

Values, ethics, policy There remains one other cross-cutting category to examine in this brief excursus into mutual implications of the behavioral sciences and medicine. That category is one that groups together values, ethics, and policy considerations. These three terms, often considered sufficiently separate and autonomous each in itself to form the basis of an entire field of inquiry, are grouped here because they share an underlying common conceptual definition: they each are rooted in statements or conceptions of what *should* be, not in what *is*.

The study of values in the behavioral sciences has long held a significant position, and this conceptual realm has been approached through a variety of terms aside from "value": belief theme, assumption, premise, sentiment, and the like. Those values which carry the connotation of "oughtness" have often been referred to by the term familiar to behavioral scientists, "norm"; while another disciplinary group of scholars, still concerned with statements of what *should* be the case as contrasted to basic empirical propositions about what does exist, prefer the term "ethical rule" and examine the field of moral conduct.

Viewed in this way, ethical propositions are a subset of the broad realm of values (Kluckholn 1951) – a domain shared (in its interest) by both the behavioral sciences and humanities as broad clusters of disciplinary fields, and in this domain we find another nexus between the behavioral sciences and medicine. In the last decade or so we have become "ethics-conscious" in many activities of society: in research (especially that involving human subjects); in the professional behavior of politicians as well as pundits; in matters of equality and distributive justice with respect to various sub-groups of the society (women, homosexuals, children, the elderly, and, of course, ethnic minority groups).

In a newer form than that contained in the Hippocratic Oath, medicine, too, has begun to feel the impact of ethical considerations in many different contexts. Found not only in the high-heroic scenarios of when and whether to "pull the plug" on life-support equipment at the bedside of a terminal patient but also in such issues as informed consent for medical procedures or allocation of scarce funding and manpower, ethical considerations have surfaced as major items of discussion in relevant literature and aspects of training in a number of medical schools. There are journals specifically devoted to these questions (e.g., *Journal of Medicine and Philosophy; Ethics in Science and Medicine; Man and Medicine – the Journal of Values and Ethics in Health Care*); other journals in which discussions of ethical issues periodically appear (e.g., *Hastings Center Magazine; International Journal of Health Services*; occasionally even the *New England Journal of Medicine*); a recent compendium of relevant articles (*Encyclopedia of Bioethics*); and at least one professional society (Society for Health and Human Values).

The existence of so much activity is indicative of a strong sense of dys-ease on the part not only of the public but also of practitioners that a vital element in consideration of disease, its treatment, and prevention has been left out of formal consideration. That element is the question not so much of whether something *can* be done (e.g., the technological response), as it is whether it *should* be done (the values dimension, the ethical dimension).

Commonly, two different theoretical positions are advanced by scholars as the bases for determining correct conduct (i.e., ethical behavior) in a situation. These two bases are called (1) the *deontological* approach; and (2) the *utilitarian* or *consequentialist* approach (Brody 1976). In the first, the deontological basis for ethical conduct, the appeal is to ultimate authority: ethical rules *within themselves* are self-sufficient, regardless of their consequences. They are, simply, *right* and correct. In the second approach, the consequentialist approach, the ethically-informed decision-making process is structured by evaluation of the differentially-weighted implications or consequences of given alternative actions. (It is interesting, in this connection, to note certain aspects of similarity in conceptual structure between the deontological basis for ethical conduct and the *ontological* conception of disease – both static, fixed. Similarly, between the "physiological" and the "consequentialist" conceptions, both fluid, dynamic, interactive.)

With regard to these two basic types of approaches to ethical decision-making, the behavioral sciences constitute powerful ancillary resources based upon an enormous body of empirically-based research literature. The behavioral sciences overlap with the deontological approach, for example, insofar as they study the origins, diffusion, and development of particular values and values-systems in societies, their persistence in an ongoing social system, and their power to shape and influence behavior. They trace out the social and psychological consequences of a given value-set. And finally, they also speak to that absolutely indispensable concept, the notion of *cultural relativity*, by which it is asserted that for an adequate understanding of any value, as much as any behavioral act, it must, initially at least be examined in its *own* context or field of dynamic relationships and meanings and not that of any other society.

With regard to the second major approach in ethical reasoning, the *consequentialist*, again behavioral sciences provide data from the real world, for there is a considerable body of empirical data about linkages, functional interrelations, and consequences of action in an ongoing socio-cultural system. The phrases coined some time ago by Merton are apt in this regard: "manifest" versus "latent" functions of any given social phenomenon. This "functionalist" approach is, of course, simply another expression of the overall ecologically-oriented frame of reference discussed earlier as one of the chief contributions of the behavioral sciences to the study of disease, its prevention, etiology, and management.

Where the behavioral sciences and the study of ethical decision-making part company lies in the area of *methods*. Insofar as the behavioral sciences explicity call for those types of data-gathering and conceptualization that are based on a scientific approach to understanding systems of values (illustrated, for example, in Vogt 1955), they speak to different canons of verifiability and validity than does an ethical approach. The latter involves, at bottom, consideration of conflicting values that lie beyond the realm of empirical data, choices of action which must be resolved by a differential *weighting* of the values involved. In the end, this is perhaps an *arbitrary* selection; but a *reasoned*, and not capricious, arbitrary choice. In this end-stage of an ethical decision-making process, all science must stand aside – for it can give data only – and the choice is based on other modes of analysis and reasoning. With the question, for example, of whether provision of adequate medical care should be a *right* or a *privilege*, the behavioral scientists might point to the functional necessity for a given society to maintain its members in adequate health such that the necessary tasks for social unit survival are met, while the ethicist might maintain that provision of medical care should be mandated because of its enormous contribution to creating the full measure of humankind's potential.

To cite just a few examples from a vast literature, value and ethical considerations have been discussed as entering into the conceptualization of health and disease (Susser 1974; Callahan 1977; Brody 1976); into the study of the distribution of disease and the implications of such distribu-tional studies for formation of health policy (Ford 1978; Susser *et al.* 1978; McKinlay 1979; Miller 1980); in reviews of problems of utilization and access (Fuchs 1974; Chapman and Talmadge 1971); in studies of the legal and ethical parameters of the roles of health care providers (Grad 1978; Whorton and Davis 1978); in preventive medicine and health maintenance programs (Ubell 1972; Wikler 1978); in considerations of health education projects (Faden and Faden 1978); and of course in choice of therapeutic modality (Pellegrino 1978; Reiser 1977) and considerations of patients' rights (Veatch 1977; Brody 1976).

The Power of the Paradigm, Structural Constraints, and a Trans-Disciplinary Perspective

To judge from developments in medical care training curricula as well as from the diverse body of research evidence linking disease, health care, and the behavioral sciences, it would seem that an encouraging degree of articulation has been achieved between the two sets of disciplines.

While that may be, there remain some unresolved conceptual and structural issues that could well inhibit further progress along this line. Specifically, they involve the question of to what extent is there likely to be change in the fundamental conceptual approach to understanding disease phenomena which has proven to be so successful in the last 100 years or so, especially when such a model is viewed against a background of its entrenchment in professional training programs and its tenacity in functioning social institutions? Does such a change in paradigm always precede change in behavior? Beyond this, how critical is a conceptual paradigm, anyway, in the broad scheme of social action in regard to health?

Social change has been analyzed as occurring at several different levels: (1) the intellectual program, the model or the paradigm, by which (in this case) disease is conceptualized, its investigation justified, and its prevention effectuated – in medicine the type of problem which Dubos (1966), Engel (1977) or Fabrega (1974), and others have addressed; and (2) the *institutionalization* of whatever conceptual model emerges from current trends and activities. Actually, of course, in its own sphere the institutionalization of any idea includes developments at two levels – first, the level of *social action*: the groups, the organizations, the social structures which express and give visible corporate power to the implications of an idea. This is the arena of a *structural* analysis of any given phenomenon. And second, at the level of the *individual person* attempting to express or implement that socially-legitimated idea or paradigm – obviously the level of a behavioral or individualistic analysis.

Viewing the situation in current American society as the point of focus, one could suggest that we appear to be somewhere at the midpoint in a dialectical process: the thesis, "the behavioral sciences represent a body of data integral to the model for understanding, predicting, and preventing disease in its natural setting"; and the antithesis, "disease is a biological phenomenon that can best be understood and controlled by reducing its constituent elements as much as possible to a molecular (or submolecular) level." Given the considerable literature on the complexities of changing established ways of thinking and acting (e.g., Goodenough 1963), the prognosis for any specific synthesis predicted to come out of this intellectual jousting is difficult.

But let us look at these three areas in which change, to be logically complete, must occur: the paradigmatic level, the institutional level, and the individual behavioral level.

The attempt to change a paradigm through argumentation – whether that be a religious belief, political view, health habit, or scientific concept – is usually a long and difficult process. While those in science, an enterprise commonly applauded as the very citadel of rationality and evidence-based behavior, pride themselves on their ability to ground belief in evidence (and perhaps at the same time disparaging the lack of fit between evidence and behavior displayed by others in the society, e.g., people who persist in unwise health habits), there is substantial evidence concerning the frequent resistance within the academic and scientific worlds themselves to accepting new or even considering radically different conceptions or models of phenomena to explain what appear to be bizarre (because unconventional) findings. Many examples can be pointed to, of course (cf. Feyerabend 1975), but from the fields with which we are concerned here the mention of resistance by other scientists to Pasteur's proposal that it is germs, not a miasma or some other ill-defined mechanism, which are significant causative agents in transmission of infectious disease; or of the medical community's refusal to accept Semmelweis's insistence upon antiseptic procedures in the delivery room, are sufficient reminders of a whole host of other incidents of like nature (Barber 1961). Another example is the antagonism, until quite recently, to thinking of acupuncture as anything other than sheer Oriental quackery, a procedure that has recently been shown to stimulate the secretion of pain-relieving endorphins.

A paradigm change of such magnitude as we are dealing with here usually comes about in fits and starts, slowly, often more slowly than does change in the actual need-satisfying behavior that is illustrative of the import of such a paradigm. One may compare this with examples taken from attempts to introduce western ideas of health and preventive medicine into nonwestern areas (Foster and Anderson 1978). Usually, for example, it is easier to change health behavior patterns (difficult though that may be at times) than to change basic conceptions of health and disease transmission – to use water from a piped and covered supply, for instance, rather than to change ideas to conform with the germ theory of disease.

Such fundamental socially-shared conceptual changes, when they do come about, are usually not like the thunderclap alteration of belief implied by Kuhn's use of the term "revolution" (1962). Rather, they appear to follow an evolutionary model, in which many changes, some of them quite modest, crop up in diverse places, unsystematic, apparently piecemeal and unrelated to a central conceptual focus. They may take the form of first informal and then later more formally-organized associations of scholars, of interdisciplinary symposia or workshops and perhaps active research collaboration, of attention to such matters in the lay media, occasionally of what are at first disparaged and then in retrospect called "pioneering" papers, of insightful and often isolated attempts at re-formulation of the unity inherent in multiple strands of related ideas – what will later in the process be called the "state of the art" assessment. In this latter connection, as an example, one could point to Terris's recent (1976) and highly apt label, the "second epidemiologic revolution." The "first" epidemiological revolution of the last century focused upon the infectious diseases and their amelioration through environmental control. The second such "revolution" now addresses the non-infectious and chronic diseases, which constitute the principal threats to health (e.g., cardiovascular disease, cancer, suicide, accidents).

Thus, such a paradigm change comes gradually, through the efforts not only of leaders in the field – role models, opinion setters, prestigious academic spokesmen, skilled lay writers who jar the mind out of conventional ways of thinking – but also through the accumulation of research evidence that is *read* by those most centrally whom one would wish to change. In this case, for example, given the enormous investment of time put into training and practice in often quite narrowly specialized technical areas by most practitioners and researchers in medical fields, one realizes the functional obstacles standing in the way of simply displaying (as the primary mode of persuasion) evidence of the need for an enlarged and behaviorally-informed model of the disease process, a point discussed below.

But there are signs that the dominant intellectual paradigm in medical thought may be in process of evolving toward a more comprehensive or "field" view, at least at the edges of the institution. Not only has "psychosomatics" been reborn as a respectable area for research (with much of its orientation incorporated under a different label, namely, "behavioral medicine" – cf. Weiss 1980 or Matarazzo 1980 – and we know how often the application of a new label can connote new substance, as "previously owned" now takes the place of "used" in references to second-hand automobiles), but, as indicated above, there has accumulated a significant body of research that associates biological and psychosocial variables.

As often asserted, however, association does not prove "cause," and for some researchers such a methodological caution reinforces resistance to changing a fundamental belief. The familiar arguments about the relationship between smoking (a behavioral pattern) and the development of lung cancer are instructive in this regard. Where is the elusive "cause" of lung cancer to be located in this chain of linked circumstances? What is the shape of "cause" behind that veil of statistical correlation?

What is frequently demanded is explication of the mechanism, the complete process by which the association comes about, and, for many, this means analytic reduction of "the" cause to a molecular or submolecular level of events which disregards many factors of context and strips the field of co-occurring factors almost bare. The lack of clear specification of mechanisms at this level which would explain the relationship between many features of "life style" and disease, for example, or between stress and disease inhibits acceptance by some researchers of those documented relationships as fully scientific, even though theoretical formulations are available which point to the kinds of evidence needed to satisfy such critics (e.g., Selye 1973; Cassel 1974).

But, as illustrated so frequently in human history, some grow restive at this frustrating prospect of infinite regress in the search for causal linkages, and, especially in a pragmatically-oriented field like medicine, action often precedes a complete and epistemologically-satisfying explanation of what is going on. Regardless of the acknowledged need eventually to specify mechanisms at all levels and linkages among those systems, this does not necessarily preclude taking action on the basis of well-established epidemiological associations (Terris 1980). After all, much still is unknown about causes in medicine and yet effective interventions do occur, based both on the long clinical trials of folk medicine and the extensive practice repertory of individuals and groups of one's professional colleagues. Why aspirin works as it does, for example, is still unresolved, yet it is heavily used and prescribed.

Such an imperative for action in the absence of thorough theoretical satisfaction has occurred more than once, and with significant results, in the history of society's attempts to control major health problems. The famous story of John Snow comes to mind, a London physician who in the 1850s took an effective although non-germ-theory-informed action in regard to an epidemic of cholera. Inferring that the disease is water-borne, he simply removed the handle of the pump on a well at a particular epidemiologically-established focus of the epidemic (Frost 1949:xxxvi), thereby preventing the well's continuing to be used by local residents for obtaining drinking water from the polluted Thames River. The action was followed by sharp decline in the epidemic in the neighborhood. Pragmatically, "the" cause becomes, in a sense, localized to the zone in which an *effective mode of intervention* into a disease process is to be found.

In a recent article, Eric Cassell, an internist at Cornell University Medical College, provides a graphic example. The article is pertinently entitled "Changing Ideas of Causality in Medicine," and Cassell discusses what he sees as an emerging and field-oriented model for medicine, straightforwardly stating that "Medicine is now undergoing a profound and fundamental change in direction. In this shift, the sick *person*, rather than the disease, is becoming both the subject and object of medicine" (1979:728). Addressing himself to the issue of what McKinlay (1975), using Zola's powerful metaphor, has called "upstream behavior," Cassell describes the case of a patient he treated whose problems of "health-as-adaptation" were simply not well handled by the conventional medical care model and system, and he uses this case to reinforce the need to widen the boundaries of formal medical concern and action in a way reminiscent of those who speak of a socially-informed medical (or health) care system:

The idea of specific cause was originally useful in stimulating research about diseases and their cure. But in recent years, in company with the ontological idea of disease, specific etiology has been a limiting concept, holding back progress in medicine and medical care. Since that may seem an odd statement, let me illustrate with an actual case.

An elderly man was found unconscious in his fifth-floor walk-up apartment and brought to a New York City teaching hospital. He was found to have pneumococcal pneumonia. In addition, his right knee was greatly swollen; his physicians believed that he had a Charcot joint, a rare manifestation of late syphilis. I learned about the patient because of the knee. The medical student on the case had previously worked with me and she called to tell me about it as a matter of interesting conversation.

The patient's diagnosis, in classical terms, was pneumococcal pneumonia and, perhaps, tertiary syphilis. The treatment in this case seems to get at the cause. Antibiotics will eliminate the pneumococcus and cure his pneumonia. If he has syphilis, the same antibiotics will eliminate the treponema but, unfortunately, will not make his knee better (because structural damage to the joint would already have occurred).

Will this patient get better? His pneumonia almost surely will. The cause of his disease is the pneumococcus, and antibiotics effectively kill the organism. But, sadly, that is not the end of the case. What is the object of treatment? Is it to make a disease better or to make a person better? It is not new to this decade to realize that making the disease better is not sufficient. The understanding is increasingly widespread that just because the disease has been cured does not mean that the physician's responsibility has ended. And, further, that although we live in an age of cure, the diseases that afflict us – heart disease, cancer, stroke, diabetes, arthritis, and so on – are often not curable. Most of those diseases (with the possible exception of cancer) do not even fit the classical definitions of disease as specific objects.

What else do we know of this patient? He is seventy-four years old and his wife died about a year ago; the remainder of his family lives out of New York; he has no friends. The bad knee turns out to be not syphilis but "merely" osteoarthritis – degenerative disease of the joints.

Any attempt to use the modern medical language of cause would face difficulties in describing this man's case. But, avoiding the words and difficulties of concepts of cause, there is another way in which his case can be presented. We are able to tell the *story* of his illness.

With his wife recently dead and no close friends, this man withdrew from social contact, a common happening in the lonely aged. Often, such people will stop making real meals, instead picking at food or eating what little is required to still their hunger. Any attempt this man might have made to re-establish social connections or to improve his diet, of his own desire or at the urging of his family and acquaintances, was hampered by his disabled right knee. Walking up and down his five flights of stairs was extremely painful, and he avoided it as much as possible. A previous physician, and the patient himself, had dismissed the knee problem as "old age arthritis for which nothing could be done." The combination of malnutrition and social isolation increased his susceptibility to infection. In all probability, the pneumococcus responsible for his pneumonia had been an inhabitant of his throat for a long time before the host-parasite relationship was tilted in its favor. He was found only because a neighbor had not seen him or heard him in his apartment for more than a day.

(pp. 732–734)

... The basic point, however, is that physicians are already used to the idea of intervening in the mechanisms of disease rather than merely trying to treat the cause. What is needed, then is not a radical reorientation in the way of thinking but in the scope of that thought – intervention not only in any part of the body mechanisms or disease that will stop its progress, but (equally honored) in any part of the story of an illness that would return the sick person to function. (p. 741) ...

The point of abandoning outmoded concepts of cause and seeing illness in terms of events unfolding over time is to realize that proper treatment is that which most simply and effectively changes the story. (pp. 742–743).

With regard to the last point Cassell makes, it was just in this fashion – and for just this reason – that Geiger, operating the Tufts-Delta Health Center in an impoverished county in Mississippi, wrote out food lists on prescription pads, lists which were honored at local grocery stores, the stores themselves being reimbursed out of the drug budget for the project (Geiger 1969). *Grocery* lists? Why grocery lists if this is a *medical* clinic? As he said in numerous contexts, as a physician the best medicine he knows for the disease of malnutrition is food!

But the interventions were not limited simply to the addition of a specific substance – the "pill" of food. On the contrary, seeing problems of ill-health as influenced by multiple factors deriving from social context, the project also developed other points of entry into the problems of health and poverty (Geiger 1972). Aside from a program of comprehensive health care that included a clinic for individual patient care, project staff went into the homes to teach principles of prevention and after-care. Environmental change activities focused on provision of clean water, proper sanitation facilities, and adequate housing; nutrition services included demonstration gardens, nutritional counseling, and home management training programs to encourage proper storage and use of food. Community organization and development fostered participation in the program by the local people – giving them the feeling that it was, indeed, designed to meet *their* needs and priorities and not those of what Geiger has called the "hard core professional." Other modes of intervention into the ongoing sociomedical process included development of ancillary bureaucratic organizations required to process and manage many of the successes in the other programs, such as the food production, locating of jobs, ect. ; programs in training local residents with skills required to participate effectively at every level of the project; and, as an over-arching strategy, identification of the strengths of the community to be used as a factor in the total assessment and operational strategy for achieving desired outcomes – not a focus on pathology narrowly conceived, which might miss the mark of the program's effectively becoming grafted onto existing local institutions and, from them, deriving much of its strength and momentum for continued growth.

Structural constraints

But what if the dominant reductionistic paradigm in medicine were, somehow, to change? There remains still the troublesome fact that such ideas need to be translated into social action to be effective. And here, when placed in the middle of social reality, new problems may well emerge that blunt their effectuation, problems arising not from the level of intelligence of the participants nor their lack of social conscience, but from their situation in a *structure of social action*.

To be the "Devil's Advocate" for a moment and review this issue: What kind of behavioral science exposure is now being received by medical students? It ranges all the way from neurobiological phenomena through behavioral genetics, individual psychobiological and personality development, perception and motivational processes, behavior dynamics, interpersonal processes and influences, small-scale social systems such as the family, intermediate structures such as the hospital, macro-structures such as institutions and communities or cultural values and belief systems, ending finally with a broad and comprehensive framework such as human ecology – i.e., adaptive relations between a unit (person, group, community) and the total environment. As indicated earlier, a large number of selections from this cafeteria list are found at many medical schools, either in a series of courses, individual sections of courses, or an omnibus course that attempts to span the range of the several natural systems being discussed – intra/and intercellular behavior, organ system relations, "mind" and body, interactions among whole bodies, and finally interactions among those abstracted conceptualizations of behavior called roles, institutions, or social systems. The result is usually either sheer intellectual indigestion on the part of the student, or, at best, simply a broadening of his or her "general education."

But more rarely is the result the acquisition of knowledge which will later prove to be *functional* in day-to-day activities of a practitioning physician. This assertion holds especially for the latter end of the spectrum just portrayed – that which deals with the macro-structures of human relations and institutions; with such topics as the structure of the health care system, community organization and dynamics, health policy and society, etc. Granted that in the medical behavioral scientist's wisdom, in *our* model, one can see how these topics are relevant to an understanding of the total functioning of a health care system (or, more accurately, a *sickness* care system), the question is still raised by many students: however interesting it may be to know these things, how can I actually *use* such knowledge as a physician?

For this is the heart of the matter if issues of health and disease are to be left exclusively to the clinical care sector of society: role behavior of that great bulk of students graduating from medical schools. Medical care is essentially a one-on-one transaction, and it is this that most students come to medical school for, not for those broader visions of the multi-system etiologic sources of disease, and the consequent need for a multi-system strategy of prevention and health maintenance. Indeed, the conceptual leap from working with a tangible system, such as a body, to an abstract system of relationships such as a family or an institution, seems to be too much for many medical students (or their mentors for that matter) to handle comfortably. The typical medical student is a "hands-on" person, an eclectic practitioner who uses multiple sources of knowledge in performance of his role as he shapes it within the general pattern defined by society. But it still centers on a given level of system organization in nature – the body (often not even including in any very important way the mind).

How well, therefore, do our usual behavioral science offerings fare against this applied, here-and-now orientation? Obviously those aspects of the behavioral sciences that have to do with interpersonal processes, with differential perceptions of two people involved in an interaction, with communication skills – these have a better chance of being accepted simply because they are seen as important to the actual role activity of the future practitioner: dealing with patients. They are more likely to "make sense" in the student's frame of reference; in addition, of course, they appeal to typical "humanistic" interests (especially if offered during the first two years of medical school training, when the curriculum is usually otherwise barren of such enlivening subjects).

But what about other aspects of the offerings, such as the nature of bureaucratic organization, or health economics? Not so fortunate here; for unless the subject matter is directly coned down on a situation in which knowledge may be functional in this limited role sense, the mental receptors are turned off. Many of us who have struggled with purveying a larger vision of events have run aground on such more limited perspectives on the part of students.

But let us develop this a bit further and assume that we do get students actively interested in tracing out some of the psychosocial dimensions to a patient's medical problem – whether these be in the area of etiology, course of the illness, management, of therapy. Let us assume, further, that such a student proceeds through his medical school training and advances through his residency years with this broadly-based concern not just with the *diseases* that afflict his patient, but in a more general sense, with that patient's *health* and health maintenance in the manner suggested by a George Engel or Eric Cassell. He is certified after his residency and establishes a practice, modest but with all the essentials required for proper doctoring: receptionist and nurse, equipment, office space, hospital privileges, etc. He begins to see patients and tries to follow the dictates of both his teaching and conscience, exploring in great detail the background of the presenting complaint and its effects on other aspects of the patient's life, including repercussions on family and job.

While satisfied inwardly that he has done a good and thorough work-up as a physician, serious and concerned and comprehensive about data-gathering, he soon finds that he has spent an hour or more with each patient on initial intake as well as substantial time in follow-up visits that require psychosocial treatment (e.g., *listening*). And he finds that he is not making enough money to meet his bills or the debts incurred for his medical education. Soon, out of the sheer structural demands of the situation – no matter motivations otherwise – he begins to cut down the time spent with each patient and his pattern of professional activity begins to resemble that of his peers, such that he now spends about five minutes per typical patient contact, and is proud of the fact that he "processes" some 60 to 80 patients a day through his office.

In short, under conditions of a fee-for-service mode of payment for medical care, can behavioral science – even that which is most obviously relevant to patient care, such as interpersonal skills and interviewing – pay its way? And, short of opting for a career in a public health department or some such health organizational structure, students well-trained in the macro-structural knowledge that behavioral science has to offer may have a difficult time earning an appropriate salary. For there are no solo practitioners of "public health" or "preventive medicine." Although this is obviously not the place to get into these matters, perhaps, as we look to possible changes in this country's pattern of health care delivery (HMO's, prepaid group practice, "holistic" health centers, use of allied health care professionals such as physician assistants, etc. there may come about a situation in which the sheer structural factors that set the context for medical care will be more conducive to utilization of more of the behavioral science skills than is the case currently.

What has been suggested here is that behavioral science efforts in medical education have been directed at their insinuation into the formal curriculum, especially the pre-clinical years. That has been fairly successful (although less successful during the clinical years, as Petersdorf and Feinstein reminded us). At the same time, however, what is most relevant for the subsequent functional activity of most students is, in Geiger's (1974) phrase, the "*latent* curriculum" in the minds of students. The latent curriculum – the operative paradigm in their minds – consists of *the things learned for survival* as one progresses through the education system. It also includes " ... messages about how health care should be paid for, who should run the system, how the questions of quality and cost should be managed, and how health care is related to the larger society," in other words, messages about the *structural context* of medical care as currently formulated.

Disciplines and the social order

One final observation remains to be made in this overview of the topic: namely, the question which has structured this inquiry may have been interpreted too simply. It may appear that we have inadvertently succumbed to the insidious disease "hardening of the categories" when we refer to "medicine" and the "behavioral sciences" unless we press further and assess the degree of fit between the total range of *phenomena* of relevance and the scope of activities taking place under the aegis of these disciplinary labels. For one of the most significant contributions of the behavioral sciences to understanding the human enterprise is analyzing and illustrating the profound role of the symbolic process in human thought and action, and the traps of logic and behavior one can fall into in failing to recognize the difference between empirical substance and the symbolic rendering of that substance. Cassirer put it well:

> Between the receptor system and the effector system, which are to be found in all animal species, we find in man a third link which we may describe as the *symbolic system*. This new acquisition transforms the whole of human life. As compared with the other animals man lives not merely in a broader reality; he lives, so to speak, in a new *dimension* of reality.
> (Cassirer 1944: 24)

The words, "medicine," "behavioral sciences," "disease," "health" – central to this discussion – lie in that symbolic dimension. The wide range of phenomena to which they conceptually refer, however, may not always be included in the typical local institutionalization of the terms. For example, it has become almost commonplace for what is more accurately called the "medical care system" to be called the "health care system." Are the referents of these terms so close in substance that it is semantically justifiable to interchange the terms? Some degree of overlap is found, to be sure, but there is a rather large number of events and situations, for example, which are contributory to and illustrative of what "health" means, that do not lie within the circle of denotation of "medicine," nor within its institutionalized range of activities. One could argue, for instance, that an agricultural extension station at a land grant university – concerned as it is with research on improvement of food crop yields – is part of the "health care system"; or that a city's bureau of traffic control, charged with responsibility to ameliorate high fatality street intersections, similarly is an important part of the social system that functions to maintain health and prevent disease or trauma, no matter its not being included formally under the symbolic umbrella of the "health care" or even the "medical care" system. Using a "latent function" analytic mode like this, one can extend the list considerably, of course (cf. Hughes 1963).

Eberstadt (1981:26) has captured the gist of this idea nicely:

> Medicine's role in lengthening lives is conspicuous because it is basically curative; of even greater importance are those quiet facets of our daily routine which prevent illness from breaking out in the first place. Decent meals, we all know, are a vital ingredient to a healthy life; less celebrated but perhaps no less essential is the web of personal relationships which can support us against adversity. A mother's care for her baby, a family's attention to its elderly or troubled members, and the will to live which such things inculcate, in an often unnoticed way, do for the health of a . . . nation what a ministry of health could never hope to duplicate.

If we direct attention, then, not only to the scope of the formal academic disciplines concerned with the question that prompted this review, but also to those variegated processes of natural events in which the health/disease continuum is embedded, a new and instructive perspective emerges. And when one conducts such a conceptual *contextualization* of the wide range of factors, antecedents, and situations involved in the causation of disease, its treatment and prevention – or, in a more positive vein, in the promotion of health – and does not simply stop at considering the activities of those labelled "disciplines" and social institutions that have a *prima facie* charge to deal with such matters, it is patent that the behavioral sciences have had, now have, and inescapably will continue to have much to say that is relevant in the social task of understanding and taking action concerning disease.

Actually, however, to be consistent with the argument just advanced, we should not say "the behavioral sciences" will be relevant – for that is to fall into the convenient symbolic shorthand that can so easily result in the "fallacy of misplaced concreteness," as Whitehead called it. Rather, we should say that, by whatever means studied, *by whoever studies them* (or, in the applied world of real events, by whoever makes *use* of them either unknowingly or with some degree of explicit understanding of relationships), there is an extensive range of psychological, social, and behavioral phenomena involved in the disease/health process that may not have been formally captured by the disciplinary net of either "behavioral science" or "medicine."

For what is a "discipline"? Viewed in broad historical perspective, a discipline is a more or less coherent system of concepts, assumptions, and ideas that organize human activities. The boundaries of disciplines change; they expand and contract, they merge, they disappear. Especially in the last 100 years and even the last 50 years, we have seen this proliferation and shifting (Kiger 1971). Academic disciplines, as we know them, are the collective products of man's need to deal with the world, to understand it, and to solve the problems it poses for human existence. As such, disciplines are (or should be) flexible, responding like finely-tuned weathervanes to shifts in the adaptational demands of a human group. Instead, because they become embodied in social institutions variously called associations, societies, departments, and universities, they have a tendency to become fixed, to achieve a gyroscopic status that is resistant to the shifting demands of a real world. As Lynd said some time ago (1939:1), "A scholarly discipline wears a tough hide."

This, of course, is not to suggest that we dispense with the conventional terms now used for disciplines, for that would be to regress and possibly lead to more confusion. It is to suggest, however, that we use such terms heuristically, tentatively, with full realization that they themselves are part of, not coterminous with, an environing social system; and with clear recognition of what they encompass and what they may not encompass. What phenomena functionally linked to the problem at hand are being left out? Again Lynd puts the point well: "Our several specializations as social scientists play tricks with our scientific definitions of 'the situation' and all too frequently prompt us to state our problems for research as if the rest of the situation did not exist" (1939:15).

A visual depiction will help make the point that there is a wide range of events and situations related to the concept of health/disease as adaptation, and that such a wide range implies numerous points of entry or intervention for many social activities and institutions, including formal academic disciplines (Figure 3). If, for example, we see the basic problem in something of a concentric fashion, with "disease" being the focal term, but that term itself only a subset of the phenomena of "health," and that term, in its turn, referring to a subset of the phenomena of "well-being," it would appear thus:

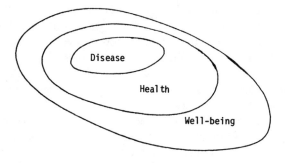

FIGURE 8.3

If one looks behind the symbolic screen which puts labels on human activities and human institutions, it seems that society has always operated on the premise that health and well-being are central values in social life, so central that the phenomena expressive of that value cannot be left solely to the tending of physicians and the "medical care system."

Indeed, long before there ever were self-conscious academic "disciplines," relationships between disease, health, and well-being and their sociocultural contexts were either known or posited by the world's peoples. Quite aside from the social development of many practices which are based not only on numerous empirical medical remedies (many of them effective) but also fairly clear ideas of preventive medicine (Hughes 1963), frequently reputed "causes" for illness are violations of some religious taboo (itself a cultural production), improper role behavior toward a member of the in-group, or malevolent actions (witchcraft) on the part of another human being. Further, the emotional and supportive power of other people long ago was (perhaps unknowingly) institutionalized in diagnostic and curative ceremonialism, the effects of which were believed vitiated if the afflicted patient were not surrounded by kinsmen or friends. Whether intended explicitly or not, therefore, the *data* of the social and behavioral sciences have been brought into the circle of folk medicine's concerns and conceptualizations from time immemorial in human societies. As stated in another place, "Religion, medicine, and morality are frequently found together in the behavioral act or event, and 'folk medicine' becomes 'social medicine' to an extent not found in industrialized societies" (Hughes 1968).

But of course one need not search the ethnographic literature for illustrations of a comprehensive conception of health and the sources of disease. The widespread social catastrophe consequent upon the Industrial Revolution in Europe in the early 19th century contributed to powerful sociopolitical movements that placed disease – ideas of cause, prevention, and treatment – in a broad and ecologically-informed framework. And it may be noted that such developments occurred before the theoretical and experimental work was accomplished which underlies much of modern biomedical theory, e.g., Pasteur's elucidation of the germ theory of infectious disease and the consequent ascendancy of the idea of a re-ductionist, specific etiology. (Which again raises, of course, the interesting question of what role is played, on the broad canvas of *social* change, by the intellectual explanatory paradigms devised from time to time.)

In a number of European nations – primarily England, France, Germany, and the Scandinavian countries – there arose strong social reformist movements which in various ways combined elements of the medical theory and practice of the time, liberal political ideology, and the application of "commonsensical" health practices. While Rudolf Virchow, a towering figure in the development of medical thought known particular-ly for his work in cellular pathology, was proclaiming with a socially-informed conscience that "medicine is a social science and politics nothing but medicine on a grand scale," concerned physicians and figures in public life across the channel in England were instrumental in passing legislation and effecting other measures that led to the "Sanitary Revolution," a movement which embodied the basic principles of old-fashioned hygiene: clean air and water, better housing, and more food (see Rosen 1947, 1958, 1972). The work of McKeown (1976), Powles (1973), and others has shown that the decline in the then dismally high mortality rates in western Europe was based much more on such socially-inspired "health promotion" efforts than upon methods of clinical medicine or the consequences of knowing the germ theory.

Especially in Europe, "social medicine" is a well-recognized discipline, a modern derivative of such an integrated and comprehensive approach to disease in its natural setting. In the United States, the term "community medicine" or "community health" is often preferred for such an approach and, in this context, is functionally more set apart from mainstream clinical medicine than is the comparable case with social medicine in European countries (Kane 1974).

Rosen has well stated the gist of a social medicine perspective:

Our illnesses and accidents in various ways reflect the world in which we live, what we do in it and with it. Dermatitis due to make-up, nylon dermatitis, and bunions are related to fashions in cosmetics and dress. Tennis elbow is a hazard in a society where the game is played. Welder's conjunctivitis, hatters' shakes, or caisson disease occur as a result of occupational activity, and of the conditions under which workers earn a living. Disease due to dietary deficiencies such as rickets and scurvy tell us a good deal about diet, living conditions, aspects of social class and other facets of a society. Moreover, this is true of the present and the past. In short, the occurrence of disease in a given population at a particular time is not just a matter of chance. It exhibits a characteristic pattern defined by etiology, incidence, prevalence and mortality as related to age, sex, social class, occupation, mode of life, or other factors connected in one way or another with the structure, culture and psychology of a society. In so far, then, as disease arises from, or affects, the social conditions or relations within which human beings live, it is a social phenomenon to be studied as such and completely comprehensible only within a biosocial context.   (1973: 234–235)

Whatever particular term is used in referring to such an overarching, comprehensive framework for viewing the etiology, prevention, and treatment of disease (whether it be "social medicine," "social hygiene," "public health," "preventive medicine," "community medicine/health," or whatever), it is therefore clear that in the scope of activities covered there is much room for the behavioral sciences to make contributions. Kennedy (1973: 789–791) has outlined a number of these points of entry, both with regard to the wide sweep of behavior implicated in response to disease problems and the kinds of institutionalized "medicines" that exist as reactions to disease situations. In an ecologically-oriented framework he discusses seven types of "health behavior" commonly found as adaptation-intended responses to illness: escape behavior, precautionary behavior, emergency response, use of curative health services, rehabilitative services, scientific research, and acceptance behavior. Similarly a comprehensive and comparative view of *medical* care activity, especially in industrialized societies, commonly includes not only scientific medicine in its three phases, professional practice, medical education, and medical research; but also religious beliefs and rituals, public health practice, folk medical practice, and public safety.

Without attempting to translate all of the suggested categories into empirical examples, it is nonetheless instructive to look briefly at the extent to which the social order itself has institutionalized diverse activities towards the goal of either disease prevention or health maintenance. A day taken at random from current American society, for example, might well include reports on various environmental and health impact studies of proposed development projects (such as the MX missile system); a report from the Food and Drug Administration – long concerned with safety of food additives and drugs (red dye, saccharine, laetrile, etc.) – about potential disease effects of birth control pills or tampons; banning of yet another synthetic textile for use in children's clothing because of its inflammability; controversy from business circles about overly stringent governmental regulation of conditions for worker safety in industrial settings; reiteration of the need for the Clean Air Act, or passage of an *indoor* anti-smoking act; another instance of a product recall because of health effects (perhaps another class of automobiles, perhaps children's toys, perhaps hairdryers); a report to the public about the danger some of its children may be in because of the type of insulation used in constructing school buildings a decade and more ago; general alarm in some localities over the discovery of yet another dumping ground for chemical wastes from industry and, spurred by that, both praise and controversy directed at the passage of a "toxic wastes control bill"; a warning from a food processor that some cans of a particular batch of its gourmet soup line have been found to contain botulism; periodic attempts to enforce the 55 mile-per-hour speed limit, perhaps with the accompanying justification of its role in decreasing the automobile fatality rate; advisement of pregnant women not to smoke cigarettes or drink alcohol (and, in the latter connection, the omnipresent warnings not to "drink and drive"); another instance of the long-standing concern over the attempt to design automobiles more safely and employ the "technological response" in devising inflatable air bags to prevent trauma in crashes – thereby, apparently, acknowledging defeat in efforts to educate the public to fasten the now universally available seat belts; the opposition of many who ride motorcycles or mopeds to wearing crash helmets.

Other instances of such health-oriented activity paid for by members of the society (therefore representing an investment in health) might include a visit from the county's construction inspector approving (or disapproving) the safety of the electrical system installed by the owner himself in the new addition to his house, or by another inspector to a different site to monitor conformance to building construction regulations intended to minimize damage and injury in earthquake-prone areas; the periodic visit by the food and sanitary inspector to the local restaurant down the block to assess the cleanliness of the premises, the hand-washing habits of its employees, and their adherence to hair-net regulations if they handle food; the availability of food stamps and the existence of school lunch programs, or special food programs for children, infants, and women, or "Meals on Wheels" for disabled elderly and shut-ins; the "Head-start Program" for socially-disadvantaged children, oriented to creating optimum conditions for intellectual and emotional growth in childhood; the proliferation of "stress management" workshops, programs, and clubs in business and other sectors of daily life; the astonishing recent growth in personal exercise activities such as jogging or tennis, and the burgeoning of sports clubs or malls; the success of many health promotive lay organizations which operate on the powerful motivational energies of peer group affiliation, such as Weight Watchers or Alcoholics Anonymous; the growth in recent years of the use of technology to create an instant social support system (such as a suicide prevention "hot-line" service or rape reporting center), or in less dramatic but no less vital a fashion the life-sustaining support offered to a person by another who has experienced the same traumatic event – the grief-work clubs for widows or widowers, or the "ostomy" clubs (e.g., colostomy) for those who have undergone major surgery and experience problems adjusting to a new life-style; the development in recent years of hostels for victims of child- or spouse-abuse ... The reader can continue with the list.

It may be worth suggesting that, given the above list (and the many other examples that could be provided in an exhaustive review), what we are seeing could be called a "cultural lag" in reverse. When the term "cultural lag" was first coined by William F. Ogburn, he referred to the slowness with which social norms change to accommodate a technological innovation, such as the automobile. It may well be that in regard to a more comprehensive view of the causes and interventional possibilities with response to disease than that provided by the conventional biomedical model, the environing social and governmental structures are proceeding with demonstrating the utility of and need for the enlarged model of health even in the absence of its full *functional* acceptance by many sectors of institutionalized medicine. That point of view was strongly evident in President Carter's retiring State of the Union message.

Perhaps, in effect, like Moliere's *Monsieur Jourdain*, society has been 'speaking the prose' of an enlarged, environmentally-inclusive model for health for some time, as though to say that there is simply too much work for any one institution, such as medicine, to do. That, indeed, is what was emphatically said by the nations of the world in the recent Alma-Ata conference of 1978, which was sponsored by the World Health Organization and the United Nations Children's Fund. Using a new term – "primary health care" – to underscope the broadly contextualized nature of health and disease that has often been referred to by the term "social medicine," the conference report notes that "primary health care"

1) reflects and evolves from the economic conditions and socio-cultural and political characteristics of the country and its communities and is based on the application of the relevant results of social, bio-medical and health services research and public health experience;

2) addresses the main health problems in the community, providing promotive, preventive, curative and rehabilitative services accordingly;

3) includes at least: education concerning prevailing health problems and the methods of preventing and controlling them; promotion of food supply and proper nutrition; an adequate supply of safe water and basic sanitation; maternal and child health care, including family planning; immunization against the major infectious diseases; prevention and control of locally endemic diseases; appropriate treatment of common diseases and injuries; and provision of essential drugs;

4) involves, in addition to the health sector, all related sectors and aspects of national and community development, in particular agriculture, animal husbandry, food, industry, education, housing, public works, communications and other sectors; and demands the coordinated efforts of all these sectors;

5) requires and promotes maximum community and individual self-reliance and participation in the planning, organization, operation and control of primary health care, making fullest use of local, national, and other available resources; and to this end develops through appropriate education the ability of communities to participate;

6) should be sustained by integrated, functional and mutually-supportive referral systems, leading to the progressive improvement of comprehensive care for all, and giving priority to those most in need;

7) relies, at local and referral levels, on health workers, including physicians, nurses, midwives, auxiliaries and community workers as applicable, as well as traditional practitioners as needed, suitably trained socially and technically to work as a health team and to respond to the expressed health needs of the community. (Primary Health Care 1978: 4–5).

Thus is the wheel continually re-invented; perhaps one day it will actually be used.

There are those who would say that not only is such a more diffused responsibility for health care socially desirable in its own right, but the need for it is reinforced, frequently, by the *maladaptive* consequences of contact with the formal medical care system. In the same manner as he called for the "de-institutionalization" of education, i.e., not only according respect to those social forces outside the formal educational institutions that function to teach the skills of life but also *encouraging* such development, Illich (1976), perhaps the best known social critic in this regard, has also spoken of the need to "*de*-mystify" medicine, to diffuse its function and purpose more broadly throughout society and decrease the over-weening dependence by people upon its current institutional forms. Mendelsohn (1979), himself a practicing physician and academician, has joined Illich in an attack upon the iatrogenic problems and pathologic consequences of contact with the medical care system.

We sometimes tend to forget that all institutions – be they those of practice and application or those of study – arise from and are ultimately accountable to the society which has charged them with amelioration of particular problem areas. At the same time, the fundamental needs of the life process as vested in a human social system cannot be left exclusively to the tending of any designated subsystem – needs having to do with survival, well-being, education, and, of course, health. When such a division of labor proves inadequate to the task – when the experts fail – the social order in its self-sealing way devises and fosters new institutional responses. When, for example, out of a sense of the need to consolidate findings and theory, a discipline becomes fixed and rigid, offering pat answers to petty questions, too quickly crystallized into dogma, society may well withdraw its licence and implicitly open the task to others. We see this, on the one hand, in the extent of dissatisfaction and malaise felt by many people with care received by the conventional medical system and the parallel growth of many "alternative" therapies; and, on the other, with strong expressions of the lack of "relevance" to current problems by much of what occurs in the behavioral sciences.

Perhaps the problem posed for this paper presents a key opportunity for renewal, especially if both sets of disciplines fully accept and implement the label now frequently applied, namely, "*life* sciences."

In his usual way, Dubos (1959:179) has put the point most eloquently:

Life is like a large body of water moved by deep currents and by superficial breezes. We have gained some understanding of the winds and can adjust our sails to them. But the really powerful forces which determine population trends are deep currents of which we know little, the fundamental physical and biological laws of the world, the habits and beliefs of mankind with their roots deep in the past. It is intellectual deceit to be dogmatic in these matters on the basis of scientific knowledge, because information is so incomplete.

And it is always dangerous to bring about radical and sudden social changes, because the complexity of the interrelationships in the living world inevitably makes for unforeseen consequences, often with disastrous results. The use of knowledge must be tempered by humility and common sense, and for this reason medical utopias must be taken with a great deal of salt.

What is being suggested, of course, is not a thorough de-institutionalization of either medicine or the behavioral sciences, but rather a renewal of their grasp of the ramifying nature of the problem. David A. Hamburg, President of the Institute of Medicine of the National Academy of Sciences, leaves us with such a challenging vision (1978:48–50):

The health of our population is related to the enormous transition that our species has brought about since the industrial revolution and especially in the twentieth century. Rapid population growth in most of the world, urbanization with its difficult ramifications, environmental damage and resource depletion, the risks of weapons technology, and new patterns of disease – all are largely products of changes that have occurred only in the most recent phase of human evolution. We have changed our diet (e.g., high fat); our activity patterns (e.g., sedentary life); our technology (e.g., transportation); the substances of daily use and exposure (e.g., in the work place); our patterns of reproductive activity; of tension relief (e.g., smoking and alcohol); and of human relationships. Many of these changes are truly epochal in character, laden with new benefits and new risks, and most of the long-term consequences are poorly understood. Natural selection over millions of years shaped our ancestors in ways that suited earlier environments. We do not know how well we are now suited biologically and behaviorally to the world our species has so rapidly made.

This situation provides a powerful stimulus for the life sciences, broadly defined. A wide spectrum of research is needed to meet long-range health problems. We are now entering an era of testing the extent to which the methods of the sciences can be brought to bear on the entire range of factors that determine the health of the public – not only through medical care but also in the way we manage our personal behavior patterns and our changing environment.

Surely, the present conditions of human life represent one of the most drastic transformations any species has ever brought about in so short a time. Its consequences – planned and unplanned, witting and unwitting, beneficial and adverse – deserve a high priority in the science of the future. This is not merely a medical problem or even a health problem. In this framework, the scholars of many disciplines can be brought together in ways I believe they will find stimulating and socially helpful. The enormous transformation of this poignant moment of evolutionary time increases the urgency of our need to know – above all about ourselves. Not just about our health, but about our environment, our behavior, our relations with each other as individuals, as institutions, and as nations. Here is a challenge we cannot afford to overlook. If we have the vision, we can deal with problems of utmost significance, not only for our health, but for our future as a species.

REFERENCES CITED

Ackerknecht, Erwin H., 1968. *A Short History of Medicine*, New York: Ronald Press.

Adair, John, and Kurt W. Deuschle, 1970. *The People's Health: Medicine and Anthropology in a Navajo Community*, New York: Appleton-Century-Crofts.

Aday, Lu Ann, 1975. Economic and noneconomic barriers to the use of needed medical services, *Medical Care* **XIII**: 447–456.

Ader, Robert, 1980. Psychosomatic and psychoimmunologic research, *Psychosomatic Medicine* **42**: 307–321.

Andersen, Ronald, Anita Francis, Joanna Lion, and Virginia S. Daugherty, 1977. Psychologically related illness and health services utilization, *Medical Care XV* (Supplement): 59–73.

Andersen, Ronald, 1978. Health status indices and access to medical care, *American Journal of Public Health* **68**: 458–463.

Antonovsky, Aaron, 1972. Social class, life expectancy and overall mortality, in *Patients, Physicians, and Illness: A Sourcebook in Behavioral Science and Health* (2nd ed.). E. Gartly Jaco (ed.), pp. 5–30, New York: Free Press.

Antonovsky, Aaron, 1979. *Health, Stress, and Coping: New Perspectives on Mental and Physical Well-Being*, San Francisco: Jossey-Bass.

APHA (American Public Health Association), 1975. *Heath and Work in America: A Chart Book*, Washington, DC: American Public Health Association.

Apple, Dorrian, 1960. How laymen define illness, *Journal of Health and Human Behavior* **1**: 219–225.

Balint, Michael, 1972. *The Doctor, His Patient and the Illness*, New York: International Universities Press, Inc.

Barber, Bernard, 1961. Resistance by scientists to scientific discovery, *Science* **132**: 596–602.

Barnett, Clifford R., P. Herbert Leiderman, Rose Grobstein, and Marshall Klaus, 1970. Neonatal separation: The maternal side of interactional deprivation, *Pediatrics* **45**: 197–205.

Becker, Marshall H., and Lawrence W. Green, 1975. A family approach to compliance with medical treatment: A selective review of the literature, *International Journal of Health Education* **XVIII**: 2–11.

Becker, Marshall H., Don P. Haefner, Stanislav V. Kasl, John P. Kirscht, Lois A. Maiman, and Irwin D. Rosenstock 1977. Selected psychosocial models and correlates of individual health-related behaviors, *Medical Care* (Supplement) **XV**: 27–46.

Belloc, Nedra B., and Lester Breslow, 1972. Relationship of physical health status and health practices, *Preventive Medicine* **1**: 409–421.

Benson, Herbert, 1975. *The Relaxation Response*, New York: Avon.

Berelson, Bernard, 1968. Behavioral sciences, in *International Encyclopedia of the Social Sciences* **2**: 41–44, New York: Macmillan and Free Press.

Berkanovic, Emil, 1976. Behavioral science and prevention, *Preventive Medicine* **5**: 92–105.

Berkman, Lisa F., and S. Leonard Syme, 1979. Social networks, host resistance and mortality: Nine year follow-up study of Alameda county residents, *American Journal of Epidemiology* **109**: 186–204.

Bernarde, Melvin A., and Evelyn W. Mayerson, 1978. Patient–physician negotiation, *Journal of the American Medical Association* **239**: 1413–1415.

Bloom, Samuel W., 1971. The medical school as a social system: A case study of faculty-student relations, *Mibank Memorial Fund Quarterly* **XIIX** (2), Part 2: v–191.

Bosk, Charles L., 1979. *Forgive and Remember: Managing Medical Failure*, Chicago: University of Chicago Press.

Bowden, Charles L., 1974. The physician's adaptation to his role, in *Psychosocial Basis of Medical Practice*, Charles L. Bowden and Alvin G. Burstein (eds.), pp. 217–223, Baltimore: Williams and Wilkins Co.

Bowden, Charles L., and Alvin G. Burstein (eds.), 1974. *Psychosocial Basis of Medical Practice: An Introduction to Human Behavior*, Baltimore: Williams and Wilkins.

Bowlby, John, 1969. *Attachment and Loss, Volume I – Attachment*, New York: Basic Books.

Brandt, Lewis W., 1973. The physics of the physicist and the physics of the psychologist, *International Journal of Psychology* 8: 61–72.

Brenner, M. Harvey, 1973. *Mental Illness and the Economy*, Cambridge: Harvard University Press.

Brenner, M. Harvey, Anne Mooney, and Thomas J. Nagy (eds.), 1980. *Assessing the Contributions of the Social Sciences to Health*, A.A.A.S. Selected Symposium 26. Washington, D.C.: American Association for the Advancement of Science.

Breslow, Lester, 1978. Risk factor intervention for health maintenance, *Science* **200**: 908–912.

Brody, Howard, 1976. *Ethical Decisions in Medicine*, Boston: Little, Brown and Co.

Brown, George W., and Tirrill Harris, 1978. *Social Origins of Depression: A Study of Psychiatric Disorder in Women*, New York: Free Press.

Bullough, Bonnie, 1972. Poverty, ethnic identity and preventive health care, *Journal of Health and Social Behavior* **13**: 347–359.

Callahan Daniel, 1977. Health and society: Some ethical imperatives, in *Doing Better and Feeling Worse: Health in the United States*, John H. Knowles (ed.), pp. 23–33, New York: Norton.

Campbell, Donald T., 1969. Ethnocentrism of disciplines and the fish-scale model of omniscience, in *Interdisciplinary Relationships in the Social Sciences*, M. Sherif and C. Sherif (eds.), pp. 328–348, Chicago: Aldine.

Cannon, Walter B., 1942. "Voodoo" death, *American Anthropologist* **XLIV**: 169–181.

Caplan, Gerald, 1974. Support systems, in *Support Systems and Community Mental Health: Lectures on Concept Development*, Gerald Caplan, pp. 1–40, New York: Behavioral Publications.

Cassel, John C., 1974. Psychosocial processes and "stress": Theoretical formulation, *International Journal of Health Services* **4**: 471–482.

Cassell, Eric J., 1976. *The Healer's Art: A New Approach to the Doctor–Patient Relationship*, Philadelphia: J. P. Lippincott.

Cassell, Eric J., 1979. Changing ideas of causality in medicine, *Social Research* **46**: 728–743.

Cassirer, Ernst, 1944. *An Essay on Man: An Introduction to a Philosophy of Human Culture*, New Haven: Yale University Press.

Caudill, William, 1958. *The Psychiatric Hospital as a Small Society*, Cambridge: Harvard University Press.

Caudill, William, F.C. Redlich, H.R. Gilmore, and Eugene B. Brody, 1952. Social structure and interaction processes on a psychiatric ward, *American Journal of Orthopsychiatry* **22**: 314–334.

Chapman, Carleton B., and John M. Talmadge, 1971. *The Evolution of the Right to Health Concept in the United States*, Pharos, January: 30–51.

Clark, Margaret, 1959. *Health in the Mexican–American Culture: A Community Study*, Berkeley: University of California Press.

Clements, Forrest E., 1932. Primitive concepts of disease, *University of California Publications in American Archaeology and Ethnology* **32**: 185–252.

Cobb, Sidney, 1976. Social support as a moderator of life stress, *Psychosomatic Medicine* **38**: 300–312.

Cobb, Sidney, and Robert M. Rose 1973. Hypertension, peptic ulcer, and diabetes in air traffic controllers, *Journal of the American Medical Association* **224**: 489–492.

Coburn, David, 1978. Work and general psychological and physical well-being, *International Journal of Health Services* **8**: 415–435.

Coburn, David, and Clyde R. Pope, 1974. Socioeconomic status and preventive health behavior, *Journal of Health and Social Behavior* **15**: 67–68.

Coombs, Robert H., 1978. *Mastering Medicine: Professional Socialization in Medical School*, New York: Free Press.

Cousins, Norman, 1979. *Anatomy of an Illness: As Perceived by the Patient*, New York: Norton.

Crawford, Robert, 1977. You are dangerous to your health: The ideology and politics of victim blaming, *International Journal of Health Services* **7**: 663–680.

Dohrenwend, Barbara S., and Bruce P. Dohrenwend, 1974. *Stressful Life Events: Their Nature and Effects*, New York: Wiley.

Dubos, Rene, 1959. *Mirage of Health: Utopias, Progress and Biological Change*, New York: Harper and Bros.

Dubos, Rene, 1966. *Man Adapting*, New Haven: Yale University Press.

Dubos, Rene, 1968. *Man, Medicine, and Environment*, New York: Praeger.

Duff, Raymond S., and August B. Hollingshead, 1968. *Sickness and Society*, New York: Harper and Row, Publishers.

Eberstadt, Nick, 1981. The health crisis in the USSR, *The New York Review of Books* **XXVIII**: 26–33, 19 February.

Egbert, Lawrence D., George E. Battit, Claude E. Welch, and Marshall K. Bartlett, 1964. Reduction of postoperative pain by encouragement and instruction of patients: A study of doctor–patient rapport, *New England Journal of Medicine* **270**: 825–827.

Einstein, Albert, and Leopold Infeld, 1961 ed. *The Evolution of Physics*, New York: Simon and Schuster.

Eisenberg, Leon, 1977. The search for care, in *Doing Better and Feeling Worse: Health in the United States*, John H. Knowles (ed.), pp. 235–246, New York: Norton.

Eisenberg, Leon, and Arthur Kleinman (eds.), 1980. *The Relevance of Social Science for Medicine*, London/Boston/Dordrecht, Holland: D. Reidel Publishing Co.

Engel, George L., 1961. Is grief a disease? A challenge for medical research, *Psychosomatic Medicine* **XXIII**: 18–22.

Engel, George L., 1977. The need for a new medical model: A challenge for biomedicine, *Science* **196**: 129–136.

Engel, George L., 1980. The clinical application of the biopsychosocial model, *American Journal of Psychiatry* **137**: 535–543.

Engelhardt, H. Tristram, 1974a. The concepts of health and disease, in *Evaluation and Explanation in the Biomedical Sciences*, H. Tristram Engelhardt and Stuart F. Spicker (eds.) pp. 125–141, Dordrecht, Holland/Boston: D. Reidel Publishing Co.

Engelhardt, H. Tristram, 1974b. Explanatory models in medicine: Facts, theories, and values, *Texas Reports on Biology and Medicine* **32**: 225–239.

Epstein, Samuel S., 1979. *The Politics of Cancer*, Garden City, New York: Anchor Books.

Eyer, Joseph, and Peter Sterling, 1977. Stress-related mortality and social organization, *Review of Radical Political Economics* **9**: 1–44.

Fabrega, Horacio, 1974. *Disease and Social Behavior*, Cambridge: MIT Press.

Faden, Ruth R., and Alan I. Faden, 1978. The ethics of health education as public health policy, *Health Education Monographs* **6**: 180–197.

Falk, Vilma, 1979. Planning health education for a minority group: The Mexican Americans, *International Journal of Health Education* **XXII**: 113–121.

Farquhar, John W., 1978. The community-based model of life style intervention trials, *American Journal of Epidemiology* **108**: 103–111.

Feyerabend, Paul, 1975. *Against Method: Outline of an Anarchistic Theory of Knowledge*, London: Verso.

Field, Mark G., 1980. The health system and the polity: A contemporary American dialectic, *Social Science and Medicine* **14A**: 397–413.

Finlayson, Angela, 1976. Social networks as coping resources: Lay help and consultation patterns used by women in husbands' post-infarction career, *Social Science and Medicine* **10**: 97–103.

Fletcher, Richard C., 1972. *A Study for Teaching Behavioral Sciences in Schools of Medicine, II: Empirical Studies*, Washington: National Center for Health Services Research and Development. Contract No. HSM 110–69–211.

Ford, Amasa B., 1978. Epidemiological priorities as a basis for health policy, *Bulletin of the New York Academy of Medicine* **54**: 10–22.

Foster, George, and Barbara Gallatin Anderson, 1978. *Medical Anthropology*, New York: John Wiley and Sons.

Frank, Jerome, 1975. The faith that heals. *The Johns Hopkins Medical Journal* **137**: 127–131.

Friedman, Meyer, and Ray H. Rosenman, 1974. *Type A Behavior and Your Heart*, New York: Alfred A. Knopf.

Friedman, Stanford B., and Lowell A. Glasgow, 1966. Psychologic factors and resistance to infectious disease, *Pediatric Clinics of North America* **13**: 315–335.

Freidson, Eliot, 1959. Client control and medical practice, *American Journal of Sociology* **65**: 374–382.

Frost, Wade Hampton, 1949. *Snow on Cholera: Being a Reprint of Two Papers by John Snow*, New York: Commonwealth Fund.

Fry, John, and W.A.J. Farndale, 1972. *International Medical Care: A Comparison and Evaluation of Medical Care Services Throughout the World*, Oxford and Lancaster (U.K.): Medical and Technical Publishing Co., Ltd.

Fuchs, Victor, 1974. Who Shall Live? in *Who Shall Live: Health, Economics, and Social Choice*, Victor Fuchs, pp. 30–55, New York: Basic Books, Inc.

Gajdusek, D. Carleton, 1977. Unconventional viruses and the origin and disappearance of kuru, *Science* **197**: 943–960.

Galdston, Iago, 1954. *Beyond the Germ Theory: The Roles of Deprivation and Stress in Health and Disease*, New York: Health Education Council.

Gallagher, Eugene B., 1976. Lines of reconstruction and extension in the parsonian sociology of illness, *Social Science and Medicine* **10**: 207–218.

Geiger, H. Jack, 1969. Community control – or community conflict? *Bulletin, National Tuberculosis Association* **54–55** (November): 4–10.

Geiger, H. Jack, 1972. A health center in Mississippi–a case study in social medicine, in *Medicine in a Changing Society*, Lawrence Corey, Steven E. Saltman, and Michael F. Epstein (eds.), pp. 157–167, St. Louis: C.F. Mosby, 1st. ed.

Geiger, H. Jack, 1974. Educational implications of changing methods of health care provision, *American Journal of Diseases of Children* **127**: 554–558.

Georgopoulous, Basil S., and Aleksander Matejko, 1967. The American general hospital as a complex social system, *Health Services Research* **2**: 76–112.

Glass, George S., 1975. Incomplete role reversal: The dilemma of hospitalization for the professional peer, *Psychiatry* **38**: 132–144.

Goodenough, Ward H., 1963. *Cooperation in Change*, New York: Russell Sage.

Gove, W.R., and J.F. Tudor, 1973. Adult sex roles and mental illness, *American Journal of Sociology* **78**: 812–835.

Grad, Frank P., 1978. Medical ethics and the law, *Annals of the American Academy of Political and Social Science* **437**: 19–36.

Greene, William A., Sidney Goldstein, and Arthur J. Moss, 1972. Psychosocial aspects of sudden death, *Archives of Internal Medicine* **129**: 725–732.

Haggerty, Robert J., 1977. Changing lifestyles to improve health, *Preventive Medicine* **6**: 276–289.

Hamburg, Beatrix A., and Marie Killilea, 1979. Relation of social support, stress, illness, and use of health services, in *Healthy People: The Surgeon General's Report of Health Promotion and Disease Prevention. Background Papers.* pp. 253–276. Washington: DHEW Publication No. 79–55071A.

Hamburg, David A., 1978. *Disease Prevention: The Challenge of the Future. The Sixth Annual Matthew B. Rosenhaus Lecture*, Washington, D.C.: American Public Health Association.

Harlow, Harry F., 1971. *Learning to Love*, New York: Ballantine Books.

Harwood, Alan, 1971. The hot-cold theory of disease: Implications for treatment of Puerto Rican patients, *Journal of the American Medical Association* **216**: 1153–1158.

Haynes, Suzanne G., Manning Feinleib, Sol Levine, Norman Scotch, and William B. Kannel, 1978. The relationship of psychosocial factors to coronary heart disease in the Framingham study. II. Prevalence of coronary heart disease, *American Journal of Epidemiology* **105**: 384–402.

Health Status of Minorities and Low-Income Groups, 1979. *Health Status of Minorities and Low-Income Groups*, pp. 5–14. Washington: DHEW Publication No. (HRA) 79–627.

Hippocrates, 1964. *The Theory and Practice of Medicine*, New York: The Citadel Press.

Holden, Constance, 1980. Behavioral medicine: An emergent field, *Science* **209**: 479–481.

Holmes, Thomas H., and Richard H. Rahe, 1967. The social readjustment rating scale, *Journal of Psychosomatic Research* **11**: 213–218.

House, James S., 1974. Occupational stress and coronary heart disease: A review and theoretical integration, *Journal of Health and Social Behavior* **15**: 12–27.

House, James S., Anthony J. Michael, James A. Wells, Berton H. Kaplan, and Lawrence R. Landerman, 1979. Occupational stress and health among factory workers, *Journal of Health and Social Behavior* **20**: 139–160.

Hughes, Charles C., 1963. Public health in nonliterate societies, in *Man's Image in Medicine and Anthropology*, Iago Galdston (ed.), pp. 157–233, New York: International Universities Press.

Hughes, Charles C., 1966. Health and well-being values in the perspective of sociocultural change, in *Comparative Theories of Social Change*, Hollis Peter (ed.), pp. 118–162, Ann Arbor: Foundation for Research on Human Behavior.

Hughes, Charles C., 1968. Ethnomedicine, in *International Encyclopedia of the Social Sciences* **10**: 87–92.

Hughes, Charles C., 1976. *Custom-Made: Introductory Readings for Cultural Anthropology*, Chicago: Rand McNally.

Hughes, Charles C., March-Adelard Tremblay, Robert N. Rapoport, and Alexander H. Leighton, 1960. *People of Cove and Woodlot: Communities from the Viewpoint of Social Psychiatry*, New York: Basic Books.

Hurley, Rodger, 1972. The health crisis of the poor, in *The Social Organization of Health*, Hans P. Dreitzel (ed.), pp. 83–122, New York: Macmillan.

Hurst, Michael W., C. David Jenkins, and Robert M. Ross, 1976. The relation of psychological stress to onset of medical illness, *Annual Review of Medicine* **27**: 301–312.

Illich, Ivan, 1976. Medical nemesis: The expropriation of health, New York: Pantheon Books.

Insel, Paul M., and Rudolf H. Moos (eds.), 1974. *Health and the Social Environment*, Lexington, Mass: D.C. Heath Company.

Ireland, Lola M., 1971. Health practices of the poor, in *Low-Income Life Styles*, Lola M. Ireland (ed.), pp. 51–65, Washington: DHEW, SRS-ORD-175-1971.

Jaffe, Dennis T., and David E. Bresler, 1980. The use of guided imagery as an adjunct to medical diagnosis and treatment, *Journal of Humanistic Psychology* **20**: 45–59.

Jenkins, C. David, 1976. Recent evidence supporting psychologic and social risk factors for coronary disease, *New England Journal of Medicine* **294**: 987–994 and 1033–1038.

Jenkins, C. David, 1979. An approach to the diagnosis and treatment of problems of health related behavior, *International Journal of Health Education* **XXII** (Supplement):1–24.

Kagan, Audrey R., and Lennart Levi, 1974. Health and environment – psychosocial stimuli: A Review, *Social Science and Medicine* **8**: 224–241.

Kane, Robert L. (ed.), 1974. *The Challenges of Community Medicine*, New York: Springer.

Kaplan, Berton H., John C. Cassel, and Susan Gore 1977. Social support and health. *Medical Care* **XV**: 47–58.

Kasl, Stanislav V., Sidney Cobb, and George W. Brooks 1968. Changes in serum uric acid and cholesterol levels in men undergoing job loss, *Journal of the American Medical Association* **206**: 1500–1507.

Katz, Roger C., and Steven Zlutnick (eds.), 1975. *Behavior Therapy and Health Care: Principles and Applications*, New York: Pergamon Press Inc.

Kelman, Sander, 1980. Social organization and the meaning of health, *The Journal of Medicine and Philosophy* **5**: 133–144.

Kennedy, Donald A., 1973. Perceptions of illness and healing, *Social Science and Medicine* **7**: 787–805.

Kiger, J.C., 1971. Disciplines. in *The Encyclopedia of Education*, New York: Macmillan and Free Press **3**: 99–105.

Kitagawa, Evelyn M., and Philip M. Hauser, 1973. *Differential Mortality in the United States: A Study in Sociodemographic Epidemiology*, Cambridge: Harvard University Press.

Kleinman, Arthur M., 1973. Toward a comparative study of medical systems, *Science, Medicine, and Man* **1**: 55–65.

Kleinman, Arthur M., 1978a. Clinical relevance of anthropological and cross-cultural research: Concepts and strategies, *American Journal of Psychiatry* **135**: 427–431.

Kleinman, Arthur M., 1978b. Concepts and a model for the comparison of medical systems as cultural systems, *Social Science and Medicine* **12**: 85–93.

Kleinman, Arthur, Leon Eisenberg, and Byron Good, 1978. Culture, illness, and care: Clinical lessons from anthropologic and cross-cultural research, *Annals of Internal Medicine* **88**: 251–258.

Kluckhohn, Clyde, and others, 1951. Values and value-orientations in the theory of action: An exploration in definition and classification, in *Toward a General Theory of Action*, Talcott Parsons and Edward A. Shils (eds.), pp. 388–433, Cambridge: Harvard University Press.

Kluckhohn, Clyde, Henry A. Murray, and David M. Schneider (eds.), 1953. *Personality in Nature, Society, and Culture*, New York: Alfred A. Knopf.

Knowles, John H. (ed.), 1977a. *Doing Better and Feeling Worse: Health in the United States*, New York: Norton.

Knowles, John H., 1977b. The responsibility of the individual, in *Doing Better and Feeling Worse: Health in the United States*, John H. Knowles (ed.), pp. 57–80, New York: Norton.

Koos, Earl Lomon, 1967. *The Health of Regionville: What the People Thought and Did About It*, New York: Hafner Publishing Co.

Kosa, John, and Irving K. Zola, 1975. *Poverty and Health: A Sociological Analysis*, Cambridge: Harvard University Press.

Kuhn, Thomas S., 1962. *The Structure of Scientific Revolutions*, Chicago: University of Chicago Press.

La Barre, Weston, 1954. *The Human Animal*, Chicago: University of Chicago Press.

Lalonde, Marc, 1974. *A New Perspective on the Health of Canadians: A Working Document*, Ottawa: Government of Canada.

Lederer, Henry D., 1952. How the sick view their world, *Journal of Social Issues* **8**: 4–15.

Leighton, Alexander H., 1959. *My Name is Legion:Foundations for a Theory of Man in Relation to Culture*, New York: Basic Books.

Leighton, Dorothea C., John S. Harding, David B. Macklin, Allister M. Macmillan, and Alexander H. Leighton, 1963. *The Character of Danger: Psychiatric Symptoms in Selected Communities*, New York: Basic Books.

Leventhal, Howard, 1973. Changing attitudes and habits to reduce risk factors in chronic disease, *American Journal of Cardiology* **31**: 571–580.

Levine, Sol, and Norman A. Scotch (eds.), 1970. *Social Stress*, Chicago: Aldine.

Lewin, Kurt, 1951. *Field Theory in Social Science: Selected Theoretical Papers*, Dorwin Cartwright (ed.), New York: Harper and Bros.

Lipowski, Z.J., and Anne M. Stewart, 1973. Illness as subjective experience, *Psychiatry in Medicine* **4**: 155–171.

Litman, Theodore J., 1974. The family as a basic unit in health and medical care: A social-behavioral overview, *Social Science and Medicine* **8**: 495–519.

Lynch, James J., 1977. *The Broken Heart: The Medical Consequences of Loneliness*, New York: Basic Books, Inc.

Lynd, Robert, 1939. *Knowledge for What? The Place of Social Science in American Culture*, Princeton: Princeton University Press.

Mabry, John H., 1964. Lay concepts of etiology, *Journal of Chronic Disease* **14**: 371–386.

Matarazzo, Joseph D., 1980. Behavioral health and behavioral medicine: Frontiers for a new health psychology, *American Psychologist* **35**: 807–817.

Mauksch, Hans, 1973. Ideology, interaction and patient care in hospitals, *Social Science and Medicine* **7**: 817–830.

Mckeown, Thomas, 1976. *The Role of Medicine: Dream, Mirage, or Nemesis?* London: Provincial Hospitals Trust.

McKinlay, John B., 1973. Social networks, lay consultation, and help-seeking behavior, *Social Forces* **51**: 275–292.

McKinlay, John B., 1975. A case for refocussing upstream – The political economy of illness, in *Applying Behavioral Science to Cardiovascular Risk*, Allen J. Enelow and Judith B. Henderson (eds.), pp. 7–17. New York: American Heart Association.

McKinlay, John B., 1979. Epidemiological and political determinants of social policies regarding the public health, *Social Science and Medicine* **13A**: 541–558.

Mechanic, David, 1972. Social psychologic factors affecting the presentation of bodily complaints, *New England Journal of Medicine* **286**: 1132–1139.

Medical Anthropology Newsletter, 1980. Open forum: Clinical anthropology, *Medical Anthropology Newsletter* **12**: 14–25.

Mendelsohn, Robert S., 1979. *Confessions of a Medical Heretic*, Chicago: Warner Books.

Miller, A.B., 1980. The epidemiology of malignant disease: A basis for public policy. *Health Communications Informatics* **6**: 283–294.

Miller, Neal E., 1969. Learning of visceral and glandular responses, *Science* **163**: 434–445.

Navarro, Vicente, 1978. The crisis of the western system of medicine in contemporary capitalism, *International Journal of Health Services* **8**: 179–211.

Palmore, Erdman, 1969. Predicting longevity: A follow-up controlling for age, *Gerontologist* **9**: 247–250

Parker, Seymour, 1958. Leadership patterns in a psychiatric ward, *Human Relations* **11**: 287–301

Parkes, Colin M., 1964. Effects of bereavement on physical and mental health – A study of the medical records of widows, *British Medical Journal* **2**: 274–279.

Parkes, Colin M., B. Benjamin, and R.G. Fitzgerald, 1969. Broken heart: A statistical study of increased mortality among widowers, *British Medical Journal* **1**: 740–743.

Peck, Bruce B., 1974. Physical medicine and family dynamics: The dialectics of rehabilitation, *Family Process* **13**: 469–479.

Pellegrino, Edmund D., 1978. Ethics and the moral center of the medical enterprise, *Bulletin of the New York Academy of Medicine* **54**: 625–640.

Pelletier, Kenneth R., 1977. *Mind as Healer, Mind as Slayer: A Holistic Approach to Preventing Stress Disorders*, New York: Dell Publishing Co.

Petersdorf, Robert G., and Alvan R. Feinstein, 1980. An informal appraisal of the current status of 'medical sociology,' in *The Relevance of Social Science for Medicine*, Leon Eisenberg and Arthur Kleinman (eds.), pp. 27–45, London and Dordrecht: D. Reidel Publishing Co.

Pomerleau, Ovide, Frederic Bass, and Victor Crown, 1975. Role of behavior modification in preventive medicine, *New England Journal of Medicine* **292**: 1277–1282.

Powles, John, 1973. On the limitations of modern medicine, *Science, Medicine, and Man* **1**: 1–30.

Primary Health Care, 1978. *Primary Health Care*. Report of the International Conference on Primary Health Care. Alma-Ata, USSR, 6–12 September 1978. Geneva: World Health Organization.

Quesada, Gustavo M., and Peter L. Heller, 1977. Sociocultural barriers to medical care among Mexican Americans in Texas, *Medical Care* **XV** (Supplement): 93–101.

Rabkin, Judith G., and Elmer L. Struening, 1976. Life events, stress, and illness, *Science* **194**: 1013–1020.

Rahe, Richard H., 1974. Life change and subsequent illness reports, in *Life Stress and Illness*, E.K. Eric Gunderson and Richard H. Rahe (eds.), pp. 58–78, Springfield: Charles C. Thomas.

Ramazzini, Bernardino, 1964 (ed.), *Diseases of Workers*, New York: Hafner.

Reiser, Stanley Joel, 1977. Therapeutic choice and moral doubt in a technological age, in *Doing Better and Feeling Worse: Health in the United States*, John H. Knowles (ed.), pp. 47–56, New York: Norton.

Relman, Arnold S., 1980. The new medical-industrial complex, *New England Journal of Medicine* **303**: 963–970.

Renaud, Marc, 1975. On the structural constraints to state intervention in health, *International Journal of Health Services* **5**: 559–571.

Richards, N. David, 1975. Methods and effectiveness of health education: The past, present and future of social scientific involvement, *Social Science and Medicine* **9**: 141–156.

Roghmann, K., and R.J. Haggerty, 1972. Family stress and the use of health services, *International Journal of Epidemiology* **1**: 279–286.

Rosen, George, 1947. What is social medicine? A genetic analysis of the concept, *Bulletin of the History of Medicine* **XXI**: 674–732.

Rosen, George, 1958. *A History of Public Health*, New York: MD Publications.

Rosen, George, 1972. The evolution of social medicine, in *Handbook of Medical Sociology*, Howard E. Freeman, Sol Levine, and Leo G. Reeder (eds.), pp. 30–60, Englewood Cliffs, N.J.: Prentice-Hall, Inc.

Rosen, George, 1973. Health, history and the social sciences, *Social Science and Medicine* **7**: 233–248.

Rosenstock, Irwin M., 1960. What research in motivation suggests for public health, *American Journal of Public Health* **50**: 295–302.

Ryan, William, 1976. *Blaming the Victim*, New York: Vintage Books.

Sackett, David L., and R. Brian Haynes, 1976. A critical review of the "determinants" of patient compliance with therapeutic regimens, in *Compliance with Therapeutic Regimens*, David L. Sackett and R. Brian Haynes (eds.), pp. 26–39. Baltimore: Johns Hopkins University Press.

Scotch, Norman A., 1963. Sociocultural factors in the epidemiology of Zulu hypertension, *American Journal of Public Health* **53**: 1205–1213.

Selye, Hans, 1973. The evolution of the stress concept, *American Scientist*, **61**: 692–699.

Selye, Hans, 1976. *The Stress of Life*, New York: McGraw-Hill Book Co.

Sherif, Muzafer, and Carolyn W. Sherif (eds.), 1969. *Interdisciplinary Relationships in the Social Sciences*, Chicago: Aldine.

Simon, Herbert A., 1980. The behavioral and social sciences, *Science* **209**: 72–78.

Skipper, James K., and Robert C. Leonard, 1968. Children, stress, and hospitalization: A Field Experiment, *Journal of Health and Social Behavior* **9**: 275–287.

Smith, Harvey L., 1958. Two lines of authority: The hospital's dilemma, in *Patients, Physicians and Illness: A Sourcebook for Behavioral Science and Medicine*, E. Gartly Jaco (ed.), pp. 268–477, Glencoe: Free Press.

Snow, Loudell F., 1974. Folk medical beliefs and their implications for care of patients: A review based on studies among black Americans, *Annals of Internal Medicine* **81**: 82–96.

Sokolowska, Magdalena, 1973. Two basic types of medical orientation, *Social Science and Medicine* **7**: 807–815.

Solomon, G.F., and A.A. Amkraut, 1972. Emotions, stress, and immunity, *Frontiers of Radiation Therapy and Oncology* **7**: 84–96.

Somers, Anne Ramsay, 1980. Life-style and health, in *Maxcy-Roseneau, Public Health and Preventive Medicine*, John M. Last (ed.), pp. 1046–1065, New York: Appleton-Century-Crofts.

Spitz, Rene A., 1965. *The First Year of Life: A Psychoanalytic Study of Normal and Deviant Development of Object Relations*, New York: International Universities Press.

Stein, Howard F., 1979. The salience of ethno-psychology for medical education and practice, *Social Science and Medicine* **13B**: 199–210.

Stimson, Gray V., 1974. Obeying doctor's orders: A view from the other side, *Social Science and Medicine* **8**: 97–104.

Stoeckle, John D., Irving K. Zola, and Gerald E. Davidson, 1963. On going to see the doctor: The contribution of the patient to the decision to seek medical aid, *Journal of Chronic Diseases* **16**: 975–989.

Stone, George C., Frances Cohen, and Nancy E. Adler (eds.), 1979. *Health Psychology – A Handbook: Theories, Applications, and Challenges of a Psychological Approach to the Health Care System*, San Francisco: Jossey-Bass Publishers.

Straus, Robert, 1957. The nature and status of medical sociology, *American Sociological Review* **22**: 200–204.

Strauss, Anselm L., 1969. Medical organization, medical care, and lower income groups, *Social Science and Medicine* **3**: 143–177.

Surgeon General, 1979. *Healthy People: The Surgeon General's Report on Health Promotion and Disease Prevention*, Washington, D.C. : U.S. D.H.E.W. (PHS) Publication No. 79–55071.

Susser, Mervyn, 1974. Ethical components in the definition of health, *International Journal of Health Services* **4**: 539–548.

Susser, Mervyn, Zena Stein, and Jennie Klein, 1978. Ethics in epidemiology, *Annals of the American Academy of Political and Social Science* **437**: 128–141.

Syme, S.L., M.G. Marmot, A. Kagan, H. Kato, and G. Rhoads, 1975. Epidemiologic studies of coronary heart disease and stroke in Japanese men living in Japan, Hawaii, and California: Introduction, *American Journal of Epidemiology* **102**: 477–480.

Syme, S. Leonard, and Lisa Berkman, 1976. Social class, susceptibility, and sickness, *American Journal of Epidemiology* **104**: 1–8.

Tao-Kim-Hai, Andre M., 1960. Orientals are stoic, in *Social Science in Nursing*, Frances C. MacGregor (ed.), pp. 313–326, New York: Russell Sage Foundation.

Taylor, Carol, 1970. The hospital patient's social dilemma, in *Horizontal Orbit: Hospitals and the Cult of Efficiency*, Carol Taylor, pp. 76–86, New York: Holt, Rinehart and Winston.

Temkin, Oswei, 1963. The scientific approach to disease: Specific entity and individual sickness, in *Scientific Change: Historical Studies in the Intellectual, Social and Technical Conditions for Scientific Discovery and Technical Invention, from Antiquity to the Present*, A.C. Crombie (ed.), pp. 629–647, New York: Basic Books.

Terris, Milton, 1976. The epidemiologic revolution, national health insurance and the role of health departments, *American Journal of Public Health* **66**: 1155–1164.

Terris, Milton, 1980. Epidemiology as a guide to health policy, *Annual Review of Public Health* **1**: 323–344.

Turbayne, Colin Murray, 1970. *The Myth of Metaphor* (Rev. ed.), Columbia: University of South Carolina Press.

Twaddle, Anthony C., 1972. The concepts of the sick role and illness behavior, *Advances in Psychosomatic Medicine* **8**: 162–179.

Ubell, Earl, 1972. Health behavior change: A political model, *Preventive Medicine* **1**: 209–221.

Useem, John, and Ruth Useem, 1958. Social stresses and resources among middle management men, in *Patients Physicians, and Illness: Sourcebook in Behavioral Science and Medicine*, E. Gartly Jaco (ed.), pp. 74–91, New York: Free Press.

Vaillant, George E., Nancy C. Sobowale, and Charles McArthur, 1972. Some psychological vulnerabilities of physicians, *New England Journal of Medicine* **287**: 372–375.

Veatch, Robert M., 1977. The dying infant and the needs of others, in *Case Studies in Medical Ethics*, Robert M. Veatch, pp. 36–42, Cambridge: Harvard University Press.

Vogt, Evon Z., 1955. *Modern Homesteaders: The Life of a Twentieth-Century Frontier Community*, Cambridge: Harvard University Press.

Waitzkin, Howard, 1980. A Marxist analysis of the health care systems of advanced capitalist societies, in *The Relevance of Social Science for Medicine*, Leon Eisenberg and Arthur Kleinman (eds.), pp. 333–369, London/Boston/Dordrecht, Holland: D. Reidel Publishing Co.

Waitzkin, Howard, and Barbara Waterman, 1974. *The Exploitation of Illness in Capitalist Society*, Indianapolis and New York: Bobbs-Merrill Co., Inc.

Walker, Kenneth N., Arelene MacBride, and May L.W. Vachon, 1977. Social support networks and the crisis of bereavement, *Social Science and Medicine* **11**: 35–41.

Wallston, Barbara S., and Kenneth A. Wallston, 1978. Locus of control and health: A review of the literature, *Health Education Monographs* **6**: 107–116.

Weber, Max, 1952. The essentials of bureaucratic organization: An ideal-type construction, in *Reader in Bureaucracy*, Robert K. Merton, Ailsa P. Gray, Barbara Hockey, and Hanan C. Selvin (eds.), pp. 18–27, Glencoe: Free Press.

Webster, Thomas, 1979. Behavioral scientists in schools of medicine. Paper presented at Fall meeting, Association for Behavioral Science and Medical Education.

Weiss Paul A., 1977. The system of nature and the nature of systems: Empirical holism and practical reductionism harmonized, in *Toward a Man-Centered Medical Science*, Karl E. Schaefer, Herbert Hensel, and Ronald Brady (eds.), pp. 17–63, Mt. Kisco, N.Y.: Future Publishing Co.

Weiss, Stephen M., 1980. Behavioral medicine in the United States: Research, clinical, and training opportunities, *International Journal of Mental Health* **9**: 182–196.

Weissman, Myrna M., and Gerald L. Klerman, 1978. Epidemiology of mental disorders, *Archives of General Psychiatry* **35**: 705–712.

Whorton, Donald, and Morris E. Davis, 1978. Ethical conduct and the occupational physician, *Bulletin of the New York Academy of Medicine* **54**: 733–741.

Wikler, Daniel I., 1978. Persuasion and coercion for health: Ethical issues in government efforts to change life-styles, *Health and Society* **56**: 303–338.

Williams, Roger J., 1963. *Biochemical Individuality*, New York: Wiley.

Wilson, Robert N., 1963. The social structure of a general hospital, *Annals of the American Academy of Political and Social Science* **346**: 67–76.

Wolf, Stewart, 1961. Disease as a way of life: Neural integration in systemic pathology, *Perspectives in Biology and Medicine* **4**: 288–305.

Work in America, 1973. Work and health, in *Work in America. Special Task Force to the Secretary of Health, Education, and Welfare*, pp. 76–92, Cambridge: MIT Press.

Yeracaris, Constantine A., and Jay H. Kim, 1978. Socioeconomic differentials in selected causes of death, *American Journal of Public Health* **68**: 342–351.

Yinger, J. Milton, 1965. *Toward A Field Theory of Behavior: Personality and Social Structure*, New York: McGraw-Hill.

Yudkin, Simon, 1961. Six children with coughs: The second diagnosis, *The Lancet* **2**: 561–563.

Zola, Irving K., 1973. Pathways to the doctor – From person to patient, *Social Science and Medicine* **7**: 677–689.

Index